VISUAL QUICKSTART GUIDE

Painter 4

FOR MACINTOSH

Elaine Weinmann
Peter Lourekas

Peachpit Press

This book is dedicated to our siblings, Harriet and Nia.

Visual QuickStart Guide
Painter 4 for Macintosh
Elaine Weinmann and Peter Lourekas

Peachpit Press
2414 Sixth Street
Berkeley, CA 94710
510/548-4393
800/283-9444
510/548-5991 (fax)

Find us on the World Wide Web at: http://www.peachpit.com

Peachpit Press is a division of Addison Wesley Longman

Copyright © 1996 by Elaine Weinmann and Peter Lourekas
Cover design: The Visual Group
Interior design: Elaine Weinmann
Production: Elaine Weinmann and Peter Lourekas
Illustrations: Elaine Weinmann and Peter Lourekas, except as noted

Colophon
This book was created with QuarkXPress 3.3 on a Macintosh
Quadra 650 and Power Macintosh 8500. The fonts used were
Sabon and Gill Sans from Adobe Systems Inc.

ISBN 0-201-88665-0
9 8 7 6 5 4 3 2 1

Printed and bound in the United States of America

Welcome to the Painter Visual QuickStart Guide

You can do things in Painter that can't be done with traditional media, like use art supplies that never run out, paint without washing your hands or brushes and without inhaling turpentine, change paper textures midway through a drawing, build up wet brush strokes with no drying time, erase a watercolor, apply oil paint over pastel on paper, or instant-replay a picture, stroke by stroke. Yet Painter's brushes work uncannily like traditional media: watercolor strokes bleed into the paper like real watercolor, oil strokes smear like real oil paint, and you can even make paint drip.

If Painter's brushes don't interest you, take a look at Painter's special effects commands: an arsenal of intriguing ways to enhance, develop, and rearrange images that simply can't be replicated in traditional media. Many of the artists featured in this book still use traditional media—palette table, drafting table, or silkscreening table right next to their Macintosh. The computer is merely a new tool in their lifelong creative process.

We think the best way to inspire you to learn and explore Painter's features is to show them in the context of drawings and paintings, and we've tried to include a wide range of art styles in this book (we happen to love diversity). Abstract or representational, Painter-ly or illusionistic, messy or neat—you're the artist. We're pretty square when we describe Painter's basic techniques, though, because we know you want to paint, not read. Our aim is to give you enough technical information about Painter to get you started without stifling your creative juices.

We took notes as we created the illustrations for this book so we could write intelligible captions. If you're not a note-taker and you would like to record your methods (the brush you used, at what opacity, etc.), you can use Painter's script commands to record and then replay a brush stroke or even a whole work session. Who knows, the next brush stroke you draw might be a "stroke of genius," and you'll be glad you made a record of it.

On the other hand, most of the artists showcased in this book don't remember an iota about how they produce their work because they're so absorbed in art-making and each piece they create is one-of-a-kind. They enjoy surprises and exploring the mysterious workings of new software, and they like the fact that the computer challenges them to try new methods. Trying to find out what commands or brushes they use is like trying to transcribe a recipe from someone's grandmother. We're grateful when they remember they've used Painter!

Speaking of methods, feel free to be disrespectful to this book. Read it in the bathtub, read it on the bus, fold down the corners, scribble notes on the pages, bend back the spine. We're thrilled when we see beat up copies of our books, because we know they're being used as learning tools. *Painter 4 for Macintosh: Visual QuickStart Guide* is not a coffee table book—it's a computer art class-in-a-book. ■

Table of Contents

Chapter 3: **Default Brushes**

Chapter 4: **More Painting**

Chapter 5: **Selections/Paths**

Chapter 6:   **Floaters**

Chapter 7: **Shapes**

Chapter 8: Fills

Chapter 9: Masks

Bare Essentials 1

Rodney Alan Greenblat (created for the Lands' End Kids' Catalog; detail).

Hardware

CPU

We hesitate to recommend specific models because the Macintosh hardware world changes so fast. By the time this book reaches the bookstores, no doubt there'll be newer models on the market. The faster the machine, the better, because many Painter commands are processor intensive. Painter will run fastest, of course, on a Power Mac. Running Painter on a slow machine requires enormous patience. If you're not using a Power Mac, you won't be able to access all Painter's features unless your machine has an FPU (Floating Point Unit). Make sure you have enough empty hard disk space for Painter to use as a scratch disk when it needs more RAM for processing. Painter requires System 7.0 or later.

Color monitor

Color monitors display 8-bit, 16-bit, or 24-bit color, depending on the type of video card or the amount of video RAM (VRAM). With an 8-bit card, the screen displays up to 256 colors; with a 24-bit card, 16.7 million colors are available. With an 24-bit card, every possible color can be represented on screen. All Painter 3.1 pictures are saved as 24-bit. Some video cards also accelerate the time needed to redraw images on screen.

Mouse or stylus?

You don't have to use a pressure-sensitive tablet and stylus combo with Painter, but we highly recommend that you do so. With a stylus and tablet you'll be able to create more idiosyncratic and personal brush strokes in a wider range of thick-to-thin and dark-to-light variations, and control how much paper grain is revealed by pressure. And since a stylus is held more like a pen or brush, you'll probably find it to be more comfortable than using a mouse. Tablets by Wacom, CalComp, Summagraphics, Hitachi, and Kurta work with Painter. If you use a pressure-sensitive tablet, you should set Brush Tracking Preferences at the beginning of each work session (see page 237).

Third-party plug-ins

Painter supports third-party plug-ins, including those created for use with Photoshop. In order to access your plug-in files you must install them all together in one folder. You can tell Painter where this folder is when you install the application, or you can use the Edit > Preferences > Plug-ins dialog box. Plug-ins are accessed from Painter's Effects menu.

Memory allocation

To learn how much RAM you have available to allocate to Painter, launch Painter and any other applications that you want to run at the same time, then choose About This Macintosh from the Apple menu. Total Memory is the amount of hardware RAM installed, and Largest Unused Block is the amount of RAM still available. The applications you launched and their RAM allotments are also displayed.

If possible, you should allocate at least 10 to 12 megabytes (MB) of RAM to Painter. To do this, quit Painter, click the Painter application icon in the Finder, choose Get Info from the File menu, then enter the desired amount in the Preferred size field. To enter 10MB, for example, type in "10000". Be sure to reserve enough RAM to run the System.

Can you guess how many megabytes this book weighs? Look for the answer later in the book!

The Painter building blocks

The background of every Painter image is called the **canvas**. The Painter canvas is a bitmap, which means that color areas, however they're applied, are actually composed of tiny pixels.

The feature that makes Painter unique is its dazzling assortment of **brushes**, from diaphanous watercolor to gloppy oil. You can even create your own brushes.

Second only to Painter's brush assortment is its rich selection of **paper textures** and methods for applying textures to images, both while and after an image is created. You can create your own paper textures using a variety of techniques, and you can also create **brush looks**—brush-and-paper combinations—that can be saved and reused later. Let's say you have a habit of using your custom Zen brush with a custom "handmade rice paper" texture—you can save it as a brush look and grab it quickly whenever the whim strikes you.

There are other ways to recolor pixels: fill an area with a **gradation**, a **weave**, or a **pattern**; spray imagery using the strange and wonderful **Image Hose**; create **mosaic** tiles; or apply any number of Effects menu (**image editing**) commands (they're like Photoshop filters).

You can also create **shapes** in Painter, which are vector-based, mathematically defined objects that can be moved, resized, and recolored independently of the background canvas (like objects in Illustrator or FreeHand).

Floaters are similar to shapes in that they can be moved, resized, or recolored independently of the background canvas, but floaters are pixel-based, which means that floater imagery can be blended with the underlying canvas by choosing a Composite Method (like Photoshop's layer modes).

If you want to isolate an area of the canvas for editing and protect the rest of the image (i.e., you want to add a nice sunset to the background of your portrait of Aunt Bea without messing up the figure), you can **select** the area you want to isolate, or you can protect it using a **mask**.

Using Painter's **cloning** commands, you can re-create all or part of an image in new media—as a charcoal sketch or an oil painting, for example. You can draw the brush strokes yourself or fold your arms and watch it happen automatically. You can also use cloning commands to restore original areas from the source document or make brush strokes look three dimensional.

Once you get rolling in Painter, you'll start to accumulate custom paper textures, Image Hose nozzles, brushes, brush looks, floaters, paths, scripts, gradations, patterns, weavings, and lighting effects. These resources are collected and organized in **libraries** so you can actually find them again.

Using Painter's **script** commands you can make a record of how you create an image. You can edit the script, if you like, and then replay it. Let's say you're pleased with everything in an image except a particular color choice (you don't know what you were thinking). You can substitute a new color and replay the script—no one will ever know. You can also record and replay an individual brush stroke.

If creating individual paintings in Painter isn't enough, you can create, paint on, add texture to, or apply Effects menu commands to a **movie**, do a group painting with other participants on a **network**, or display your Painter image on the World Wide Web. Of course you could also output the durn thang on acid-free paper, frame it, and hang it on the wall—we've heard there are still people out there who do that.

To launch Painter:
Double-click the Painter application icon inside the Painter application folder or on the Launcher.

Painter 4.0

Follow these instructions to create a new, blank document. To paint on scanned imagery, see the scanning info on pages 23–24 and the instructions for opening a file on page 7.

To create a new file:

1. Choose File menu > New (Command-N).
2. Choose a unit of measure for the Width and Height **2**.
3. Enter Width and Height values **3**.
4. Enter a Resolution value **4**.
5. *Optional:* To choose a different background color, click the Paper Color rectangle, click a color on the color wheel, adjust the Hue, Saturation, or Lightness, if necessary, then click OK. (To reset the Paper Color to pure white, enter Hue, Saturation, and Lightness values of 0, 0, and 65535, respectively.)
6. Click OK or press Return **5**.

About resolution

■ Resolution is a measurement of the number of pixels in a file. One pixel in a file displays as one pixel on screen when the image is displayed at 100% view. When a file is printed, pixels are converted into dots, whose size will vary depending on the resolution of the output device. The higher a file's resolution, the larger its storage size and the longer image edits will take to process.

■ For video, choose a resolution of 72 ppi unless you'll be zooming in on part of the image. For printing, your resolution should be double the line screen your print shop is going to use for color output, or one and a half times the line screen for grayscale output. A lower resolution than that might be adequate for a very painterly image; a picture with sharp line work would require a very high resolution.

■ When all the values in the New dialog box are in pixels, choosing a resolution above 72 ppi (pixels per inch) will reduce the file's dimensions without changing the file's storage size (RAM). If the Height and/or Width is specified in a unit other than pixels, the higher the resolution, the more pixels in the file and thus the larger the file's storage size.

■ Using Painter's scripts feature, you can record the creation of a picture at one resolution and then replay it later in a new document at a different resolution (see page 212).

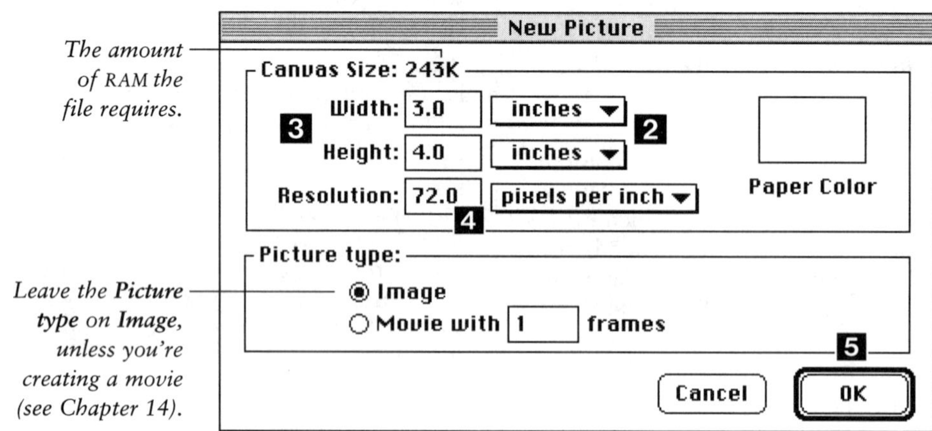

The amount of RAM the file requires.

Leave the Picture type on Image, unless you're creating a movie (see Chapter 14).

The Painter image window

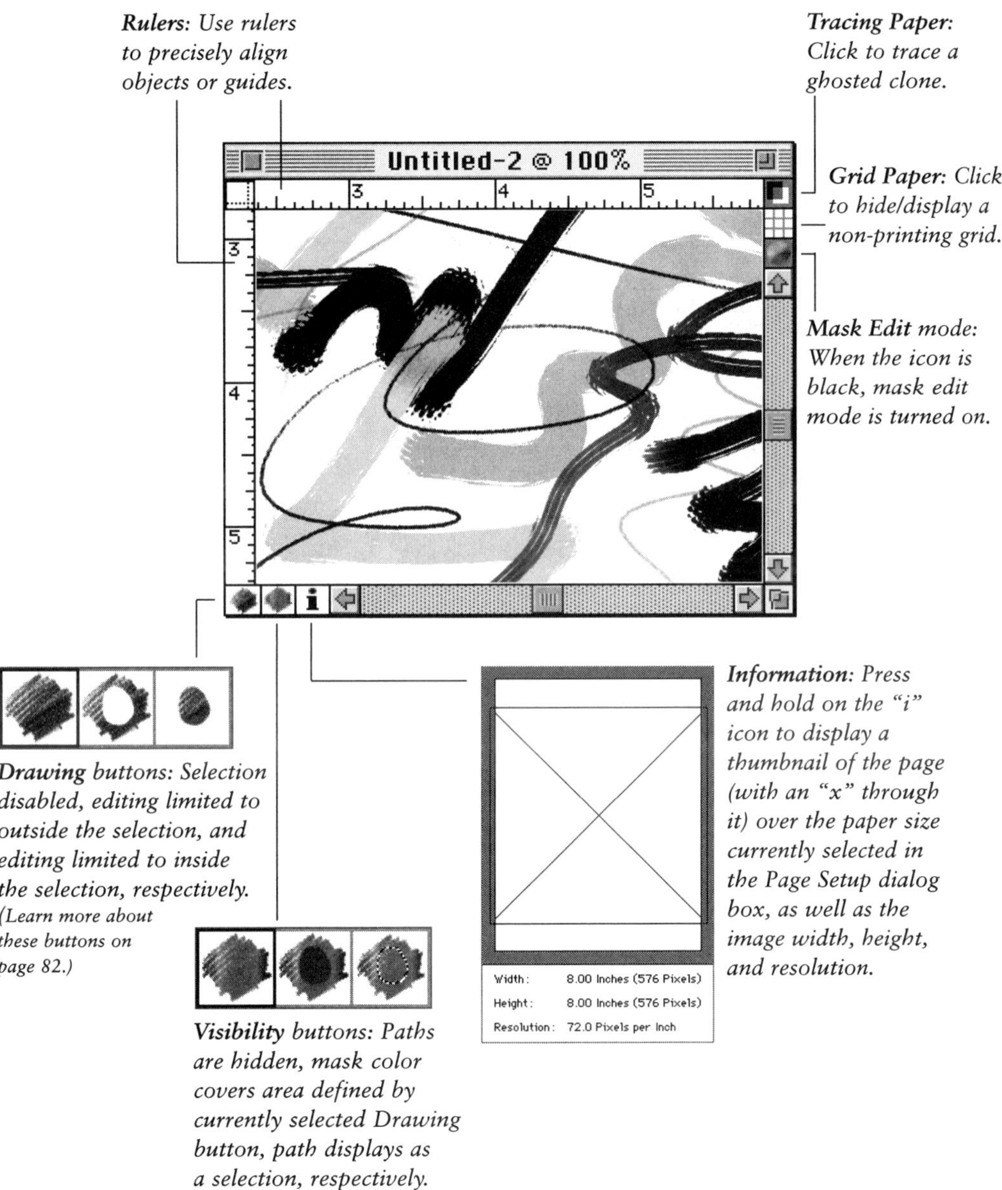

Rulers: *Use rulers to precisely align objects or guides.*

Tracing Paper: *Click to trace a ghosted clone.*

Grid Paper: *Click to hide/display a non-printing grid.*

Mask Edit *mode: When the icon is black, mask edit mode is turned on.*

Drawing *buttons: Selection disabled, editing limited to outside the selection, and editing limited to inside the selection, respectively.* (Learn more about these buttons on page 82.)

Visibility *buttons: Paths are hidden, mask color covers area defined by currently selected Drawing button, path displays as a selection, respectively.*

Information: *Press and hold on the "i" icon to display a thumbnail of the page (with an "x" through it) over the paper size currently selected in the Page Setup dialog box, as well as the image width, height, and resolution.*

The Painter Image Window

You just can't wait to pick up a brush and start painting?

After you read this chapter, read **QuickStart Paint on page 26.**

After you save your document for the first time, just choose Save from the File menu (Command-S) the next time you want to save it.

To save a new file:

1. Choose File menu > Save As. If you've already starting painting, you can choose Save (Command-S).

2. Enter a name for the file in the Save Image As field **2**.

3. Choose a file format from the Type pop-up menu **3**.

4. Choose a location in which to save the file **4**.

5. Click Save or press Return **5**.

Use the Save As command to save a file in a different format after it's already been saved.

What file format Type should I choose?

RIFF is Painter's default native format. You must use this format if you want to save your document with floaters, color annotations, editable mosaics, or Wet Paint layer brush strokes. Leave the Uncompressed box unchecked to save file storage space. Floaters are also preserved in the Photoshop 3.0 format, but color annotations are not.

Information about other file formats for opening Painter files in other applications is on pages 246–247.

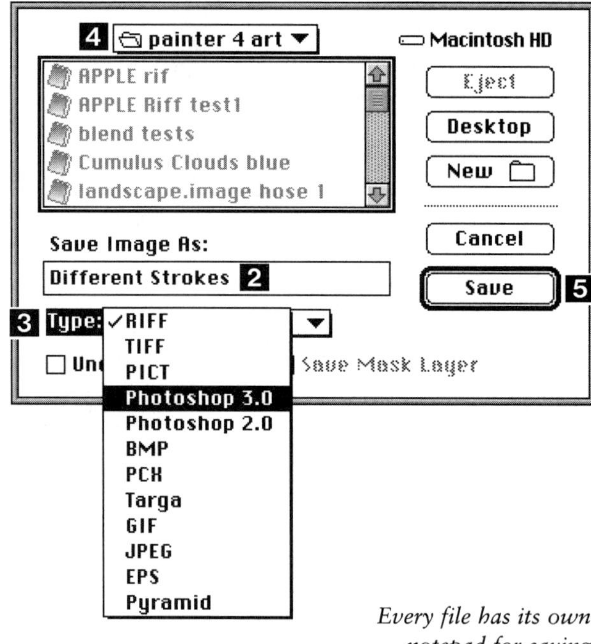

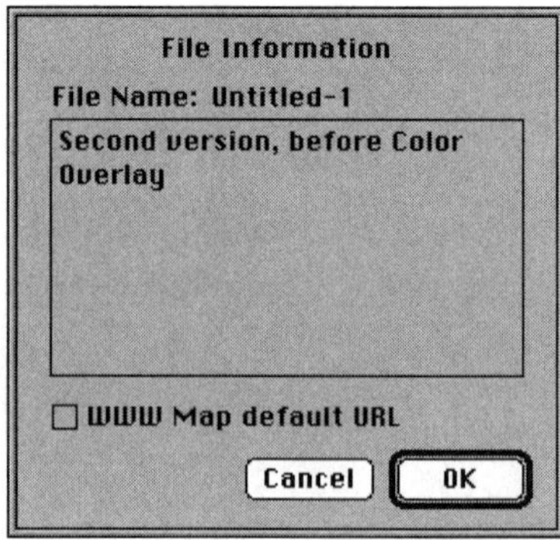

Every file has its own notepad for saving messages or instructions. With the file open, choose Get Info from the File menu, then type anything you want in the information field.

Save a New File

What happens to a Photoshop file if it's opened in Painter 4?

- Layers will be converted into floaters in Painter and paths in the Photoshop file will be converted into paths in Painter.

- If the Photoshop file contains a layer mask, it will be converted into a floater with a mask in Painter. If you reopen the document in Photoshop, however, the layer mask effect will become permanent and the mask itself will be deleted.

- The fourth channel in a Photoshop file will be viewable in Painter as a mask if there were no paths in the original Photoshop 3.0 file. To display the mask in Painter and force its name to appear on the Objects: P. List palette, choose the Path Adjuster tool and click in the document window or click the third Visibility button on the P. List palette. The channel will be blank if you reopen the file in Photoshop.

- If you import a Photoshop file that has a transparent background, a white background will be created for it in Painter. If you reopen the file in Photoshop, the file will have a new, white background layer, which will contain any brush strokes that were applied to the background in Painter.

- If you apply a layer blending mode to a layer in Photoshop and then open the image in Painter, the mode effect may look different, but the original effect will reappear if you reopen the file in Photoshop.

These file formats can be opened in Painter: RIFF, TIFF, PICT, BMP, PCX, GIF, JPEG, Pyramid, Targa, Photoshop 2.0, and Photoshop 3.0. **All** Painter images are in **RGB** color mode—you can't even open CMYK color mode file in Painter.

To open a file in Painter:

1. Choose File menu > Open (Command-O).

2. Highlight the file you want to open, then click Open.
   or
   Click Browse to view thumbnails of pictures in the currently open folder, then double-click a thumbnail to open that picture (or click a thumbnail, then click Open or press Return).

   You can also open a Painter file by clicking its icon in the Finder.

   To open a Photoshop image in Painter, first save the image in Photoshop in RGB Color or Grayscale mode, and in Photoshop 2.5 or 3.0 file format.

   To open an Illustrator or FreeHand file as shapes, see page 134. You can't open an EPS directly into Painter.

   To open a PhotoCD file directly into Painter, use Kodak's PhotoCD Acquire plug-in module. Or open your PhotoCD file in Photoshop, save it in RGB Color mode and Photoshop 3.0 format, then open it in Painter.

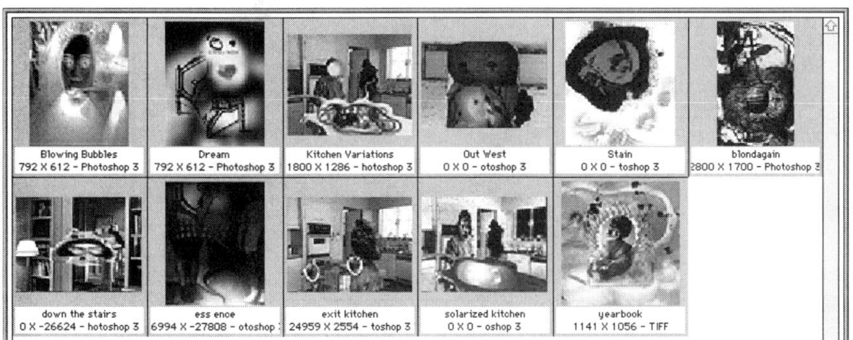

*Painter's terrific **Browse** feature, with its large thumbnails, makes it easy to identify and open pictures. Double-click a thumbnail to open that file. (Artwork by David Humphrey)*

Palettes

You'll be using one or more of the six main palettes for most of your work in Painter. To open a palette, choose the palette name from the Window menu or use the keyboard shortcut listed at right.

The Brush, Art Materials, and Objects palettes have subpalettes. To open a subpalette from the Art Materials or Objects palette, click its icon at the top of the main palette (except for the Paths and Floaters palette, which open from Objects palette submenus). Open subpalettes from the Brushes palette from the Brush, Controls, and Nozzle pulldown menus. To display a subpalette by itself, make sure it isn't currently displayed (click a different icon), then drag its icon away from the main palette. To restore a subpalette to its main palette, just click its close box.

If you want your screen to look neat and tidy, you can manually snap your palettes together edge-to-edge (you'll need a large monitor to do this). To restore the palettes to their default locations—snapped together—choose Window menu > Clean Up Palettes.

The Painter palettes

*Show/hide
palette shortcut*

Command 1   **Tools**

Command 2   **Brushes**
Subpalettes: **Looks, Brush Controls, Advanced Controls**

Command 3   **Art Materials**
Subpalettes: **Color, Paper, Grad, Pattern, Weave**

Command 4   **Objects**
Subpalettes: **P. List, Paths, F. List, Floaters, Scripts, S. List, Network**

Command 5   **Controls**
Command 6   **Color Set**
Command H   Hide all open palettes or display all previously open palettes

Many Painter commands are accessed from palette pull-down menus.

To close a palette, click its close box or use the shortcut.

To expand a palette, click its grow box.

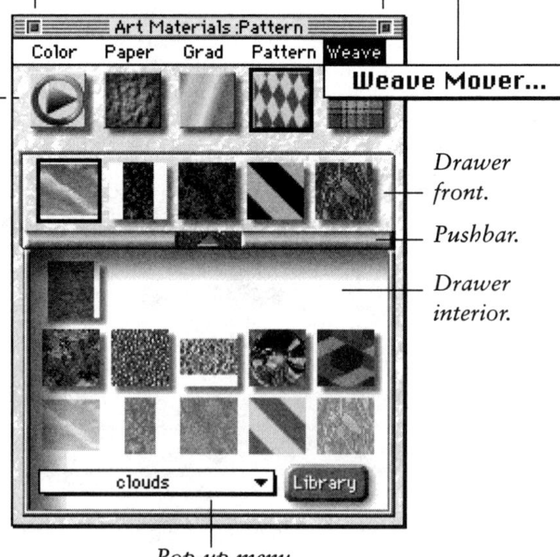

Drawer front.

Pushbar.

Drawer interior.

Pop-up menu.

The Color palette displayed separately from the Art Materials palette. We usually display our Color palette separately because we use it so frequently.

Palette backgrounds

You may have noticed that our palettes have a different background texture than yours. We thought the background texture on the default interface was too distracting for our illustrations. If you'd like to change yours, turn to page 238.

Palette drawers

To make a selection from any palette that has a drawer, click an icon on the drawer front. Or click the pushbar to open the drawer, then click an icon in the drawer or choose from the pop-up menu. When you click an icon in a drawer, the icon is placed on the drawer front and the same icon in the drawer becomes grayed out. The drawer front contains the last five most recently used icons.

To lock an icon on the drawer front, press and hold on the icon for a couple of seconds until a green dot appears under the icon. Press and hold on the icon again to unlock it. Up to four items can be locked at a time.

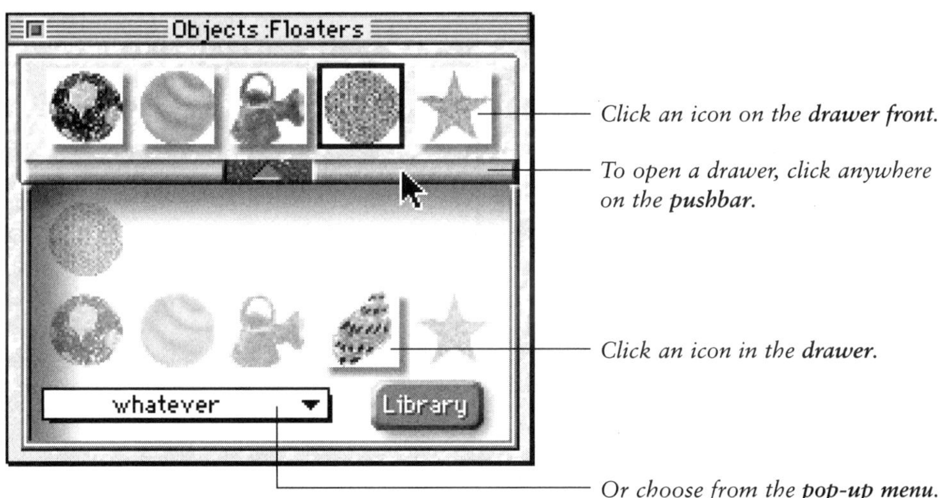

Click an icon on the **drawer front**.

To open a drawer, click anywhere on the **pushbar**.

Click an icon in the **drawer**.

Or choose from the **pop-up menu**.

Palettes

Sliders

Many Painter palettes and dialog boxes have sliders.

Click anywhere in the **bar**.

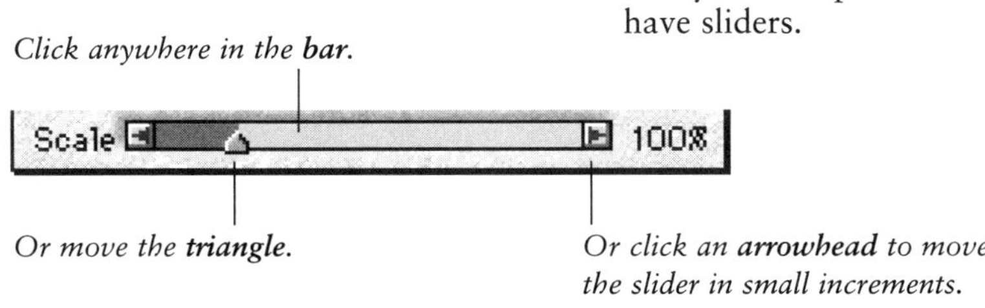

Or move the **triangle**.

Or click an **arrowhead** to move the slider in small increments.

The main palettes

Open the Color, Paper, Grad, Pattern, or Weave palette by clicking its icon on the Art Materials palette.

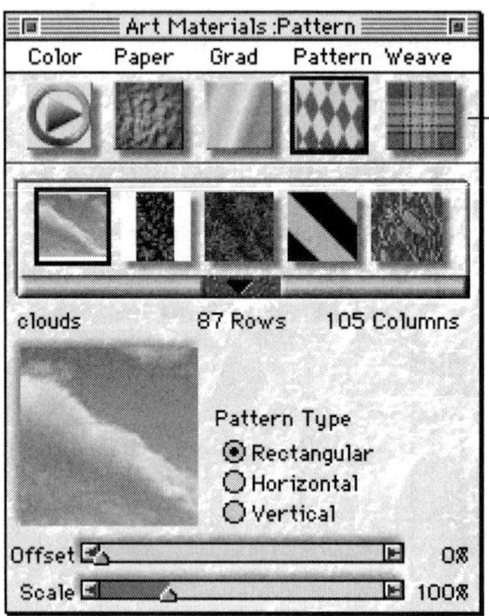

The Art Materials palette.

The three Color palette types (choose from the Color pull-down menu on the Art Materials palette)

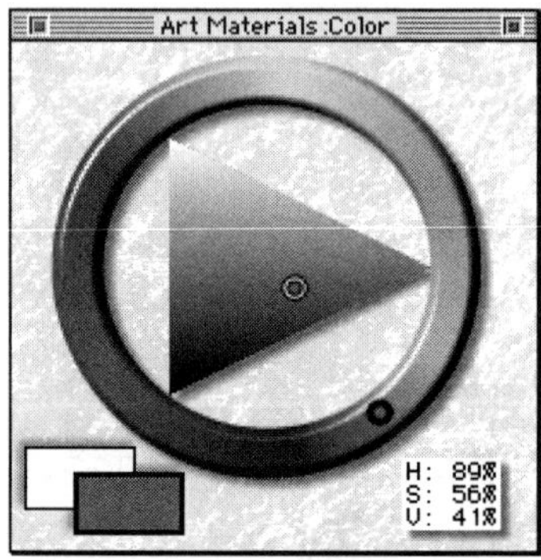

Standard Colors (Color) palette.

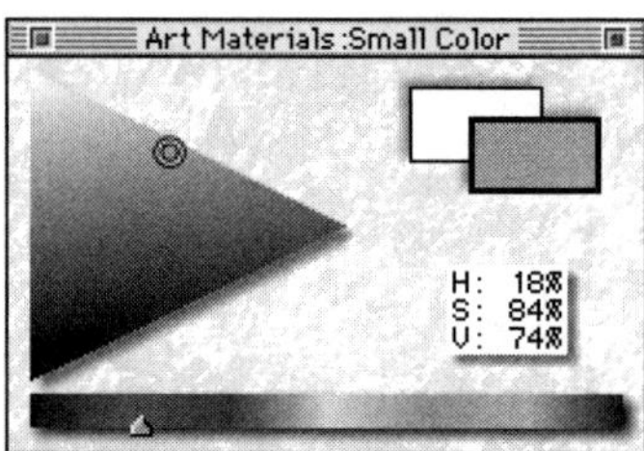

Compact Colors (Small Color) palette. We like to use this configuration because it takes up the least amount of screen space.

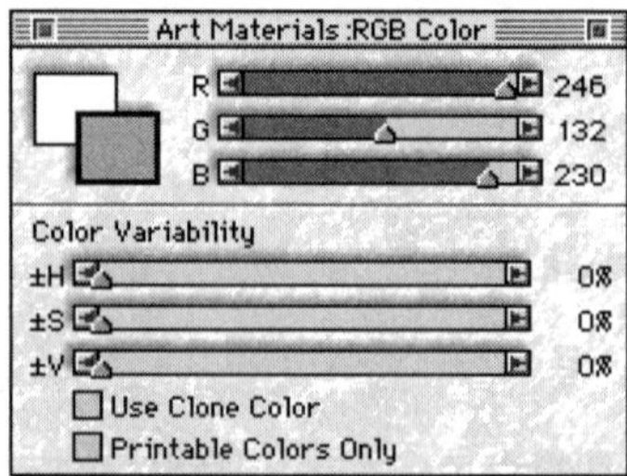

RGB Colors palette. Use this palette type if you want to mix RGB colors by number.

A note regarding the instructions in this book

Pull-down menus appear on palettes. Menus appear, of course, on the standard Macintosh menu bar. To distinguish between the two, we use the following system:

To choose from the menu bar:

Edit menu > Cut *-or-*

Edit menu > Paste > Normal

To choose from a palette pull-down menu:

Brushes palette > Nozzle menu > Load Nozzle

Palettes

Shrink your palettes

If you're using Painter 4.0 and System 7.5 or later, you can use the WindowShade feature. Turn it on from the Control Panels submenu under the Apple menu. With WindowShade on at a setting of 2 clicks, you can double-click any window or palette title bar to shrink the palette to a title bar. Double-click it again to enlarge the palette. To shrink the Objects palette or the Art Materials palette to just its drawer front, click the currently highlighted icon on the palette.

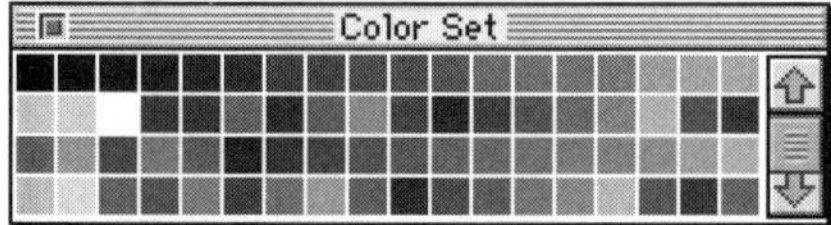

The **Color Set** palette.

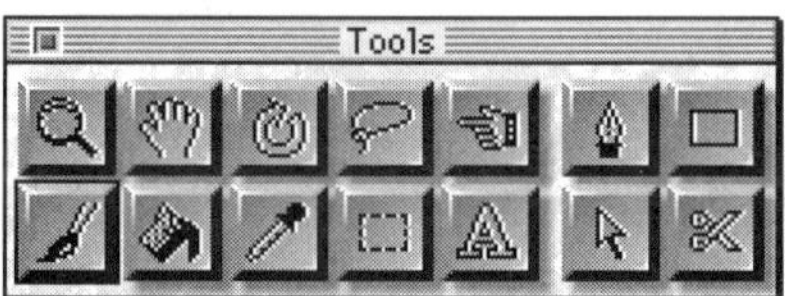

The **Tools** palette.

*Open the **P. List**, **F. List**, **Scripts**, **S. List**, or **Network** subpalette by clicking its icon on the Objects palette.*

The **Objects** palette.

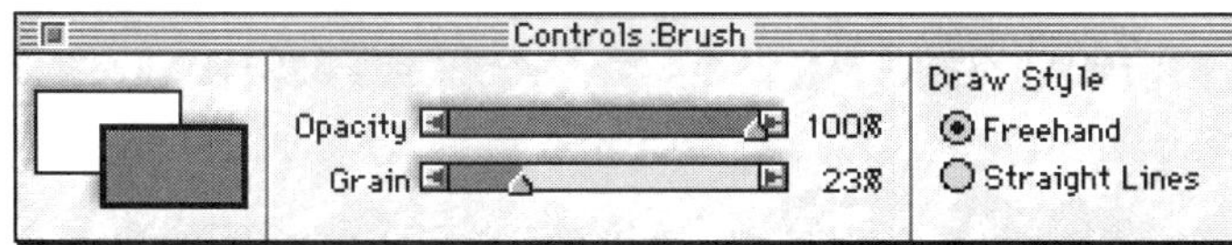

The **Controls** palette.

*Open the **Brush Controls** and **Advanced Controls** palettes (Size, Spacing, Random, Bristle, Rake, Well, Water, and Sliders) from the Controls pull-down menu.*

To open the Nozzle palette, choose Nozzles from the Nozzle pull-down menu.

*To open the **Looks** palette, choose Brush Looks from the Brushes pull-down menu.*

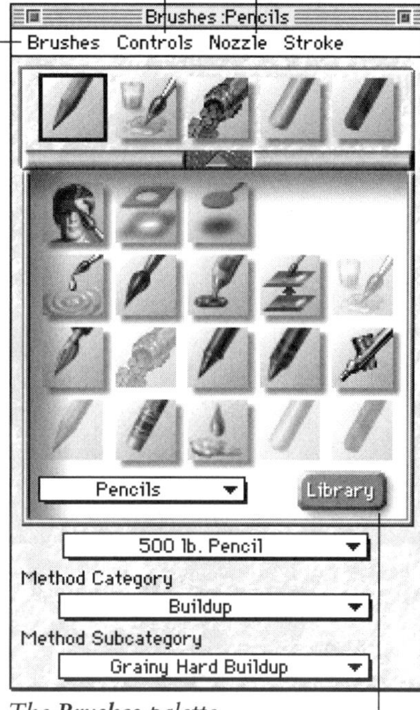

The **Brushes** palette.

A **library** is collection of papers, paths, brushes, patterns, nozzles, brush looks, scripts, lighting effects, floaters, weaves, or gradations that is supplied with Painter or that you create yourself. Only one library can can be open and displayed per palette, but you can quickly load a different library onto a palette. To do so, click Library, click Open, highlight the library you want to open, then click Open again. To create a new library, see page 21. To edit a library, see page 22.

Tools

The Tools palette contains 22 tools. To open the Tools palette, choose
Window menu > Tools (Command-1). To choose a tool, click once on its
icon or press the tool's assigned letter on the keyboard (in boldface, below).
Some tools are combined on the palette to conserve space. To access a related tool, press on the currently visible tool. Or click the currently visible tool,
then click the desired tool's icon on the Controls palette. Once a tool is chosen, you can also choose special attributes for it from the Controls palette.

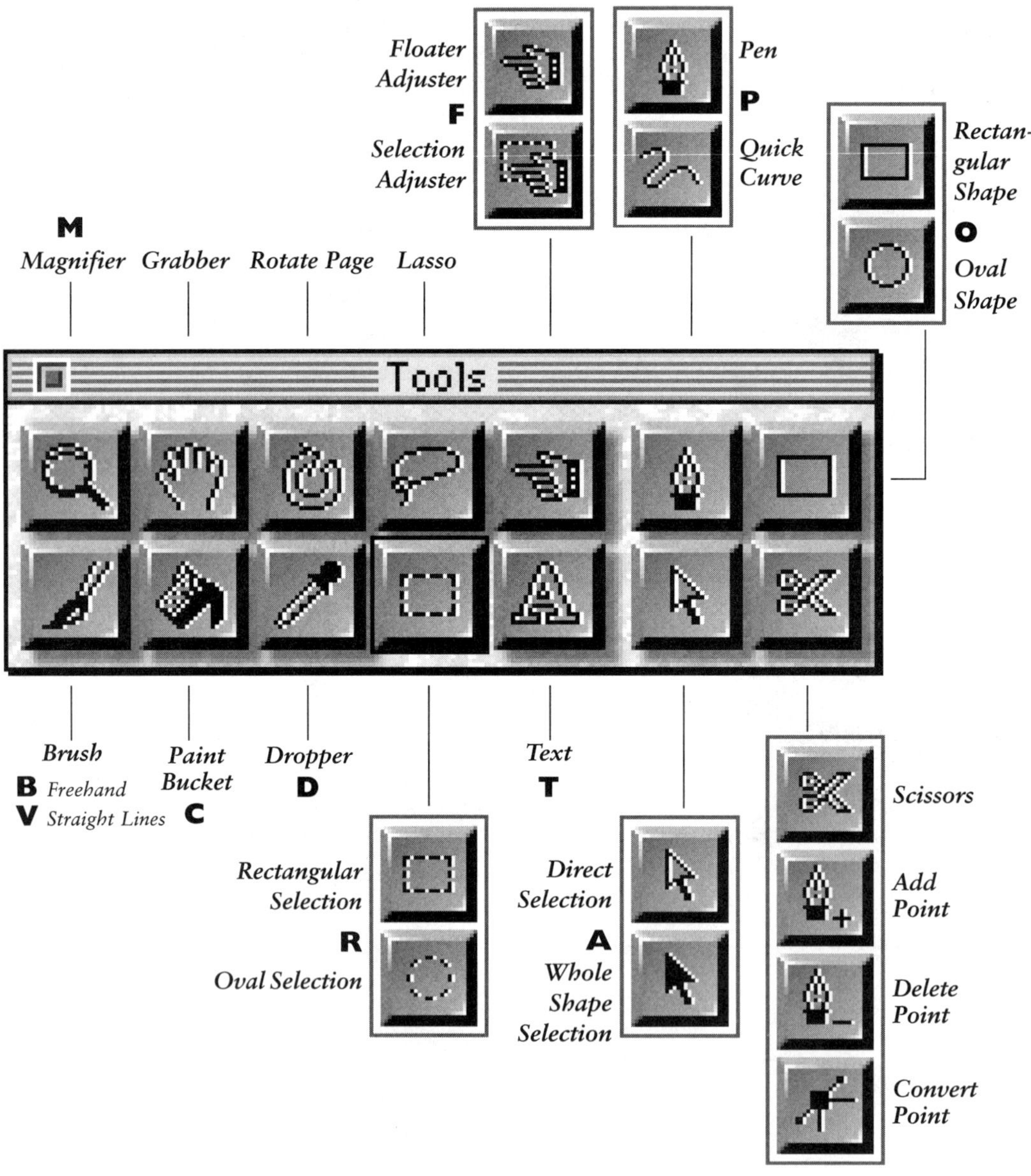

Tool descriptions

Magnifier
Changes the picture's screen display size.

Grabber
Moves the picture in the image window. (Hold down Space bar to access the Grabber when another tool except the Text tool is selected.)

Rotate Page
Rotates the canvas for drawing comfort. (Hold down Option and Space bar to rotate the page when another tool is selected.)

Lasso
Creates freehand selection paths or open shapes.

Floater Adjuster
Turns an ordinary selection into a floater; selects, moves, or transforms an existing floater or shape.

Selection Adjuster
Selects, moves, and transforms selection paths.

Pen
Creates straight-sided or Bézier curve shapes.

Quick Curve
Creates freehand shapes.

Rectangular Shape
Creates rectangular or square shapes.

Oval Shape
Creates oval or circular shapes.

Brush
Painter's basic painting tool. Choose individual brushes (Pen, Chalk, etc.), brush variants, method categories, and method subcategories from the Brushes palette.

Paint Bucket
Fills with color where you press or drag the stylus or click or drag the mouse.

Dropper
Selects a Primary color (front color rectangle highlighted on the Art Materials: Color palette) or a Secondary color (back color rectangle highlighted on the Color palette) from a picture. (Press Command to access the Dropper when another tool is selected.)

Rectangular Selection
Creates rectangular or square selection paths.

Oval Selection
Creates oval or circular selection paths.

Text
Creates text shapes.

Direct Selection
Selects components of shapes (segments, anchor points, or wings).

Whole Shape Selection
Selects whole shapes.

Scissors
Splits shape segments.

Add Point
Adds anchor points to shapes.

Delete Point
Removes anchor points from shapes.

Convert Point
Converts curve anchor points into corner anchor points, and vice versa.

Changing your mind (undo options)

It's easy to backtrack if you learn the following techniques.

Choose Edit menu > **Undo** (Command-Z) to undo the last operation. Repeat to undo the second-to-last operation, etc. You can undo up to 32 operations (the combined total for all open documents), depending on the Undo Preferences setting (choose Edit menu > Preferences > Undo and enter a number 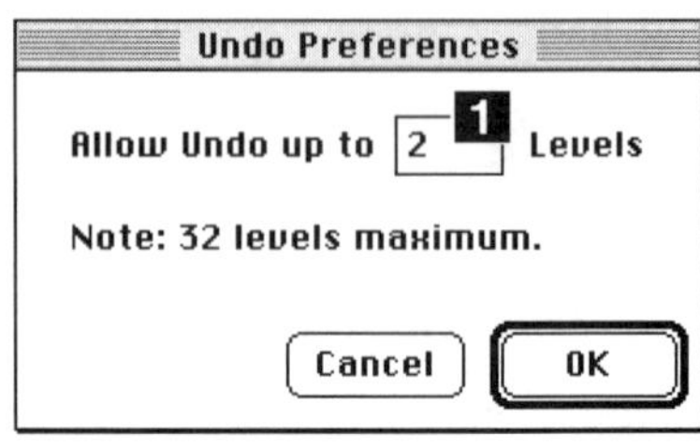). The whole picture is saved for each Undo level, so you may want to limit the number of levels to conserve disk space. To take advantage of the Undo command, draw short brush strokes when you're painting. You can Undo after you save your file, as long as it's still open.

Choose File menu > **Redo** (Command-Y) to redo the last undone operation.

Choose File menu > **Revert,** then click Revert to restore the last saved version of your document.

Choose Edit menu > **Clear** (or press Delete) to fill the current selection with the current paper color. Choose Edit menu > Select All first if you want to clear your whole picture.

A pat on the back to Fractal Design for the **Fade** command, which reduces the last modification in increments. Choose Edit menu > Fade, then watch the preview in the Fade dialog box as you move the Undo Amount slider 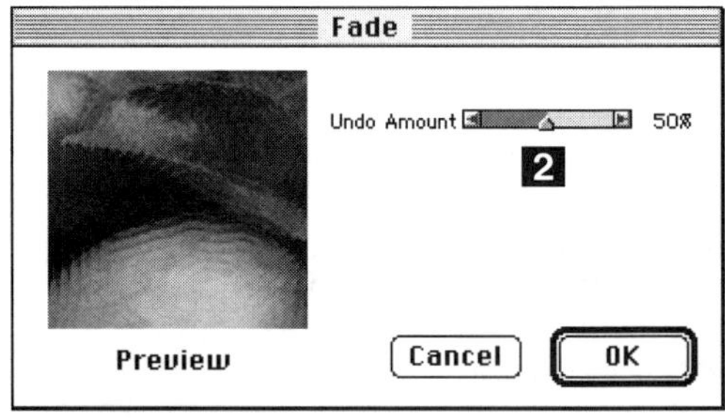. If you choose Undo after executing the Fade command, both the Fade and the previous command will be undone.

Another way to backtrack on an image is to record its creation as a **script**. Then you can edit the script: add or delete steps or copy steps from another script. Chapter 13 is devoted entirely to scripts.

And finally, if you **clone** a whole document and then work in the clone image window, you can restore areas from a source document. This technique is discussed in Chapter 10.

How to remove brush strokes
Choose Edit menu > Undo (Command-Z).
or
Erase using an Eraser brush variant or using the Eraser method category for a non-Eraser brush.
or
Paint with a background color or the current paper color (you can use the Dropper tool to choose a color from the picture).

Magnifier tool

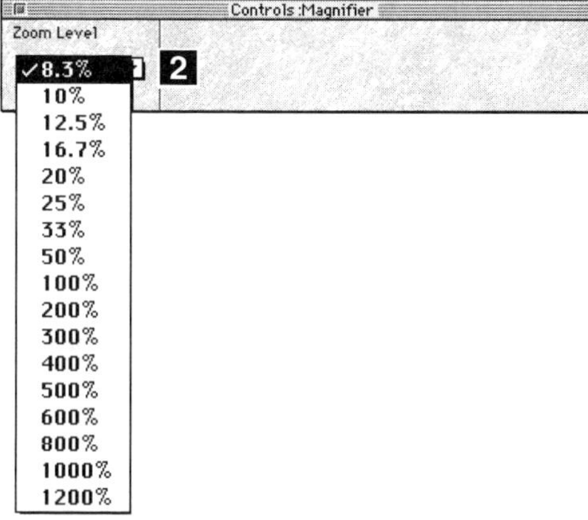

To change the view size without using the Magnifier tool

TO ENLARGE THE VIEW SIZE:
Command-+ *-or-* **Command-Space bar-click in the image window**

TO REDUCE THE VIEW SIZE:
Command-– ** *-or-* **Command-Option-Space bar-click in the image window

Grabber tool

To change a picture's display size:

1. Choose the Magnifier tool (M).

2. To enlarge the view size, click in the image window.
   or
   To reduce the view size, hold down Option and click in the image window.
   or
   Choose a Zoom Level from the Controls: Magnifier palette pop-up menu **2**.
   or
   Press and drag in the image window. The area you marquee will be magnified.

   The current level of magnification will be indicated on the document title bar.

   To center the image, hold down Space bar and click in the image window.

   To display your entire picture at the largest possible size for your screen, choose Window menu > Zoom to Fit Screen or double-click the Grabber tool.

To move the image in the image window:

1. Choose the Grabber tool.

2. Press and drag in the image window.

   Click in the image window with the Grabber tool to center the image in the window.

   Hold down Space bar to use the Grabber tool while another tool is selected.

   When the Grabber tool is selected, you can choose a Zoom Level from the Controls palette.

Like an artist working in traditional media, you can rotate the paper/canvas to reach an area of a picture from a more comfortable position, or simply to study the composition from a different angle. **The picture will print from its original orientation.**

To work on a picture from a different angle:

1. Choose the Rotate Page tool **1**.

2. Press and drag in a circular direction in the image window. The arrow will point to the top of the original image as you drag **2**a–b.

To restore the original vertical orientation, click in the image window with the Rotate Page tool, or Option-Space bar-click in the image window with any tool selected except the Text tool, or double-click the Rotate Page tool.

Hold down Option and Space bar to use the Rotate Page tool while another tool is selected.

Hold down Shift while dragging to rotate to the nearest 90° angle.

1 *Rotate Page tool*

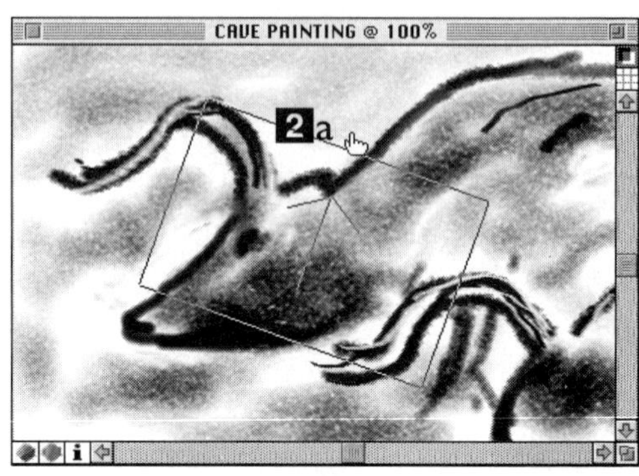

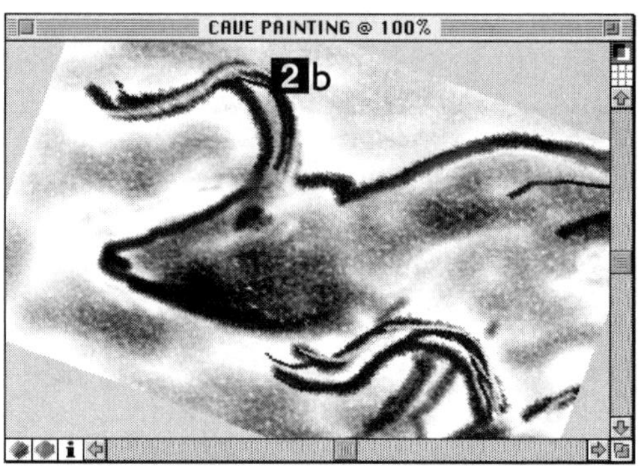

Tip

To prevent clicking in the Finder when you stroke off the edge of your paper, make the image window slightly larger than the picture.

Work on a Picture from a Different Angle

The cropped image appears in a new, untitled image window.

This method is a bit cumbersome, but it works.

To crop an image:

1. Choose the Rectangular Selection tool.
2. Select the area you want to keep **2**.
3. Choose Edit menu > Copy (Command-C).
4. Choose Edit menu > Paste > Into New Image.

🖌 To replace the old document with the new document, choose File > Save As, and use the same document name as the original. To preserve the original, save the new document under a different name.

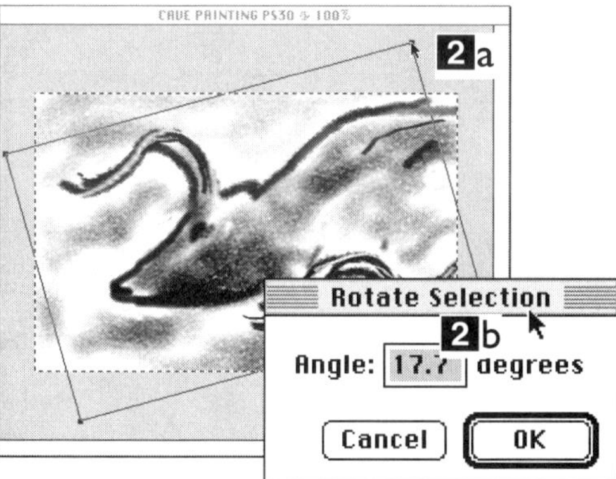

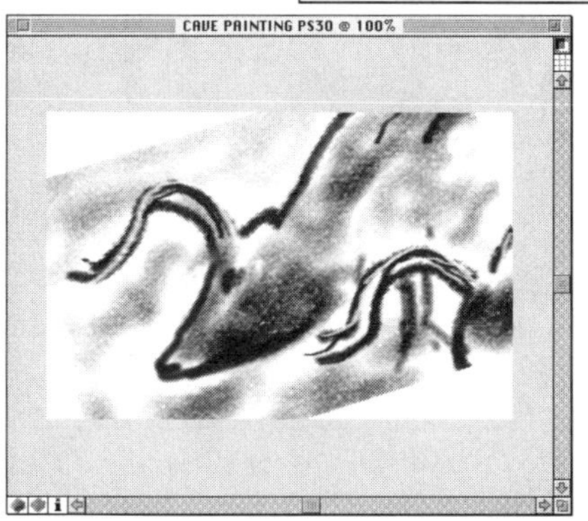

The rotated image.

Use the Rotate command to save and print a picture from a new orientation. The Rotate command will turn your picture into a floater, and it will blur it slightly on screen (it will print okay).

To rotate the image:

1. Choose Effects menu > Orientation > Rotate. Move the Rotate Selection dialog box out of the way, if you like.
2. Press and drag a corner of the image in the image window **2**a.
   or
   Enter a number in the Angle field **2**b.
3. Click OK or press Return.
4. Choose Edit menu > Deselect (Command-D).
5. *Optional:* To drop the floater onto the canvas, click the F. List icon on the Objects palette, then click Drop.

🖌 To create a vertical or horizontal mirror image of your picture, choose Effects menu > Orientation > Flip Horizontal or Flip Vertical. The image won't become a floater.

Use the Canvas Size command to add new, editable pixels to any of a picture's four sides. **You must turn off Wet Paint to access the Canvas Size command.**

To enlarge the canvas size:

1. *Optional:* The new border area will be the Paper Color you chose when you created your document. To change the paper color, choose a Primary color from the Art Materials: Color palette, then choose Canvas menu > Set Paper Color.

2. Choose Canvas menu > Canvas Size.

3. Enter the number of pixels you want to add to the image in any of the Increase Size fields **3**. To calculate the number of pixels to enter, multiply the number of inches you want to add by your file's pixels per inch resolution, then divide by two.

4. Click OK or press Return.

5. Click the image window grow box (upper right corner) to enlarge the window and display the added pixels.

Toggle your screen mode

To display your picture in the center of your screen with the image window title bar and scroll bars hidden, choose Window menu > Screen Mode Toggle (Command-M). The picture is editable in this mode. Choose the same command again to restore the normal viewing mode.

Enlarge the Canvas Size

The original picture.

Pixels added to all four sides of the picture and the image window enlarged.

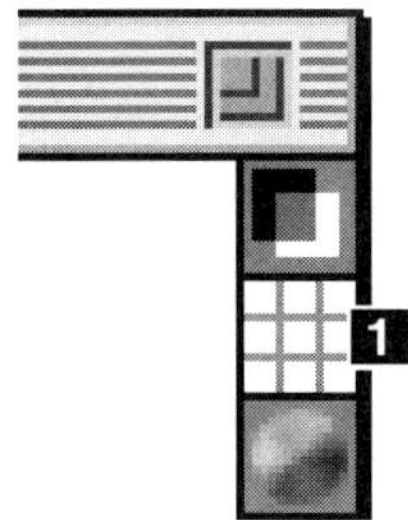

To display a non-printing grid:

1. Choose Canvas menu > Grid >
View Grid.
or
Click the grid icon in the upper right
corner of the image window ◼.

2. *Optional:* Choose Canvas menu >
Grid > Grid Options, then change the
Grid type, Horizontal or Vertical
Spacing (space between lines), Line
Thickness, or Grid Color (line color).
When the Transparent Background
box is unchecked, the grid will have a
semi-transparent background. When
it's checked, you'll see the image at
full strength behind the grid. Click
OK to display the modified grid.

To turn the grid off, choose Canvas
menu > Grid > View Grid or click the
grid icon again.

To create a grid that *is* part of the
image and does print, choose Effects
menu > Esoterica > Grid Paper **before**
you start painting (this command
clears the whole canvas).

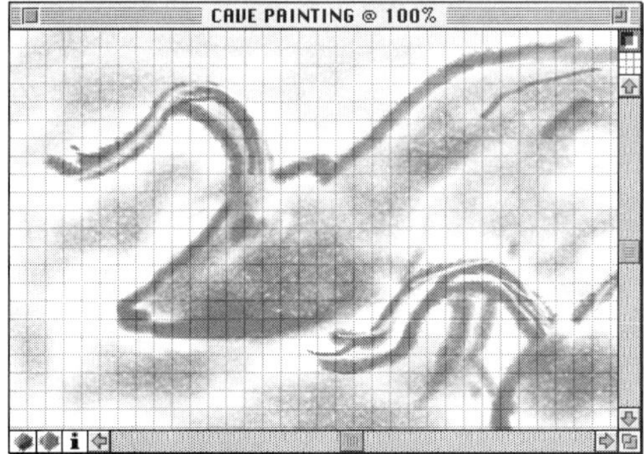

*Show Grid turned on and the Transparent Background
box unchecked in the Grid Options dialog box.*

Display a Non-Printing Grid

Read about rulers and guides on page 65.

To change a picture's storage size and/or resolution:

1. Choose Canvas menu > Resize (Command-Shift-R).

2. To change the file's storage size and not its resolution, choose pixels from the pop-up menus and enter a new number in the Width or Height field **2**. The Constrain File Size box will uncheck automatically if it was originally checked. Don't recheck it unless you want to restore the original file size.

   or

   To change the file's resolution and overall dimensions but not its storage size, choose an increment other than pixels from the Width and Height pop-up menus, check the Constrain File Size box, then enter a new number in the Width, Height, or Resolution field. (To change resolution *and* storage size, uncheck the Constrain File Size box first.)

3. Click OK or press Return.

   To add pixels to any of the image's four sides, use the Canvas menu > Canvas Size command (see page 18). If you use the Edit menu > Orientation > Scale > command to resize a whole image, the image will become a floater.

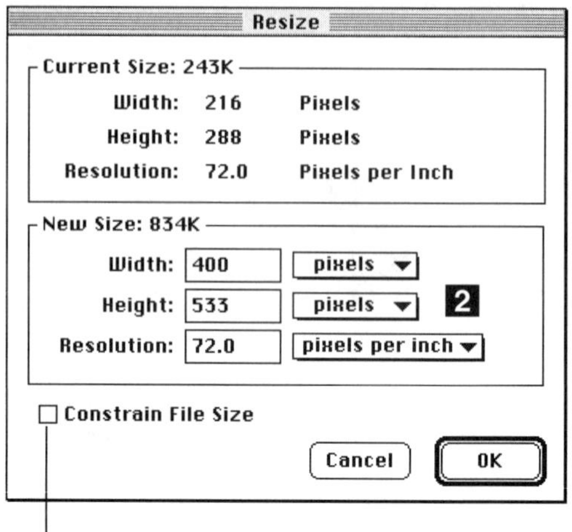

*If the **Constrain File Size** box is checked and you change a picture's width, height, or resolution, the picture's on-screen display size will remain the same, with no loss of pixels. With the Constrain File Size box unchecked, the image is resampled, which means its on-screen size and file storage size change. Resampling down causes pixels to be permanently deleted from the file, and resampling up causes pixels to be added based on existing colors in the picture. Resampling will diminish a picture's crispness, but the degree to which the change will be noticeable depends on how much the resolution is changed and whether the picture contains sharp line work.*

To access the movers

Type of library	Choose
Brush	Brushes palette > Brushes menu > Brush Mover
Brush Look	Brushes palette > Brushes menu > Brush Look Mover
Nozzle	Brushes palette > Nozzle menu > Nozzle Mover
Path	Objects palette > P. List menu > Path Mover
Floater	Objects palette > F. List menu > Floater Mover
Script	Objects palette > Scripts menu > Script Mover
Paper	Art Materials palette > Paper menu > Paper Mover
Gradation	Art Materials palette > Grad menu > Grad Mover
Pattern	Art Materials palette > Pattern menu > Pattern Mover
Weave	Art Materials palette > Weave menu > Weave Mover
Lighting	Command-Shift-L

How many items should I put in a library?

A maximum of 25 icons can be displayed in the palette drawer at a time, so you might want to limit the number of items you place in one library to that number. If the drawer contains more than 25 items, you'll need to use the scroll bar or arrows to access the ones on the bottom. Also, keeping your libraries small will help Painter run efficiently.

To create a library:

1. Choose the name of the mover from the appropriate palette (see the list at left).

2. Click New.

3. Enter a name for the library.

4. Choose a location in which to save the library. The Painter application folder is the usual spot.

5. Click Save.

6. Highlight the gradation, weave, etc. on the left side of the Mover dialog box that you want to move into the library. (If the item isn't listed, click Close, then click Open to open the correct library.)

7. Click Copy.

8. *Optional:* To change the name of a library entry, highlight the entry name, click Change Name, enter a new name, then click OK.

9. Click Quit or press Return.

   Note: The methods for adding current items to libraries vary widely, so they're covered in relevant chapters throughout this book. For example, to add a path to a path library, you'll simply drag it onto the Objects: Paths palette. To add a nozzle to a nozzle library, you'll choose Brushes palette > Nozzle menu > Add Nozzle To Library.

To delete a whole library, drag its icon from the Finder to the trash.

Create a Library

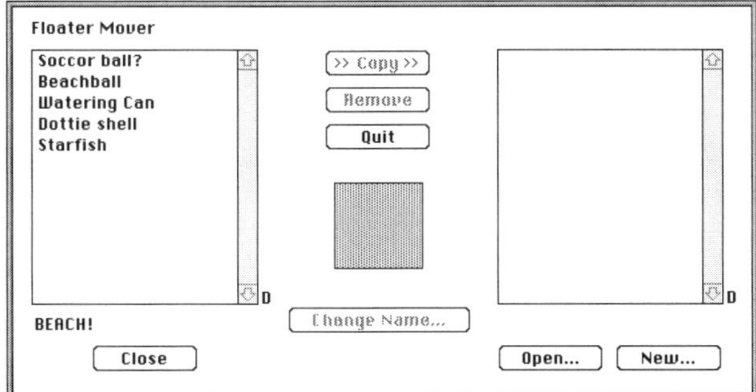

The Floater Mover. In this illustration, a new library called "BEACH!" has been created, and it contains five items.

To edit a library:

1. Choose name of the mover from the appropriate palette pull-down menu (see the previous page).

2. *Optional:* To open a different library at any time, click Close, if necessary, click Open, highlight the library you want to open, then click Open.

3. To **delete** an item from a library, highlight it, then click Remove.

   To **rename** an item, highlight it, click Change Name, enter a new name, then click OK or press Return.

   To **copy** an item from one library to another, open the library you want to copy from and highlight the item you want to copy on the left side of the dialog box, open the library you want to move the item to on the right side of the dialog box, then click Copy.

4. Click Quit or press Return.

About default libraries

If you inadvertently remove an item from one of Painter's default libraries, you'll have to reinstall Painter to retrieve it.

In the General Preferences dialog box (Edit > Preferences > General), you can choose which libraries will load automatically when you launch Painter.

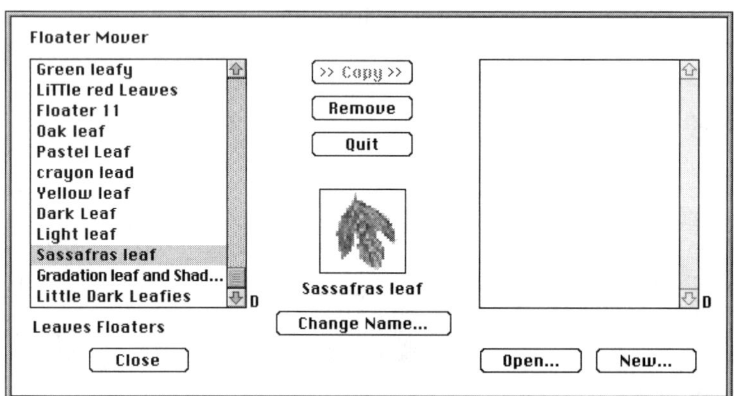

To close a file:

Choose File menu > Close (Command-W). If you've edited your image since it was last saved, a warning prompt will appear. Click Save or Don't Save—whichever you prefer.

To quit Painter:

Choose File menu > Quit (Command-Q).

Scanning

Using a scanning device and scanning software, a slide, flat artwork, or a photograph can be digitized so you can open it and paint on it in Painter. If you install the correct plug-in file, you can scan directly into Painter. (Painter can only access plug-ins from one folder, so install your scanner plug-in with the rest of the plug-ins you want to use in Painter.) If you scan outside Painter, make sure to save the scan in a file format that Painter imports, such as TIFF.

Scanners

The quality of a scan depends on the type of scanner you use. If you are going to apply a lot of brush strokes or Effects menu commands to the image in Painter, you can use an inexpensive flat-bed scanner. If color accuracy is critical, scan a transparency on a slide scanner. Scan a picture that is going to be printed electronically on a high-resolution CCD scanner, such as a Scitex Smart-Scanner, or on a drum scanner. A high-quality scan can be obtained from a service bureau. Unfortunately, high-resolution scans usually have very large file sizes, and they are sometimes saved in CMYK color mode, which Painter cannot open. You can use another application, like Photoshop, to convert a CMYK color file into an RGB color file, which Painter can open.

Scanner software

Scanning software usually offers most of the following options, although terminology may vary. The quality and file storage size of a scan are affected by the mode, resolution, and scale you specify, and whether you crop the image. Set the scanning parameters carefully, weighing such factors as your final output device and storage capacity.

Preview: Place the art in the scanner, then click Preview or PreScan.

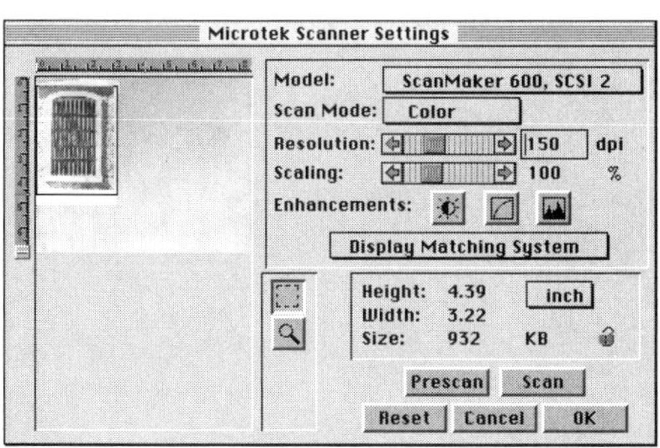

(Continued on the next page)

Scan mode: Choose Black-and-White Line Art (no grays), Grayscale or Color. A picture scanned in color will be approximately three times larger in file size than in grayscale.

Resolution: Scan resolution is measured in pixels per inch (ppi). The higher the resolution, the better the scan, and the larger its file size. Choose the minimum resolution necessary to obtain the best possible printout from your final output device. Choosing a higher resolution than is required will just make the picture take up more disk space than is necessary and it will take longer to render on screen and to print, with no improvement in output quality.

For multimedia or video work, choose the monitor's resolution (72 ppi). Before selecting a resolution for printing, ask your print shop what halftone screen frequency they will be using. As a general rule, your image resolution should be one-and-a-half times the printer's halftone screen frequency (lines per inch) for a grayscale picture and twice the halftone screen frequency for a color picture. (If your printer plans to use a 133-line screen for grayscale printing, for example, scan your image at 200 ppi.) We've been told this rule can be broken, though. For smudgy, chalky, or painterly color images, one-and-a-half times screen frequency may be adequate. For crisp line art, use a very high scan resolution (600 ppi or higher), then lower the resolution in Painter to the appropriate output resolution.

Cropping: If you're going to use only part of the image in Painter, move the handles of the selection box in the preview window to reduce the scan area. Cropping will reduce the scan's storage size.

Scale: To enlarge the image's dimensions, choose a scale percentage larger than 100%. This is the time to enlarge your image, if you need to. Enlarging the image in Painter may make it blurry because mathematical "guesswork" is used to fill in needed pixel information. A source picture's original information is recorded only at the time of scanning.

Scan: Click Scan and choose a location in which to save the file.

Video capture

To digitize (capture) video frames to edit in Painter, a video board and its accompanying software must be installed in your computer. The necessary hardware and software to capture video is built into AV (audio-visual) Macs and 7500, 7600, and 8500 PCI Power Macs.

You'll need to use the proper cables to connect the video source (like a VCR) to the Mac. In Painter, choose File menu > Acquire, and select the appropriate plug-in name for video. In the video capture software dialog box, set such parameters as the video encoding standard used by the input signal (like NTSC for United States video recordings), the source encoding method of the video (like composite or S-video), and the size of the captured video image. A 640 by 480 pixel resolution will produce a full video frame on a 14-inch monitor.

With the video capture dialog box open, start the source video, then click the Grab button (or a similarly-named capture button) to grab a "frame" of the video. If your Mac has built in video capture capability (AV and 7500 or 8500 PCI Macs), use that software to capture a video frame, save the captured image in the PICT or TIFF file format, then open it in Painter.

Keep in mind that the quality of a video captured image will depend on the quality of hardware and software you use to capture and of course the quality of the original videotape.

Painting Basics 2

*Ron Gorchov, **Clone of Herophile** (detail).*

Follow these instructions if you'd like to get started painting right away using Painter's default brushes. After you learn these basic steps, you'll want to learn more about brushes, paper textures, and color. These topics are covered in this chapter and in the next two chapters.

QuickStart Paint:

■ *Choose a brush.*

1. Click the **Brush** tool on the Tools palette (B).

2. Click a brush icon on the Brushes palette drawer front **2**a (Command-2 or double-click the Brush tool to hide/show the Brushes palette).
   or
   Click the pushbar to open the drawer, then click a brush icon in the drawer **2**b or choose a brush from the pop-up menu **2**c. (If an item is already on a palette drawer front, its icon in the drawer will be dimmed.)

3. Choose a variant for the brush from the variant pop-up menu **3**.

■ *Choose a paper texture.*

Note: Brush strokes will reveal the paper texture only if your brush has a Grainy method subcategory.

1. Click the **Paper** icon on the Art Materials palette **1** (Command-3 to open/close the Papers palette).

2. Click a paper texture icon on the Papers palette drawer front **2**a.
   or
   Click the pushbar to open the drawer, then click a paper texture icon in the drawer **2**b or choose a paper texture from the pop-up menu **2**c.

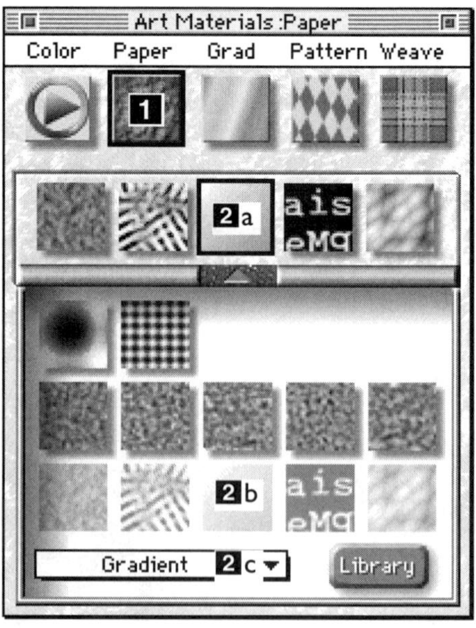

■ *Choose a color.*

1. Click the **Color** icon on the Art Materials palette .

2. Make sure the Primary (frontmost) rectangle is highlighted **2**. (Click on it to activate it.)

3. To choose a hue, click on the color ring or move the little circle on the color ring **3**. If you're using the Compact Colors (Small Color) palette (Art Materials palette > Color menu), click on the color bar to choose a hue.

4. Click on the triangle or move the circle on the triangle to choose a value and a saturation of that hue **4**.

■ *Paint!*

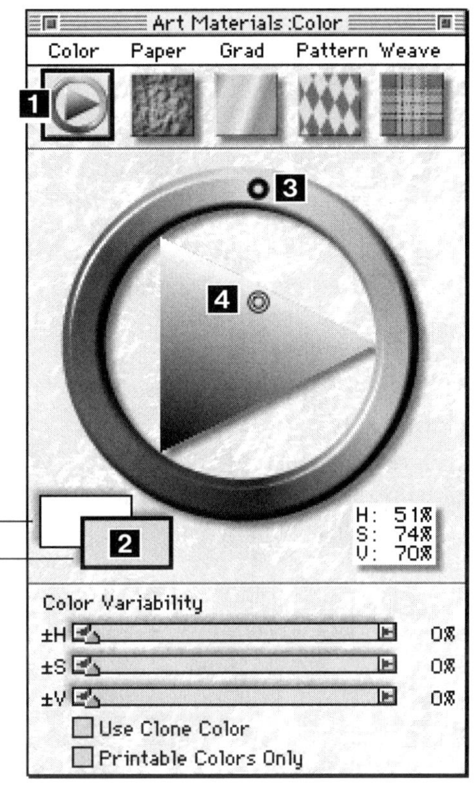

Secondary color rectangle

Primary color rectangle

How to remove brush strokes
Choose Edit menu > Undo (Command-Z).
or
Erase using an Eraser brush variant or a non-Eraser brush with the Eraser method category.
or
Paint with a background color or the current paper color (you can use the Dropper tool to choose a color from the picture).

(To delete the whole image, choose Edit menu > Select All (Command-A), then press Delete.)

The Controls: Brush palette

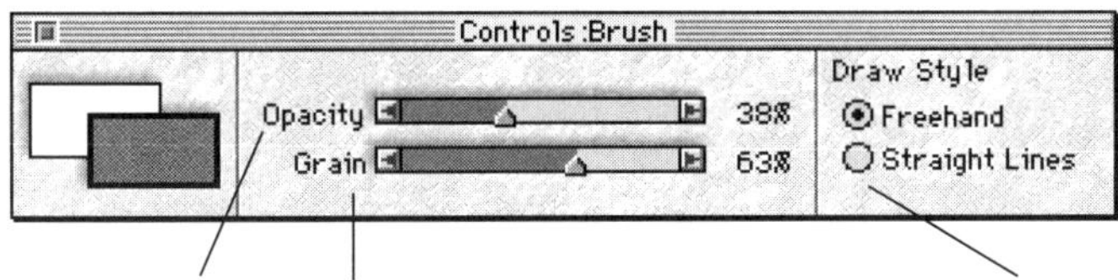

*Move the **Opacity** slider to adjust the transparency of the stroke. Or press a corresponding keypad key (0=100%, 1=10%, 2=20%, etc.)*

*If you choose for your brush a sub-method category that contains the word "Grainy," moving the **Grain** slider to the left will usually make the paper texture more prominent in your brush strokes. The higher the Grain setting, the more strokes penetrate the paper surface and the less the grain shows.*

*Drag with your mouse or stylus when the **Freehand Draw Style** is selected. Click with your mouse or stylus to create **Straight Lines**. To end a Straight Lines stroke as an open shape, click the Freehand button. To end it as a closed shape, press Return.*

Choose a Color

Color

Most of the time you will paint with what Fractal Design calls the **Primary** color. The current Primary color is displayed in the front color rectangle on the Art Materials: Color palette and on the Controls: Brush and Controls: Dropper palettes. You may occasionally choose a **Secondary** color (the back color rectangle)—for the Graduated Brush, to mix a color into the Image Hose, or to create a Two-Point gradient.

To choose a Primary color:

1. Click the Color icon on the Art Materials palette **1**.

2. Make sure the Primary (frontmost) rectangle is highlighted **2**. (Click on it to activate it.)

3. Click on the color ring (or the color bar, if you're using the Compact Colors palette) on the Color palette to choose a hue **3**.
   or
   To choose a color from a picture, choose the Dropper tool, then click on a color in any open image window.
   or
   Choose Window menu > Color Set, then click a swatch. To open a different color set, see the next page.

4. On the Color palette, click on the triangle or move the little circle on the triangle to choose a different value or saturation of that hue **4**.

5. *Optional:* Check the Printable Colors Only box on the expanded Colors palette to restrict subsequently chosen colors to colors that can be printed on a four-color press **5**.

   To convert existing colors in a picture into their closest printable equivalents, choose Effects menu > Tonal Control > Printable Colors, then click OK. To convert existing colors to video legal colors (NTSC for the U.S., PAL for Europe), choose Video Legal Colors from the same submenu.

In Painter, you can choose colors based on their **Hue, Saturation, and Value (HSV)** components or their **Red, Green, and Blue (RGB)** components. You can't choose **CMYK** colors in Painter.

In the HSV color model, hue is the component that gives a color its name, such as red or green; saturation is the intensity of a color; value is the amount of white or black in a color (brightness).

Use the RGB Colors palette to mix **RGB colors** by number (Choose Art Materials > Color menu > RBG Colors).

 *Dropper tool*

Tip
To quickly choose white, drag from anywhere inside the triangle on the Color palette upward off the triangle. To choose black, drag downward.

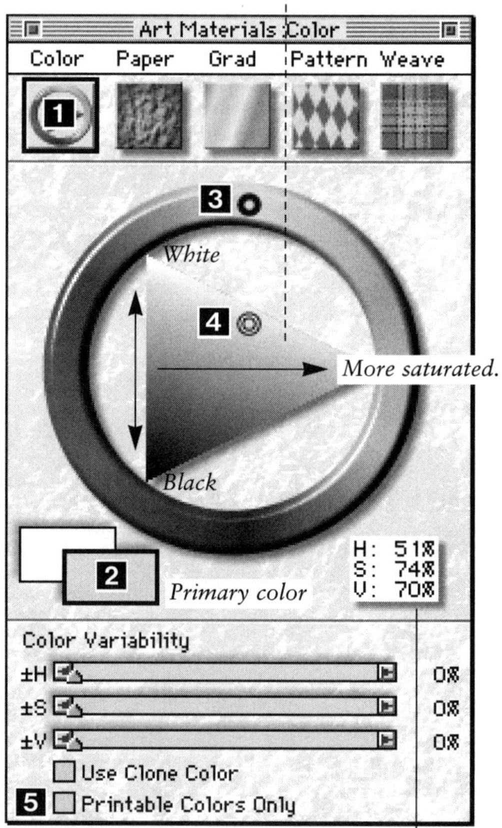

Click this box to switch between HSV and RGB color readouts.

The Color Set swatch palette displays one group of color swatches at a time that you can choose from to paint with. To display the Color Set palette, choose Window menu > Color Set (Command-6). Choose Color Set again to close the palette, or click the palette close box. To choose a color in a set, simply click on a swatch.

The color you choose from the Color Set palette will also be displayed in whichever color rectangle is currently active on the Art Materials: Color palette and the Controls: Brush palette.

Painter Colors is Painter's default color set. The Pantone Colors set and many other color sets, including Grayscale, Muted Tones, and Candy, are also supplied with Painter. You can create your own color sets to make it easier to grab colors that you use frequently or to assemble special colors for specific projects.

To display a different color set:

1. Choose Art Materials palette > Color menu > Adjust Color Set.

2. Click Library **2**.

3. Locate and highlight the color set you want to open. The Painter Colors color set is on the first level of the application folder. The other Painter color sets are in the Colors, Weaves, Grads folder. Color sets that you create may be stored anywhere you like.

4. Click Open.

✎ Read more about color sets in Chapter 4, More Painting.

✎ Use Painter's Grayscale color set to create a grayscale picture **3**.

✎ You can choose which color set will open when you launch Painter via the Edit menu > Preferences > General dialog box.

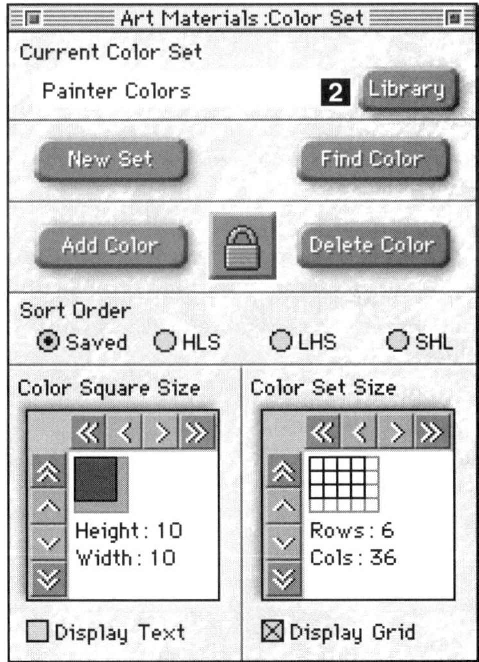

3 *The Grayscale color set.*

Paper Textures

There is a rich assortment of methods for applying paper textures in Painter. If you use a brush for which you've chosen a Grainy method subcategory, the paper texture currently selected on the Art Materials: Paper palette will be revealed under your brush strokes. You can choose a different paper texture at any time while you're painting. Many Effects menu commands, including Adjust Colors, Adjust Selected Colors, Apply Screen, Apply Surface Texture, Color Overlay, Dye Concentration, Express Texture, and Glass Distortion, apply a texture to a whole painting or to a selected area. If you use an Eraser brush on a texture applied using either method, you'll **erase texture** along with color.

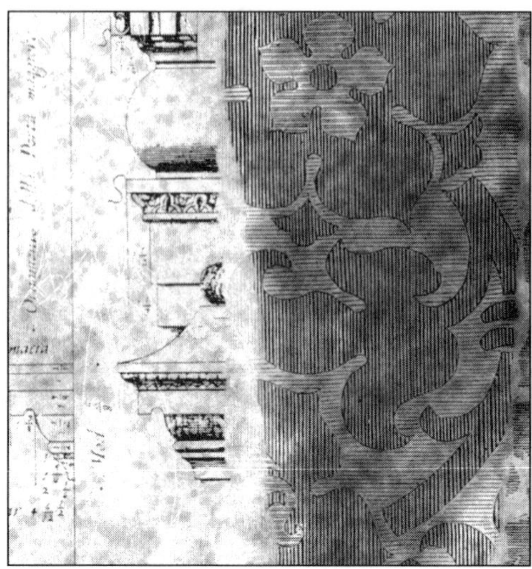

Fabric Effects, Inc. (detail)

Grainy brushes used to add texture.

To reveal a paper texture under brush strokes:

1. *Optional:* To choose a different paper texture, click the Paper icon on the Art Materials palette, then click a paper texture icon on the palette drawer front or in the drawer.
2. Make sure the brush method subcategory you have selected contains the word "Grainy."
3. Paint.
4. *Optional:* To make the paper texture more prominent, move the Controls: Brush palette Grain slider to the left.

HELP!

You chose a brush and color, tried to paint, and nothing happened?

Make sure the Brush tool is still selected.

Still nothing?

Check to make sure your paint color doesn't match your background color (i.e., white-on-white).

Still nothing?

Make sure you haven't unintentionally activated a floater or a selection path (check on the Objects: F. List and P. List palettes).

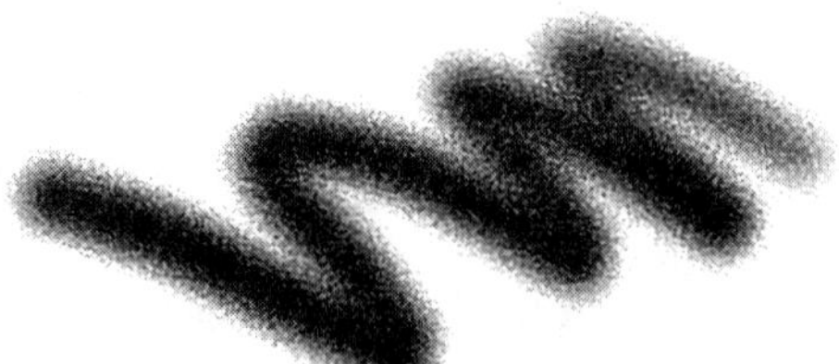

Default Charcoal variant, Grainy Hard Cover method subcategory: Brush stroke reveals paper texture.

Default Charcoal variant, Soft Cover method subcategory: Brush stroke doesn't reveal paper texture.

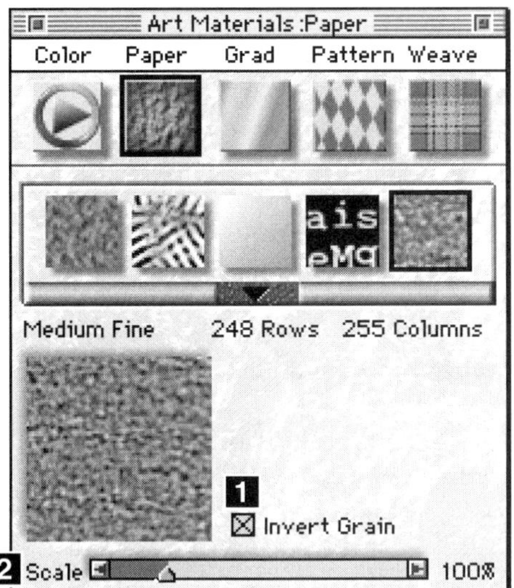

If you're ready to expand beyond the default Paper Textures library...

To choose Art Materials: Paper palette options:

- To switch the raised and depressed areas of the paper, check the Invert Grain box **1**.

- To shrink or enlarge the texture, move the Scale slider **2**.

- To display a different paper texture library, open the drawer, click Library, highlight a library, then click Open. Several paper texture libraries are supplied with Painter (in the Paper folder inside the Goodies folder on the Painter 4 CD-ROM), and of course you can create your own paper textures and paper texture libraries.

Painter's default Hatching paper texture.

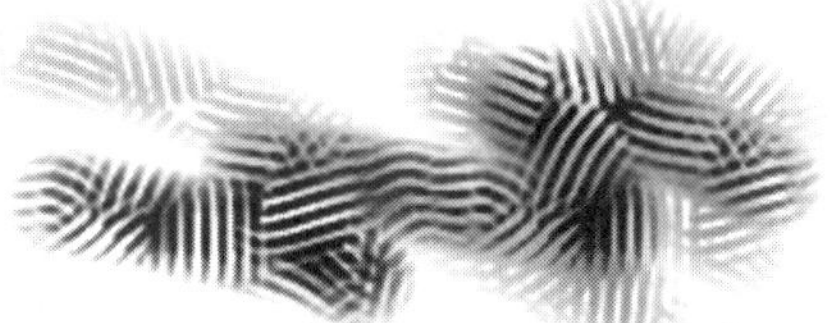

To create a two-color texture, move the Grain slider on the Controls: Brush palette to the left and stroke with the Invert Grain box checked, then uncheck the Invert Grain box and stroke with a second color.

Texture and then a brush stroke (Grainy Buildup method subcategory) applied to the top part of the image with the Invert Grain box unchecked. The brush stroke darkens the positive areas of the texture.

Texture applied with the Invert Grain box unchecked, and then a brush stroke applied with the Invert Grain box checked (Water Color brush, Grainy Wet Abrasive method subcategory). The brush stroke affects the negative areas.

Brushes

When you use a default brush **variant**, a **method category** and **method subcategory** are selected for you automatically. To customize a brush, you can start by choosing a different category or subcategory from the expanded Brushes palette. For the Pencil brush, for example, you can choose a variant like the 2b Pencil, then choose a different method category like Cover, and then choose a different method subcategory, like Soft Cover. There are an immense number of possible variant/category/subcategory combinations. Other ways of customizing brushes are discussed on pages 62–63 and 66–74.

Default brush settings

- ■ If you choose non-default settings for a brush and then choose a different brush or variant, your non-default settings will be lost. To save a customized variant so you can choose it again, follow the instructions on page 63.

- ■ You can preview and test brush variants and brush-and-paper combinations in the Brush Look Designer dialog box before you use them in your picture.

- ■ To restore a brush's default settings while keeping the brush selected, Option-click its icon on the Brushes palette.

Brush Method Categories

THE METHOD CATEGORIES

Buildup *strokes combine with existing strokes underneath them, producing darker areas where they crisscross. Choose a light Opacity from the Controls: Brush palette to slow down the buildup.*

Cover *strokes cover existing strokes underneath them. Choose a light Opacity from the Controls: Brush palette to make cover strokes less opaque.*

Eraser *strokes erase completely to the current paper color when the Controls: Brush Opacity slider is at 100%. Choose a lower Opacity to partially erase strokes (we chose 40% for the eraser stroke above). And of course you can use of the Eraser brush itself, with its own variants.*

Drip *strokes smear existing colors. The Liquid brushes automatically have the Drip method category.*

Mask *strokes create masked (protected) areas. (See Chapter 9)*

Cloning *brush strokes reproduce pixels in a clone document from the source document. (See Chapter 10)*

Wet *strokes stay wet on the special Wet Paint layer until you choose Canvas > Dry. Water Color brush variants automatically have this method category. (Before drawing the Large Simple Water brush stroke above, the Diffusion slider on the Advanced Controls: Water palette was moved to 13.)*

THE METHOD SUBCATEGORIES

Soft: Smooth, anti-aliased edge.

Flat: Hard, jagged edge.

Edge: Thick, opaque edge.

Hard: Semi-anti-aliased edge.

Grainy: Brush strokes reveal paper texture.

Cover method subcategories hide underlying pixels.

Flat Cover *Hard, jagged edge. Doesn't reveal paper grain.*

Soft Cover *Anti-aliased edge. Doesn't reveal paper grain.*

Grainy Flat Cover *Paper grain sensitive, hard-edged.*

Grainy Soft Cover *Paper grain sensitive, anti-aliased.*

Grainy Edge Flat Cover *Hard-edged, paper grain visible only on the brush stroke edge. Unaffected by opacity setting on Brush Controls palette.*

Grainy Hard Cover *Paper grain sensitive, semi-anti-aliased.*

You can see the difference between Cover and Buildup brush strokes where the stroke crisscrosses itself.

Buildup method subcategories build up to black.

Soft Buildup *Anti-aliased.*

Grainy Soft Buildup *Paper grain sensitive, anti-aliased.*

Grainy Edge Flat Buildup *Paper grain sensitive, hard-edged.*

Grainy Hard Buildup *Paper grain sensitive, semi-anti-aliased.*

How can I change my brush size?

To change the brush size interactively, hold down Command and Option and drag in the image window. If you make the brush tip large, you may get a prompt to Build the brush when you start to use it.

To change the brush size another way, choose Brushes palette > Controls menu > Size, move the Size slider, and click Build, if the button lights up. (More about Brush Controls in Chapter 4.)

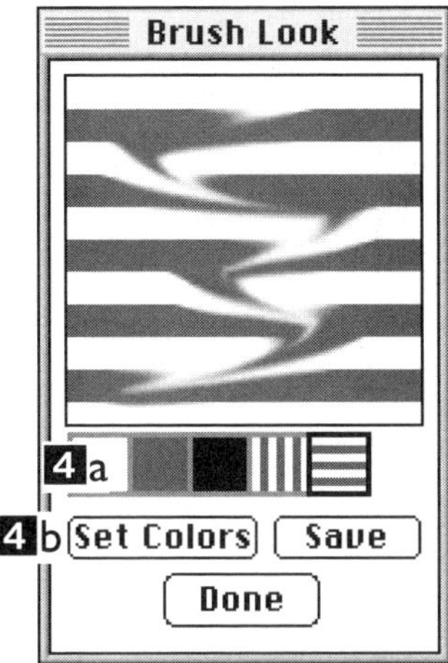

*The **Brush Look Designer***

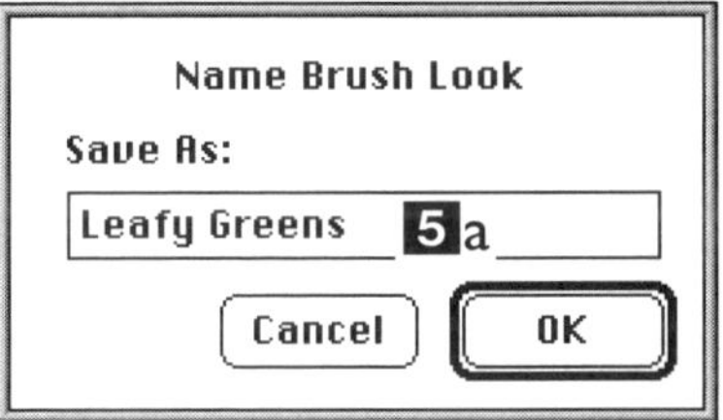

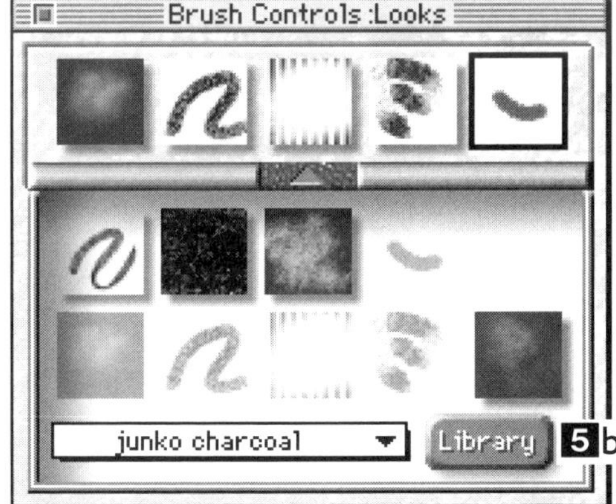

To choose a saved brush look

Choose Brushes palette > Brushes menu > Brush Looks, then click an icon on the drawer front or in the drawer or choose from the pop-up menu. (To create or edit a brush looks library, see pages 21–22.)

You can use the Brush Look Designer simply to preview a brush variant or a customized brush before you use it. Or use the Brush Look Designer to save a brush look, which is a brush-and-paper texture combination. Once a brush look is saved, it can be reused at any time.

To preview and save brush-and-paper combinations (Brush Look Designer):

1. Open the palettes you want to use (Art Materials, Brushes, Color Set, etc.).

2. Choose Brushes palette > Brushes menu > Brush Look Designer.

3. Draw a stroke in the preview window.

4. Do any of the following:
   Choose a different brush, variant, method category, method subcategory.
   Change the brush size (see page 66).
   Choose a different paper texture.
   Choose a different Primary color.
   Fine-tune the brush using any Brush Controls or Advanced Controls palette.
   Click a different background color icon for the preview window **4**a: White, the last color applied using Set Colors, Black, or stripes. Use the stripey background to test a Liquid or Water brush or the Drip or Wet method category.
   To change the background color for the Brush Look dialog box, choose a Primary color from the Art Materials: Color palette, then click Set Colors in the Brush Look dialog box **4**b.

5. Click Done if you don't want to save the current brush look.
   or
   To save the brush look in the currently open brush looks library, click Save, enter a name for the brush look **5**a, then click OK. (To open a different library, choose Brushes palette > Brushes menu > Brush Looks, click Library in the Looks palette drawer **5**b, then locate and double-click a library.) An icon for the new brush look will appear on the Looks palette.

Diane Margolin

Margolin is a computer graphics instructor, so of course she's fluent in many software programs, but she likes to explore novel ways of using program features. She builds rich textures by applying different kinds of brush strokes at a low opacity, often with custom brushes that she creates using Painter's Capture Brush command, and by applying a series of commands or filters. For her figurative work, Margolin draws her initial image directly on the computer, though she sometimes refers to an actual photograph as she draws. She rarely uses scanned imagery. Sometimes she'll mask an image based on luminosity and then layer another image over it. Margolin uses other applications—Photoshop, Illustrator, ColorStudio, Gallery Effects, Director, and Paint Alchemy—in conjunction with Painter. In addition to her other professional work, Diane Margolin has created a series of over one thousand original textures and patterns designed for print, multimedia, and video, a collection that was conceived as an imaginative, functional, and innovative alternative design solution to the standard photographic products.

Default Brushes 3

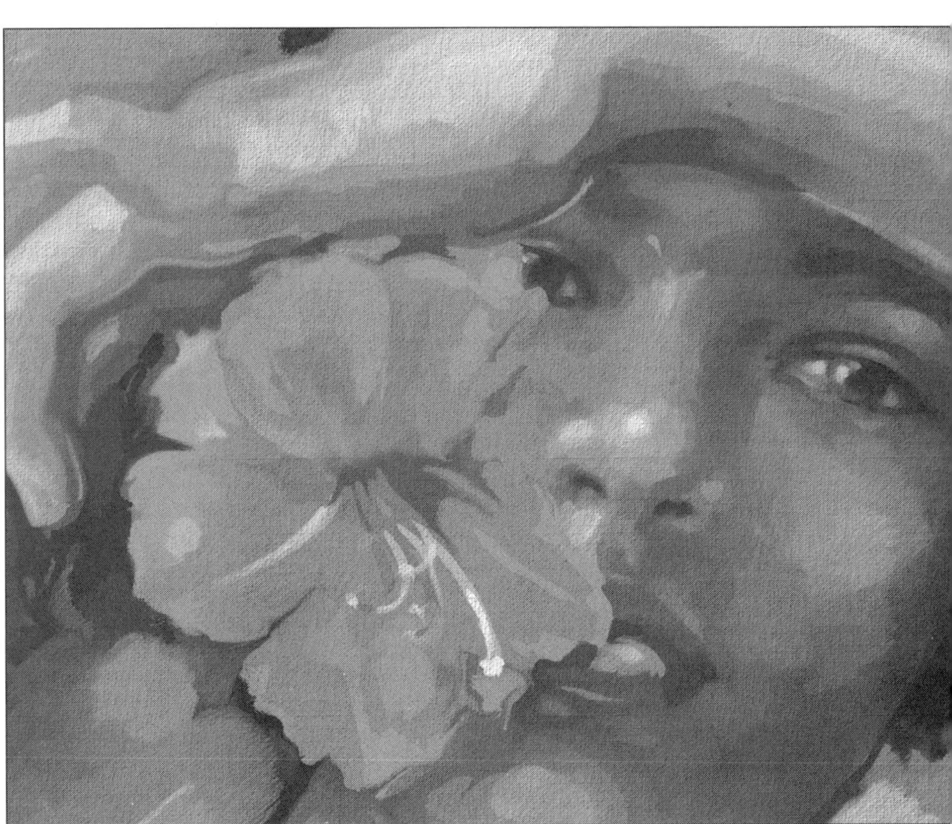

*Nancy Stahl, **Island Woman** (detail).*

Brushes that apply color

The following is a description of Painter's default brushes, which are designed to mimic traditional media. Illustrations of special brushes that erase, dilute, smear, lighten, or darken begin on page 49.

Various methods for customizing brushes—choosing a different brush size, method category or subcategory, etc.—are covered on pages 32–34 and in Chapter 4, More Painting.

Terms you'll see in the brush variant descriptions in this chapter:

ANTI-ALIASED
Smoothed edges. Semi-anti-aliased edges are semi-smoothed.

PRESSURE AFFECTS OPACITY/REVEAL PAPER GRAIN/PRESSURE AFFECTS STROKE WIDTH
The harder you press with your stylus, the more opaque and the less apparent the paper grain, and/or the wider the stroke.

DIRECTION AFFECTS STROKE WIDTH
Vertical strokes are wider than horizontal strokes, or vice versa.

SPEED AFFECTS STROKE WIDTH
The faster you drag the mouse or stylus, the thinner the stroke.

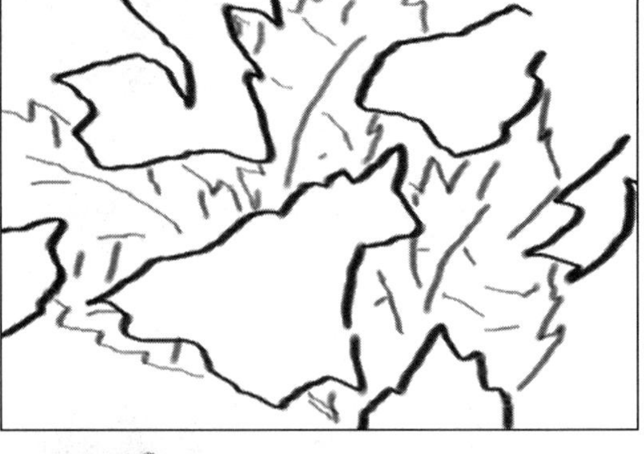
Weinmann

Pencils

PENCILS

Main characteristics
Reveal paper grain.
Pressure affects opacity.
Buildup method category.

2B Pencil
Thin, soft, anti-aliased.

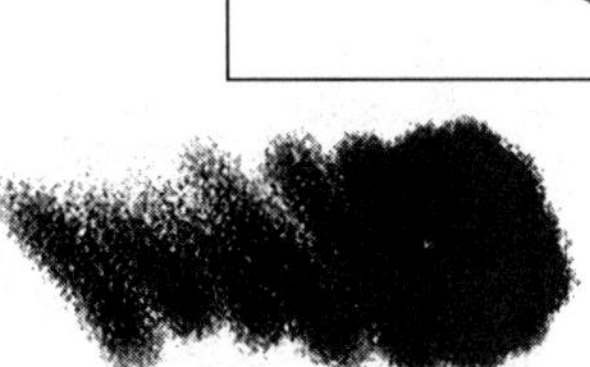

500 lb. Pencil
Fat, semi-anti-aliased.

Colored Pencils
Semi-anti-aliased.

Sharp Pencil
Thin, hard, semi-anti-aliased.

Single Pixel Scribbler
One pixel wide.

Thick & Thin Pencils
Semi-anti-aliased. Stylus/mouse direction and stylus pressure produce widely variable stroke widths.

CHALK

Main Characteristics
Like pastels.
Pressure affects opacity.
Reveal paper grain.
Cover method category.

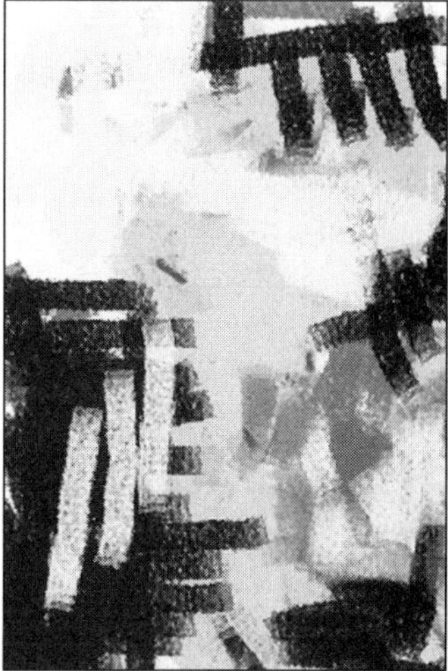

Square chalk

Artist Pastel Chalk
Medium width, semi-anti-aliased.

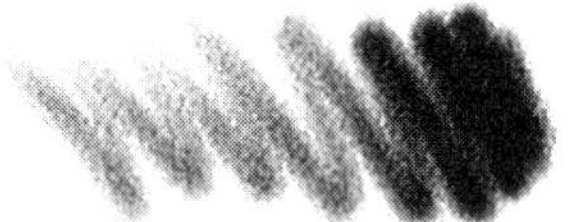

Large Chalk
Wider version of Artist Pastel Chalk.

Oil Pastel
Captured triangular tip. Smears underlying colors and applies color.

Sharp Chalk
Thinner, anti-aliased version of Artist Pastel Chalk.

Square Chalk
Like Artist Pastel Chalk with a square, captured rectangular tip.

Chalk

CHARCOAL

Main Characteristics
Pressure affects opacity.
Reveal paper grain.
Cover method category.

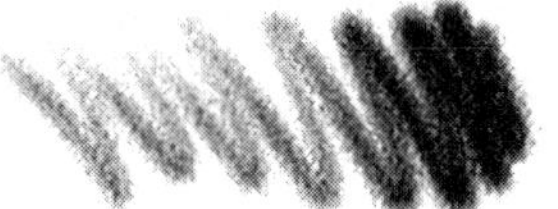

Default Charcoal
Grainy, semi-anti-aliased.

Gritty Charcoal
Semi-anti-aliased. Stylus/mouse direction affects stroke width.

Soft Charcoal
Soft, anti-aliased.

PENS

Main Characteristics
Like ballpoint or fountain pens.
Pressure doesn't affect opacity.
All Cover method category, except
Fine Point and Smooth Ink Pen.

Calligraphy
Opaque. Stylus/mouse direction and stylus pressure affect stroke width. Like India ink.

Fine Point
Like a ballpoint pen. Reveals paper grain. Buildup method category.

Flat Color
Very wide, consistent width.

Leaky Pen
Ink drops. The more slowly you drag the stylus/mouse, the larger the blobs become.

Pen and Ink
Opaque, smooth. Stylus/mouse speed affects stroke width.

Pixel Dust
Fine, random spray of pixels.

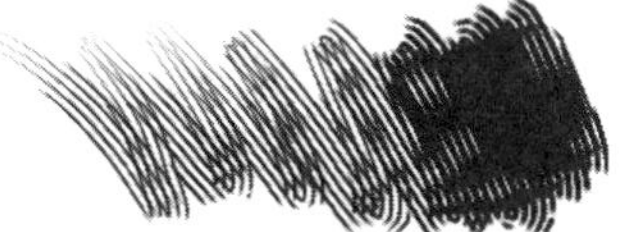

Scratchboard Rake

Multi-bristle stroke. Use for crosshatching. Pressure affects width and opacity. Adjust via Advanced Controls: Rake palette.

Scratchboard Tool

Like a traditional scratchboard tool. Try it on a Black background (choose Black as the paper color when you start your new document). Stylus pressure affects stroke width.

Single Pixel

Not pressure sensitive.

Smooth Ink Pen

Like pen-and-ink. Stylus pressure affects stroke width. Reveals paper grain. Buildup method category.

Tip

To create a leaky pen effect with the Scratchboard Tool, move the Brush Controls: Size palette Size Step slider above 50% and move the Advanced Controls: Sliders palette Size slider to Velocity.

Two images created with the Scratchboard Tool

Steve Gorney

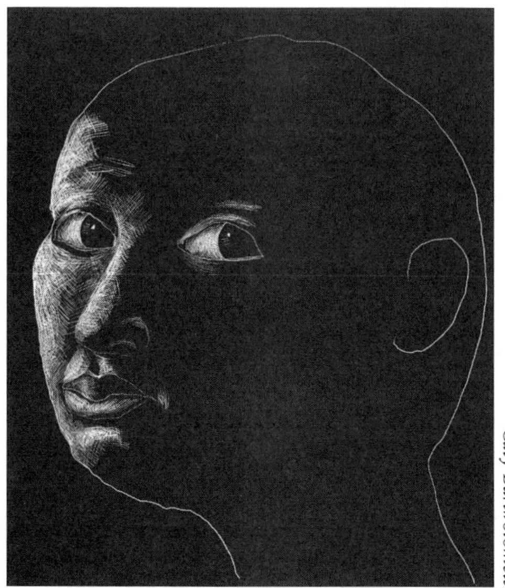

Caty Bartholomew

Calligraphy pen "tips"

Use the Rotate Page tool to tilt your page to a comfortable angle for writing.

To display non-printing horizontal lines to help you align the letters, choose Canvas menu > Grid > Grid Options, and choose Horizontal Lines from the Grid type pop-up menu. Then click the grid icon in the upper right corner of the image window.

Are you left-handed? You can change the brush angle via the Brush Controls: Size palette Angle slider.

FELT PENS 

Main Characteristics
Smooth, anti-aliased.
Buildup method category.
Pressure affects opacity.

Weinmann

Dirty Marker
*Direction affects stroke width.
Fast buildup.*

Fine Tip Felt Pens
Thin.

Single Pixel Marker
Ultra thin version of Fine Tip.

Felt Marker
*Lighter than Felt Pens.
Direction affects stroke width.*

Medium Tip Felt Pens
*Medium width. Stylus/mouse
speed affects stroke width.*

CRAYONS 

Main Characteristics
Semi-anti-aliased.
Pressure affects opacity.
Reveal paper grain.
Buildup method category.

Default
Crayon–crayon.

Waxy Crayons
*Smears underlying color with
paint color.*

Lourekas

AIRBRUSH

Main Characteristics
Sprays color.

Cover method category.

Anti-aliased (except Spatter Airbrush).

Pressure affects opacity.

Doesn't reveal paper grain (except Spatter Airbrush).

Fat Stroke
Wide, soft, medium opacity.

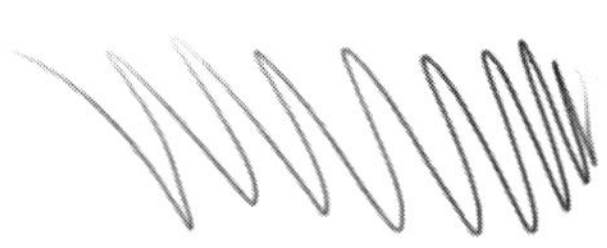

Feather Tip
Narrow, more opaque.

Single Pixel Air
Very narrow spray.

Spatter Airbrush
Semi-anti-aliased. Reveals paper grain.

Thin Stroke
Thinner version of Fat Stroke.

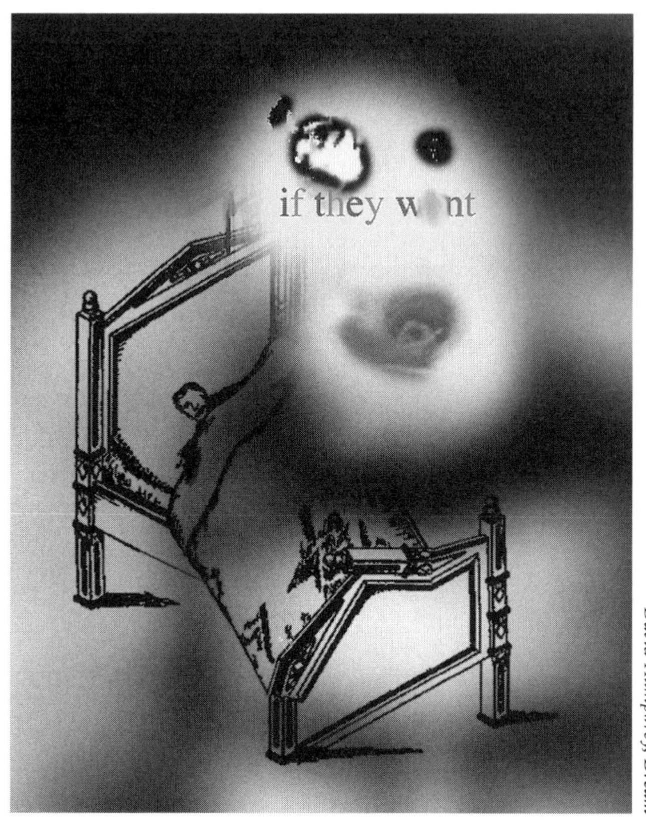

David Humphrey, Dream

Airbrush

BRUSH

Main Characteristics
Like acrylics and oils.

Full coverage.

Pressure affects opacity.

Some variants reveal paper grain, and some don't.

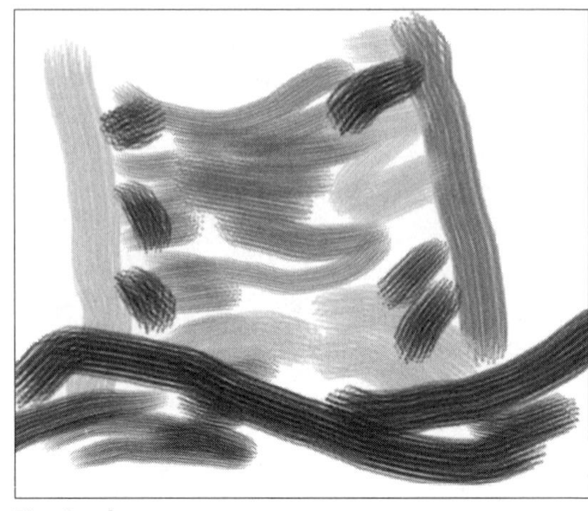

Lourekas

Fine Brush

Big Wet Ink
Wide, dark inky stroke, with hard-edged bristles.

Big Loaded Oils
Wide, raked, multicolored bristle stroke. Stylus pressure affects width and opacity.

Big Rough Out
Stylus/mouse speed affects stroke width. Reveals paper grain.

Big Wet Oils
Wide, raked, multicolored bristle stroke. Similar to Big Loaded Oils, but less opaque.

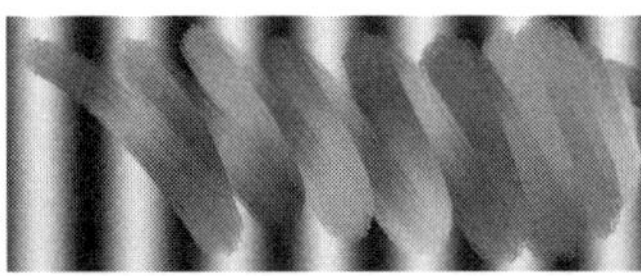

Brushy
Runs out of paint as the stroke finishes. Multi-bristle. Smears existing paint. Stylus pressure affects stroke width.

Camel Hair Brush
Anti-aliased, opaque, raked stroke. Stylus/mouse speed affects bristle width.

Coarse Hairs
Noticeable bristles. Stylus pressure easily affects width and opacity.

Cover Brush
Anti-aliased, raked. Doesn't reveal paper grain. Stylus pressure affects width.

Digital Sumi
Uniform, raked, noticeable bristles. Stylus pressure affects stroke width.

Fine Brush
Smooth, but noticeable bristles. Stylus pressure easily affects width and opacity.

Graduated Brush

Semi-anti-aliased. Reveals paper grain. Stylus pressure affects stroke width. Uses Primary and Secondary colors with strong or light stylus pressure, respectively.

Hairy Brush

Semi-anti-aliased, bristle stroke. Takes time to render, so use short strokes. Reveals paper grain. Stylus pressure affects width and opacity. Experiment by changing the Spacing or Bristle palette settings or the Color Variability sliders (Color palette).

Huge Rough Out

The widest version of Rough Out. Reveals paper grain.

Loaded Oils

Medium size version of Big Loaded Oils.

Oil Paint

Hard, aliased. Reveals paper grain. Stylus pressure affects opacity and stroke width.

Penetration Brush

Hard, aliased rake stroke. Stylus pressure affects opacity and width. Reveals paper grain.

Rough Out

Reveals paper grain, opaque. Speed affects stroke width.

Sable Chisel Tip Water

Smears existing color; doesn't apply color. Soft bristle stroke. Pressure affects width. This is a beauty.

Small Loaded Oils

Smaller version of Loaded Oils.

Smaller Wash Brush

Thin, closely spaced bristles. Soft, translucent stroke. Applies color and smears existing color.

Ultrafine Water Brush

Wider version of Smaller Wash Brush, with thinner bristles.

Big Dry Ink

Wide, dark stroke, with noticeable, but soft, bristles.

To make brush strokes look more three dimensional, clone an image, apply brush strokes to the clone, then use the Apply Surface Texture command (Using: 3D Brush Strokes).

ARTISTS

You can control the color range for these multicolored brush variants using the Color Variability sliders on the Color palette.

Auto Van Gogh

Use this variant to create a "Van Gogh" clone (instructions on page 169).

Flemish Rub

A 16th Century massage? No, it's a brush that smears underlying pixels (Flemish Smear?). Doesn't apply color.

Impressionist

Multicolored, orzo-shaped dabs. Smears paint when the Opacity slider is at a low setting.

Piano Keys

We admit we slept through some of our art history classes, but as far as we know, Piano Keys wasn't an artist. This brush falls into the miscellaneous category. Creates wide, multicolored ribbons, as if applied with a palette knife. Try using at a low opacity.

Seurat

Multicolored, anti-aliased dot clusters. Use the Brush Controls: Size palette to adjust dot size.

Van Gogh and Van Gogh 2

Oh that it were so easy to be Van Gogh! We differ with Fractal Painter's description of Van Gogh's paint strokes as "multicolored brush strokes." Van Gogh actually applied clean strokes, but when he worked wet-on-wet, his brush strokes dragged color from underneath. Painter's Van Gogh brushes are multicolored, anti-aliased, full coverage, similar to Small Loaded Oils. Pause between short strokes.

Van Gogh brush strokes appear after they're drawn; Van Gogh 2 brush strokes are precomputed (you'll see color as you draw). Otherwise, there's little difference between the two.

(The Auto Van Gogh variant is discussed on page 169.)

Textile designer Bernice Mast uses the Seurat variant to create flower centers.

Artists

WATER COLOR

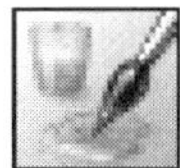

Water Color brush strokes automatically appear on the Wet Paint layer. Choose Canvas menu > Wet Paint to turn it on or off. To save a picture with its Wet Paint layer still wet, choose the RIFF file format. Choose Canvas menu > Dry to dry Wet Paint layer strokes and merge them into the background. To layer translucent brush strokes, apply them at a low opacity (or use the Fade command), and then dry them periodically as you work. Selection tools, masking tools, and Effects menu commands don't affect the Wet Paint layer.

Stylus pressure affects stroke width and opacity for all Water Color variants except Wet Eraser. The Grain slider on the Brush Controls palette works the reverse of normal—move it to the right to accentuate the paper grain. All Water Color variants have the Circular Dab Type (Brush Controls: Size palette).

To adjust the pooling (concentration of color at the edges) or diffusion (pigment bleed into paper) of Water Color strokes, use the Brushes palette > Controls menu > Water palette (see page 74). To diffuse all the Wet Paint brush strokes into the current paper texture after they're created, use the Shift-D shortcut.

To remove Wet Paint layer strokes, choose the Wet Remove Density method subcategory for any Water Color variant, or choose the Wet Eraser Water Color variant.

Broad Water Brush
Wide, bristle stroke.

Diffuse Water
Stroke edges bleed after stroke is drawn.

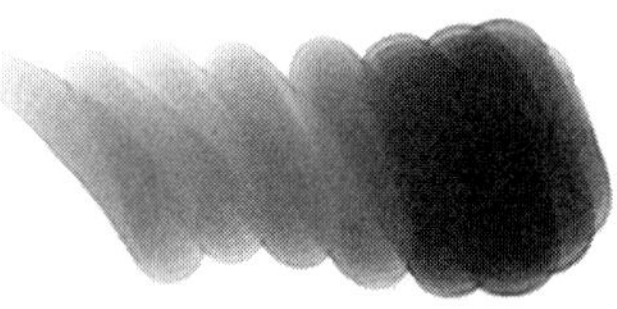

Large Simple Water
Very large version of Simple Water. Stylus pressure affects opacity and width.

Large Water
Wider version of Simple Water.

Simple Water
Smooth, non-bristle stroke. Pressure affects opacity and stroke width.

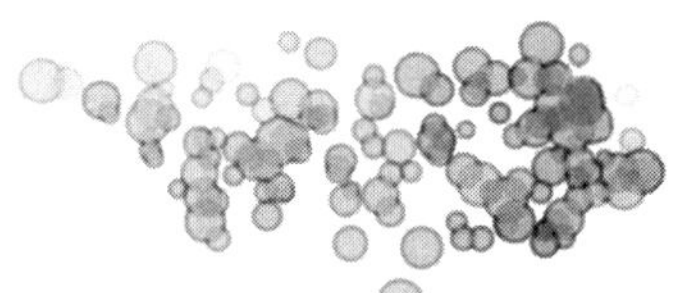

Spatter Water
Sprays random droplets. High Wet Fringe setting (Water palette).

Water Brush Stroke
Bristle. Pause between strokes.

Wet Eraser
Erases on the Wet Paint layer only. Stylus pressure affects the amount of erasure.

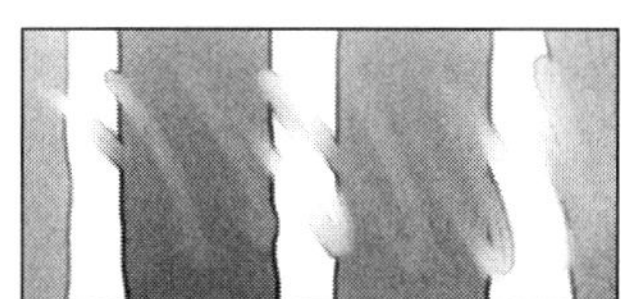

Pure Water Brush
Smears existing brush strokes. Doesn't apply color.

An advantage of using Painter's watercolor brushes over traditional watercolor: You can apply strokes on the Wet Paint layer without smudging a chalk or charcoal drawing on the underlying canvas layer. To build up translucent layers, dry Painter's Wet Paint layer periodically as you work.

Lourekas

Fabric Effects, Inc.

Fabric Effects, Inc. is a textile firm whose services run the gamut of innovative computer-assisted design and manufacture on the one hand, and traditional fabric design, hand painting, dyeing, and silkscreening techniques on the other. Many tasks formerly done by hand are now accomplished using a variety of proprietary and off-the-shelf software. To reduce electronic images to screen printable colors, create repeats, and execute other important tasks, for example, Fabric Effects uses proprietary software developed by Monarch Computex. Richard Lerner, president of Fabric Effects and of RSL Digital Consultants, specializes in system design and hardware and software integration for digital imaging, graphics, and textile design.

To create the textile designs by Fabric Effects that are reproduced in this book, scanned imagery was composited and then color and texture were applied in Painter using grainy brushes. White lines were drawn using Bleach variants of the Eraser brush.

Fabric Effects, Inc.

Special brushes

The following brush variants don't apply color—they erase, dilute, smear, lighten, or darken color (except for the Liquid brushes, which apply color when used at an Opacity above 0).

ERASER

Main Characteristic
Stylus pressure affects opacity.

Eraser "tips"

You don't have to use the Eraser brush to erase—you can choose the Eraser variant for any non-Eraser brush.

To change the color that the Eraser erases to, choose a Primary color, then choose Canvas menu > Set Paper Color. This won't change the paper color you chose when you created your document. Adjust Eraser strength via the Controls: Brush palette Opacity slider.

The Eraser variants erase to the paper color.

Flat Eraser

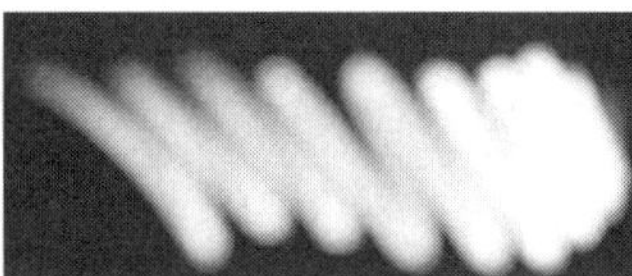

Fat Eraser

Medium Eraser

Small Eraser

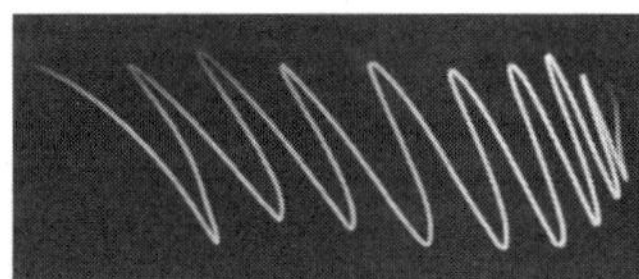

Ultrafine Eraser

©D. Margolin

The Eraser method subcategories

These categories are available when you choose the Eraser method category for any brush.

Soft Paper Color: Erases to the current paper color.

Soft Paint Remover: Erases to white.

Soft Paint Thickener: Darkens color. Similar to the Buildup method. Try using a low opacity.

Soft Grain Colorize: Applies the current paper texture using the current Primary and Secondary colors.

Soft Mask Colorize: Applies the current Primary color to opaque areas of a mask and the current Secondary color to partially masked areas when the third Drawing button is selected. To produce grayscale strokes using this subcategory, apply the Auto Mask command (Using: Image Luminance), then draw with black as the Primary color and white as the Secondary color.

The Bleach variants erase to white, regardless of the paper color.

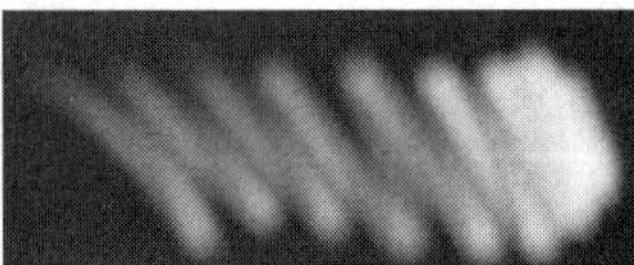

Fat Bleach

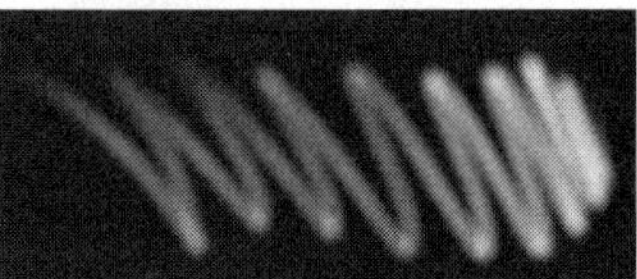

Medium Bleach

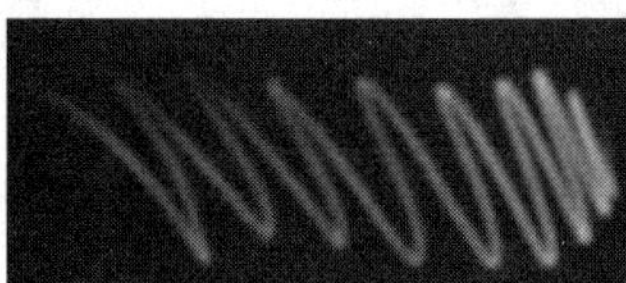

Small Bleach

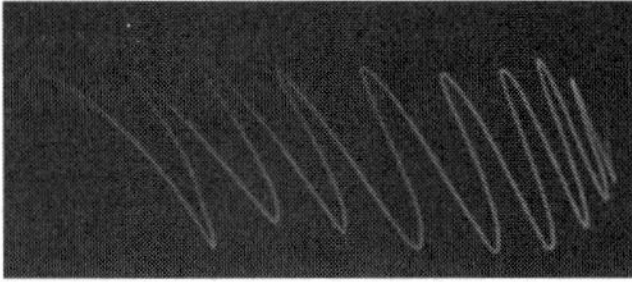

Ultrafine Bleach

Single Pixel Bleach

Textile artists Mandy Leonard and Bernice Mast both use the Bleach variants of the Eraser brush like traditional bleach—to produce white lines. See Leonard's work in the color plates section (Fabric Effects, Inc.). See Mast's work on pages 46 and 137.

The Darkeners build up and saturate color—the opposite of bleach.

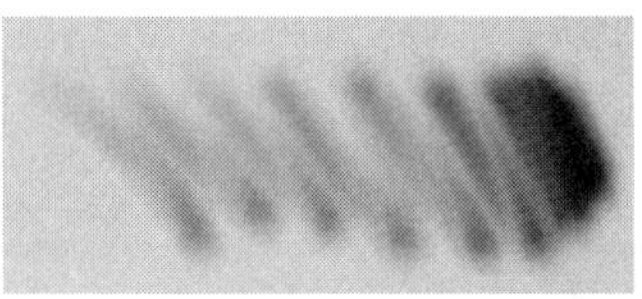

Fat Darkener

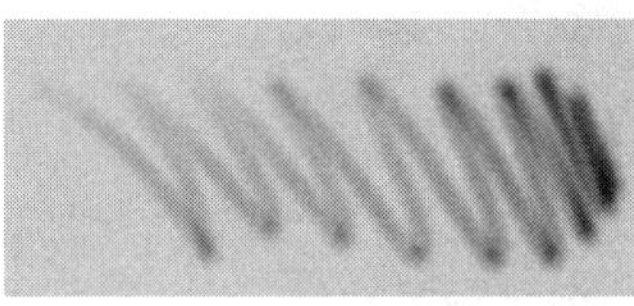

Medium Darkener

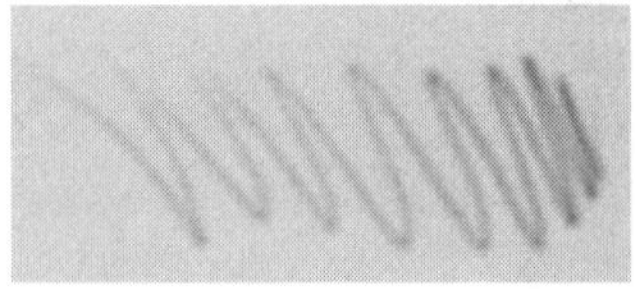

Small Darkener

Ultrafine Darkener

Note: The Burn tool works like the Darkeners, except it has a lower opacity setting, so it darkens color more slowly.

WATER

Main Characteristics

Watery smudge.

No application of color.

Stylus pressure affects the amount of smudge.

Most reveal paper grain.

The Water brushes work on the background canvas, not on the Wet Paint layer.

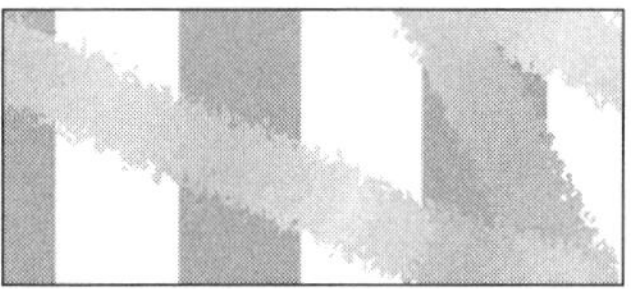

Big Frosty Water
Larger version of Frosty Water.

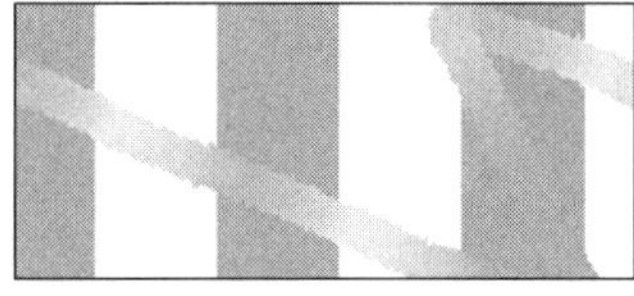

Frosty Water
Hard, aliased stroke. Reveals paper grain.

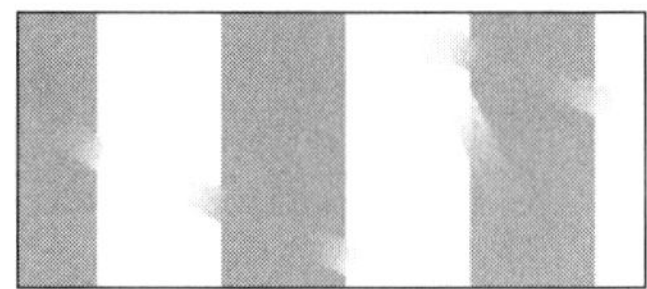

Grainy Water
Reveals paper grain.

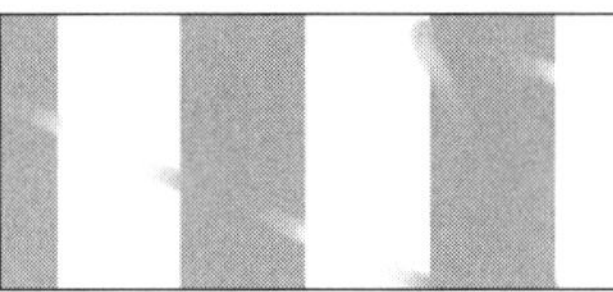

Just Add Water
Smooth, anti-aliased stroke. Smudges paper grain.

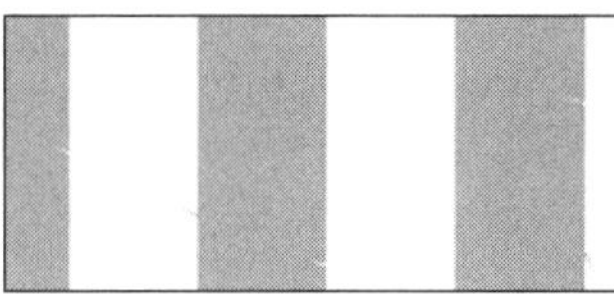

Single Pixel Water
Very thin.

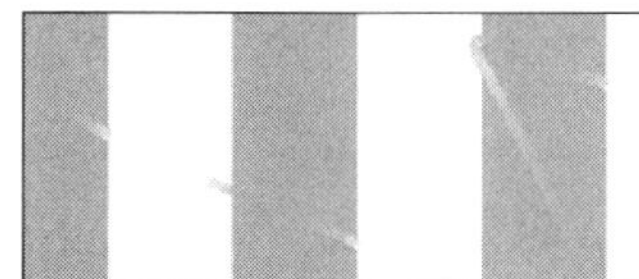

Tiny Frosty Water
Smaller version of Frosty Water. Reveals paper grain.

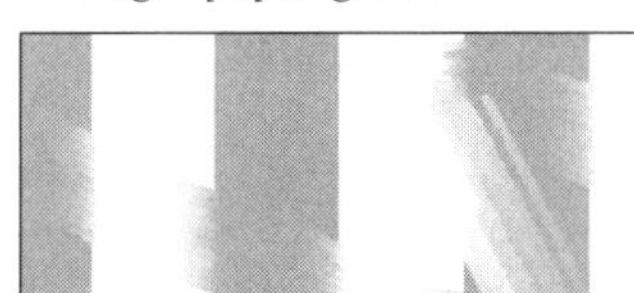

Water Rake
Wide, bristle stroke. Reveals paper grain.

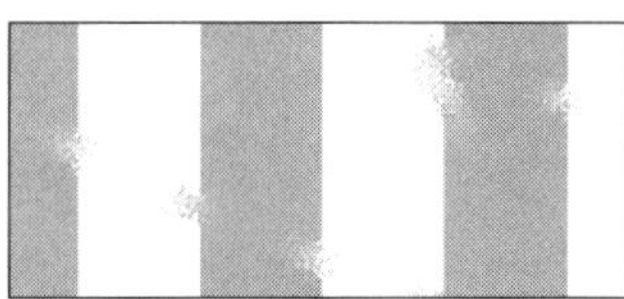

Water Spray
Water mist.

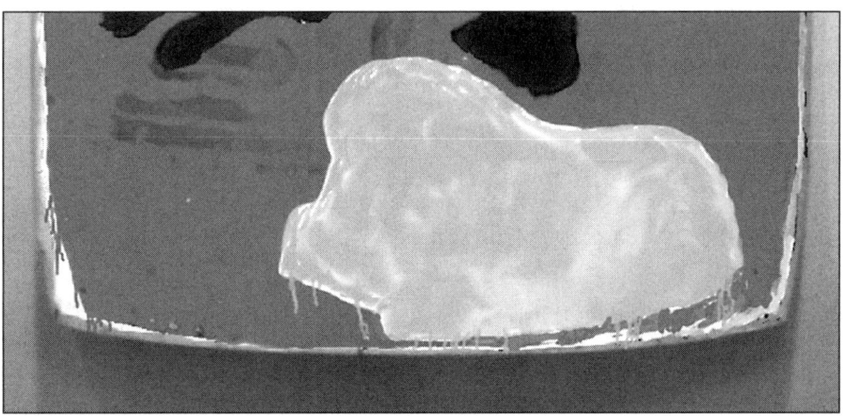

*Ron Gorchov, **Knossos** (detail). Gorchov uses Water brush variants to create drips.*

LIQUID

Main Characteristics

At zero opacity (Controls: Brush palette), the Liquid variants smear existing color without applying color, like a palette knife. At an opacity greater than zero, they smear existing color and apply the current Primary color.

With the exception of the Tiny Smudge variant, stylus pressure affects stroke width, the degree of smearing, and the amount paper grain is revealed.

Illustrator Nancy Stahl likes to use the Camel Hair Brush variant and the Smeary Mover variant of the Liquid brush. She also creates her own paper textures, which she applies using grainy brushes or the Apply Surface Texture command. Take a look at her work in the color plates section.

Coarse Distorto
Semi-anti-aliased. Smears existing paint only. Doesn't apply color.

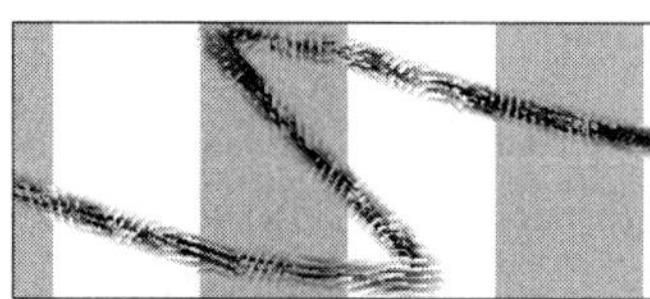

Coarse Smeary Bristles
Semi-anti-aliased version of Smeary Bristles. Applies and smears color.

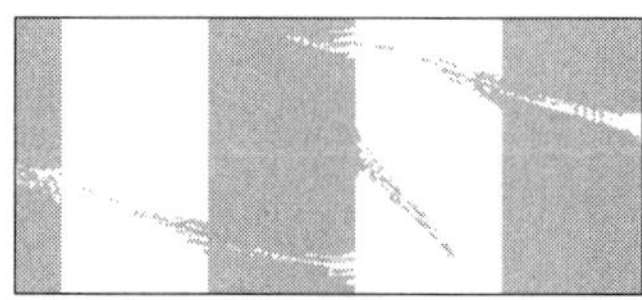

Coarse Smeary Mover
Smears existing paint only. Semi-anti-aliased.

Distorto
Wet, smooth mover. Doesn't reveal paper texture. Smears existing paint. Stylus/mouse speed affects stroke width.

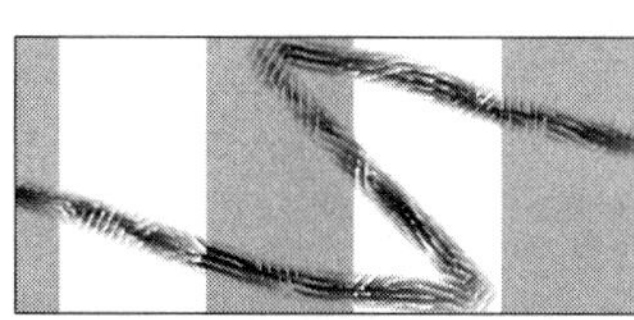

Smeary Bristles
Pressure affects grain/opacity. Applies color. Stylus/mouse speed affects stroke width.

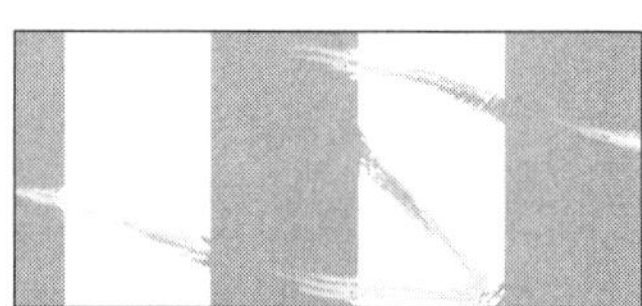

Smeary Mover
Zero opacity version of Smeary Bristles. Doesn't apply color.

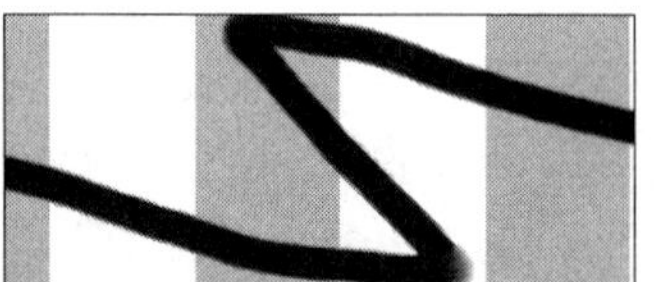

Thick Oil
Thick, oily, wet, cover brush. Applies color.

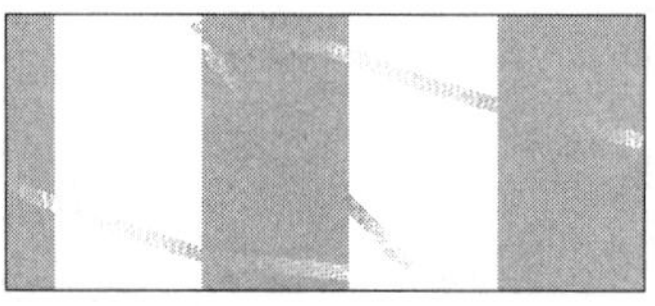

Tiny Smudge
Zero opacity, thin, multibristled smudger.

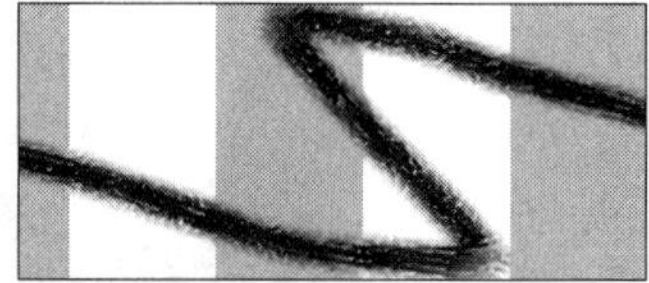

Total Oil Brush
Thinner version of Smeary Bristles.

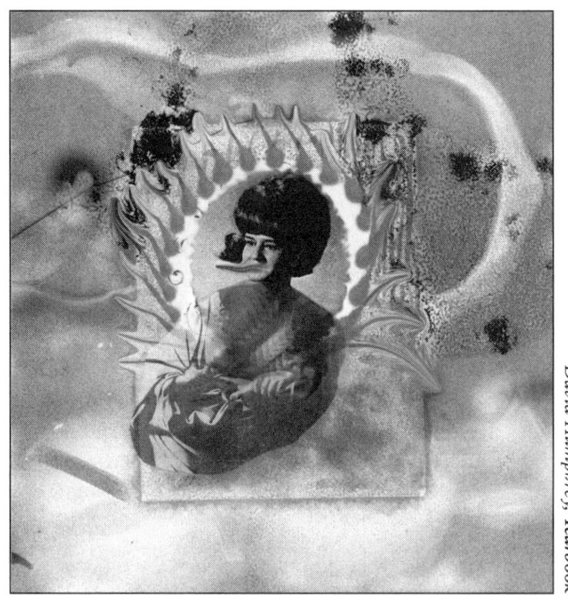

David Humphrey, Yearbook

Two examples of Distorto

David Humphrey, Essence

BURN

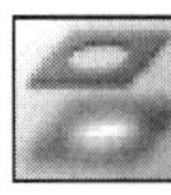

Main Characteristics
Darkens existing color.

DODGE

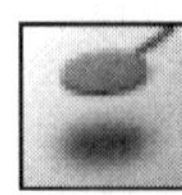

Main Characteristics
Lightens existing color.

MASKING

The Masking brush variants are discussed on page 151.

IMAGE HOSE

The Image Hose, which sprays imagery, is discussed on pages 110–114.

CLONERS

The Cloners brush variants are discussed on pages 166–167.

David Humphrey

Painter David Humphrey has had numerous one-man shows in New York City and his first retrospective, last year, at the Contemporary Arts Center in Cincinnati, Ohio. He has been making computer images for a few years in conjunction with his traditional media paintings and drawings, and he frequently combines traditional media and computer techniques. He uses various methods to digitize imagery: he uses a digital camera; scans his own traditional media drawings, sculpture, photographs, and photocopies of photographs; and he captures video images with his AV Macintosh.

Humphrey has been working with images from his own family albums for several years, exploring the process of remembering. Ironically, Humphrey discovered that a horror movie was filmed in the house in which he lived as a child, and his family had sold long ago. For his piece *Solarized Kitchen* (see the color insert), he video-captured a shot of his family kitchen from the movie, digitally removed the film actors, and then added brush strokes in Painter.

Humprey likes to use the computer because it challenges him to work in new, less comfortable ways, and, like many artists, he is partial to the Water Color, Liquid, and Water brushes. Humphrey feels his work on the computer has influenced his continuing work in traditional media. "The computer," he says, "has altered how I think about organizing pictures. I think that the computer helped me develop different voices within a picture. I'm also interested in how the computer can give photography some of the powers that painting has; that increased power to retouch. What I've been trying to do in some of these paintings is to act out the notion of retouching as a living component of remembering. We seem to remember according to conditions of the present. The computer can rehearse this process in anticipation of the paintings. Some computer imaging software was designed to imitate effects of painting. In some of my newer works I'm trying to make representations of the effects the computer uses to imitate paintings. There's a feedback loop."

From an interview with Elaine A. King, curator of Humphrey's Contemporary Arts Center exhibition.

More Painting 4

*Ray Rue, **Minotaur** (detail).*

Color

To create a new color set:

1. Choose Art Materials palette > Color menu > Adjust Color Set.

2. Click New Set **2**. A tiny Color Set palette will appear on your screen.

3. Click on a color in any open image window using the Dropper tool or choose a color from the Art Materials: Color palette.

4. Click Add Color.

5. Repeat steps 3 and 4 for any other colors you want to add to the set.

6. To save the new color set, click Library, click Save, enter a name for the set, choose a location in which to save it, click Save, then click Cancel. (We wish there was a Save button on the Art Materials: Color Set palette.)

To change the colors in a color set:

1. Open the color set you want to edit, and display the Color Set palette.

2. If the color set is locked (closed padlock icon), click the padlock icon.

3. To add a color, choose a color from the Color palette or click on a color in any open image window with the Dropper tool, then click Add Color (Command-Shift-K).

   To **delete** a color, click the color swatch, click Delete Color, then click Yes.

   To **replace** a color, choose a color from the Colors palette or from a picture using the Dropper tool, then hold down Option and click on the color swatch you want to replace.

   To **name** or **rename** a color, double-click the swatch, type a name, then click OK.

4. To save the edited color set, click Library, click Save, open the set's folder, click Save, click Replace, then click Cancel.

The currently open color set.

A new color set...

...with three colors added to it.

Dropper tip

Hold down Command to use the Dropper while the Oval Selection, Rectangular Selection, Brush, Floater Adjuster, or Paint Bucket tool is selected.

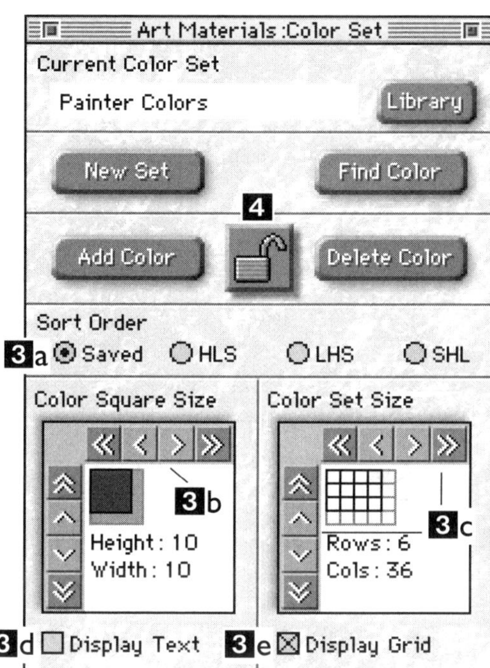

To change a color set's display style:

1. Choose Art Materials palette > Color menu > Adjust Color Set.

2. If the color set is locked (closed padlock icon), click the padlock icon.

3. On the expanded Color Set palette, do any of the following:

   Click a different **Sort Order** button to rearrange the swatches **3**a. "Saved" is the default arrangement. Click HLS to arrange colors by hue, luminance, and saturation, click LHS to arrange colors by luminance, hue, and saturation, or click SHL to arrange colors by saturation, hue, and luminance.

   Click a single **Color Square Size** arrow **3**b to enlarge or shrink the swatches by one pixel each, or click a double arrow to enlarge or shrink the swatches by half their current size.

   Click a single or double down **Color Set Size** arrow **3**c to make the palette taller or shorter, and/or click the left or right arrow to make the palette wider or narrower.

   Check the **Display Text** box **3**d to display color names, if there are any, below the swatches. Make sure the swatches are wide enough for the text to appear. The Pantone Colors are automatically named.

   Uncheck the **Display Grid** box **3**e and the Display Text box to eliminate the white grid lines between swatches. Colors are harder to distinguish without grid lines.

4. Click the padlock **4** to lock the palette.

5. *Optional:* To save the edited color set, click Library, click Save, open the set's folder, click Save, click Replace, then click Cancel.

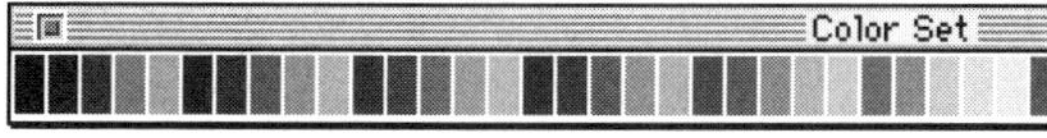

The default Hi Key color set.

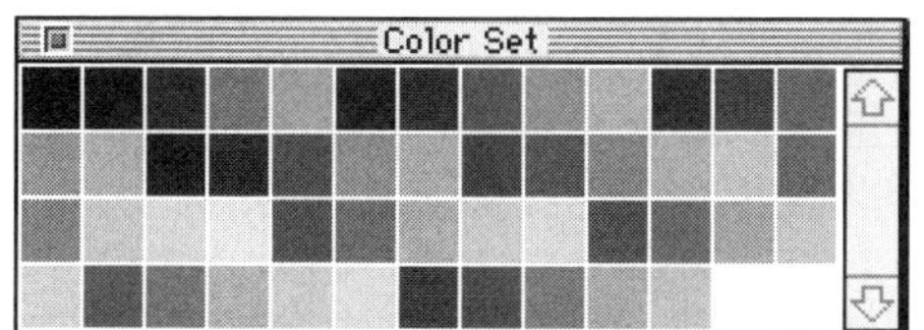

The Hi Key color set with modified display settings, as shown in the Art Materials: Color Set palette screenshot, above. The swatches were widened and the palette was made taller.

You can search for a color by name or search for the closest color to the current Primary color. The color set you search through **must** be the Current Color Set (the currently open set), but the Color Set swatch palette **doesn't** have to be open.

To find a color in a color set:

1. Choose Art Materials palette > Color menu > Adjust Color Set.

2. Click Find Color.

3. Click "By name" and enter a color name. Be sure to enter the correct word spacing. For example, enter a space between Pantone numbers and letters (100 CV, etc.).
or
Click "Closest to current color."

4. Click Search.

5. Click OK. If the OK button is unavailable, the color name you entered was not found. If the Color Set swatch palette is open, the found swatch will be highlighted.

To produce multicolored brush strokes:

On the expanded Art Materials: Color palette, move the **H**(hue) Color Variability slider **1** to add more hues to the stroke. Note how the color changes in the Primary color rectangle.
and/or
Move the **S**(saturation) slider to increase the saturation range in the stroke.
and/or
Move the **V**(value) slider to increase the range of brightness values in the stroke.

- For a nice effect, raise the H and V settings. The default Loaded Oils and Hairy Brush variants of the Brush brush and the Van Gogh and Seurat variants of the Artists brush produce multicolored strokes.

- To produce multicolored strokes another way, choose a Primary and Secondary color, then move the Color slider on the Sliders palette (Brushes palette > Controls menu > Sliders) to Direction or Pressure.

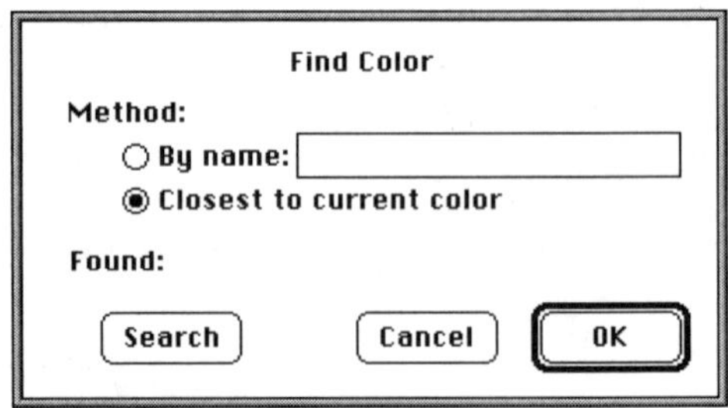

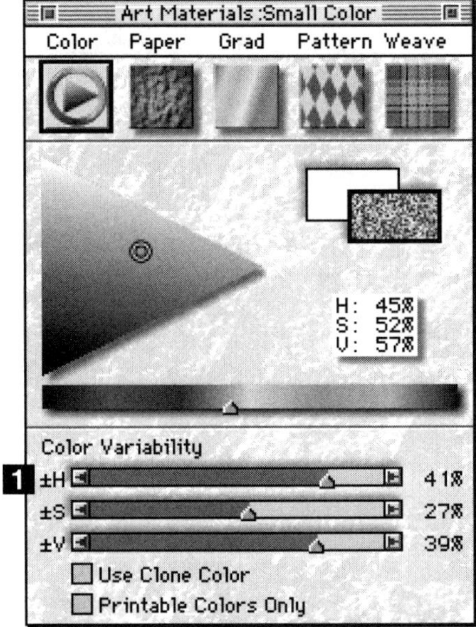

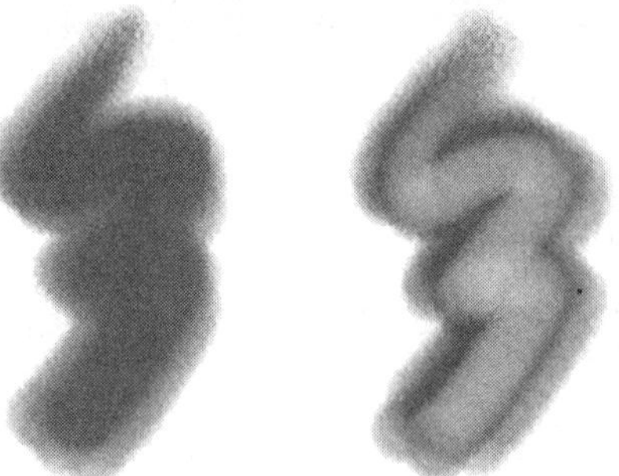

The Hairy brush variant of the Brush brush, normal Color Variability.

The same brush, with the V Color Variability slider at 48%.

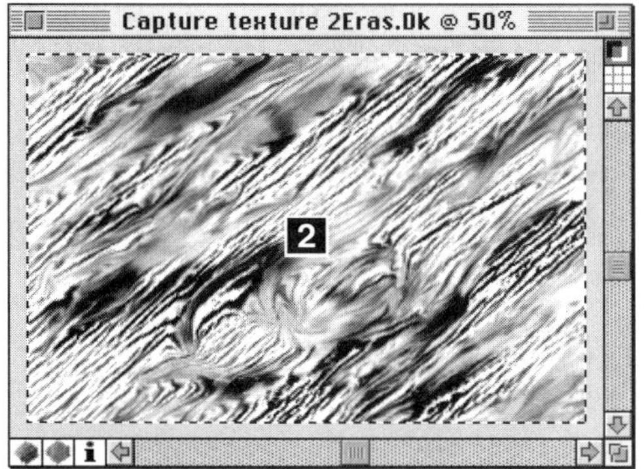

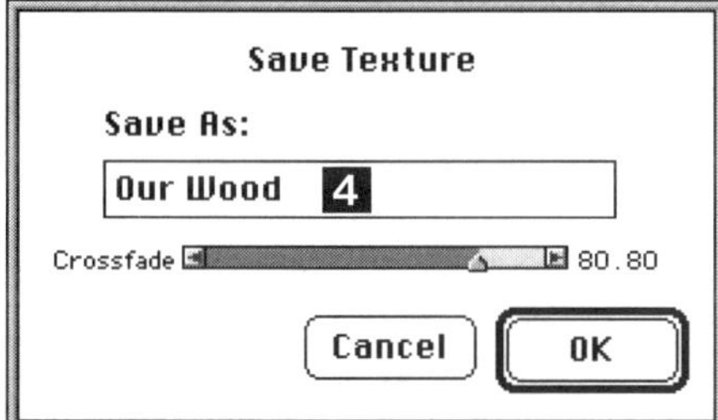

Paper textures

In addition to the paper textures that Painter supplies, you can create your own textures using the Capture Texture or Make Paper Texture command. Apply a texture that you create as you would any other texture: use an Effects menu > Surface Control submenu command or use a brush with a Grainy submethod category.

To capture a paper texture from a picture:

1. Choose the Rectangular Selection tool.

2. Select an area of a painting **2**. You can select an area filled with a pattern or weave. (Hold down Shift before and while dragging to create a square selection.)

3. Choose Art Materials palette > Paper menu > Capture Texture.

4. Enter a name for the texture **4**.

5. Choose a Crossfade setting. The higher the Crossfade, the more the borders between paper texture tiles will be blended.

6. Click OK or press Return. The new texture will appear on the Art Materials: Paper palette and it will be added to the currently open paper library. (To create a papers library, see page 21.)

Capture Paper Texture

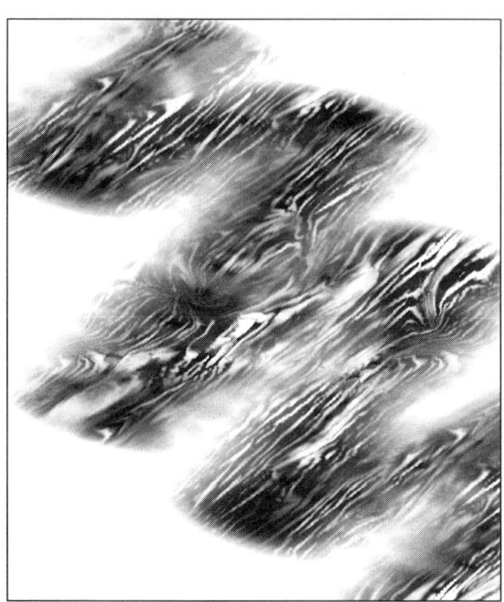

The texture applied in a brush stroke.

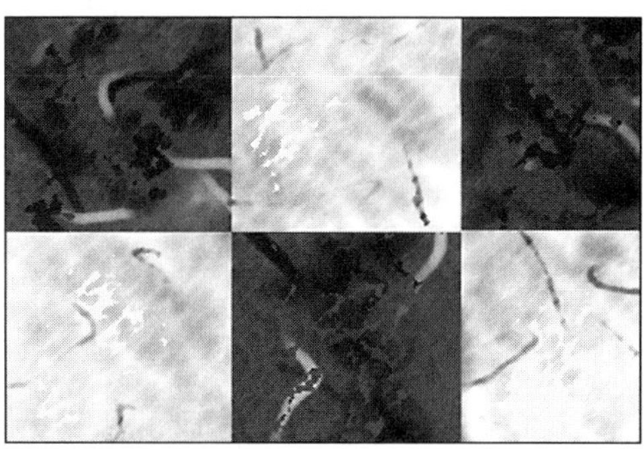

Our Marble texture.

To create a paper texture from an existing texture:

1. Choose Art Materials palette > Paper menu > Make Paper Texture.

2. Choose from the Pattern pop-up menu **2**.

3. Move the Spacing slider to change the size of the pattern.
   and/or
   Move the Angle slider to rotate the pattern.

4. Enter a name for the paper texture in the Save As field.

5. Click OK or press Return. The texture will appear on the Art Materials: Paper palette and it will be saved in the currently open paper library.

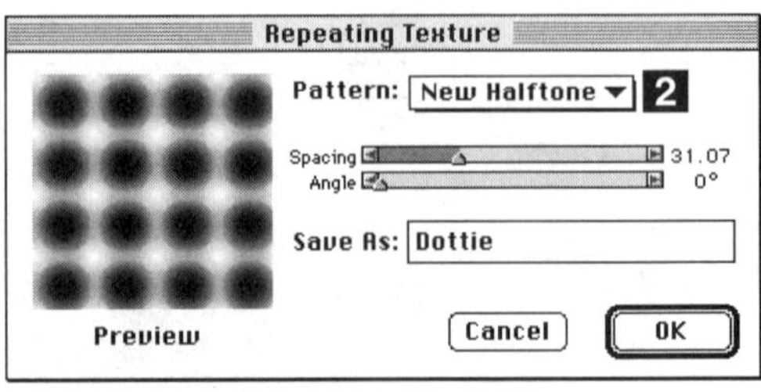

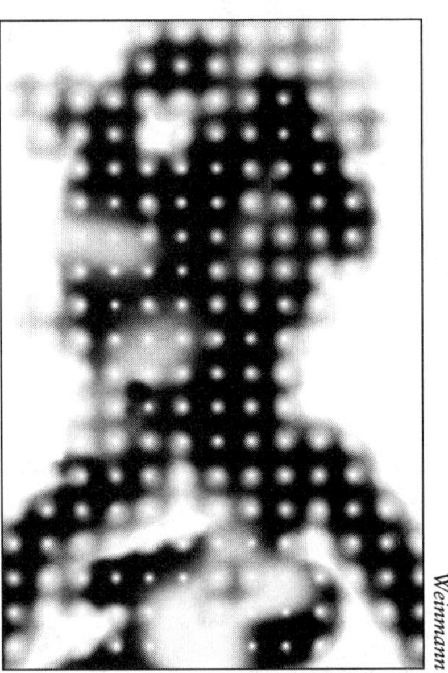
Weinmann

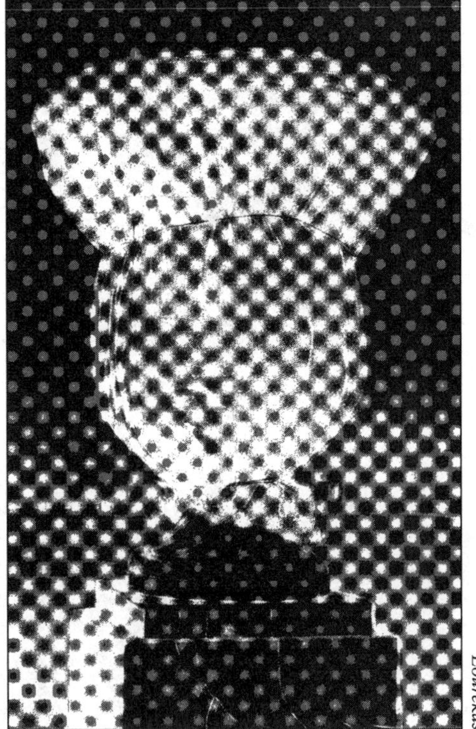
Lourekas

The **Make Fractal Pattern** command produces irregular grayscale patterns in a new document whose size you select. Alone, Painter's fractal patterns make good cloud, stone, or fabric textures, but you can develop them further using any Effects menu command or the Express in Image command (see page 139).

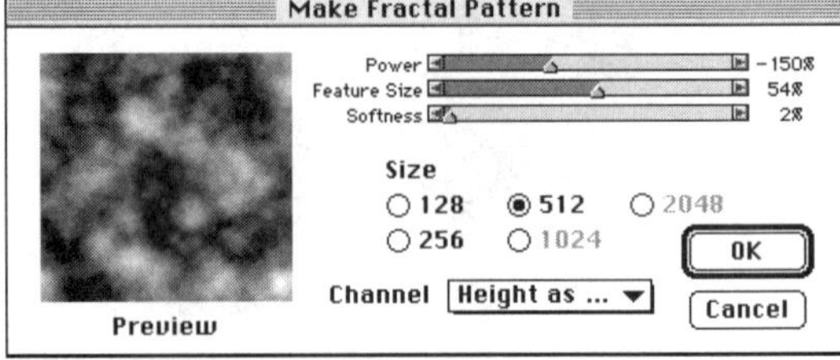

Make Paper Texture; Make Fractal Pattern

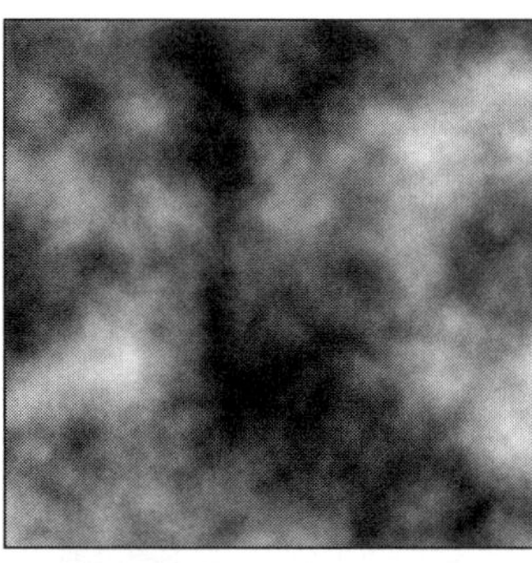

*Power –139%,
Feature Size 69%,
Softness 16%.*

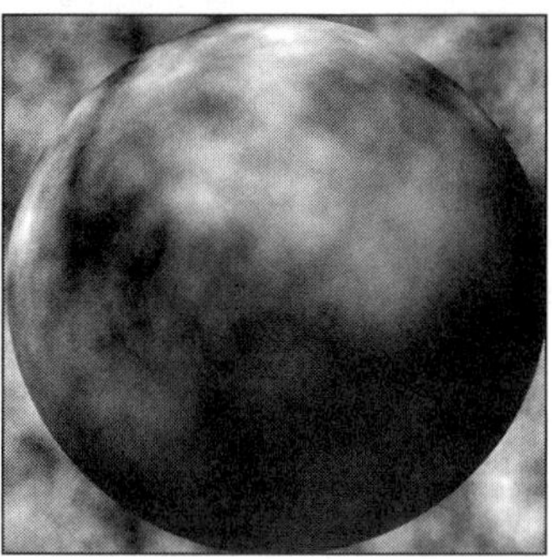

*The above pattern
after applying
Kai's Power Tools
Glass Lens
Normal filter.*

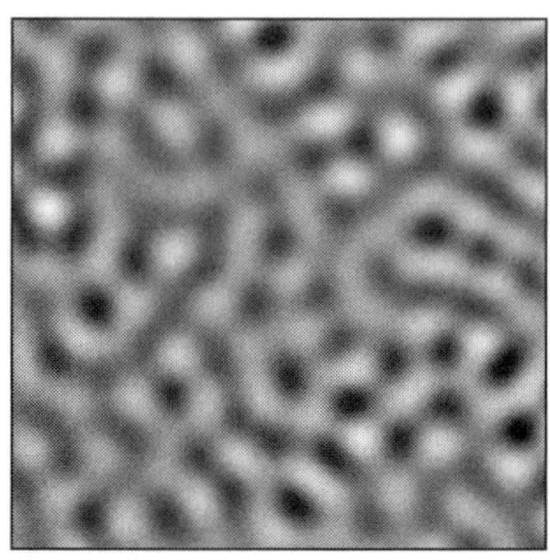

*Power –194%,
Feature Size 8%,
Softness 95%.*

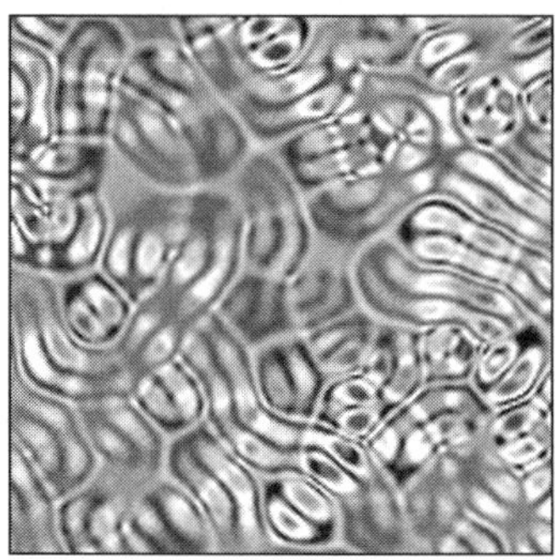

*The above pattern
after applying
Effects menu >
Focus > Glass
Distortion, (Image
Luminance, Amount
1.63, Variance 1),
and Effects menu >
Tonal Control >
Brightness/Contrast.*

You can apply a Fractal Pattern to your image as you would any paper texture or pattern. To add it to the currently open paper texture library, follow the instructions on page 59. Or use the Capture Pattern command and use the pattern as a fill (see page 145).

To make a fractal pattern:

1. Choose Art Materials palette > Pattern menu > Make Fractal Pattern.

2. Do any of the following:

   Move the **Power** slider to the left to enlarge the shapes in the pattern or to the right to make them smaller.

   Move the **Feature Size** slider to the left to increase the number of repetitions per tile.

   Move the **Softness** slider to increase/decrease blending between pattern elements.

   Click a **Size** button—the pattern's tile size (document size) in pixels. The dpi will be 72. The number of available Size buttons depends on the amount of RAM allocated to Painter.

   From the **Channel** pop-up menu, choose Height as Luminance for a grayscale pattern. For an interesting color effect, choose Gradient Bearing or Surface Normal.

3. Click OK or press Return.

   Use Effects menu > Surface Control > Color Overlay command (Using: Paper Grain or Mask, and Hiding Power option) to colorize the pattern.

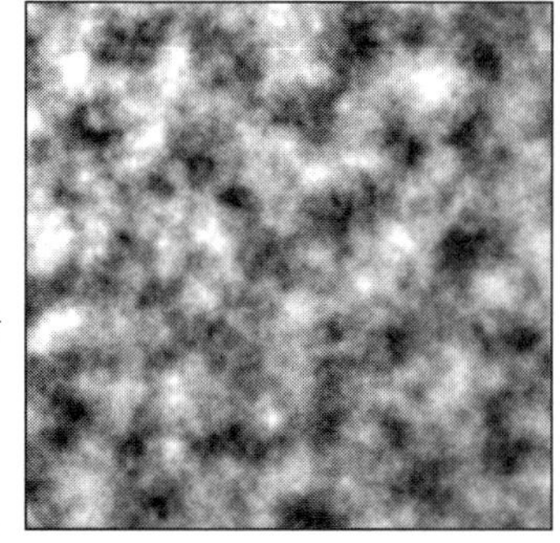

*Power –126%,
Feature Size
17%, Softness
0%, then
Effects menu >
Surface Control >
Apply Lighting.*

Brushes

As we said earlier in this book, if you choose non-default settings for a brush and then choose another brush or variant, you'll lose your non-default settings. To save a customized brush so you can choose it again, save it as a new variant for an existing brush (such as a Zen variant of the Water Color brush) or save it over an existing variant. You can also create a whole new brush category (like Pencils or Crayons), and then create variants for it. To save a brush using the Brush Look Designer, see page 35.

To create a new brush category:

1. Create an image for the brush's icon that will appear on the Brush palette drawer, or open an existing picture.

2. Choose the Rectangular Selection tool.

3. Hold down Shift and drag to create a square selection **3**.

4. Choose Brushes palette > Brushes menu > Variants submenu > Save Brush.

5. Enter a name for the brush **5**.

6. Click OK. An icon for your new brush will appear on the Brushes palette drawer front **6**, but it won't have any variants. To create variants for it, follow the instructions on the next page.

Use the Brush Look Designer to preview brush variations.

To change the brush name, choose Brushes palette > Brushes menu > Brush Mover, highlight the name you want to change, click Change Name, enter a new name, click OK, then click Quit.

To change the brush icon, follow steps 1 through 3 above, choose Brushes palette > Brushes menu > Brush Mover, highlight the name of the brush whose icon you want to change, click Change Picture, click OK, then click Quit.

Select an area to become the new brush icon. This is Ray Rue's Eraser brush icon.

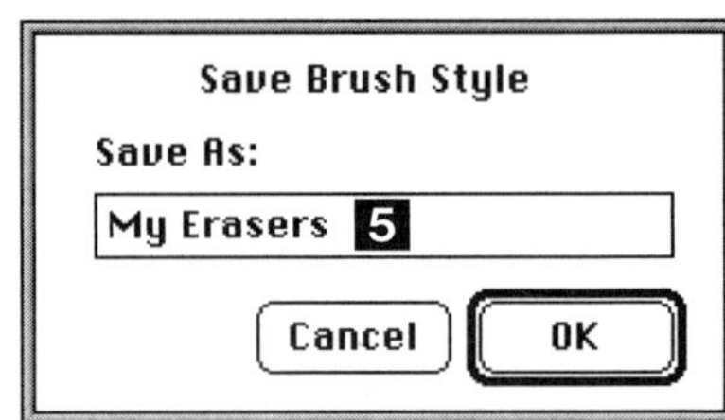

Enter a name for the new brush.

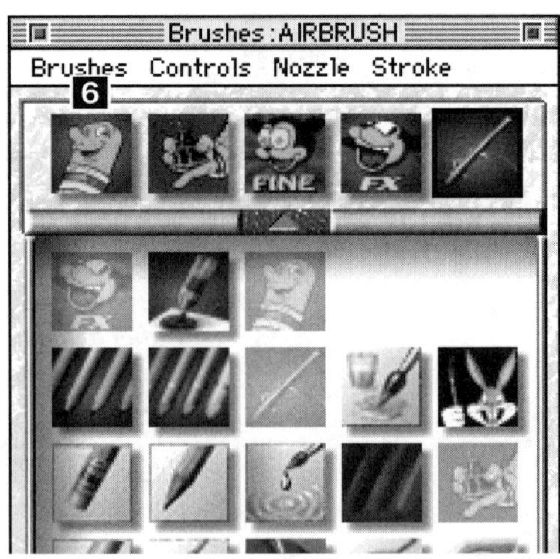

The new brush icon appears on the Brushes palette. (Ray Rue's Brushes palette)

Ray Rue's custom variants.

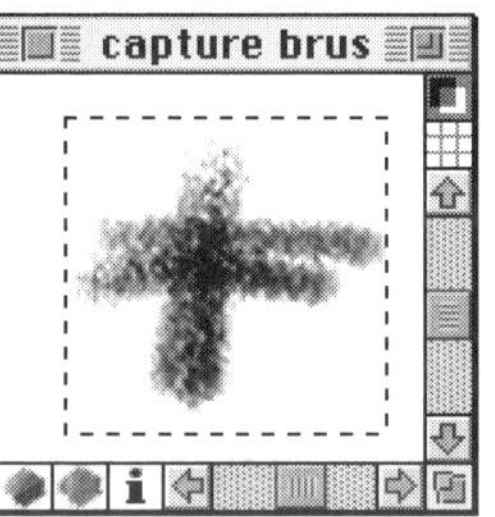

Select an area to become the brush tip.

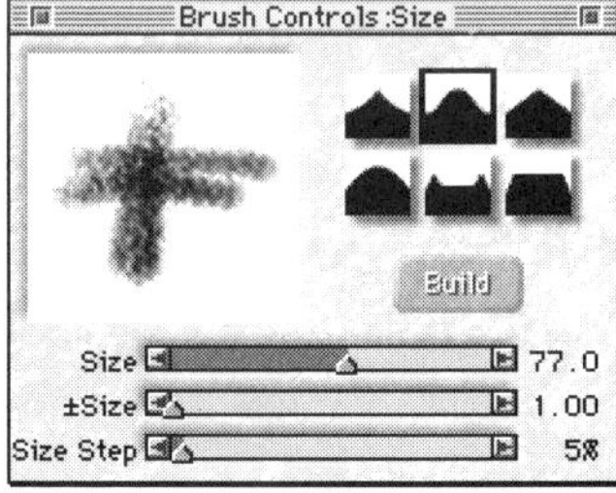

You can adjust the captured brush size using the Brush Controls: Size palette, but don't over-enlarge it. It's best to capture a tip at about the size you plan to use it.

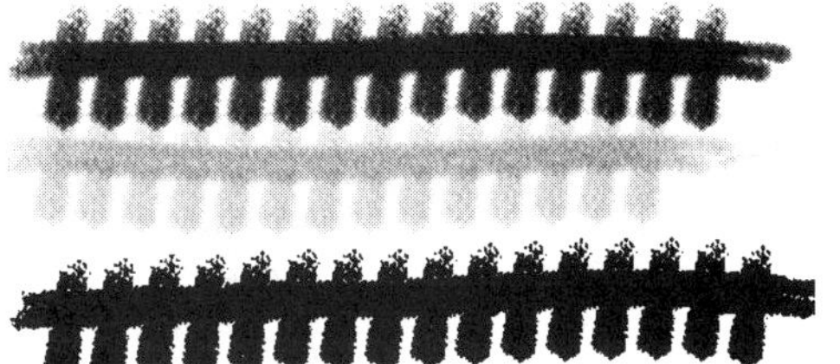

Captured brush strokes drawn with the Soft Buildup, Grainy Soft Cover, and Grainy Edge Flat Cover submethod categories chosen.

A brush can have up to 32 variants.

To save a new or modified brush variant:

1. Customize your brush any way you like (method category or subcategory, Color Variability, Brush Controls, etc.).

2. To add the variant to the variant pop-up menu, choose Brushes palette > Brushes menu > Variants > Save Variant, enter a name, then click OK.
   or
   To save over the currently selected variant, choose Brushes palette > Brushes menu > Variants > Save Built Variant.

To restore a brush's original default variant, make sure the variant is selected, then choose Brushes palette > Brushes menu > Variants > Restore Default Variant. Choose Delete Variant from the same submenu to delete a variant altogether.

To capture a brush from a painting:

1. Open an existing image. Or draw with 100% black on a white background to define opaque parts of the brush tip and a lower opacity brush to define semi-transparent areas. Soft edges work well.

2. Choose the Rectangular Selection tool.

3. Hold down Shift and drag to create a square selection.

4. Choose Brushes palette > Brushes menu > Capture Brush. The brush will display in the preview window on the Brush Controls: Size palette.

5. *Optional:* Modify the new tip using the Brush Controls: Size palette. Move the Spacing/Size slider on the Brush Controls: Spacing palette to adjust the spacing between dabs. Click the Build button, if necessary.

6. Save the new brush variant. If you don't save it, it will disappear as soon as you choose a different brush.

Use the Record Stroke command to record any single stroke, including a stroke made with the Cloners brush. This command was used to create many of the brush stroke illustrations in this book. You can save, close, then reopen a file in which you've recorded a stroke and still replay it, but the stroke will be **lost** if you quit Painter.

To record a brush stroke:

1. Choose Brushes palette > Stroke menu > Record Stroke.

2. Draw a brush stroke.

To replay a recorded brush stroke:

1. Choose Brushes palette > Stroke menu > Playback Stroke.

2. Choose the Brush tool.

3. *Optional:* Choose a different brush, variant, Primary color, or paper texture, or customize the brush.

4. Click in the image window. Keep clicking to replay additional strokes.

5. Choose Playback Stroke again to turn the feature off.

If you record a new stroke and then want to replay it, you'll need to choose Playback Stroke again, even if the command has a check mark next to it.

You can choose Playback Stroke again to replay the same recorded stroke at any time, and in any document, until a different stroke is recorded or you quit Painter.

To replay a recorded brush stroke randomly:

1. *Optional:* Create a selection to confine the Auto Playback to that area.

2. Choose Brushes palette > Stroke menu > Auto Playback.

3. Click your mouse or press with your stylus to stop the playback. You can choose new art materials and then choose Auto Playback again.

A recorded stroke.

The stroke played back several times, the brush and color changed once. To produce this illustration, we enlarged our image window so we could click outside the "live" image area.

Auto Playback.

Use rulers and guides to place objects:

- To **display the rulers**, choose Canvas menu > Rulers > Show Rulers (choose Hide Rulers from the same submenu to hide the rulers). Tip: To place a floater very precisely, use the floater's attributes dialog box (see page 98).

- To **create guides**, make sure the rulers are displayed, then press and drag in the horizontal or vertical ruler where you want the guide to appear. If the guides don't appear, choose Canvas menu > Guides > Show Guides (choose Hide Guides from the same submenu to hide the guides). If you want the guides to snap to the ruler tick marks, choose Canvas menu > Rulers > Snap to Ruler Ticks.

- To **move a guide**, drag its marker.

- To **change the ruler units**, hold down Option and click in the ruler, or choose Canvas menu > Rulers > Ruler Options.

- To make objects and most tool cursors **snap to a guide** when dragged within six pixels of the guide, choose Canvas menu > Guides > Snap to Guides.

- To **recolor a guide**, double-click its marker on the ruler, click the Guide Color swatch **1**, then choose a color. To make all the guides the same color again, check the Same Color for All Guides box in the same dialog box.

- To **lock a guide**, double-click its marker on the ruler, then click the Locked Guide box **2**.

- To **remove a** horizontal **guide**, drag its marker upward or downward out of the image window. To remove a vertical guide, drag its marker to the left or the right. To **remove all guides**, double-click anywhere in the ruler, click Delete All Guides **3**, then click Yes.

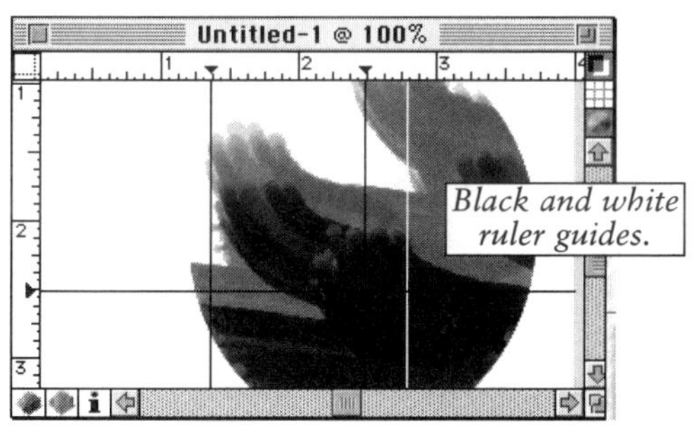

Black and white ruler guides.

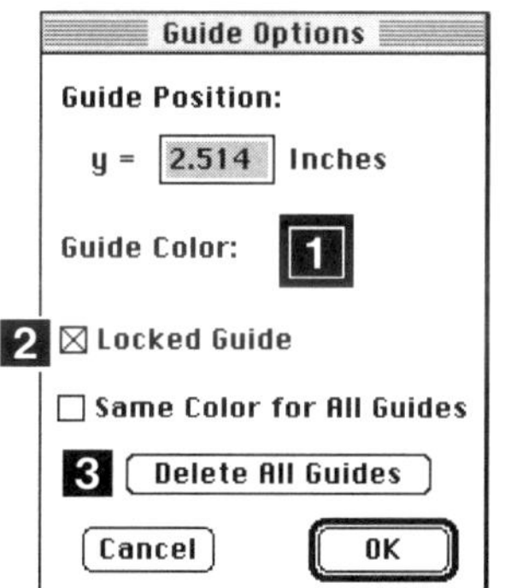

The Brushes palette > Controls pull-down menu.

The Brush Controls and Advanced Controls palettes

Using the Brush Controls and Advanced Controls palettes—Size, Spacing, Random, Bristle, Rake, Well, Water, and Sliders—you can fine tune your brushes to suit your painting style. These palettes are discussed on the remaining pages in this chapter. To open any of them, choose the palette name from the Controls pull-down menu on the Brushes palette. You can test Brush Controls settings using the Brush Look Designer.

To change brush size and/or shape (Brush Controls: Size palette):

SIZE

Move the **Size** slider to the right to make the tip wider. Large tips take longer to preview and render on screen.

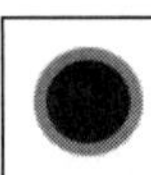

Move the **± Size** slider to the right to increase the amount the stroke width can vary with stylus pressure. A large ± Size setting takes more time to build.

The **Size Step** slider controls the smoothness of the transition between the thin and thick parts of the stroke. Move the slider to the right to make the transition more abrupt.

ANGLE CONTROL *(expanded Size palette)*

The **Squeeze** slider controls the shape of the tip. Rounder to the right...

...more elliptical to the left.

The **Angle** slider changes the angle of the tip relative to the horizontal axis. The Angle slider has no effect if the tip is a circle (100% Squeeze). 0° Angle is a horizontal tip. Lefties, this is for you! You can rotate the tip to a more natural angle for your hand.

DAB TYPES

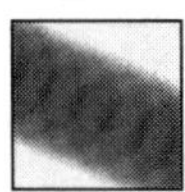

The Dab Type is the dab shape. The **Circular** Dab Type is a single round shape. The spacing between Circular dabs is controlled via the Brush Controls: Spacing palette.

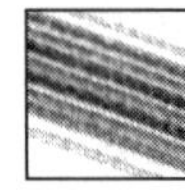

The **Bristle** Dab Type is comprised of multiple dots. Adjust the character of the bristle dabs using the Brush Controls: Bristle palette.

Speed tips

- Click Build (Command-B), if the button lights up, after you've made *all* your Size, Spacing and Bristle palette adjustments.

- To change the brush size without using the Size palette, hold down Command and Option and drag in the image window. If you make the brush tip large, you may get a prompt to Build the brush when you start to use it.

- To restore a whole brush category's default settings, Option-click the brush's icon on the Brushes palette.

Click here to toggle between a preview of the overall brush shape (right) or the individual dabs in the brush tip (left) (shown at the same time here just for illustration purposes). *These profiles are illustrated on the next page.*

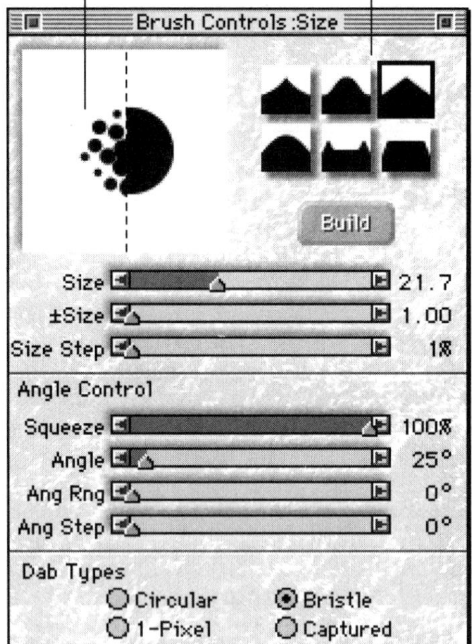

A **Captured** dab is created when you create your own brush tip (see page 63).

To turn a variant (like Small Wash) into a calligraphic brush, choose the Circular Dab Type, move the Squeeze slider to the left, and adjust the Angle slider.

Brush tip profiles

The brush tip profiles on the Brush Controls: Size palette affect color flow. Brush tip profile changes are noticeable with "hard" media brushes, like the Felt Pens, Pencils, Chalk, Crayons, and Charcoal.

To produce a coiled "Slinky" stroke, choose a hard medium brush, choose the Water Color profile and the Circular Dab Type on the extended Size palette, and choose the Single or Multi Stroke Type from the Spacing palette.

<table>
<tr><td align="center">TOP ROW</td><td align="center">BOTTOM ROW</td></tr>
</table>

Pointed profile. Color is densest at the center of the stroke and falls off quickly toward the edge. The narrowest profile.

Dull profile. Color spreads over a wide area. More density at the edge than the Linear profile.

Medium profile. Like the Linear profile, except with a wider area of density, and thus a wider stroke.

Water Color profile. Color is concentrated at the edge of the stroke. This is the default Water Color profile.

Linear profile. Color is concentrated in the center of the stroke and falls off smoothly towards the edge.

One-pixel edge profile. Very wide density. Color falls off rapidly at the one-pixel, anti-aliased edge.

To change dab spacing (Brush Controls: Spacing palette):

Pigment is actually applied in dabs, the flow of which you can adjust via the Brush Controls: Spacing palette.

The **Spacing/Size** slider controls the continuousness of the dab flow. Move to the right to produce a less dense stroke.

The **Min Spacing** slider controls the minimum spacing between dabs. For maximum space between dabs, move both the Spacing/Size and Min Spacing sliders to the right.

The **Stroke Types** and **Bristles** sliders control the number of bristle paths in the stroke:

Single creates one path of bristle dabs per stroke. Single Stroke Type brushes are affected by both the Spacing/Size and Min Spacing sliders.

Multi strokes are comprised of a group of dab paths that are precomputed, so they take time render. Draw short strokes and pause between them for this Stroke Type. The Min Spacing slider affects this Stroke Type more.

Rake strokes are comprised of grouped dab paths with uniform spacing between each path. The Digital Sumi, Penetration Brush, Loaded Oils, and Camel Hair Brush variants of the Brush brush and the Scratchboard Rake variant of the Pen brush are Rake brushes. The Min Spacing slider affects this Stroke Type more.

If you change the Stroke Type from Single to Rake and the stroke is too light, raise the Resaturation slider setting on the Advanced Controls: Well palette to add pigment to the paint flow.

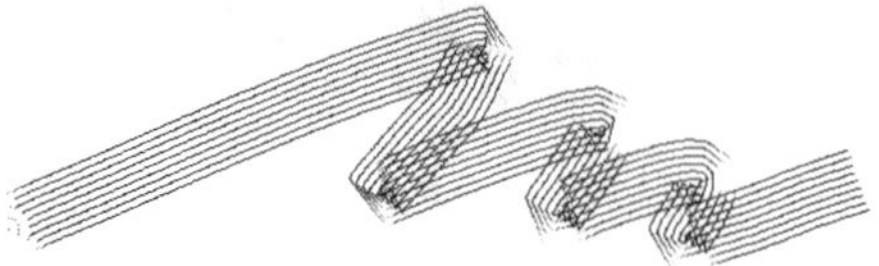

Rake Stroke Type—Digital Sumi

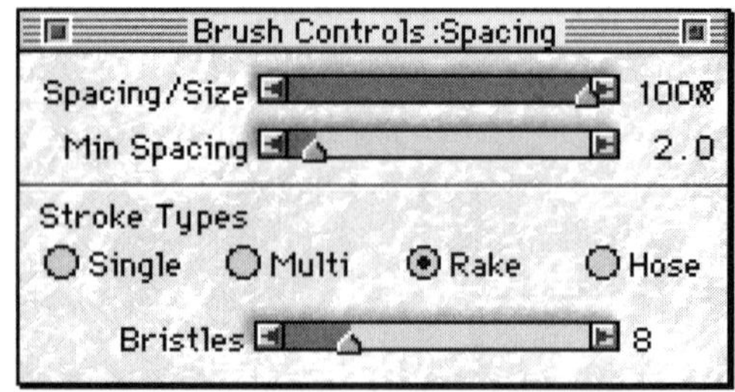

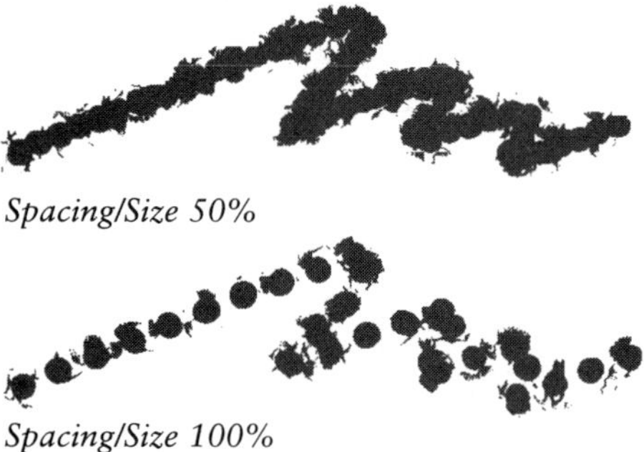

Spacing/Size 50%

Spacing/Size 100%

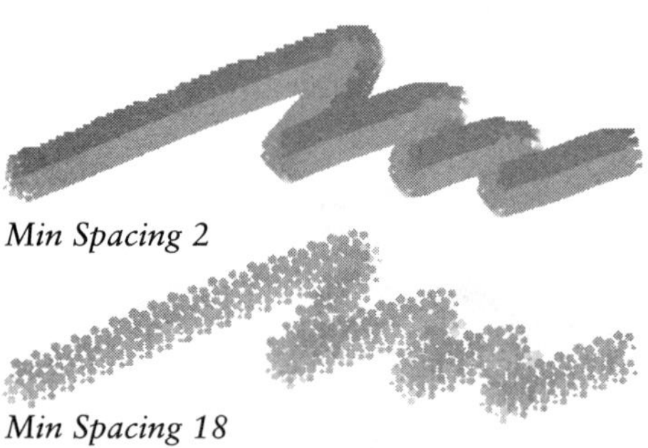

Min Spacing 2

Min Spacing 18

Multi Stroke Type—Hairy Brush. Increasing Color Variability (expanded Color palette) produces nice effects with this Stroke Type.

Spacing Palette

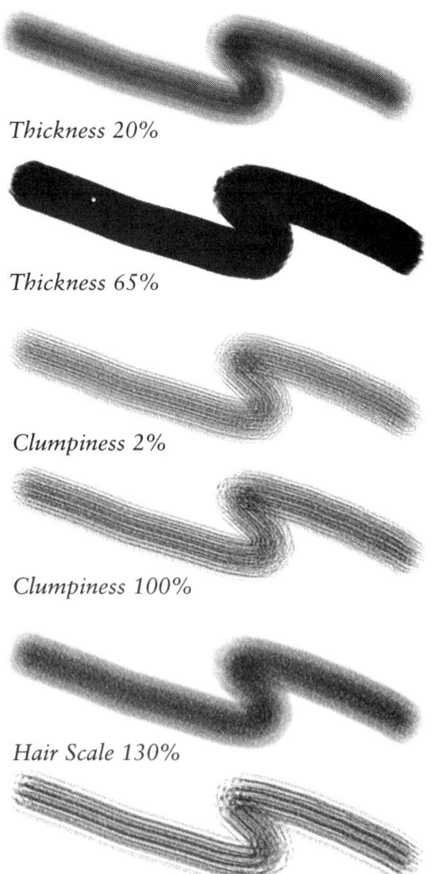

Thickness 20%

Thickness 65%

Clumpiness 2%

Clumpiness 100%

Hair Scale 130%

Hair Scale 900%, Thickness 30%

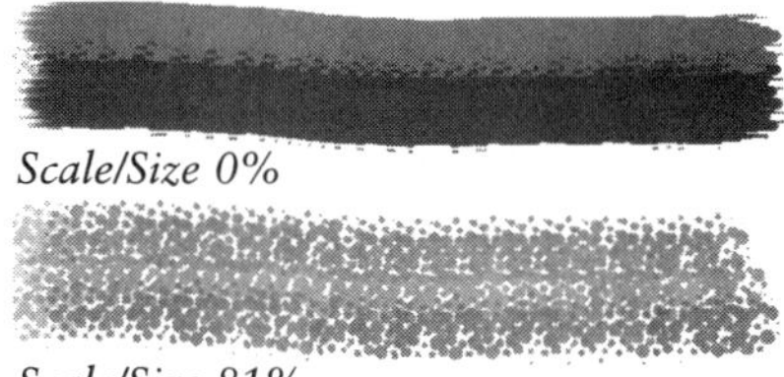

Scale/Size 0%

Scale/Size 81%

[Brush strokes on this page: Loaded Oils, Soft Cover submethod category.]

To change stroke character (Brush Controls: Bristle palette):

You must choose the Bristle Dab Type on the Brush Controls: Size palette for your brush for Bristle palette settings to have any effect. You can preview the Brush Controls: Bristle palette changes on the Size palette—just drag the Size palette away from the main Brush Controls palette and click the preview to display the bristle dots.

The higher the **Thickness**, the thicker the bristles and the denser the stroke.

The higher the **Clumpiness**, the more bristles clump together.

The higher the **Hair Scale**, the larger and denser the bristle dots and the more separate and noticeable are the bristles.

The **Scale/Size** slider controls jumps in size variations in the bristle dots in the tip. For the Scale/Size slider to have any effect, the Brush Controls: Size palette ± Size setting must be above 1.0. Scale/Size changes are noticeable with these bristly variants of the Brush brush: Big and Small Loaded Oils, Big Wet Oils, and Smaller and Ultrafine Wash Brush.

Brush variants: Fine Wet Oils and Smaller Wash Brush; Bristle Thickness and Clumpiness lowered, Hair Scale raised.

To fine-tune a raked brush (Advanced Controls: Rake palette):

Before using the Rake palette, you must choose the Rake Stroke Type from the Brush Controls: Spacing palette.

The **Contact Angle** slider controls how much of the brush touches the canvas. The higher the Contact Angle, the wider the stroke or the more pigment is applied.

The higher **Brush Scale**, the wider bristles are spread. Adjust in small increments!

The higher the **Turn Amount**, the more bristles will lift up sporadically as you move the stylus in a new direction, mimicing traditional brush behavior.

With the **Spread Bristles** box checked, bristles are spread apart. Stroke width will vary with stylus pressure.

With the **Soften Bristle Edge** box checked, bristles edges are more transparent.

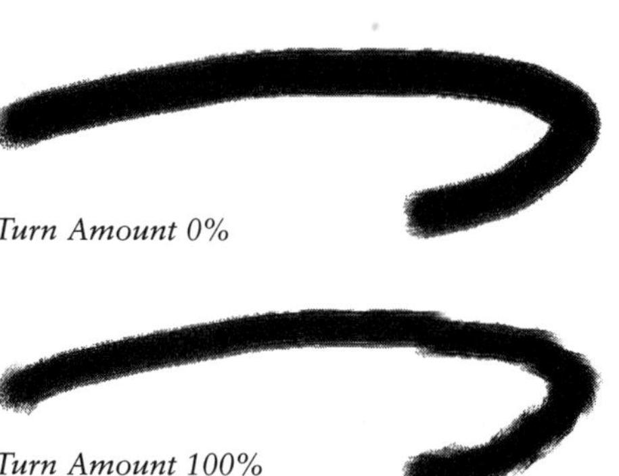

Turn Amount 0%

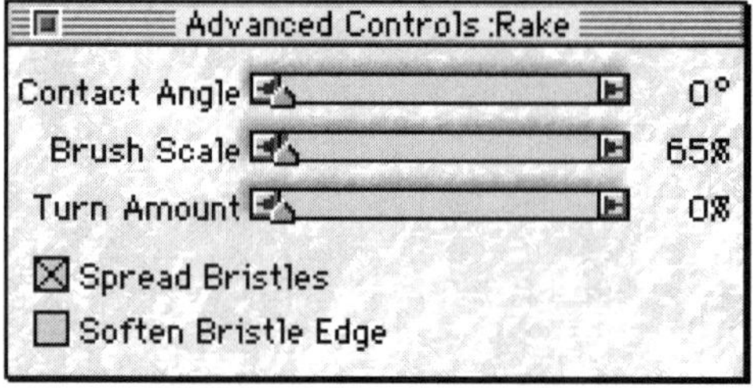

Turn Amount 100%

[Brush strokes on this page: Brush brush, Loaded Oils, Soft Cover submethod category.]

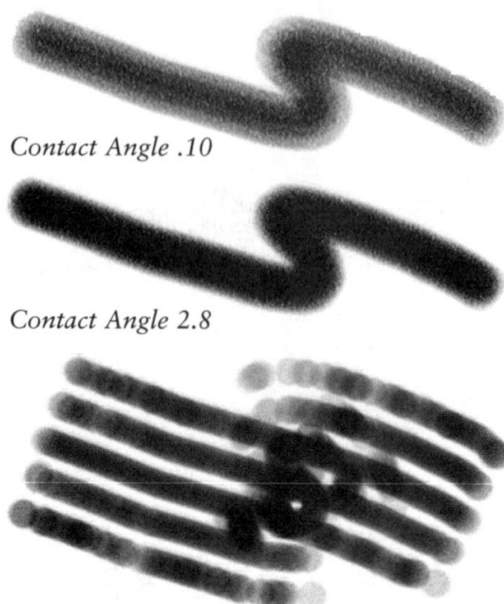

Contact Angle .10

Contact Angle 2.8

Contact Angle 2, Brush Scale 400%

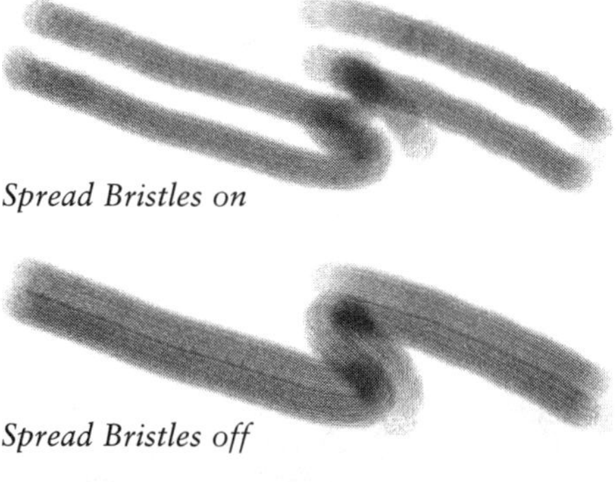

Spread Bristles on

Spread Bristles off

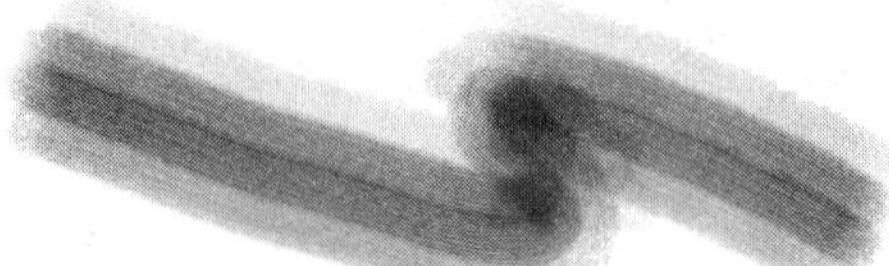

Soften Bristle Edge on, Contact Angle 1.44

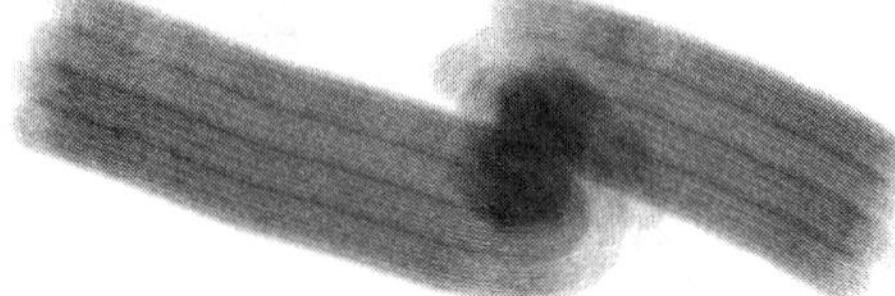

Soften Bristle Edge off

Resaturation 10%

Resaturation 88%

Bleed 15% (low Resaturation setting)

Bleed 90% (low Resaturation setting)

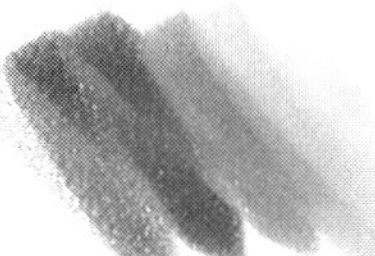

Dryout 1285

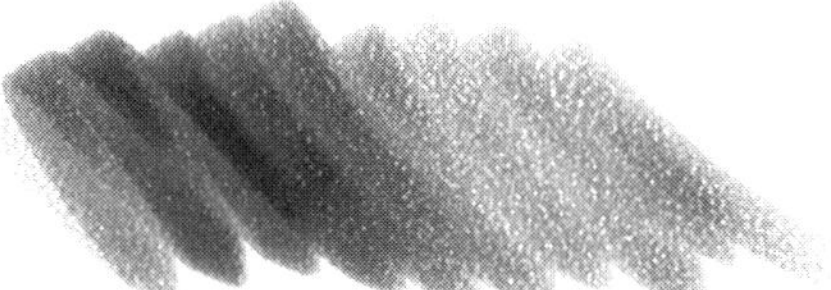

Dryout 22026

[Brush strokes on this page: Brush brush, Cover Brush variant, Buildup method category, Soft Buildup submethod category.]

To change the paint flow (Advanced Controls: Well palette):

The higher the **Resaturation** setting, the more concentrated the color in the paint flow.

The higher the **Bleed** setting, the more a brush stroke bleeds into colors beneath it. You may have to lower the Resaturation setting to observe any Bleed effect.

The higher the **Dryout** setting, the more slowly a brush stroke runs out of paint. There is no dryout when the Dryout slider is at its rightmost setting or when the Bleed slider is at zero.

Dryout works with brushes that have the Single or Multi Stroke Type (Spacing palette). Brushes of this type include the Water Color brush variants, the Coarse Hairs, Fine Brush, Brushy and Smaller Wash Brush variants of the Brush brush when the Bleed setting is above 0%, the Oil Pastel variant of the Chalk brush, the Dirty Marker and Medium Tip Felt Pens variants of the Felt Pens brush, and the Waxy Crayons variant of the Crayons brush.

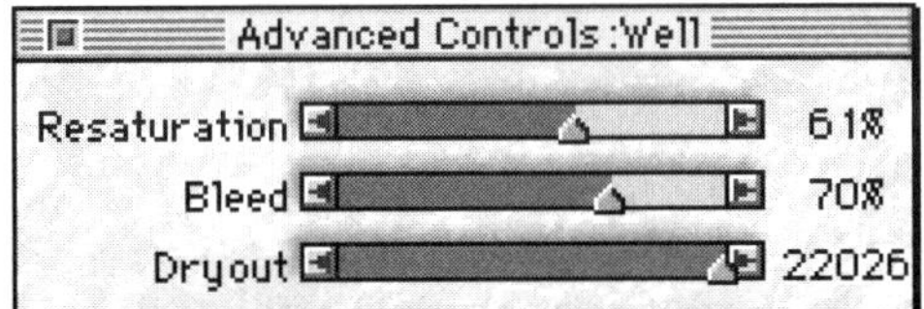

Well Palette

To change a stroke's randomness (Advanced Controls: Random palette):

Use the Random palette to control how variegated your strokes are.

Move the **Dab Location: Placement** slider to the right to scatter the dabs in the stroke and produce a noticeable "jitter." Most noticeable when the Single Stroke Type is selected for the brush (Brush Controls: Spacing palette).

Check the **Random Brush Stroke Grain** box to make the current paper texture appear more randomly. Choose a Grainy method subcategory for your brush and a paper texture with a large pattern.

Dab Location Placement .15

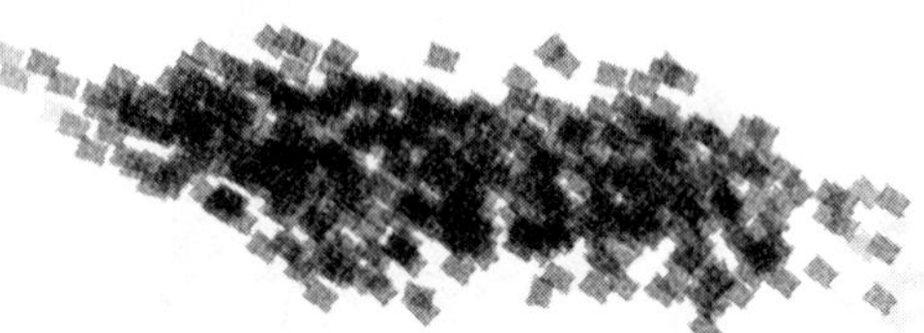

Dab Location Placement 3.41

[Square Chalk variant, Grainy Soft Cover sub-method category.]

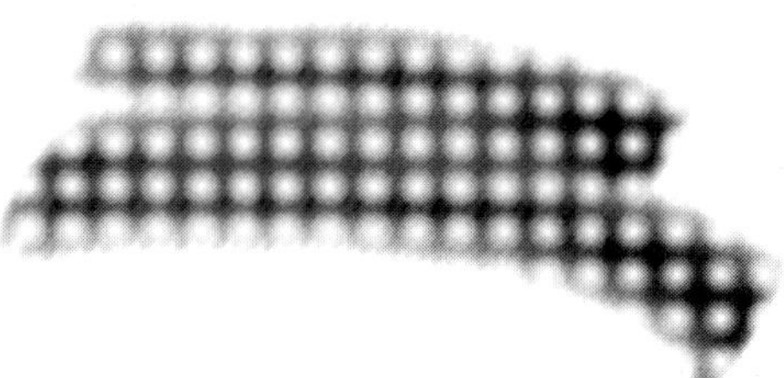

Random Brush Stroke Grain box unchecked

Random Brush Stroke Grain box checked

[Gritty Charcoal brush, Grainy Soft Cover sub-method category, Dottie paper texture.]

To clone areas of a source image more haphazardly, push the **Clone Location: Variability** slider to the right. Check the **Random Clone Source** box for maximum haphazardness. The further left the **How Often** slider is, the more frequently areas are displaced as you clone, and the rougher the stroke (set Variability above 0).

The Seurat variant of the Artists brush has a high Dab Location Placement setting (flower center).

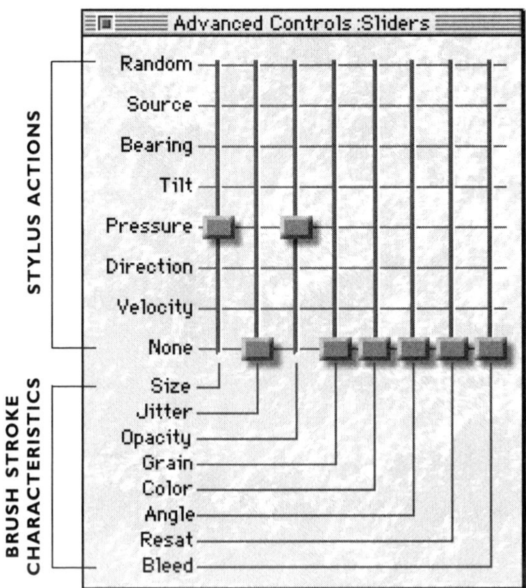

STYLUS/MOUSE ACTIONS:

Link any of these stylus actions to any of the stroke characteristics described at right.

Random sets the level of the selected stroke characteristic randomly.

Source uses the source document's light and dark distribution to assign different amounts of the selected brush stroke characteristic in the clone document.

Bearing and **Tilt** are functions found only on some styluses.

Most brushes have their Size and Opacity set to **Pressure** as a default.

Direction of stylus or mouse affects the selected stroke characteristic.

Velocity (speed) of stylus or mouse affects the selected stroke characteristic.

None—the stroke characteristic is unaffected by cursor motion.

To change the stylus/mouse–stroke connection (Advanced Controls: Sliders palette):

The Sliders control how stylus or mouse characteristics, like speed, direction, and pressure, express themselves through stroke characteristics, like size, jitter, and opacity.

If you're using a stylus/tablet, you might want to set stroke characteristics to Pressure. If you're using a mouse, experiment with Direction or Velocity.

BRUSH STROKE CHARACTERISTICS:

Size affects brush tip size when the ± Size slider setting on the Brush Controls: Size palette is above 1.2.

Jitter affects the randomness of the placement of brush dabs. Jitter parameters are set on the Advanced Controls: Random palette.

Opacity affects how quickly colors mix to black when a brush Buildup method category is selected or what level of coverage a brush has when the Cover method category is selected.

Grain affects how much the current paper texture shows through a stroke.

Color controls how the Primary and Secondary color mix in a brush stroke, in conjunction with the Color Variability sliders on the Art Materials: Color palette.

Angle sets the direction (orientation) of the brush dabs.

Resat(uration) controls the level of color concentration that flows from a brush, in conjunction with the Resaturation setting on the Advanced Controls: Well palette.

Bleed controls how much colors mix together, in conjunction with the Bleed slider on the Well palette.

Water Palette

To fine-tune a Water Color brush (Advanced Controls: Water palette):

Water palette settings only affect strokes made on the Wet Paint layer. When you choose a default Water Color brush or choose the Wet variant for any other brush, the Wet Paint layer is turned on automatically (Canvas menu > Wet Paint). If you want to experiment with different Water palette settings, choose Canvas menu > Dry periodically as you work to merge the Wet Paint layer strokes with the underlying canvas.

When the **Diffusion** setting is above zero, pigment will feather outward from the edge of brushstrokes into the current paper texture, like traditional watercolor on wet paper. Diffusion may take a few seconds to render.

The higher the **Wet Fringe** setting, the more paint pools at the edges of wet strokes, like traditional watercolor pigment on dry paper. The Wet Fringe slider affects **all** strokes currently on the Wet Paint layer.

To diffuse strokes after they're made

The Shift-D shortcut diffuses all existing strokes on the Wet Paint layer in small increments. Repeat the shortcut to diffuse more.

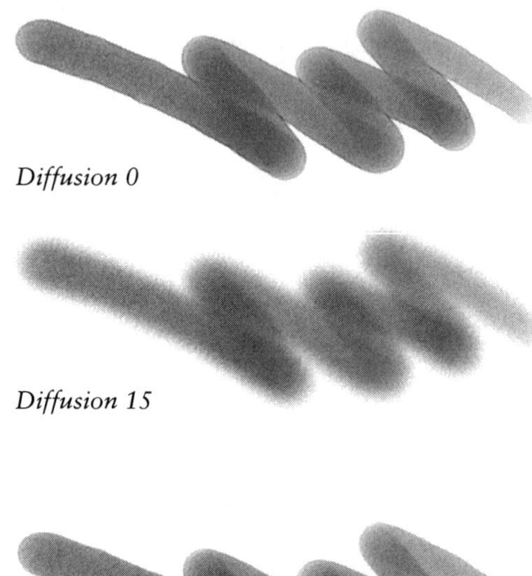

Diffusion 0

Diffusion 15

Wet Fringe 15

Wet Fringe 90

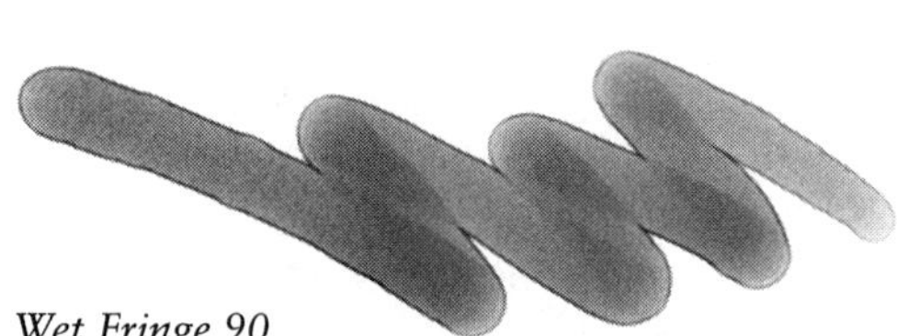

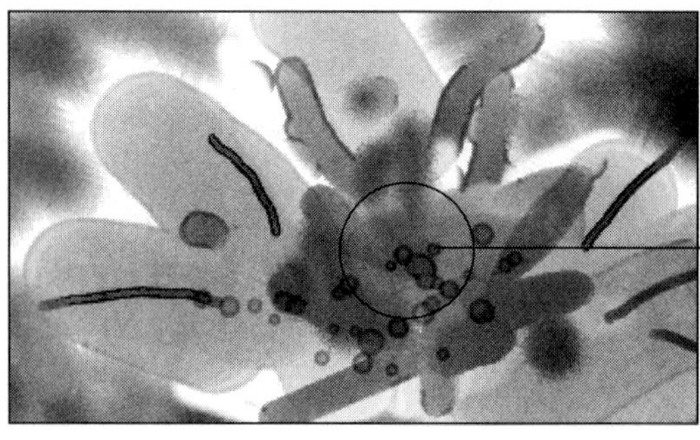

[The default Spatter Water variant of the Water Color brush has a high Wet Fringe setting.]

Peter Lourekas,
Figure & Shroud.

Peter Lourekas, **Simi.**

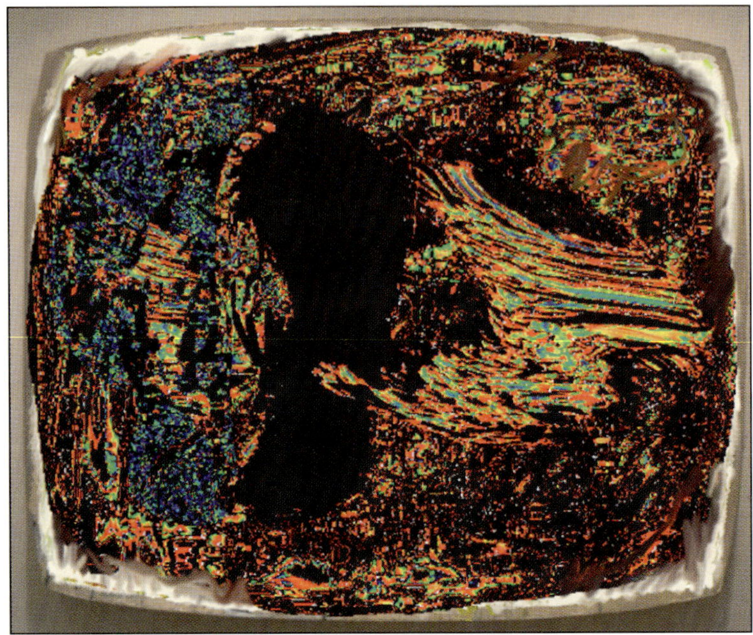

Ron Gorchov,
Clone of Herophile.

Ron Gorchov,
Low Comedy II.

Ron Gorchov, **Knossos**.

Ron Gorchov,
Year of the Boar.

David Humphrey, *Yearbook*.

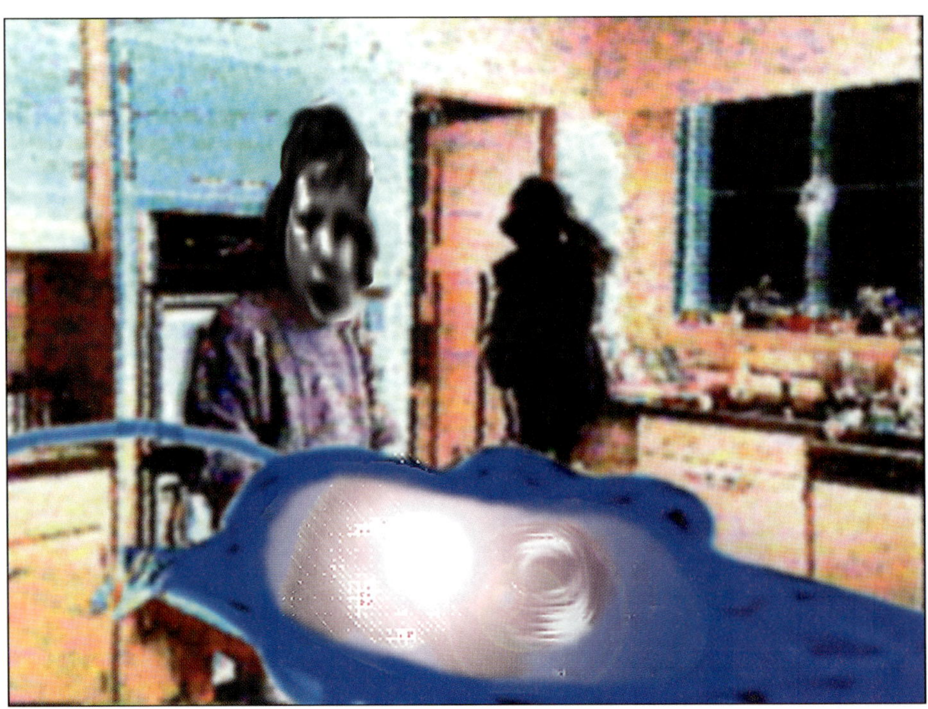

David Humphrey, *Solarized Kitchen*.

Phil Allen

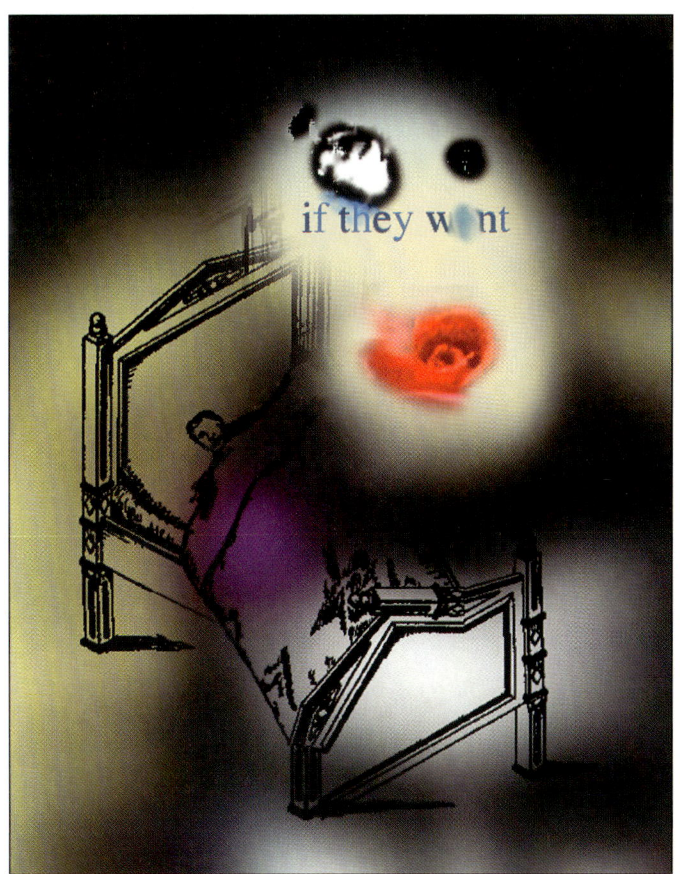

David Humphrey, **Dream**.

*David Humphrey, **Blond Again**.*

*Elaine Weinmann, **Unfolding**.*

*Elaine Weinmann, **Synthesis**.*

Rodney Alan Greenblat.

*Rodney Alan Greenblat, **Springing**.*

IMAGES

*Diane Margolin, **Self Portrait**.*

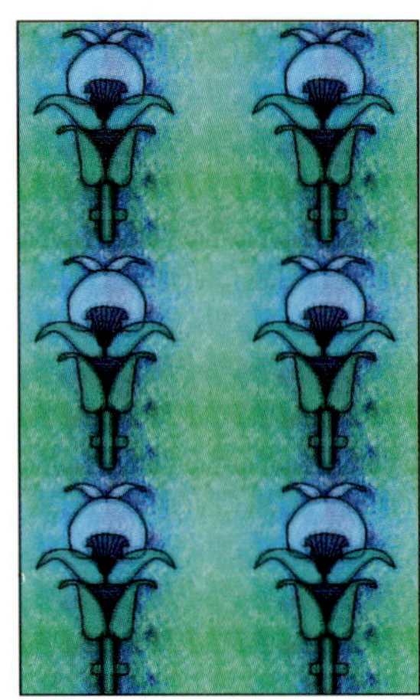

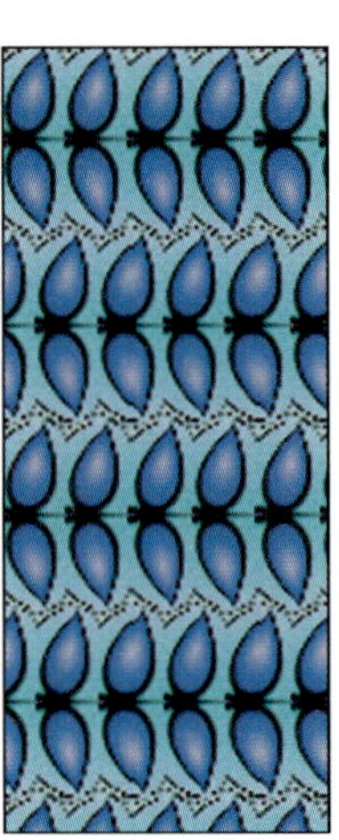

Patterns and textures by Diane Margolin.

Diane Margolin, *Nicky and Zoe.*

Fabric Effects, Inc.

Fabric Effects, Inc.

Nancy Stahl, **Jacket**.

Jaime Davidovich.

Nancy Stahl, **Island Woman**.

Nancy Stahl, *Greenish Head.*

*Ray Rue, **Minotaur**.*

*Ray Rue, **Arc Library**.*

Selections/Paths 5

Elaine Weinmann (detail).

Selections/Paths

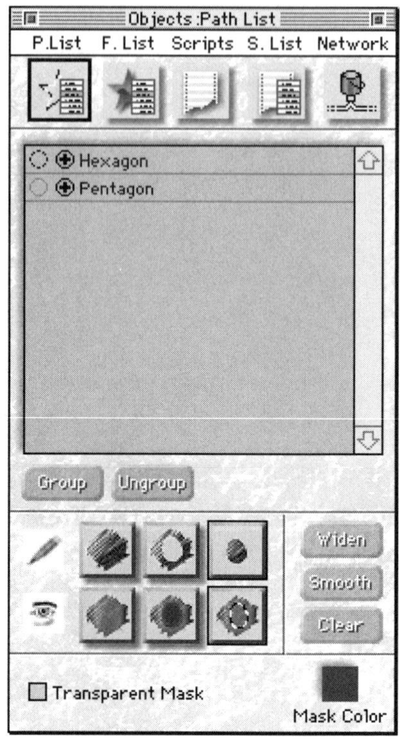

If you create a selection path using the Oval Selection, Rectangular Selection, or Lasso tool, the area inside the path will automatically be selected. In the image window, a selection path will have a black dashed marquee; on the Objects: P. List palette, selection path names appear in blue (except those created with the Rectangular Selection tool, which are not listed on the P. List). If you fill a selection or apply any Painter editing feature to a selection, only the pixels inside it will be modified—not the surrounding, unselected areas.

You can move, reshape, resize, rotate, skew, or feather an Oval Selection or Lasso tool selection path without affecting the background pixels. To reshape a path very precisely, convert it into a shape, adjust its control points and wings, and then convert it back into a selection. Paths are automatically saved with the document in which they are created, but if you save a path in a paths library, you can then place the path onto any picture.

The Objects: P. List palette is used to highlight and activate selections; to control whether a path is displayed as a marquee or as a mask; to control whether painting and editing occurs inside or outside an active selection or ignores the selection altogether; and to group/ungroup, widen or shrink, smooth, and clear (delete) paths. More than one path can be active at a time.

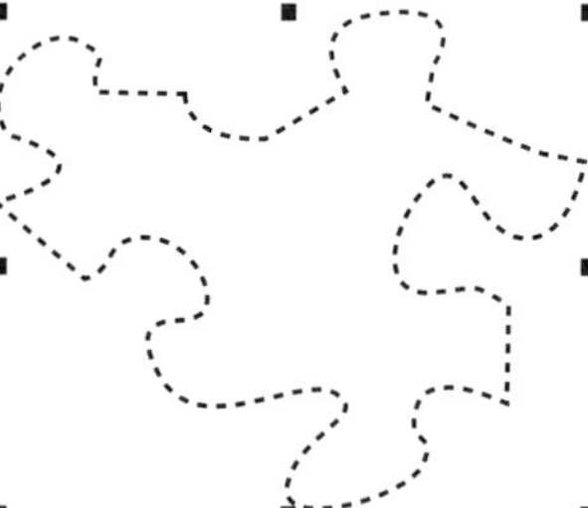

A selection path selected with the Selection Adjuster tool.

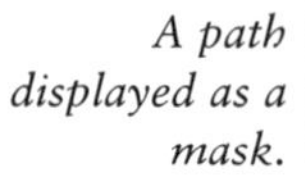

A path displayed as a mask.

Ways to create a selection

- ■ **Draw with the Oval Selection, Rectangular Selection, Pen, or Lasso tool**
- ■ **Convert a mask or a shape into a selection**
- ■ **Use the Magic Wand command.**

Selections/Paths

Rectangular Selection tool

To select an entire picture:

Double-click the Oval Selection or Rectangular Selection tool. If you already have a selection on your picture, double-click the tool twice.

or

Choose Edit menu > Select All (Command-A). **Note:** If you choose Select All when the Selection Adjuster tool is chosen and a path is displayed as a selection (its circle icon is dashed), you will select all the file's paths instead of selecting the image.

Press Delete to fill the entire selected picture with the current paper color.

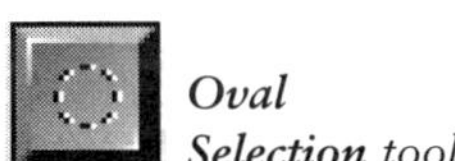

Oval Selection tool

To create an oval selection:

1. Choose the Oval Selection tool. If the Oval Selection tool isn't displayed on the Tools palette, you can access it by pressing on the Rectangular Selection tool or by clicking the Rectangular Selection tool and then clicking the Oval Selection tool icon on the Controls: Selection palette.

2. Drag diagonally to create a selection.

Hold down Shift before and while dragging to create a circular selection. Release the mouse before you release Shift.

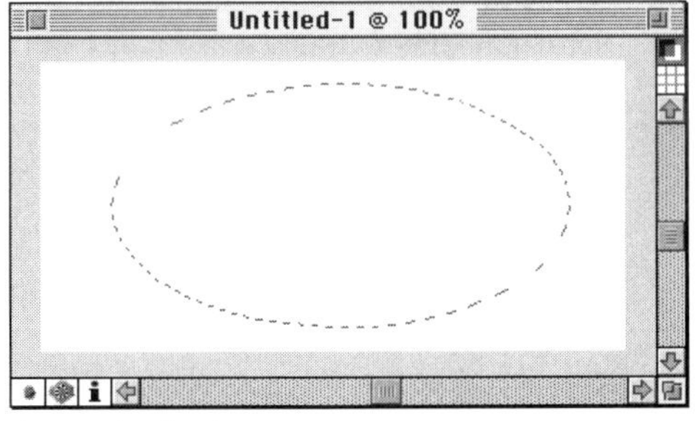

An oval selection.

To switch the selected and unselected areas:

Choose Edit menu > Mask > Invert Mask (Command-Shift-I). The selection is now a mask group.

Use Invert Mask to make unselected parts of an image editable when you apply an Effects menu command.

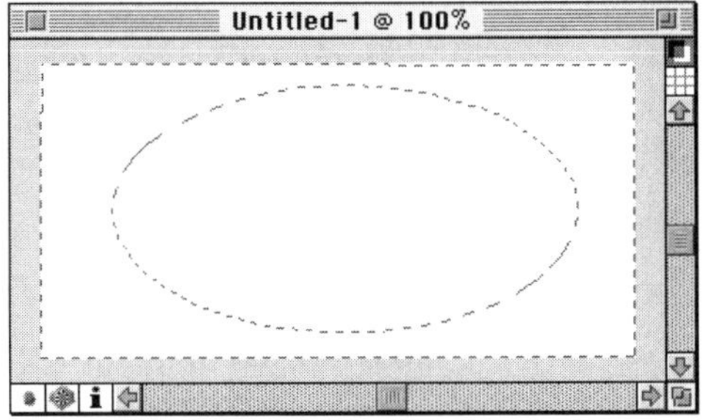

*After choosing the **Invert Mask** command. The selection is now a mask group.*

The **Rectangular Selection** tool creates a temporary rectangular or square selection area that functions differently from other Painter paths and from rectangular selections in other programs in that it won't limit paint strokes. A rectangular selection *will* limit Effects menu commands, however.

To create a rectangular selection:

1. Choose the Rectangular Selection tool. If the Rectangular Selection tool isn't displayed on the Tools palette, you can access it by pressing on the Oval Selection tool or by clicking the Oval Selection tool and then clicking the Rectangular Selection tool icon on the Controls: Selection palette.

2. Drag diagonally over the area of the picture you want to select.

   Hold down Shift before and while dragging to create a square selection. Release the mouse before you release Shift.

To resize a rectangular selection:

To resize a selection manually, using the Rectangular Selection tool, hold down Control and drag toward or away from any corner of the rectangle. (You don't have to click right on the corner.)
or
To resize a rectangular selection using a dialog box, choose Objects palette > P. List menu > Edit Rectangular Selection (Command-Shift-E), enter new Height and/or Width values, then click OK. (Click Show Bottom and Right to resize the selection using the bottommost and rightmost position values.)

   In the Edit Rectangular Selection dialog box, enter a position number in pixels in the Top field to move the selection vertically or enter a number in the Left field to move the selection horizontally. These numbers reflect the exact location of the rectangle relative to the top and left edge of the image.

Rectangular Selection tool

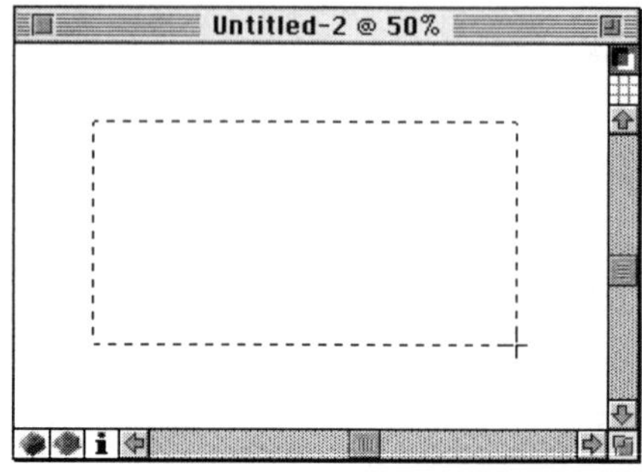

To limit brushstrokes to a rectangular selection

Choose the Rectangular Shape tool, draw a rectangle, resize it if you wish, then choose Shapes menu > Convert To Selection. The shape will no longer be listed on the F. List palette, but the new selection will be listed on the P. List palette. You can use the Selection Adjuster tool to further adjust the selection. Effects menu commands and brush strokes will be limited to the selection. Press Return to deselect the selection when you're finished.

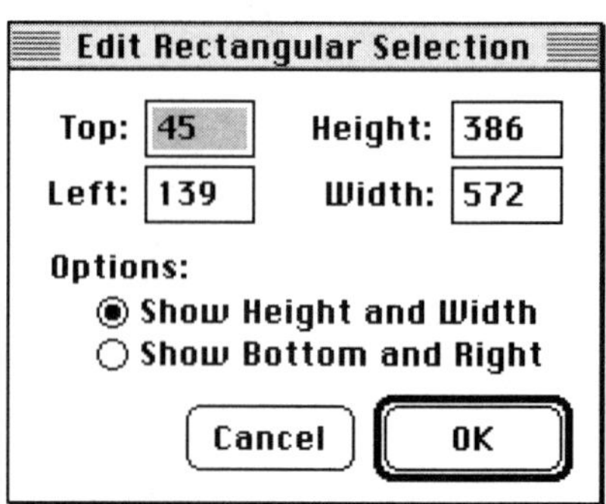

1 *Lasso* tool

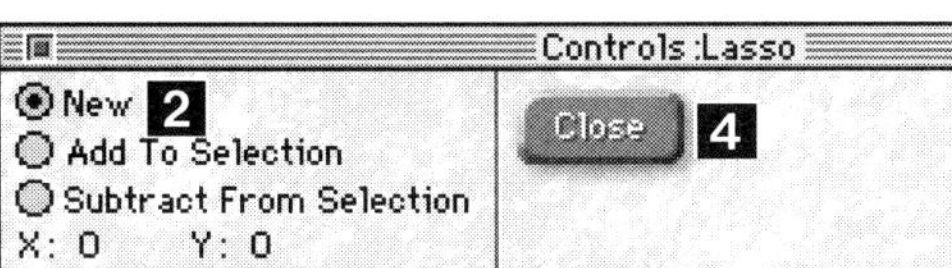

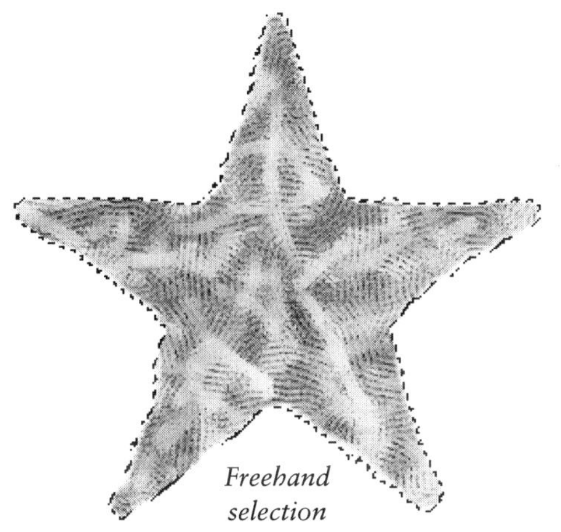

Freehand selection

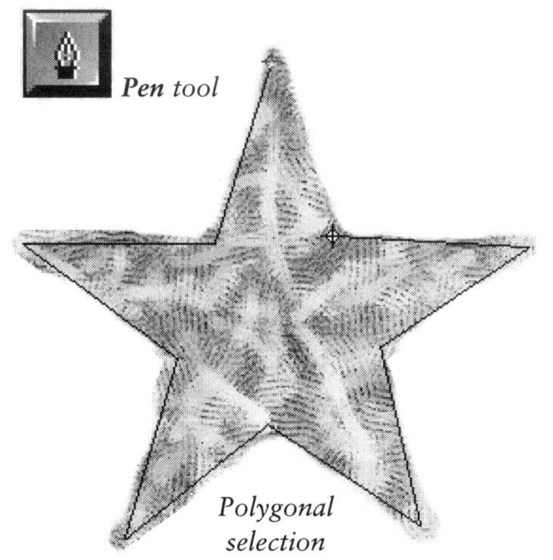

Pen tool

Polygonal selection

To draw a freehand selection:

1. Choose the Lasso tool **1**.

2. On the Controls: Lasso palette, click New **2**.

3. Press and drag to create a selection area on your picture.

4. Close the selection right away using one of these methods (otherwise, the open selection will become a shape):

   Drag back over the starting location.
   or
   Click Close on the Controls: Lasso palette **4**.
   or
   Press Enter.

   The selection path will be listed on the Objects: P. List palette with the next higher number.

To create a polygonal selection:

1. Choose the Pen tool.

2. Click in the image window to create anchor points and define the path.

3. Click the Make Selection button on the Controls: Shape Design palette.

To convert a selection into a shape:

1. Click the path name on the Objects: P. List palette.

2. Choose Objects palette > P. List menu > Convert to Shape. The selection name will be removed from the P. List palette, and the new shape name will appear on the F. List palette.

The **Magic Wand** command usually selects *adjacent* pixels that are similar in hue, saturation or value to the pixel you click on in the image window. To select similar *non-adjacent* pixels by color, choose Edit menu > Select All or create a selection using the Rectangular Selection tool before you choose the Magic Wand command, or use the Color Mask command instead (page 155).

To create a Magic Wand (color) selection:

1. *Optional:* Choose Edit menu > Select All.

2. Choose Edit menu > Magic Wand.

3. Click on a color or shade in the image window.
   or
   Drag across an area of varying color to select a wider range of colors.

   The color bars in the Magic Wand dialog box will reflect the hue, saturation, and value range in the selection.

4. *Optional:* Hold down Shift and click or drag on adjacent pixels in the picture to add to the selection. If you chose Select All before you chose the Magic Wand command, you can add similar, non-adjacent pixels.

5. *Optional:* To widen or narrow the hue, saturation, or value range in the selection, press and drag either end of the H, S, or V color bar. Shorten the bar to narrow the range. Try moving the V slider first.

6. Click OK or press Return. The selection will display as a moving marquee and a new Wand Group will be listed at the top of the P. List palette.

To remove the Magic Wand selection after clicking OK, click the Wand Group name at the top of the Objects: P. List palette, then click Clear.

The first pass over the boy's sweater with the Magic Wand selected only the dark stripes. After moving the Value slider slightly to the right...

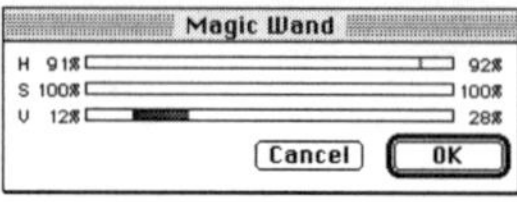

...the entire sweater is selected.

Rodney Alan Greenblat

Rodney Alan Greenblat's interactive stories on CD—Dazzeloids and Rodney's Wonder Window—have won wide acclaim for their humor, invention and artistry. He writes and illustrates his CDs, and composes and records the soundtracks for them. He's also written and illustrated several children's books, including Uncle Wizmo's New Used Car, Aunt Ippy's Museum of Junk, and Thunder Bunny.

Greenblat starts an illustration with a traditional media pencil-and-paper sketch. He scans the sketch, traces over it and refines the shapes in FreeHand, and then imports his FreeHand EPS files into Painter as shapes. He converts the shapes into selections, fills them with color using the Paint Bucket tool, and then applies brush strokes using charcoal and colored pencil brushes. Greenblat, whose background is in traditional painting and sculpture media, loves the painterly look that he achieves using Painter. (See Rodney Alan Greenblat's work in the color plates section.)

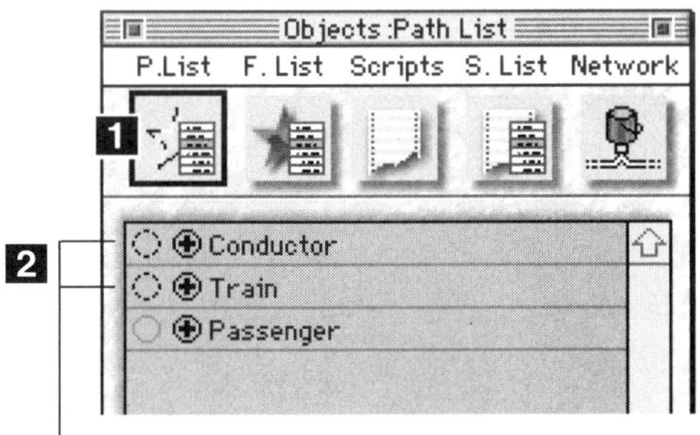

These two paths are displayed as selections.

When a path's selection icon on the Objects: P. List palette (the circle next to the path name) is dashed, the path is displayed in the image window with a moving marquee. More than one path can be displayed as a selection at one time.

To activate a selection path:

1. Click the P. List icon on the Objects palette **1**.

2. Click the leftmost circle icon for the path you want to activate **2**.
or
Click the path name on the palette, then press Return.

To deactivate the path, click the dashed circle again or with the path name highlighted, press Return again.

The Edit menu > Deselect command (Command-D) activates the first Drawing and Visibility buttons. The selection path will be active, but it won't restrict painting.

Choose Edit menu > Reselect to reselect a path after choosing the Deselect command.

If path handles are visible (the Selection Adjuster tool is chosen) and you click the selection's circle icon, only the path's handles will remain visible.

To rename a selection path, double-click the path name, type in the Name field, then click OK.

A path displayed as a selection.

Rodney Alan Greenblat's **Springing** (detail)

To choose editing and display options for a selection path:

1. Make sure the path is displayed as a selection: On the Objects: P. List palette, the selection (circle) icon next to the path name should be dashed. Click on it, if necessary.

2. Click a Drawing (pencil) button on the extended Objects: P. List palette **2**.

3. Click a Visibility (eye) button **3**.

Tips

■ You can also choose Drawing and Visibility options from the bottom left corner of the image window at any time.

■ A warning prompt will appear if all of a document's paths are deselected and you attempt to work on the image while the third Drawing button is selected. Click on the first Drawing button to work on the image.

■ If you click on a path name on the Objects: P. List palette, the third Drawing and Visibility buttons will select automatically.

2 **DRAWING BUTTONS**

Painting/editing limited to outside the selected area.

Disables the selection. Painting/editing can occur anywhere on the picture.

Painting/editing limited to inside the selected area.

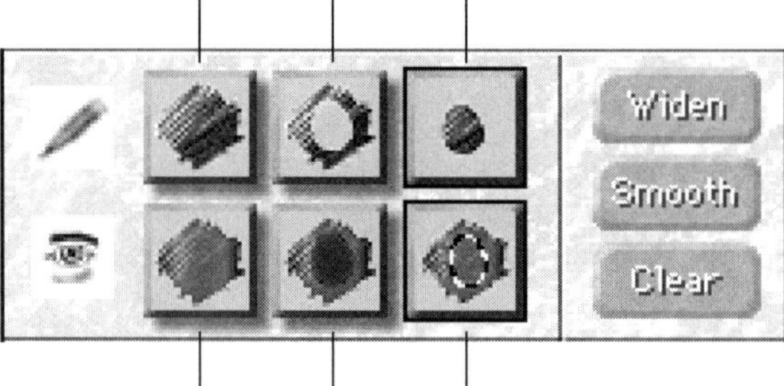

All the paths are hidden, but active paths remain active.

The active path displays as a selection marquee.

A mask covers the selected or unselected area, depending on which Drawing button is currently selected.

3 **VISIBILITY BUTTONS**

Selection Adjuster tool

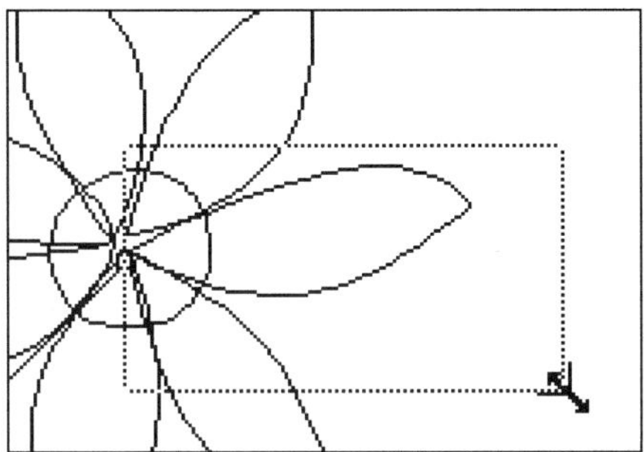

Hold down Shift and drag a corner handle to resize a selection proportionally.

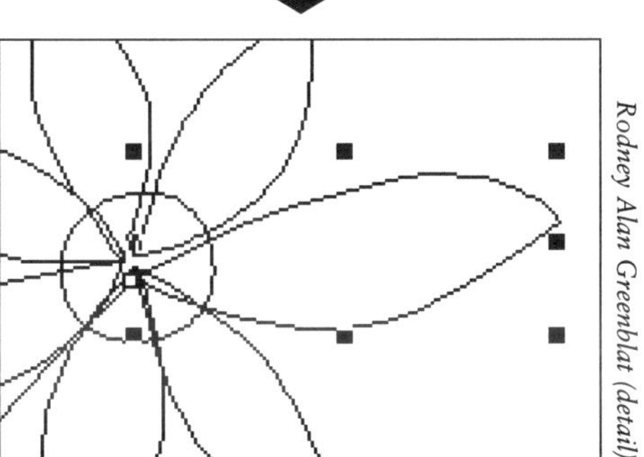

Rodney Alan Greenblat (detail)

The following operations will modify a selection path's outline, but not the path's contents.

To move, resize, rotate, slant, or copy a selection path:

1. Activate the selection on the P. List palette.

2. Choose the Selection Adjuster tool. (If the Selection Adjuster tool isn't visible on the Tools palette, press on the Floater Adjuster tool to access it.)

3. To **move** the whole path, press and drag inside it.
   or
   To **resize** the path, drag any of the path's handles. Hold down Shift while dragging to resize proportionally.
   or
   To **rotate** the path, hold down Command and drag a corner handle.
   or
   To **slant** a path, hold down Command and drag a midpoint handle.
   or
   To **copy** the path, hold down Option and drag inside it. (To copy and paste a selection to a different file, follow the instructions for copying and pasting a floater on page 96.)

To resize a selection path and its contents (and turn the path into a floater), use the Effects menu > Orientation > Scale command. The original selection will remain on the P. List palette and a new floater name will be listed on the F. List palette.

Move, Resize, Rotate, Slant, or Copy a Selection Path

By default, all selection paths are positive. Click the + button next to the path name on the P. List palette **1** to make a selection negative. Parts of selections that are below and overlap a negative selection are uneditable. A negative selection will have a red dashed marquee in the image window, and its name will appear in red on the P. List.

To create a new negative selection that cuts away from an existing selection path:

1. Activate a selection path (see page 81).

2. Choose the Lasso tool.

3. On the Controls: Lasso palette, click Subtract from Selection.

4. Draw a second selection that overlaps the existing selection.

5. On the P. List palette, move the negative selection name directly above the original selection name.

6. *Optional:* Group the original and negative selections.

 The Add To Selection button creates a new, separate selection.

 To add or subtract from a selection path that's part of a group, you must temporarily remove the path from the group. (Open the group list, and drag the path name out of the list. Drag it back over the group when you're finished.)

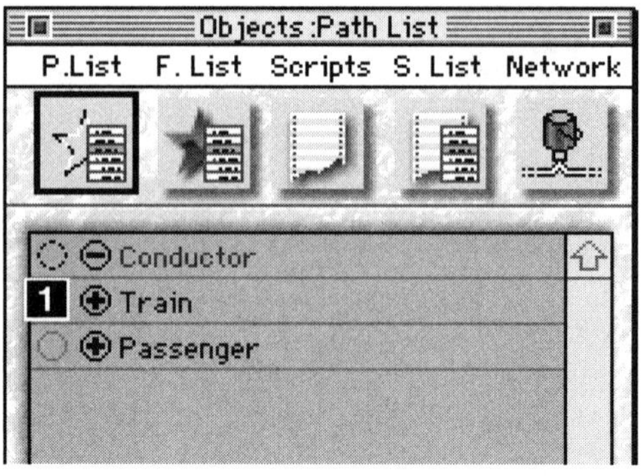

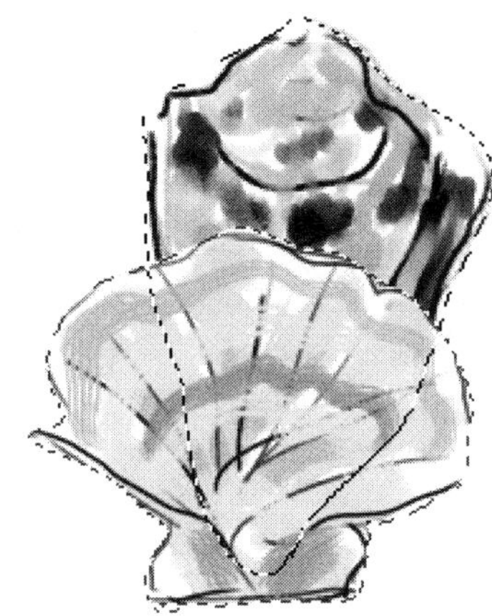

The clam shell has a negative path; the shell behind it has a positive path. With the third Drawing button selected, painting effects will be limited to the visible part of the taller shell.

To deselect a selection path:
Click the dashed circle icon next to the path name on the Objects: P. List palette.
or
Highlight the path name on the P. List, then press Return.

 See the second tip on page 81.

Create a Negative Selection Path; Deselect a Selection

*Selection
Adjuster* tool

To delete a selection path:
1. Choose the Path Adjuster tool.
2. Click on the path in the image window.
3. Press Delete.
   or
1. Click the path name on the Objects: P. List palette. (Hold down Shift and click to select multiple paths.)
2. Click Clear.

To delete the contents of a selection path:
1. Click the path name on the Objects: P. List palette.
2. Choose any tool except the Selection Adjuster tool or any Shape Design or Shape Selection tool.
3. Press Delete. The path will fill with the current paper color **3**.

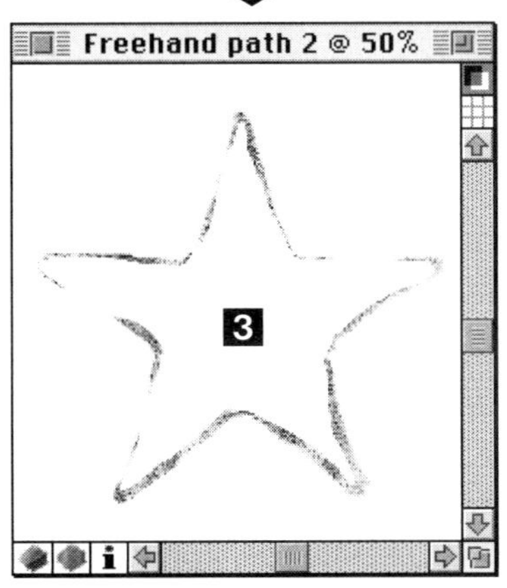

The path's contents are deleted.

Delete a Selection Path or its Contents

To feather a selection path:

1. Choose the Selection Adjuster tool.

2. Click the second Visibility (eye) button on the Controls palette or on the Objects: P. List palette so you'll be able to see the feather.

3. Move the Feather slider on the Controls palette to the right.

   The feather will be saved with the path when you save your document and if you save the path in a Paths library. The Controls: Adjuster palette Feather slider will automatically reset to zero when you reopen the image.

   Click Smooth on the P. List palette to smooth the corners of a selection. Click Smooth again to smooth more.

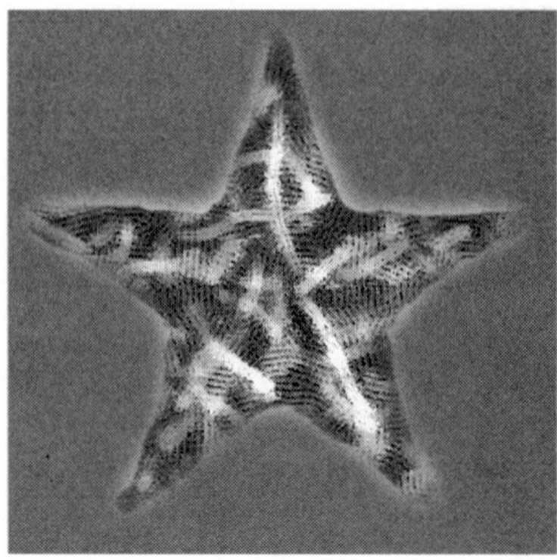

A feathered selection.

To widen or shrink a selection path:

1. On the Objects: P. List palette, click on the name of the path that you want to widen, then click Widen.

2. Enter the number of pixels by which the path will be widened **2**. Enter a negative number to shrink the path.

3. Click OK. The widened path will be listed on the P. List as a separate path from the original, but with the same name and number.

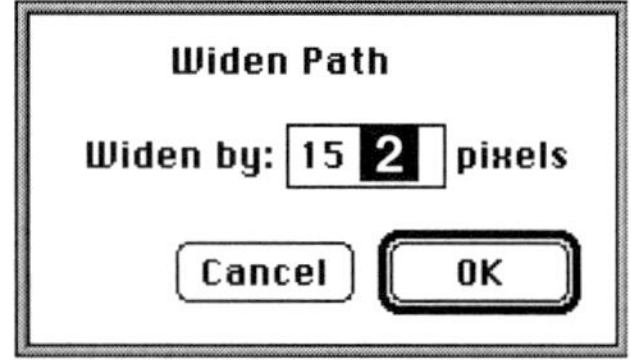

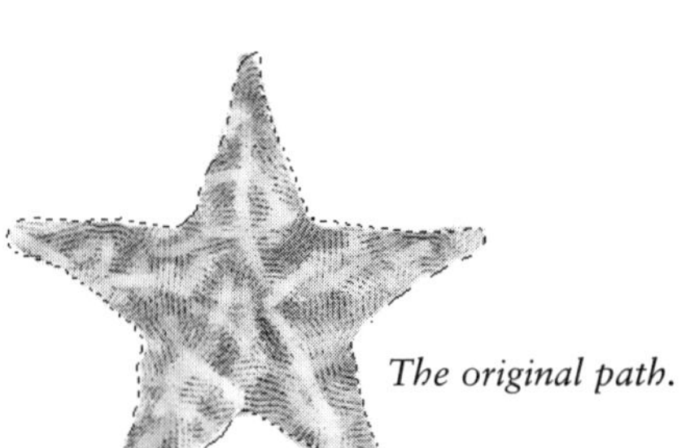

The original path.

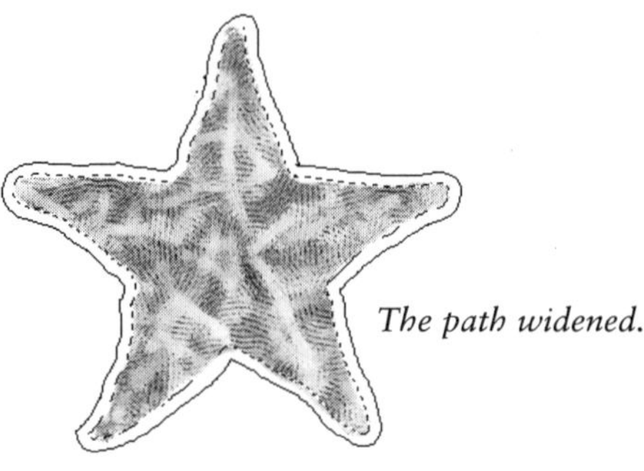

The path widened.

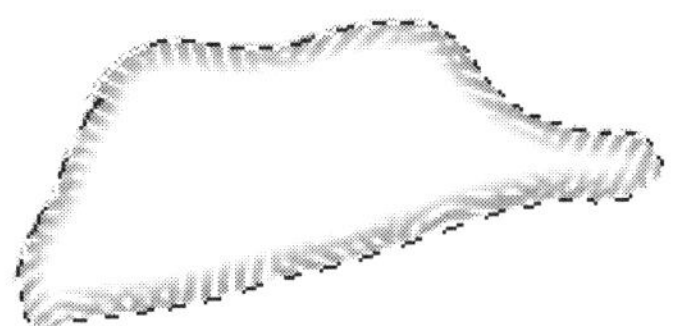

A selection stroked with a Chalk variant, grainy method subcategory.

To stroke a selection path:

1. Choose a brush, variant, Primary color, and paper texture for the stroke.

2. Click on the first, second, or third Drawing button on the P. List palette to stroke both sides, outside, or inside the selection, respectively.

3. Choose Objects palette > P. List menu > Stroke Selection.

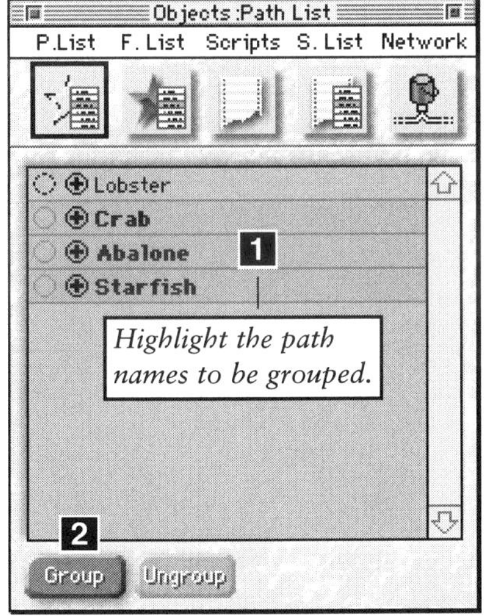

Highlight the path names to be grouped.

Grouped paths can be moved, resized, or selected/deselected as a unit.

To group selection paths:

1. Hold down Shift and, on the Objects: P. List palette, click the names of the paths you want to group **1**.
   or
   To select all the paths, click on a path name, choose the Selection Adjuster tool, then choose Edit menu > Select All (Command-A).

2. Click Group **2**. The word "Group" followed by the next sequential group number will appear on the path list.

   To close the group list, click the arrowhead next to the group name so the arrowhead points to the right. Click the arrowhead again to redisplay the individual path names in the group.

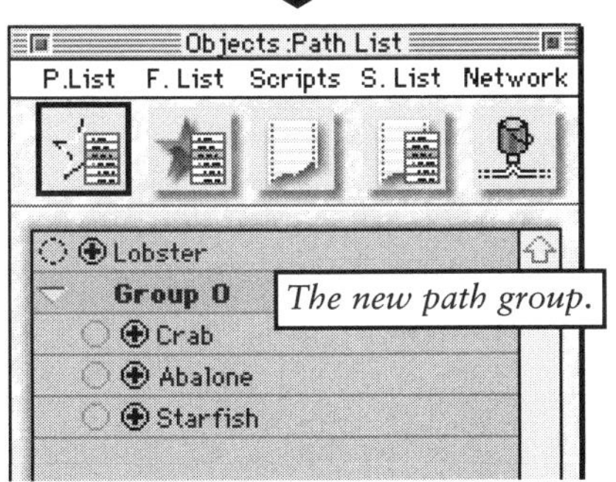

The new path group.

Stroke or Group Selection Paths

To move or resize a selection path group:

1. Make sure the group list on the Objects: P. List palette is closed (if it's not closed, click the arrowhead next to the group name).

2. Click the group name.

3. Press Return to activate all the paths in the group.

4. Choose the Selection Adjuster tool.

5. To **move** the whole group, drag inside any of the grouped paths.

   To **resize** the whole group, drag any path handle. Hold down Shift while dragging to preserve the paths' original proportions.

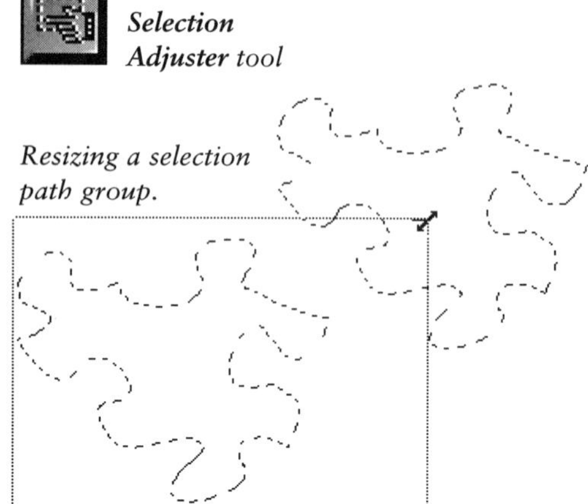

Selection Adjuster tool

Resizing a selection path group.

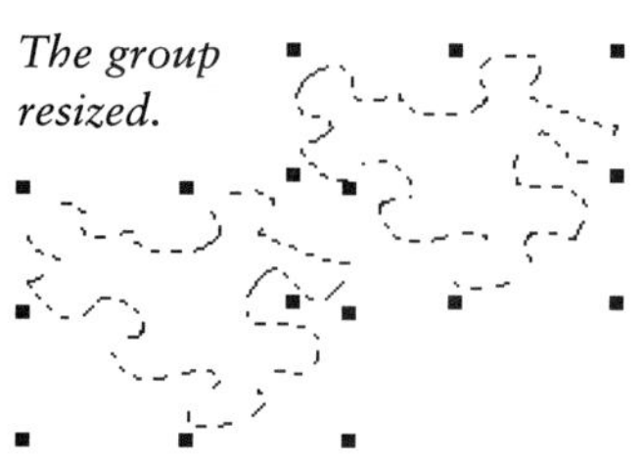

The group resized.

To add to or delete from a selection path group:

1. Make sure the group list is on the P. List palette is open (the arrowhead should point downward).

2. To **remove** a path from a group but keep the path, drag the path name upward or downward out of the group list.

   To **delete** a grouped path altogether, click on its name, then click Clear. (To delete a whole group, close the group list, then click Clear.)

   To **add** a path to a group, drag the path name into the group list.

To ungroup selection paths:

1. Click the group name on the Objects: P. List palette.

2. Click Ungroup. The group name will disappear and the names of the previously grouped paths will be highlighted.

Move, Resize, Add To, Delete From, Ungroup Path Group

*Selection
Adjuster* tool

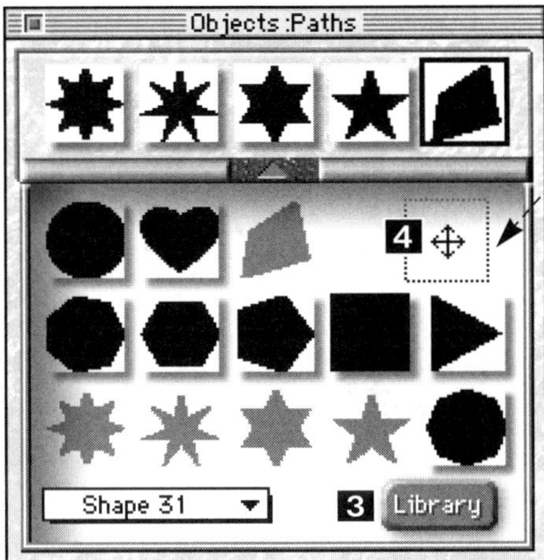

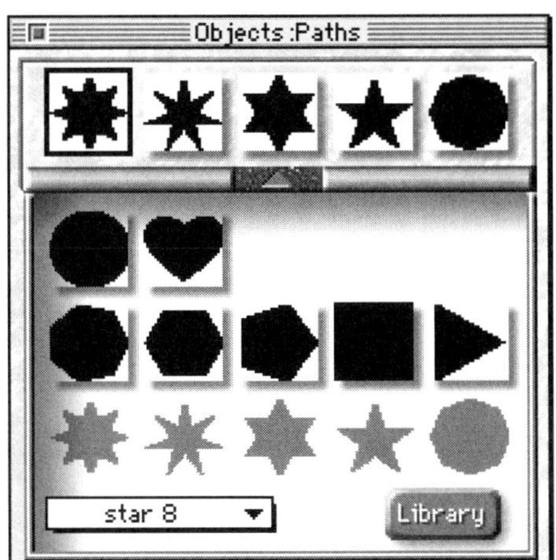

The preformed paths in the Painter Paths library.

To save a selection path in a paths library:

1. Choose the Selection Adjuster tool.

2. Choose Objects palette > P. List menu > Paths.

3. *Optional:* To place the path in other than the currently open library, click Library in the Paths palette drawer **3**, locate and highlight the library you want to open, then click Open.

4. Press and drag the path shape from the image window into the open Objects: Paths palette drawer or onto the drawer front **4**.

5. Enter a name in the Save Path dialog box.

6. Click OK or press Return. An icon for the saved path will appear on the Objects: Paths palette, and the name you entered will appear on the pop-up menu in the palette drawer.

To create a new paths library, see page 21. To edit a paths library, see page 22.

To retrieve a path from the Paths palette:

1. Choose Objects palette > P. List menu > Paths.

2. If the path you want to retrieve is not in the currently open Paths library, click Library, locate the library you want to open, then click Open.

3. Drag a path icon from the Paths palette drawer front or drawer onto the picture. The path will appear as a selection in the image window.

To retrieve a path to the same position in the same document from which you saved it to the Paths palette, drag the path's icon from the drawer onto the drawer front, then double-click it. This won't work if you changed the document's resolution or canvas size after the path was originally saved.

To import closed objects from Illustrator or FreeHand into Painter as shapes and convert them into selections:

1. For an Illustrator file, save it in the Illustrator 5.0/5.5 or 6 format in Illustrator. Make sure all the shapes you want to import are closed.

   For a FreeHand file, save it in the Illustrator 5 format in FreeHand.

2. Choose File menu > Acquire > Open Adobe Illustrator File.

3. Locate and double-click the EPS file you want to open.

4. Choose the Floater Adjuster tool.

5. Click on the shapes in the image window.

6. Choose Shapes menu > Convert To Selection.

Rodney Alan Greenblat's Bézier curve paths, created in FreeHand and imported using the File menu > Acquire > Open Adobe Illustrator File command.

After choosing Shapes menu > Convert To Selection.

To convert a path into a shape, see page 79. To export a path to Illustrator or FreeHand, first convert it into a shape, then follow the instructions on page 134.

Floaters 6

*David Humphrey, **Blond Again** (detail).*

Floaters

A floater is a shape that floats above the background pixels. Floaters add enormous flexibility to picture-making because you can repaint, restack, move, or feather a selected floater or change its opacity or composite method without affecting the background or any non-selected floaters, and vice versa. Floaters can be grouped, and each floater has its own mask.

Floaters will remain floating if you save your file in the RIFF or Photoshop 3.0 format. If you save your file in any other format, floaters will automatically be merged into the background. To drop (defloat) a floater, see page 105.

Painter supplies a few pre-made floaters, but you'll probably want to create your own and save them in a floaters library or libraries. Any selected area of a painting can be turned into a floater.

A reference floater is a special low resolution version of a standard floater. Because of its low resolution, a reference floater can be transformed (moved, resized, rotated, or skewed) more quickly than a standard floater. To produce a reference floater, you can convert a standard floater into a reference floater using the Free Transform command or you can place an image in Painter using the Place command—it will automatically appear as a reference floater.

Painter floaters ↔ Photoshop layers

Now you can make a round trip without losing layers or floaters. If you save a Painter 3.1 or 4 file with floaters in the Photoshop 3.0 file format and then open it in Photoshop, each floater will be assigned its own layer. If you open a Photoshop 3.0 file in Painter 3.1 or 4, each layer will become a floater.

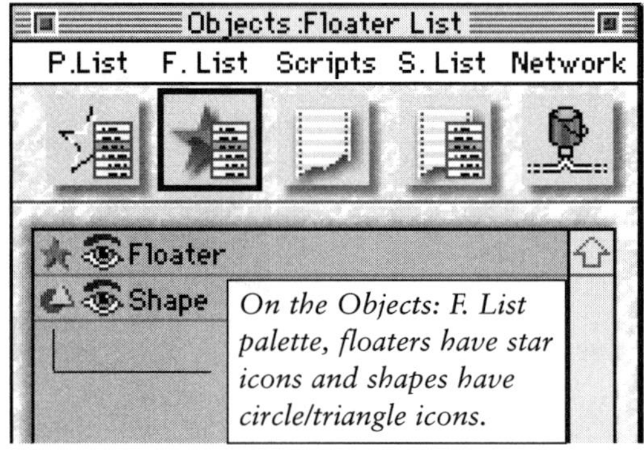

On the Objects: F. List palette, floaters have star icons and shapes have circle/triangle icons.

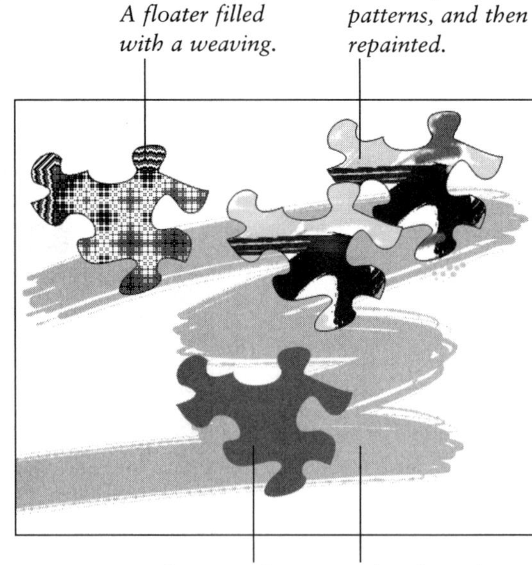

A floater filled with a weaving.

Floaters filled with patterns, and then repainted.

A floater with a solid fill.

A brush stroke painted behind the deselected floaters.

To create a floater from a shape

Highlight the shape name on the F. List, then choose Shapes menu > Convert To Floater. If you want to draw an irregular shape, use the Pen tool or the Quick Curve tool.

Rectangular Selection tool   *Floater Adjuster* tool

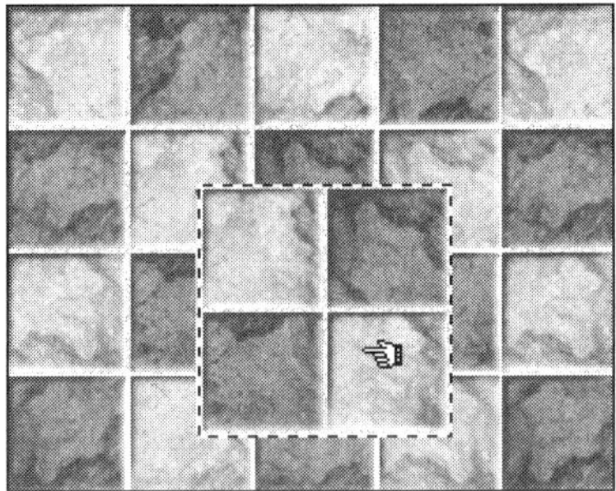

3a *If you click on a selection with the Floater Adjuster tool while holding down Option, you'll copy background pixels and you won't cut a hole in the background.*

To create a floater:

1. Create a selection using the Oval Selection, Rectangular Selection, or Lasso tool. Or create a mask, and then convert the mask into a selection by highlighting the mask name and pressing Return.

2. Choose the Rectangular Selection tool or the Floater Adjuster tool **2**.

3. Hold down Option and click inside the selection to copy it and leave the background intact **3**a.
   or
   Click inside the selection to cut the selection out of the background **3**b.

   ✎ To rename a floater, double-click its name on the F. List palette, enter a new name, then click OK.

A floater is created automatically if you:

■ **Apply the Effects menu > Orientation > Scale, Rotate, or Distort command to a selection.**

■ **Copy and paste a selection.**

■ **Open a Photoshop file containing multiple layers in Painter.**

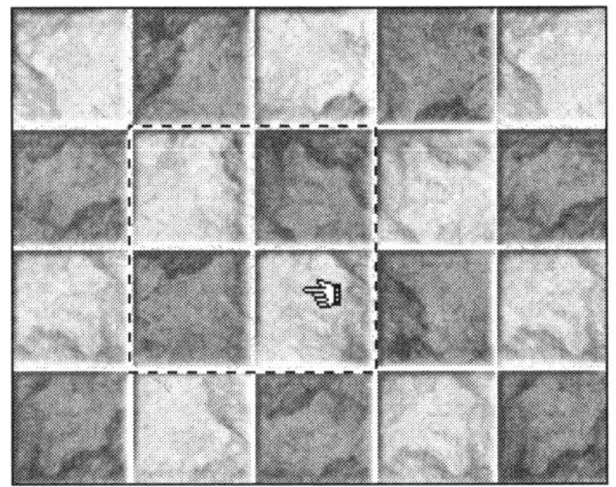

3b *If you click on a selection with the Floater Adjuster tool **without** holding down Option, you'll cut a hole in the background...*

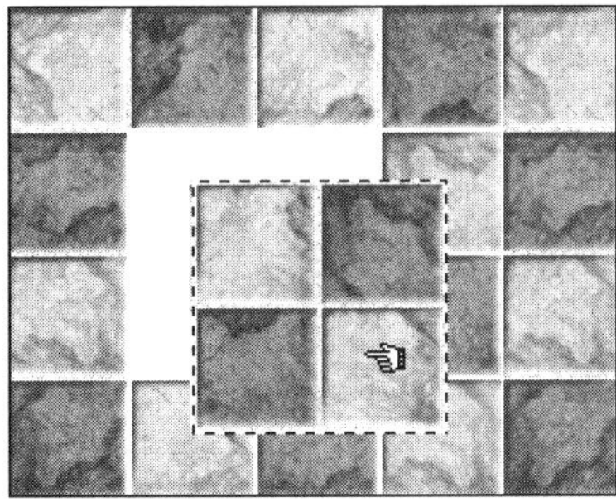

...and if you move the floater, you'll reveal the hole.

Every floater in an image window is also listed on the Objects: F. List palette. When a floater is selected, its name is highlighted and appears in bold type. **You can only modify a floater if it is selected, and only one floater or floater group can be selected at a time** (though you can highlight more than one floater name at a time and you can move multiple floaters simultaneously).

To select a floater or a floater group:

On the Objects: F. List palette, click the floater or floater group name **1**.
or
Choose the Floater Adjuster tool, then click on the floater in the image window (or Command-A to select all floaters).

To hide the floater marquee, uncheck the Show Selection Marquee box on the extended F. List palette (Command-Shift-H) **2**.

A deselected floater is uneditable, but it still floats.

To deselect a floater:

Click on the blank area below the floater names on the Objects: F. List palette.
or
Choose the Floater Adjuster tool or the Rectangular Selection tool, then click outside the floater in the image window.

To delete a floater or a floater group from an image:

1. On the Objects: F. List palette, click the name of the floater or floater group that you want to delete. If you're deleting a floater group, make sure the group list on the Objects: F. List palette is closed.
   or
   Choose the Floater Adjuster tool, then click on the floater or the floater group in the image window.

2. Press Delete.

Select, Deselect, Delete a Floater

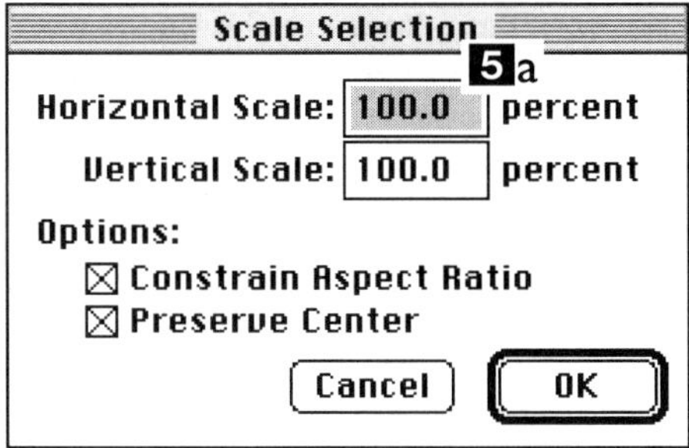

With the Scale Selection dialog box open, you can resize a selection by dragging any of its handles.

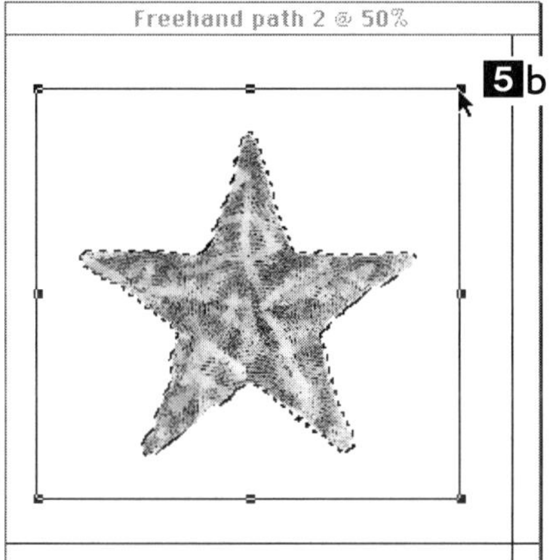

(You can also resize a selection using this command. It will turn your selection into a floater.) To resize a floater in a high resolution document more quickly, turn it into a reference floater (see page 107).

To resize a floater:

1. On the Objects: F. List palette, click on the name of the floater that you want to resize.

2. Choose Effects menu > Orientation > Scale.

3. *Optional:* Uncheck the Preserve Center box if you don't want to resize the floater from its center.

4. *Optional:* Uncheck the Constrain Aspect Ratio box if you don't want to preserve the floater's original proportions.

5. Enter the percentage amount you want to enlarge or shrink the floater in the Horizontal and/or Vertical Scale field **5**a.
   or
   Press and drag any of the floater's handles in the image window **5**b.

6. Click OK or press Return.

To copy a floater in the same file:

1. Choose the Floater Adjuster tool.

2. Hold down Option and drag the floater in the image window.

If the resolution of the original image is higher than the resolution of the destination image, the floater will increase in size when pasted, and vice versa.

If you copy a large image to the Clipboard, copy a small area when you're finished so the Clipboard contents don't occupy a large chunk of memory.

To copy a floater to a different file:

1. Choose the Floater Adjuster tool.

2. Click on the floater you want to copy.

3. Choose Edit menu > Copy (Command-C).

4. Click in the destination image window.

5. Choose Edit menu > Paste > Normal (Command-V).

 If you Copy and Paste a selection, it will become a floater.

 You could also add the floater to the Floaters palette, then retrieve it from the palette in any document (see page 99).

To align floaters or shapes:

1. Hold down Shift, and on the F. List palette, click on the names of the floaters you want to align.

2. Choose Effects menu > Objects > Align.

3. Click an alignment button: Horizontal (floaters will move horizontally to align) or Vertical (floaters will move vertically to align). Click None to disable either command.

4. Click OK or press Return.

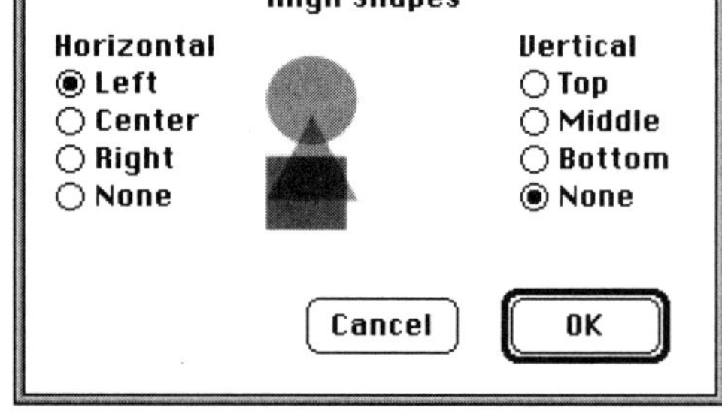

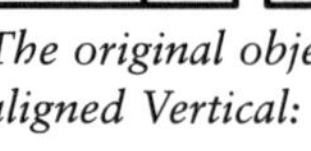

The original objects aligned Vertical: Top.

The original objects

The objects aligned Horizontal: Left.

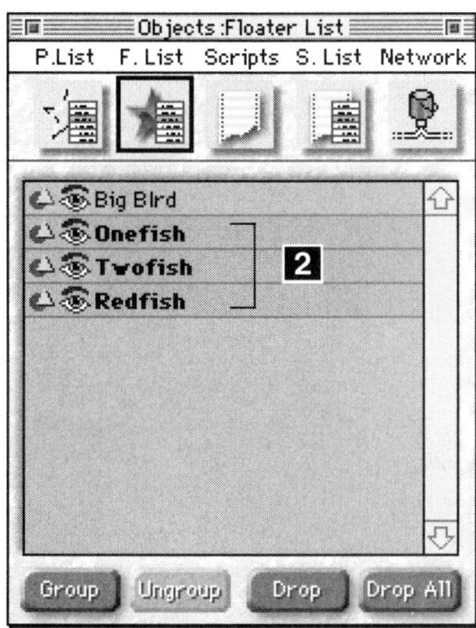

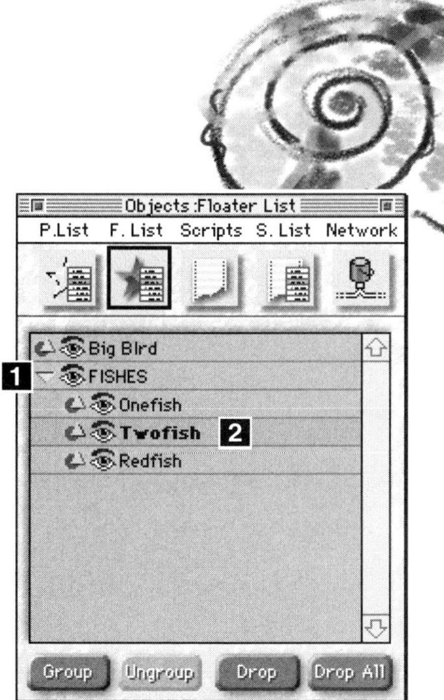

Grouped floaters can be moved easily as a unit, but they can only be edited individually, and each floater stays on its original layer. A floater group can be saved in a Floaters library.

To group floaters:

1. Open the Objects: F. List palette.
2. Hold down Shift and click on the names of the floaters you want to group **2**.
3. Click Group.
4. *Optional:* To rename the group, double-click the group name, enter a name, then click OK.

To add a floater to a group:

1. If the group list isn't open, click the arrowhead next to the group name (it should point downward).
2. Drag the name of the floater you want to add below the group name.

If you combine floaters into one, you can then paint brush strokes across them.

To combine all the floaters in a group into one floater:

1. Click on the floater group name on the Objects: F. List palette.
2. Click the Collapse button on the extended Objects: F. List palette.

To remove a floater from a group:

Drag the floater name upward or downward out of the open group list.

To select one floater in a group:

1. If the group list isn't open, click the arrowhead next to the group name (it should point downward) **1**.
2. Click on the name of the floater you want to modify **2**.

Shortcuts

To open/close the Objects palette: Command-4.

To open the F. List palette: Double-click the Floater Adjuster tool.

Floater Groups

To ungroup a floater group:

1. Make sure the group list is closed (the arrowhead should point to the right).

2. Click the floater group name on the Objects: P. List palette.

3. Click Ungroup.

To move a floater or a floater group manually:

1. Click on the floater name or floater group name on the Objects: F. List palette. For a floater group, close the group list (the arrowhead should point to the right) 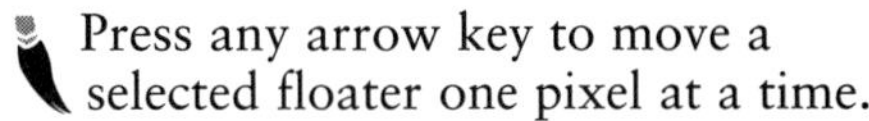.

2. Choose the Floater Adjuster tool or the Rectangular Selection tool.

3. Drag the floater in the image window.

   Note: If you dragged the floater from the Objects: Floaters palette, it won't make a hole in the background when you move it. But if you just created the floater by selecting an area of the background without holding down Option and you drag the floater for the first time, you'll create a hole in the background. If you want to refill the hole, choose Undo immediately, then re-create the floater using Option.

   Press any arrow key to move a selected floater one pixel at a time.

To move a floater or a floater group using a dialog box:

1. Double-click the floater name on the Objects: F. List palette.

2. Enter a higher number in the Position: Top field to move the floater downward or enter a lower number to move the floater upward .

   Enter a higher number in the Position: Left field to move the floater to the right or enter a lower number to move the floater to the left.

3. Click OK or press Return.

Rectangular Selection tool   *Floater Adjuster* tool

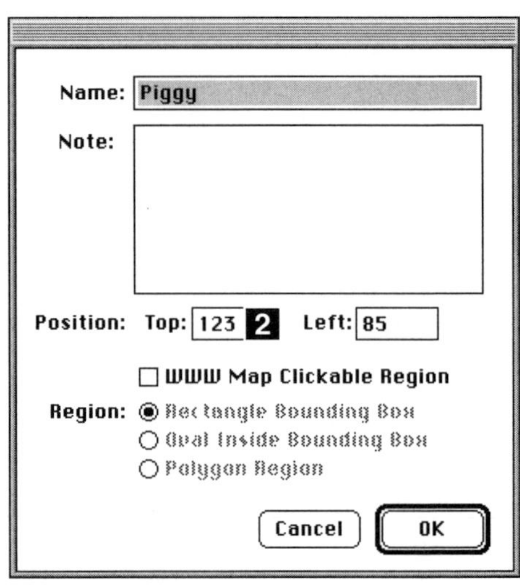

Floater Adjuster tool

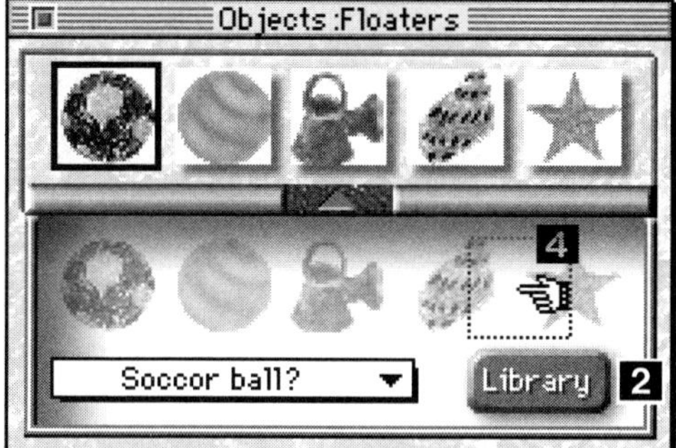

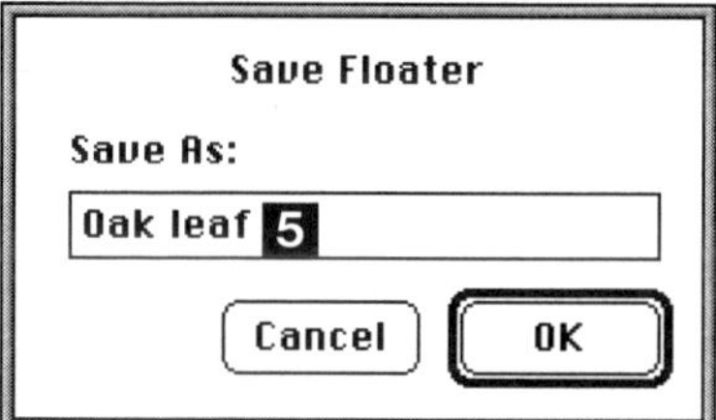

If you save a floater in a floaters library, its icon will appear on the Objects: Floaters palette and you'll be able to drag it into any open image window.

To save a floater or a floater group to the Floaters palette:

1. Choose Objects palette > F. List menu > Floaters.

2. *Optional:* To add a floater to a library that isn't currently open, click Library in the Floaters palette drawer **2**, locate and highlight the library you want to open, then click Open.

3. Choose the Floater Adjuster tool (F).

4. Drag a floater or a floater group onto the Floaters palette drawer or drawer front. The floater will be removed from your document **4**.
   or
   Hold down Option while dragging to save a copy of the floater.

5. Enter a name for the floater **5**.

6. Click OK. A thumbnail of the floater will appear on the Floaters palette.

To create or edit a floater library, see the instructions on pages 21–22.

When you retrieve a floater from the Objects: Floaters palette, it takes on the resolution of the file into which it's placed.

To retrieve a floater from the Floaters palette:

1. If the floater you want to retrieve is not in the currently open library, click Library in the Objects: Floaters palette drawer, then locate and double-click the name of the library that contains the floater you want to retrieve.

2. Drag the floater icon from the drawer front or drawer into the image window.

Ways to modify a floater:

You must select a floater before you can modify it. To select a floater, click on it in the image window with the Floater Adjuster tool (F) or click the floater name on the Objects: F. List palette.

- **Paint** using any technique except Wet Paint. Modifications will be restricted to the selected floater. To paint on the background behind the floater, first deselect the floater.

- Choose the Floater Adjuster tool (F), then change the floater's **Opacity, Feather** amount, or **Composite Method** using the Controls: Adjuster palette. (Or press keypad keys to choose 10% opacity increments: 1=10%, 2=20%, etc.)

  Note: You can only feather up what the "Floater pre-feather" amount setting was in the General Preferences dialog box at the time the floater was created. To feather beyond that amount, first click the Expand button to enlarge the floater area to accommodate a wider feathered edge. (To view the feather, place the floater over a colored background.)

- Click **Trim** on the Objects: F. List palette to shrink the floater area to the minimum area needed to contain the floater and its mask.

- Choose Effects menu > Orientation > **Scale** to resize the floater or Effects menu > Orientation > **Rotate** to rotate it. Both commands cause slight on-screen blurring.

- **Mask** part of a floater with White paint using a Masking brush variant or a non-Masking brush at 100% opacity with the Mask method category and the third Floater Visibility button selected (top row). Floater masks are discussed in depth on pages 156–158.

To produce the image below, first this entire picture was selected and turned into a floater (Option-click method to make a copy)…

…then Painter's "tri-weave" texture was applied to the floater using the Express Texture command. Finally, the Hard Light Composite Method was chosen on the Controls: Adjuster palette and the Opacity slider was lowered to reveal some of the underlying pixels.

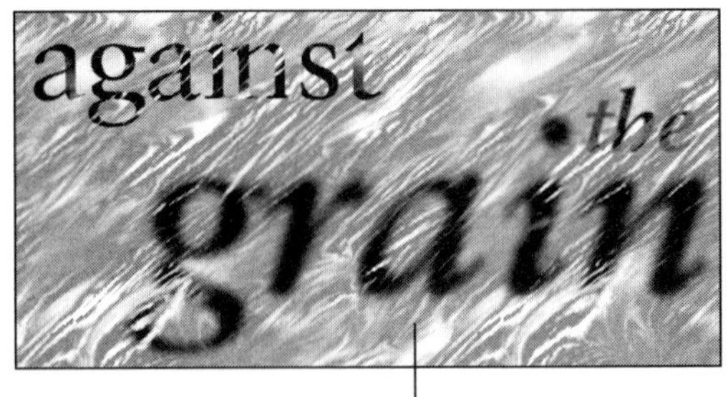

Text shapes turned into floaters and feathered using the Controls: Adjuster palette.

We placed text over Ray Rue's Yellow Quartz texture, turned it into a floater, filled it with the background texture using Color Overlay, enlarged it, and then applied the Create Drop Shadow command.

To produce the 3E effect shown on the right, first a text shape was turned into a floater, and the Create Drop Shadow command was applied to it (left). Then Effects > Surface Control > Apply Surface Texture was applied using these settings (Using: Mask, Softness slider at 16 to produce a soft, 3D effect, and the Reflection slider at 10%).

And of course you can easily hand paint your own shadows behind a floater if you don't like the uniformity of Painter's drop shadows. Try using the Airbrush.

A drop shadow can be part of the original floater or it can be a separate floater on its own. You can't preview the Drop Shadow effect.

To add a drop shadow to a floater:

1. Click on the floater or floater group name on the Objects: F. List palette.

2. Choose Effects menu > Objects > Create Drop Shadow.

3. Do any of the following:

   Enter higher **Offset** values to create a greater illusion of depth. You can enter negative Offset numbers.

   Enter an **Opacity** value for the darkest part of the shadow.

   Enter a **Radius** value for the amount of blurring. The radius is half the width of the shadow.

   Enter an **Angle** for the direction of the shadow. 0° is horizontal, 90° is vertical.

   Enter a **Thinness** percentage for the amount the shadow is blurred perpendicular to the Angle.

4. Check the **Collapse to one layer** box if you want the shadow to become part of the floater.

   Uncheck the **Collapse to one layer** box if you want the shadow to be separate from the floater. If you choose this option you'll be able to adjust the shadow's opacity, color, or position, or delete the shadow altogether. The floater and its shadow will become a floater group, which will be listed on the Objects: F. List palette as "[floater name] and Shadow."

5. Click OK or press Return.

6. *Optional:* If you unchecked the "Collapse to one layer box" when you created the drop shadow, you can adjust the shadow's opacity. Choose the Floater Adjuster tool (F), click the shadow name on the Objects: F. List palette, then move the Opacity slider on the Controls: Adjuster palette.

Add a Drop Shadow to a Floater

The intensity of the Composite Method effect will be affected by the current Controls: Adjuster palette Opacity slider setting. The Composite Methods don't truly alter underlying pixels until the floater is dropped.

To combine a floater with underlying pixels:

1. Choose the Floater Adjuster tool (F).

2. Select the floater (click on the floater in the image window or click on the floater name on the Objects: F. List palette).

3. Choose from the **Composite Method** pop-up menu on the Controls: Adjuster palette.

   Gel: Underlying pixels are tinted with the floater's color.

   Colorize: The underlying pixels' hue and saturation are replaced by the floater's hue and saturation. Underlying luminosity values are preserved.

   Reverse-Out: Underlying pixels turn into their opposite value and complementary hue.

   Shadow Map: Makes the highlight areas of the floater transparent so the background shows through. Darker areas of the floater remain, creating a shadow effect.

   Magic Combine: Floater pixels are replaced by underlying pixels, except for floater pixels that are lighter than underlying pixels.

   Pseudocolor: Translates floater and underlying luminosity values into hues on the color spectrum (darks at the Red end, lights at the Cyan end).

Floater Composite Methods

Floater Adjuster tool

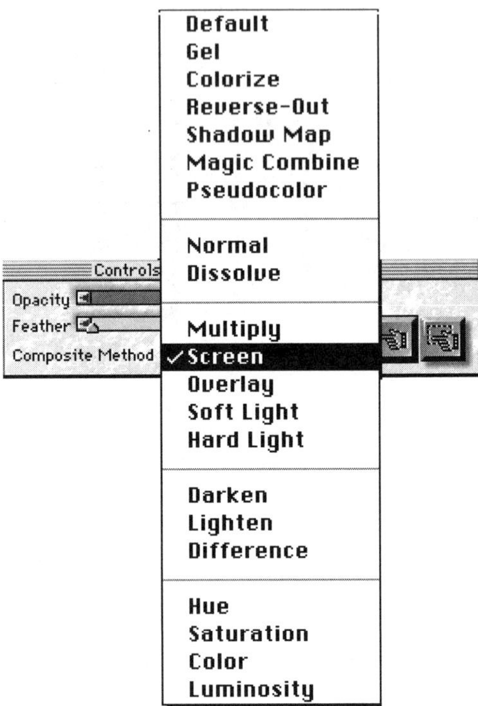

How to fill text with the canvas image

Create text shapes. Choose a bold typeface in a large point size so you'll have a wide area to fill with imagery. Deselect the text by clicking in the blank area on the Objects: F. List palette. Then choose Edit menu > Select All, click on the picture with the Floater Adjuster tool to turn the canvas into a floater, and finally, with the floater still active, choose the Magic Combine Composite Method from the Controls: Adjuster palette.

**_Photoshop modes on Painter's Controls:
Adjuster palette Composite Method
pop-up menu:_**

NORMAL:

Like Painter's Default Composite
Method.

DISSOLVE:

Combines the floater and underlying
pixels to create a stippled texture. The
higher the opacity, the more solid the
color.

MULTIPLY:

Floater pixels and underlying pixels
combine to produce a darker color.
Similar to Painter's Shadow Map.

SCREEN:

Bleaches the inverse of the floater color
and the underlying color.

OVERLAY:

Multiplies (darkens) dark pixels and
screens (lightens) light pixels. Preserves
luminosity (light and dark) values.

SOFT LIGHT:

Floater pixels that are lighter than
underlying pixels are lightened. Floater
pixels that are darker than underlying
pixels are darkened. Subtle light effect.

HARD LIGHT:

Floater pixels that are lighter than the
underlying pixels are lightened. Floater
pixels that are darker than the underlying pixels are darkened. Harsh light
effect.

DARKEN:

Underlying pixels that are lighter than
the floater pixels are modified; underlying pixels that are darker than
floater pixels are not.

LIGHTEN:

Underlying pixels that are darker than
the paint color arc modified; underlying
pixels that are lighter than floater pixels are not.

DIFFERENCE:

Subtracts the underlying pixel color
from the floater color, or vice versa,
depending on which is brighter.

HUE:

Underlying pixel's hue is replaced with
floater's hue. Saturation and luminosity
values aren't modified. Similar to
Painter's Colorize mode.

SATURATION:

Underlying pixels' saturation is
replaced with floater's saturation.
Underlying hue and luminosity values
aren't modified.

COLOR:

Underlying pixels' hue and saturation
are replaced with floater's hue and saturation. Underlying luminosity values
aren't modified.

LUMINOSITY:

Underlying pixels' luminosity values are
replaced with floater's luminosity values. Underlying hue and saturation values aren't modified.

Floaters are listed on the Objects: F. List palette in front-to-back order. Follow these instructions to change the stacking position of any floater.

To move a floater frontward or backward:

Drag the name of the floater you want to restack up or down on the Objects: F. List palette **1**.

or

Click on the name of the floater you want to move on the Objects: F. List palette and choose the Floater Adjuster tool. Then, on the Controls: Adjuster palette, click **Front** to make the floater the frontmost floater, or click **Back** to make it the backmost floater, or click the right arrow to move the floater forward one layer at a time, or click the left arrow to send the floater backward one layer at a time **2**.

The clam shell moved to the back.

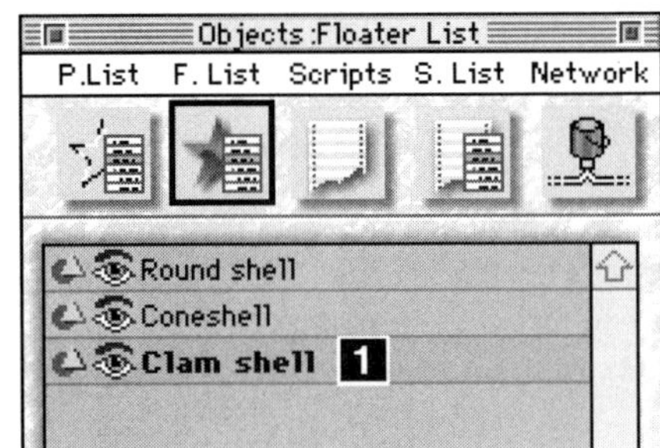

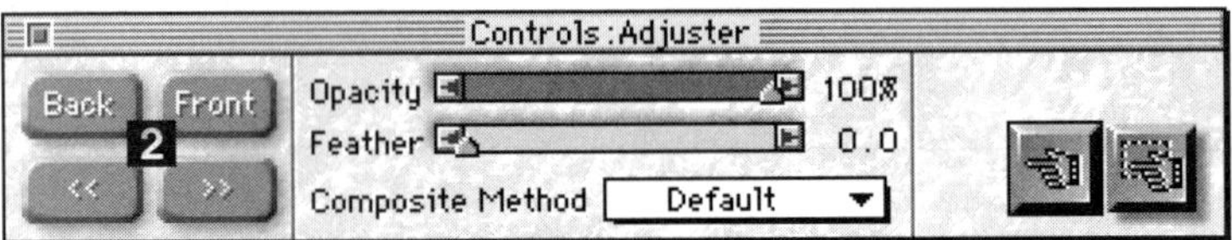

To hide a floater's marquee:

On the Objects: F. List palette, click on the name of the floater that you want to hide **1**.
and
Uncheck the Show Selection Marquee box (Command-Shift-H) **2**. (Check the Show Selection Marquee box to redisplay the marquee).

To hide a floater altogether:

On the F. List palette, click the eye icon next to the name of the floater you want to hide.

Click the shut eye icon to redisplay the floater. If the floater doesn't reappear, make sure it's not being masked by an overlapping, active selection.

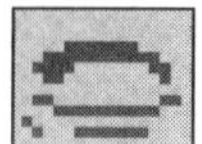

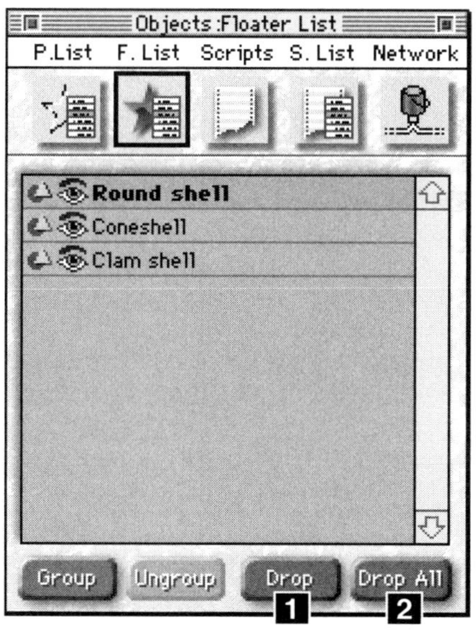

Save your document in the RIFF or Photoshop 3.0 file format to save it with floaters. Before dropping your floaters, you might want to save a copy of the original document with its floaters under another name using the Save As command and then drop the floaters into the background in the new, open document.

To drop a floater(s) into the background:

To drop one floater or one floater group, click its name on the Objects: F. List palette, then click Drop **1** or choose Edit menu > Drop (Command-Shift-D).
or
Click Drop All **2** to drop all the documents' floaters at once.

Hide or Drop a Floater

You'll need to follow these instructions to save a floater's outline as a path if the floater originated from the Floaters palette. If you drop a floater that was created in the current document, its outline will be saved as a path automatically, whether the Drop With Mask box is checked or unchecked.

To drop a floater and save its outline as a selection path:

1. On the Objects: F. List palette, click the name of the floater that you want to drop **1**.

2. Check the Drop With Mask box **2**.

3. Click the third Floater Mask Visibility button **3**. What you see in the image window is what will drop.

4. Click Drop **4**.

5. On the Objects: P. List palette, click the third Visibility (eye) button. The mask group name will appear on the list.

6. To ensure mask groups from subsequently dropped floaters don't become part of the same mask group, convert the active Mask Group into a selection by pressing Return (the name will become blue).

If you choose Undo after dropping a floater, the floater will be restored and the selection will still be listed on the P. List palette.

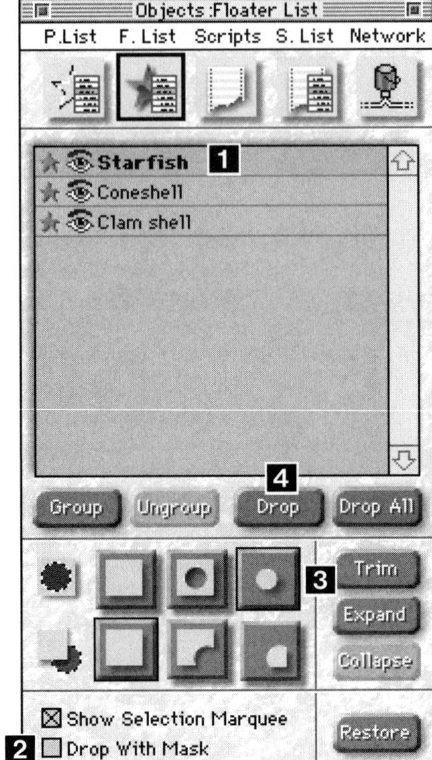

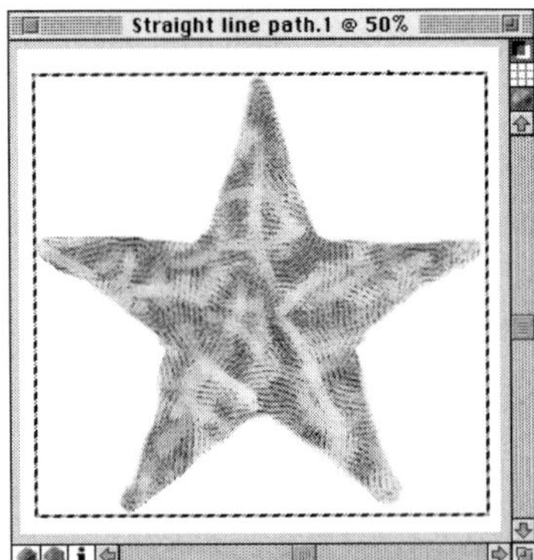

Activate the floater you want to drop.

The floater mask converted into a selection path.

Drop a Floater and Save its Outline

Reference floaters

A reference floater is a low resolution version of a standard floater. Because of its low resolution, a reference floater can be transformed (moved, resized, rotated, or skewed) more quickly than a standard floater.

To produce a reference floater, you can convert a standard floater into a reference floater using the Free Transform command or you can place an image into Painter—it will automatically appear as a reference floater. And don't worry— you can convert a standard floater into a reference floater and back again at any time without actually changing the floater's resolution. In fact, if you paint on or apply an Effects menu command to a reference floater, it will automatically convert to a standard floater.

To convert a standard floater into a reference floater:

1. Select a floater.

2. Choose Effects menu > Orientation > Free Transform. The leftmost icon for the floater name on the P. List palette will change from a star into a rectangular marquee **2**.

To place an image as a reference floater:

1. Choose File menu > Place.

2. Highlight the file you want to place.

3. Click Open.

4. Move the cursor in the image window just to see the scale of the placed image rectangle, but **don't click the mouse button yet.**

5. *Optional:* Enter new Horizontal or Vertical Scaling percentages. Check the Constrain Aspect Ratio box if you want to preserve the image's original proportions.

(Continued on the following page)

6. *Optional*: Check the Retain Mask box to place a mask, if the original image contains one, as the reference floater's mask.

7. *Optional*: If you're planning to use the image in a script, check the Create Pyramid box. A Pyramid file contains several versions of an image in different resolutions so the image can appear at the appropriate resolution for the file in which it's opened.

8. Click in the image window where you want the image to appear.
or
Click OK or press Return to place the image in the center of the image window.

Make sure you keep the original file in its original location for Painter to reference.

To transform a reference floater manually:

1. On the Objects: F. List palette, click the name of the floater you want to transform.
or
Choose the Floater Adjuster tool, then click on the floater in the image window.

2. Make sure the Show Selection Marquee box is checked on the extended Objects: F. List palette.

3. Perform any of the following transformations:

To **resize** the floater, drag any of its handles. Hold down Shift before and while dragging a corner handle to perserve the floater's proportions.

To **rotate** the floater, hold down Command and drag a corner handle in a circular direction.

To **skew** the floater, hold down Command and drag a side handle.

Rotating a reference floater.

Transform a Reference Floater

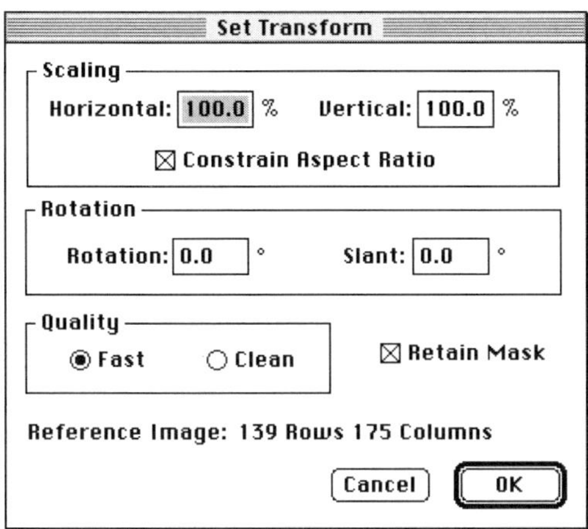

Use the Set Transform dialog box to convert a standard floater into a reference floater and transform it by entering precise scaling, rotation, or slant values.

To transform a floater via a dialog box:

1. On the Objects: F. List palette, click the name of the floater you want to set transform.
   or
   Choose the Floater Adjuster tool, then click on the floater in the image window.

2. Choose Effects menu > Orientation > Set Transform.

3. Do any of the following:

   Enter new Horizontal or Vertical Scaling percentages. Check the Constrain Aspect Ratio box to preserve the floaters's original proportions.

   Enter new Rotation or Slant angles.

   Check the Retain Mask box to preserve the floater's mask.

4. Click Quality: Fast to transform the floater quickly at a low resolution.
   or
   Click Quality: Clean to transform the floater at a higher resolution. This option produces a better quality image, but it takes longer to process.

5. Click OK or press Return.

To convert a reference floater into a standard floater:

1. On the Objects: P. List palette, click the name of the floater you want to convert.
   or
   Choose the Floater Adjuster tool, then click the floater in the image window.

2. Choose Effects menu > Orientation > Commit Transform. The floater may look sharper after Painter finishes processing the conversion, and the leftmost icon for the floater name on the F. List palette will change from a a rectangular marquee into a star.

A reference floater will be converted into a standard floater automatically if you paint on it or apply any Effects menu command to it.

The Image Hose

The Image Hose is a brush that sprays imagery. The imagery that you fill the Hose with is called the nozzle. A nozzle can be built from floaters or movie frames. To paint with the Image Hose, see the instructions on the next page.

To create an Image Hose nozzle from floaters:

1. Create a new document.

2. Move the floaters you want to put in the nozzle into the image window : Drag them from the Objects: Floaters palette or copy and paste them from another document. (To create a non-rectangular floater and eliminate the background imagery around it, select it using the Lasso tool, close the selection, then click on it with the Floater Adjuster tool).

3. Click the F. List icon on the Objects palette.

4. For any floater group, click the group name, then click Ungroup or click Collapse.

5. If you want to spray images in a sequence (like from small to large, or vice versa, or in a color, rotation, or shape progression), organize the floater names on the F. List from top to bottom in that order. (Choose a Sequential variant when you're ready to use the Image Hose.) The top floater on the list becomes the first element in the nozzle sequence, etc.

6. Hold down Shift and click on the names of the floaters you want to load into a nozzle.

7. Click Group, and leave it highlighted.

8. Click Trim to reduce excess space around the floaters.

9. With the group name still highlighted, choose Brushes palette > Nozzle menu > Make Nozzle From Group.

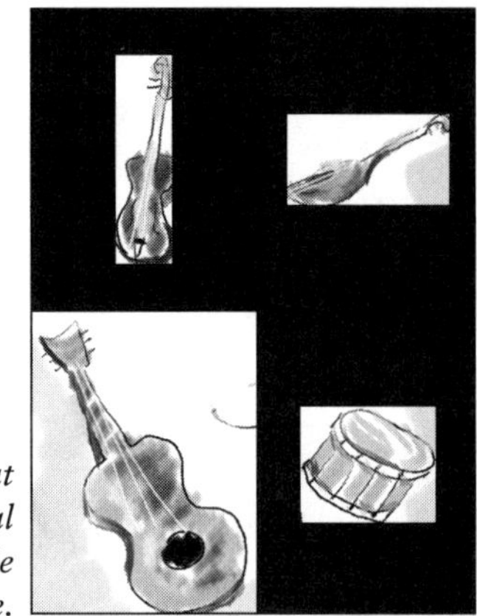

This is what an actual nozzle file looks like.

To make a nozzle from a movie

Open the movie file, choose Brushes palette > Nozzle menu > Make Nozzle from Movie, choose File menu > Save, choose RIFF from the Type pop-up menu, open a folder in which to store the nozzle, then click Save.

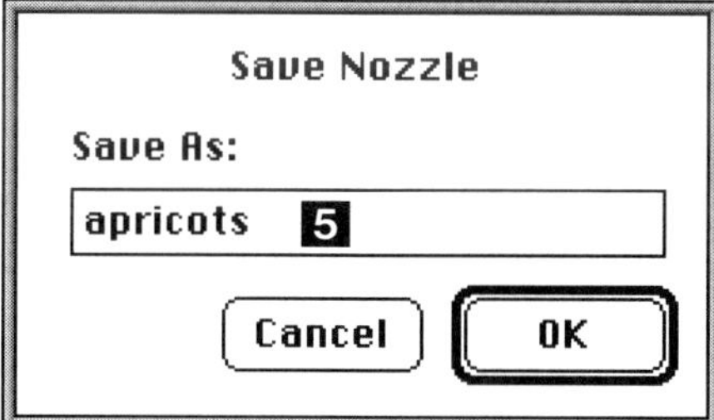

To modify a nozzle

Choose Brushes > Nozzle menu > Check Out Nozzle, and locate and double-click the nozzle you want to modify. After modifying the nozzle, choose File menu > Save As, choose a location in which to save the nozzle (preferably where all your other nozzles are stored), then follow the instructions at right (choose the name of the modified nozzle for step 3).

10. Choose File menu > Save.
11. Enter a name for the nozzle.
12. Leave the Type as RIFF, open a nozzle folder, then click Save.
13. Close both image windows.
14. Follow the instructions below to load the nozzle and add it to a library.

You can load a nozzle file that is not in a library via the Brushes palette > Nozzle menu > Load Nozzle command, but if you then click on another nozzle on the Nozzle palette or load a different nozzle, the original nozzle will no longer be loaded—you'll have to reload it if you want to use it again. Follow the instructions below to load a nozzle and add it to a library so it will stay on the Nozzle palette as long as its library is open.

To load a nozzle that's not in a library and add it to the current library:

1. Make sure the library to which you want to add the nozzle is open. To open a different library, choose Brushes > Nozzle menu > Nozzles, click Library in the Nozzle palette drawer, locate and highlight the library you want to open, then click Open.

2. Choose Brushes palette > Nozzle menu > Load Nozzle (Command-L).

3. Locate and highlight the name of the nozzle file you want to use, then click Open (or just double-click the nozzle file name).

4. Choose Brushes palette > Nozzle menu > Add Nozzle To Library to add the current nozzle to the currently open nozzle library.

5. Enter a name for the new nozzle library entry in the Save As field **5**.

6. Click OK or press Return.

To paint using the Image Hose:

1. Choose Brush palette > Nozzle menu > Nozzles.

2. Click a nozzle icon on the palette drawer front or drawer **2**. If the nozzle you want to use isn't in a library, you'll need to use the Load Nozzle command (see the previous page).

3. Choose the Image Hose brush from the Brushes palette **3**.

4. Choose a variant. **Small**, **Medium**, and **Large** refer to the space between elements, not the size of the elements.

   3 Rank R-P-D stands for Randomness, Pressure, and Directionality (2 Rank uses two of these characteristics). If you choose these variants, you can use the Brush Controls: Nozzle palette to adjust the R, P, or D settings for the current nozzle. With light stylus pressure, for example, imagery will be sprayed from the upper left position in the nozzle file.

   Random Linear: Elements are sprayed in random order where you drag.

   Random Spray: Elements are randomly placed in random order. To make the placement more random, move the Dab Location: Placement slider on the Advanced Controls: Random palette to the right.

   Sequential Linear: Elements are sprayed sequentially (1-2-3, 1-2-3) in a uniform pattern based on the top-to-bottom order of elements on the Objects: F. List palette when the nozzle was created (the top left to bottom right order in the nozzle file).

   Directional: The direction in which the mouse or stylus is moved determines which elements are sprayed.

5. Click or drag on your picture.

6. *Optional:* To resize the current nozzle elements, close the Nozzle palette drawer, then move the Scale slider.

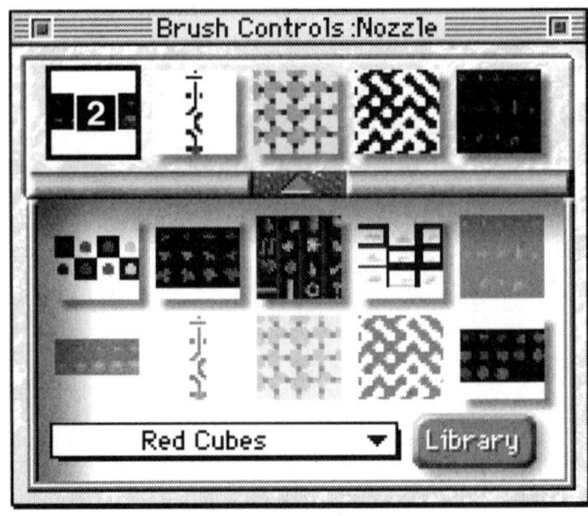

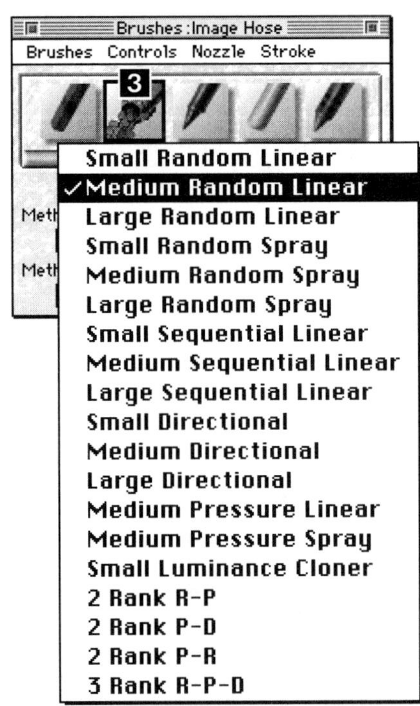

What is the Image Hose resolution?
Nozzle elements are stored at 72 ppi, but they will take on the resolution of the document they are sprayed into. The nozzle elements will change size if their resolution doesn't match the resolution of the file they are sprayed into. For example, if the nozzle resolution is lower than the document resolution, the nozzle elements will appear smaller when they're placed in the document.

Our favorite Image Hose effect: the Opacity slider on the Controls: Sliders palette pushed up to Random.

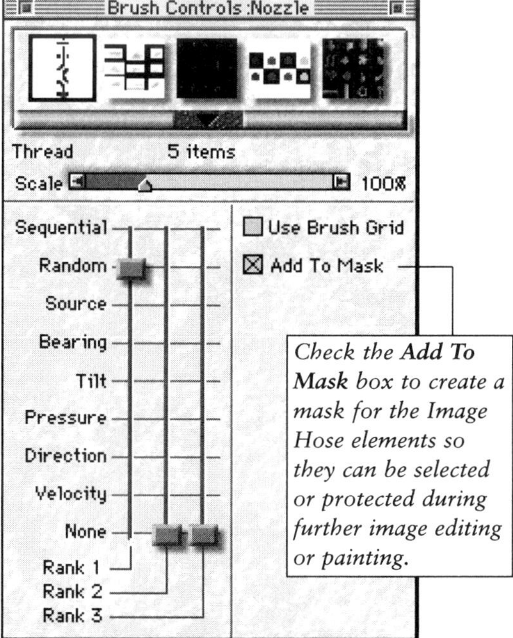

*Check the **Add To Mask** box to create a mask for the Image Hose elements so they can be selected or protected during further image editing or painting.*

To fine-tune the Image Hose:

Do any of the following:

■ Adjust the **spacing** between elements using the Brush Controls: Spacing palette Spacing/Size or Min Spacing slider. Use the Brush Controls: Size palette Size slider to increase spacing if the Spacing palette sliders are at their maximum settings. To change the **size** of the Image Hose elements themselves, use the Scale slider on the Brush Controls: Nozzle palette.

■ Adjust the **opacity** using the Controls: Brush palette.

■ Move the Grain slider to the left on the Controls: Brush palette to **tint the Image Hose elements with the current Secondary color.**

■ To make a **Random Spray** variant spray more unpredictably, move the Dab Location slider on the Brush Controls: Random palette to the right.

■ Adjust settings on the expanded Brush Controls: **Nozzle** palette (close the drawer). The default nozzle settings conform to the Image Hose variants. For example, for a Sequential variant, the Sequential option will be selected. Adjust these sliders to produce non-default variants. The Bearing, Tilt, and Pressure sliders don't work with a mouse. Adjust the Rank 1, Rank 2, Rank 3 sliders for the 3 Rank R-P-D or 2 Rank variant. Check the Use Brush Grid box to spray elements at grid intervals (sometimes on top of each other). Remember, images in a nozzle file are stored in a specific index order, so adjusting Nozzle palette sliders or choosing a different Image Hose variant will control which mouse or stylus action will affect how images are sprayed from that existing index order. You can also adjust the Advanced Controls: Sliders palette settings.

Artistic ideas often arise from unexpected sources. "I discovered this technique quite by accident," says Ray Rue, "when I took a carrots nozzle I had designed for a vitamin screen and put the setting on Small Directional. The result immediately suggested scales to me, and the dragon illustration soon followed."

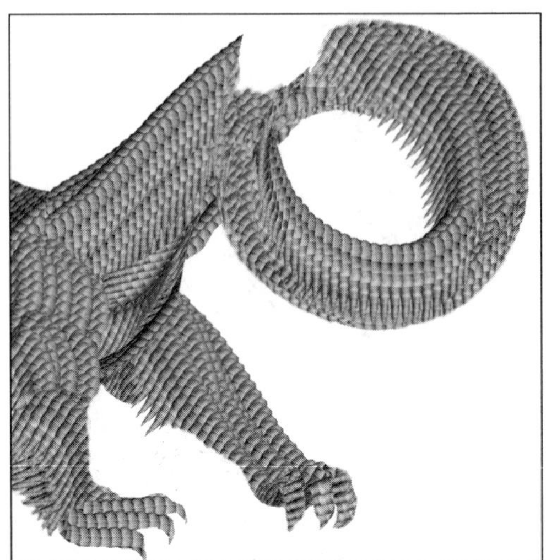

Starting to paint the dragon with the Image Hose.

The final image by Ray Rue.

Have you done something spectacular with the Image Hose? We'd like to see it! Our mailing address is listed at the bottom of page 257.

Shapes 7

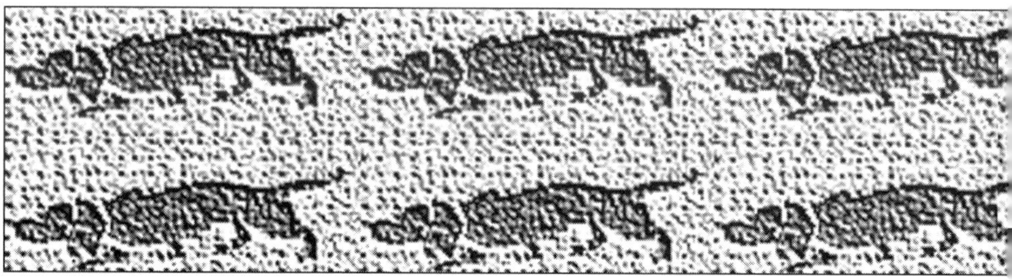

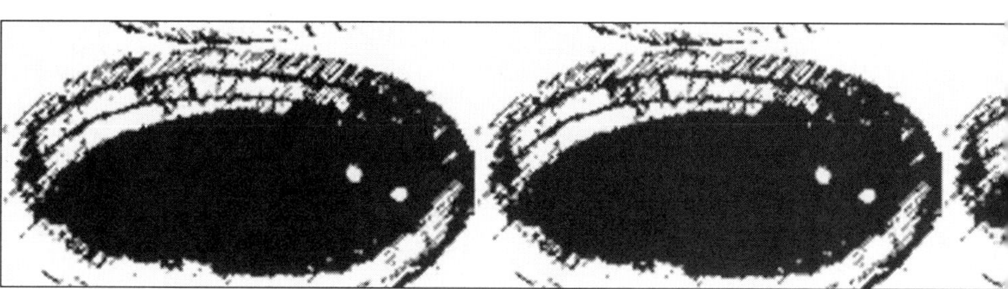

Diane Margolin.

Shapes; Shape Tools

Shapes

If you're familiar with Adobe Illustrator or Macromedia FreeHand, you already know something about shapes, which are vector-based objects in Painter. Shapes can add a whole new dimension to your work in Painter, because they'll give you the power to create precise geometric objects on their own separate layer that can be moved and modified without affecting the underlying, pixel-based canvas.

A shape is an open or closed object consisting of anchor points connected by straight and/or curved line segments. The Rectangular Shape and Oval Shape tools create closed shapes. The Pen and Quick Curve tools create open or closed shapes. You can keep your shapes as shape objects or you can turn them into selection paths or floaters.

A shape can be filled, and its edge stroked, with the current Primary color. And you can choose an opacity level for the fill and stroke on a Painter shape—unlike objects in an illustration program. You can't paint on a shape, though, or apply the Fill command or any Effects menu > Tonal Control or Surface Control command to a shape unless you first convert it into a selection or a floater.

To save shapes on separate layers, save your file in the RIFF format. Photoshop 3 format converts shapes into image floaters on separate layers.

Shapes and floaters are both accessed from the Objects: Floater List palette.

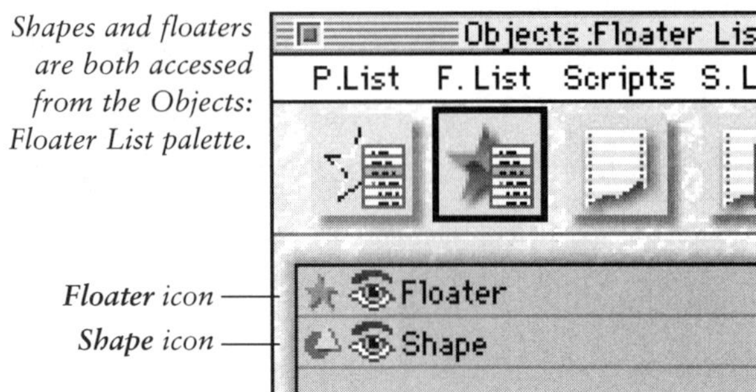

Floater icon —
Shape icon —

The shape tools

The **Shape Object** tools are used to create closed, polygonal shapes.

 *Rectangular Shape*

 *Oval Shape*

The **Shape Design** tools are used to create open or closed freeform shapes.

 *Pen (produces Bézier curves and straight line segments)*

 *Quick Curve*

The **Shape Selection** tools are used to select components of a shape or whole shapes.

 *Direct Selection*

 *Whole Shape Selection*

The **Shape Editing** tools are used to reshape shapes.

 *Scissors*

 *Add Point*

 *Delete Point*

 *Convert Point*

The **Floater Adjuster** tool is used to select shapes for resizing, rotating, moving, or skewing.

 *Floater Adjuster*

To change a shape's fill or stroke attributes, see page 126.

Rectangular Shape tool

Oval Shape tool

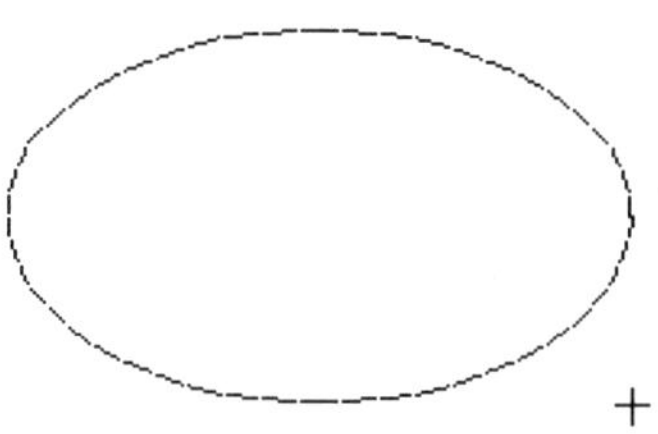

Create shapes

To create a rectangular or oval shape:

1. Choose the Rectangular Shape or Oval Shape tool.

2. Press and drag diagonally in the image window. A wireframe representation of the rectangle or oval will appear. When you release the mouse, the rectangle or oval shape will be selected and colored with the default fill and stroke attributes (see page 126), and the new shape name will be highlighted at the top of the Objects: F. List palette. Whether the shape is given a stroke and/or fill color automatically depends on the Shape Preferences settings (see page 127).

   To create a square with the Rectangular Shape tool or a circle with the Oval Shape tool, hold down Shift as you start dragging.

Quick Curve tool

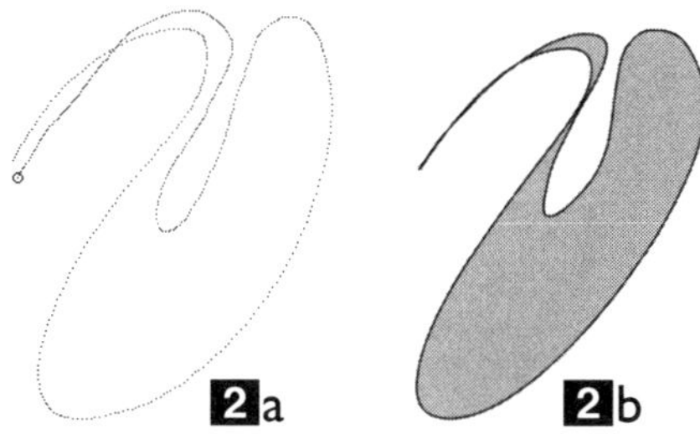

To draw a freeform line shape:

1. Choose the Quick Curve tool (press on the Pen tool to access it if it's not visible on the Tools palette).

2. Press and drag in the image window. A dotted line will appear **2**a. When you release the mouse, the shape's anchor points will be selected and the shape's edge will be colored with the current shape attributes stroke settings **2**b, and the new shape name will be highlighted at the top of the Objects: Floater List palette.

3. *Optional:* To add to the shape, drag from the red square endpoint.

4. To close the shape, click the Close button on the Controls: Shape Design palette **4**. The shape will fill with the current shape attributes fill setting.

Create a Rectangular, Oval, or Freeform Shape

The Pen tool

The Pen tool creates precise curved and straight line segments connected by anchor points. If you click with the Pen tool, you'll create corner points and straight line segments with no wings. If you drag with the Pen tool, you'll create smooth curve points and curve segments with wings, which are called Bézier curves. The distance and the direction in which you drag the mouse determines the shape of the curve segment.

Each curve segment consists of two anchor points connected by one curve segment, with at least one wing (control handle) extending from each anchor point. If an anchor point connects a curve and a straight line segment, it will have one common wing. If an anchor point connects two curve segments, it will have a pair of wings that move in tandem. The longer the wings, the larger the curve.

Pen tool

To create a straight or curved shape using the Pen tool:

1. Choose the Pen tool (P). If the Quick Curve tool is currently chosen, you'll need to press on it to choose the Pen tool, or press P, then click the Pen tool icon on the Controls: Shape Design palette.

2. To create **straight segments:**
   Click to create an anchor point, then click to create a second anchor point. A straight line segment will connect the two points.
   Then
   Click to create additional anchor points. They will be also connected by straight line segments.

   To create **curve segments:**
   Press and drag to create the first anchor point. The shape of the curve segment will be defined by the length and direction you drag the mouse.
   Then

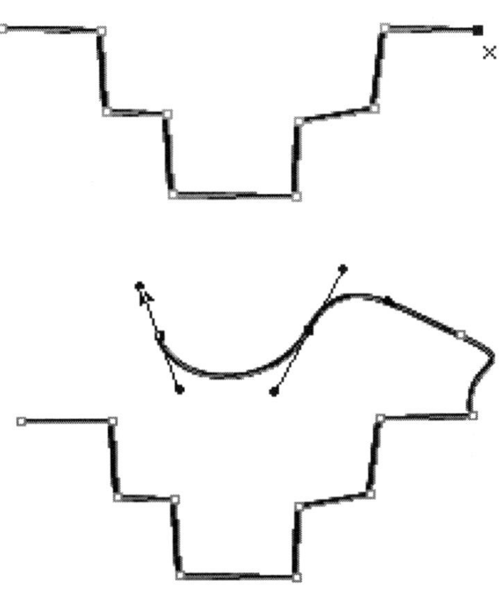

Release the mouse and move it away from the last anchor point, and press and drag in the direction in which you want the curve to go to create a second anchor point. A curve segment will connect the first and second anchor points, and a second pair of wings will be created. Remember, you can always reshape the curves later (see "Change shapes," starting on page 121).

Then

Drag to create additional anchor points and wings. The anchor points will be connected by curve segments.

3. To complete the shape as an **open shape**:

   Hold down Command and click outside the new shape to deselect it.

   or

   Click the Direct Selection or Whole Shape Selection tool, then click outside the shape.

   or

   Click on the blank area of the Objects: Floater List palette.

   To complete the shape as a **closed shape**, position the Pen pointer over the starting point (a tiny circle will appear next to the pointer), then click.

   or

   Click Close on the Controls: Shape Design palette.

   ✎ To add to an open shape, follow the steps on page 122.

   ✎ The fewer the anchor points, the smoother the shape. Too many anchor points will produce bumpy curves.

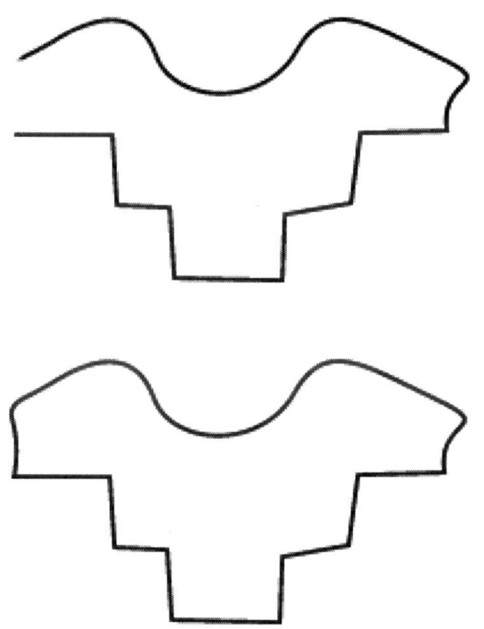

To delete a shape:

1. On the Objects: F. List palette, highlight the name of the shape you want to delete, and make sure the Direct Selection tool isn't currently chosen.

2. Press Delete.

Each text character that is created in Painter is a separate shape, is listed separately on the F. List palette, and can be filled or stroked like any other shape.

To create text shapes:

1. Choose the Text tool (T) **1**.

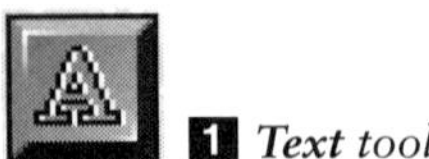

2. Move the Point Size slider on the Controls: Text palette to the desired point size **2** (or click either Point Size arrow).

3. Choose from the Font pop-up menu. If the font you want isn't on the menu, choose Other Font, choose a font **3**, then click OK.

4. *Optional:* Move the Tracking slider to adjust the spacing between letters **4**.

5. Click in the image window where you want the text to appear.

6. Enter the text. (Press Delete to delete characters one at a time. To delete all the characters at once, choose the Whole Shape Selection tool, hold down Shift and click the names of the shapes that you want to delete on the Objects: F. List palette, then press Delete.)

To reshape text shapes, you can add, delete, move, or convert their anchor points (instructions for changing shapes are on the following pages), or use the Scale, Rotate, or Distort command (Effects menu > Orientation).

To fill and stroke text shapes, see page 126.

Use the Whole Shape Selection tool to select and move multiple text shapes at once or to move individual text shapes closer together or further apart (drag inside the text path). Or use the arrow keys on the keyboard to move text shapes one pixel at a time. Group text shapes to make it easier to move them as a unit.

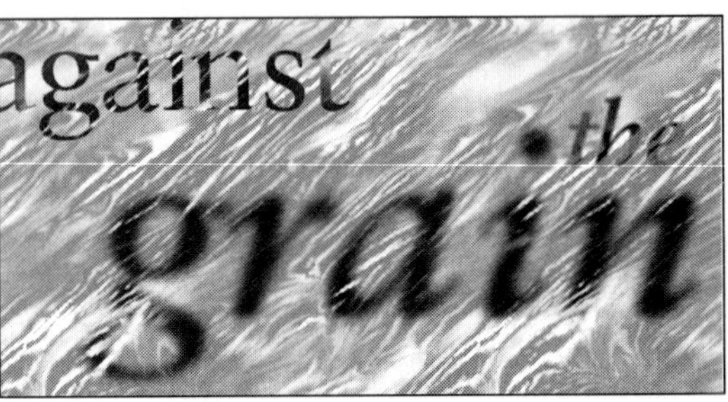

To produce this illustration, our own Woody Grain surface texture was applied using the Color Overlay command (Opacity 50%, Hiding Power). Then the type was added, turned into floaters, and the Dye Concentration command was applied to each word several times (Maximum 1–15%, Minimum 200%).

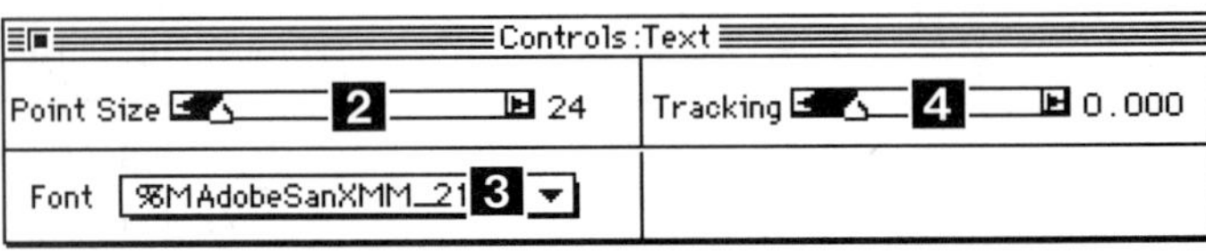

How to choose the Direct Selection or Whole Shape Selection tool

- If the Direct Selection tool isn't visible on the Tools palette, press on the Whole Shape Selection tool to access it, or vice versa.

- Or press A, then click the Direct Selection or Whole Shape Selection icon on the Controls: Shape Selection palette.

- Hold down Command to use the Direct Selection or Whole Shape Selection tool (whichever was last used) when another tool is selected.

Whole Shape Selection tool

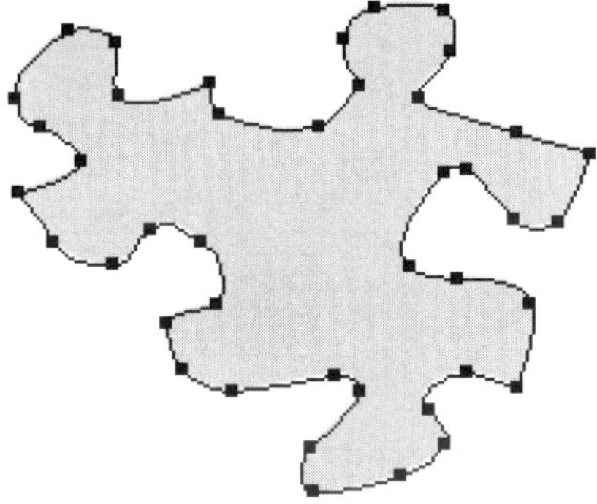

Change shapes

If you want to change a shape in any way, you must first select it. Once a shape is selected, you can add, delete, join, or average its anchor points; convert its curve anchor points into corner anchor points, or vice versa; split its segments; change its fill or stroke attributes; restack, group, copy, or transform (scale, rotate, blend, or skew) it; or convert it into a floater or a selection.

To select an entire shape:

1. Choose the Whole Shape Selection tool.
2. Click on the shape's edge or fill.
   or
   Draw a marquee around all or part of the shape (start dragging from outside the shape). All the points on the shape will be highlighted.
   or
   Click the shape name on the Objects: Floater List palette.

   To move a shape, use the Whole Shape Selection tool or the Floater Adjuster tool.

Direct Selection tool

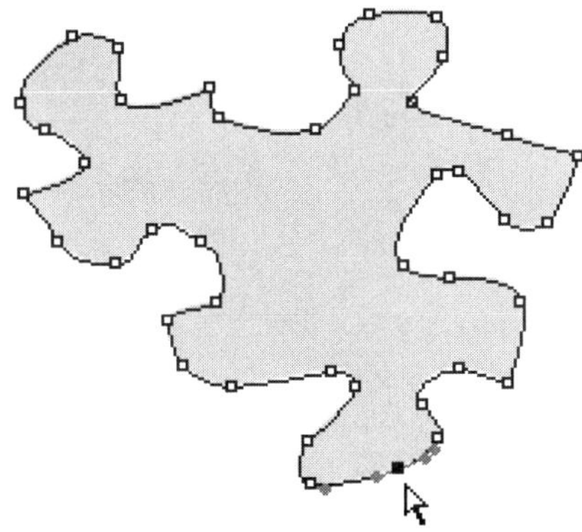

To select anchor points or segments on a shape:

1. Choose the Direct Selection tool.
2. Click on the edge of the shape to select only that segment.
   or
   Click on the shape's fill, if there is one, to select all the shape's anchor points.
   or
   Marquee only those points or segments you want to select (start dragging from outside the shape).

If you move an anchor point, segments connected to it will reshape.

To move an anchor point on a shape:

1. Choose the Direct Selection tool.
2. Click on the edge of the shape.
3. Press and drag an anchor point.

   If all the anchor points on a path are selected, you won't be able to move an individual point. Deselect the shape, then click on its edge with the Direct Selection tool.

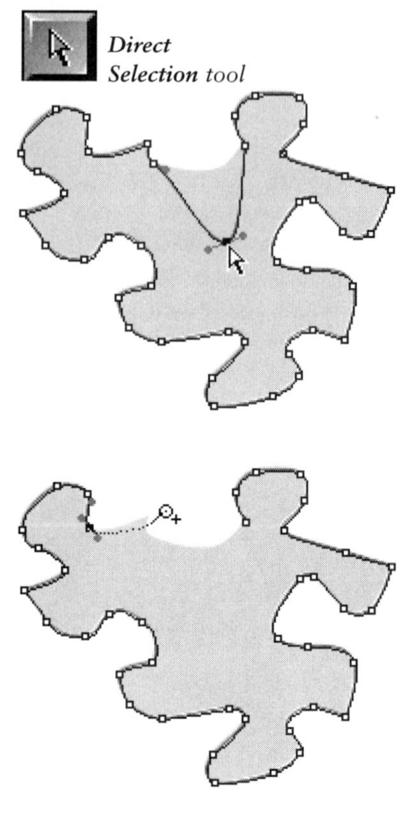

Direct Selection tool

To add to an open shape:

1. Choose the Direct Selection tool.
2. Click on the edge of the open shape.
3. Click on an endpoint.
4. Choose the Quick Curve tool.
5. Position the cursor over the highlighted endpoint (the pointer will turn into a "+" sign).
6. Press and drag to create an addition to the shape.

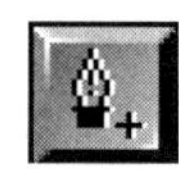

To add anchor points to a shape:

1. Choose the Direct Selection tool.
2. Click on the edge of the shape.
3. Choose the Add Point tool.
4. Click on the edge of the shape where you want the new anchor point to appear. The new anchor point will be selected. Repeat if you want to add more points. Use the Direct Selection tool to move or otherwise modify the new anchor point.

Add Point tool

To delete anchor points from a shape:

1. Choose the Direct Selection tool.
2. Click on the edge of the shape.
3. Choose the Delete Point tool.
4. Click on the anchor point you want to delete.

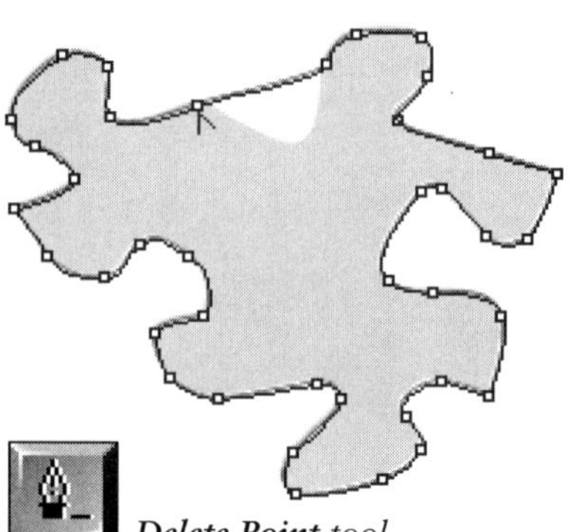

Delete Point tool

Move Anchor Point; Add/Delete Points or Segments

Scissors tool

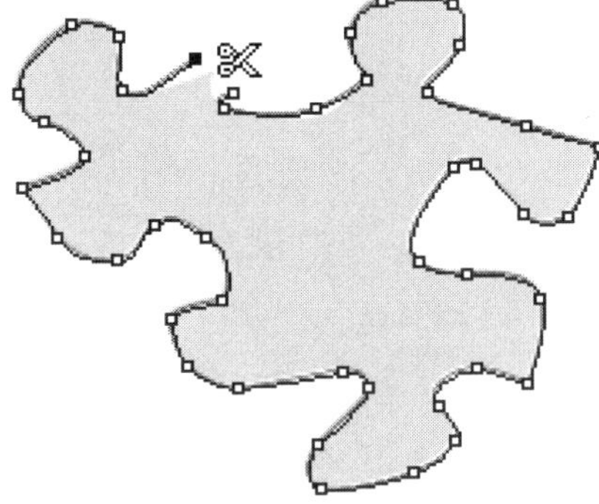

If you click on a closed shape with the Scissors tool, it will turn into a single, open shape. If you click on an open shape, it will split into two shapes. A shape can be split at an anchor point or in the middle of a segment.

To split a shape segment:

1. Choose the Direct Selection or Whole Shape Selection tool (A).

2. Click on a shape to display its anchor points.

3. Choose the Scissors tool.

4. Click on the edge of the shape.

To move the new endpoints apart:

5. To move the whole shape, choose the Whole Shape Selection tool.
   or
   To move just an endpoint, choose the Direct Selection tool.

6. Drag the new endpoint or shape.

   To apply a fill to an open shape, double-click the shape name on the F. List palette, then check the Fill box.

Convert Point tool

To convert a corner anchor point into a curve anchor point, or vice versa:

1. Choose the Direct Selection tool.

2. Click on the edge of the shape. The anchor points will be hollow.

3. Choose the Convert Point tool.

4. To convert a corner into a curve, press on the anchor point, then drag away from it. Wings will be created as you drag. The further you drag, the rounder the curve will become.
   or
   To convert a curve into a corner, click on the curve anchor point (don't drag). Its wings will disappear.

5. *Optional:* To reshape the curve, choose the Direct Selection tool, then drag an anchor point or a wing.

If a curve segment twists around the anchor point as you drag, keep the mouse button down, rotate the wing back around the anchor point to undo the twist, then continue to drag in the new direction.

To create non-continuous curves:

1. Follow the steps on pages 118–119 to create an open shape with smooth curves.

2. Choose the Direct Selection tool.

3. Click on the shape.

4. Click on the anchor point to be modified.

5. Choose the Convert Point tool.

6. Rotate the wing so it forms a "V" shape with the other wing. The curve segment will be on the same side of the anchor point as the previous curve segment.

7. Repeat to convert other anchor points. Remember, you can hold down Command to access the last used Shape Selection tool when another tool is selected.

To make a non-continuous curve continuous again, choose the Convert Point tool, then drag one of the wings of the "V."

Convert Point tool

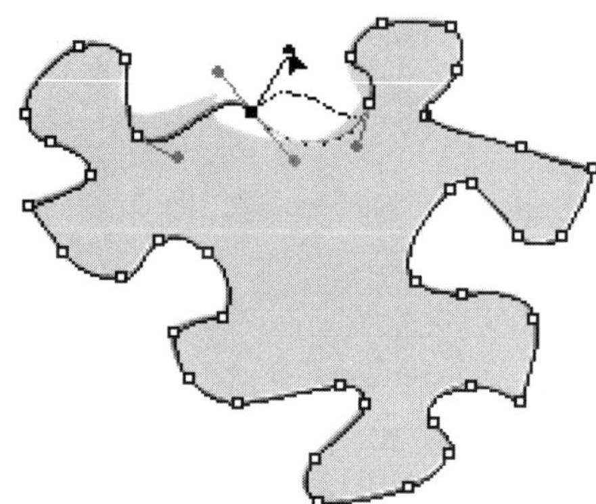

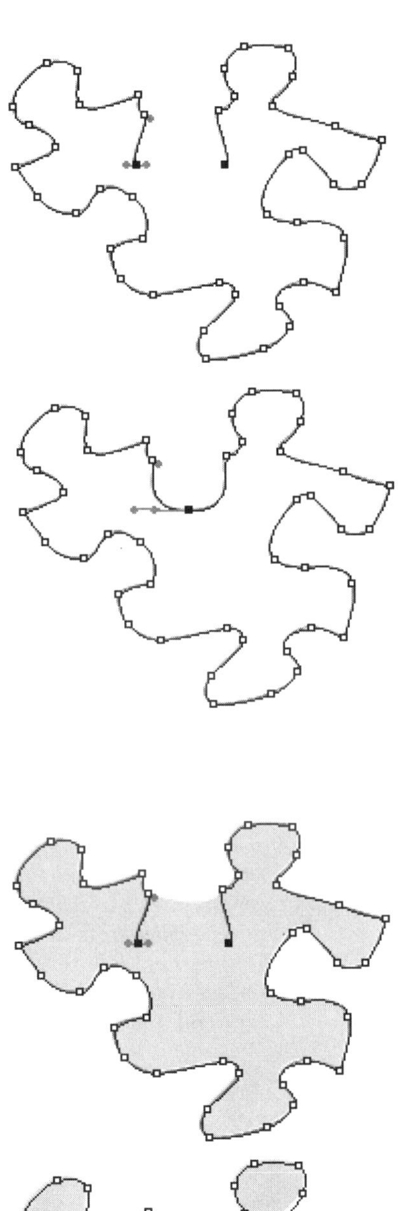

The Average Points command reshapes one or more paths by precisely realigning their endpoints or anchor points to the horizontal and/or vertical axis.

To average anchor points:

1. Choose the Direct Selection tool.

2. Hold down Shift and click on two or more anchor points.

3. Choose Shapes menu > Average Points.

4. Click **Both** to overlap the points along both the horizontal and vertical axes. Choose this option if you want to join them later into one point (instructions below).

   or

   Click **Horizontal** to align the points along the horizontal (*x*) axis.

   or

   Click **Vertical** to align the points along the vertical (*y*) axis.

5. Click OK or press Return.

If you align two endpoints on top of each other and then execute the Join command, they will combine into one anchor point. If the endpoints are not on top of each other, the Join command will create a new straight line segment between them—not a curve.

To join two endpoints:

1. Choose the Direct Selection tool.

2. *Optional:* If you want to combine two endpoints into one, move one endpoint on top of the other manually, or use the Average Points command (Both option) to align them (instructions above).

3. Hold down Shift and click on two endpoints, or marquee them.

4. Choose Shapes menu > Join Endpoints. If the endpoints are not on top of each other, the Join command will connect them with a straight line segment.

To change a shape's fill or stroke attributes:

1. Double-click the shape name on the Objects: Floater List palette.

2. Use any of the following methods illustrated below.

3. Click OK or press Return.

*To apply a **Stroke color**, check the Stroke box, click the color square, then choose a color from the Art Materials: Color palette. The new color will preview in the color square and in the shape. You can also adjust stroke **Opacity** or **Width**.*

*To apply a **Fill color**, check the **Fill** box, click the color square, then choose a color from the Art Materials: Color palette. The new color will preview in the color square and in the shape. You can also adjust fill **Opacity**.*

*Click a **Line cap** icon to change the endpoints style.*

*Click a **Line joins** icon to change the corner points style.*

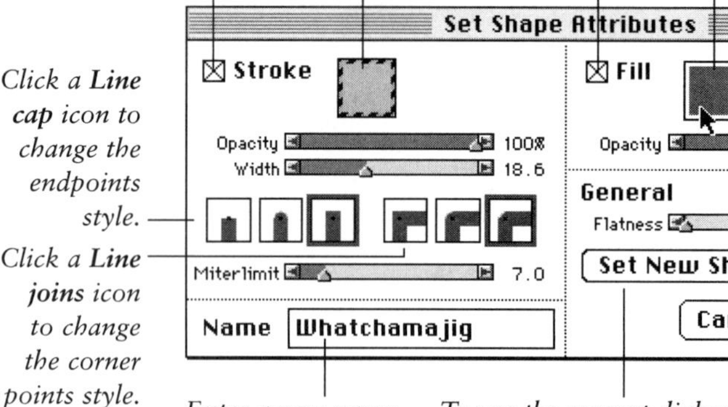

Enter a new name for the shape in the Name field.

*To use the current dialog box settings as the default for all future shapes, click **Set New Shape Attributes**. To set default attributes when no shape is selected, choose Shapes menu > Set Default Attributes, then follow the instructions in this illustration to change the attributes.*

*If the shape has overlapping segments, click the **Fill Overlap** (solid star) icon to fill overlapping areas **1**. Click the **Don't Fill Overlaps** icon if you don't want to fill overlaps **2**.*

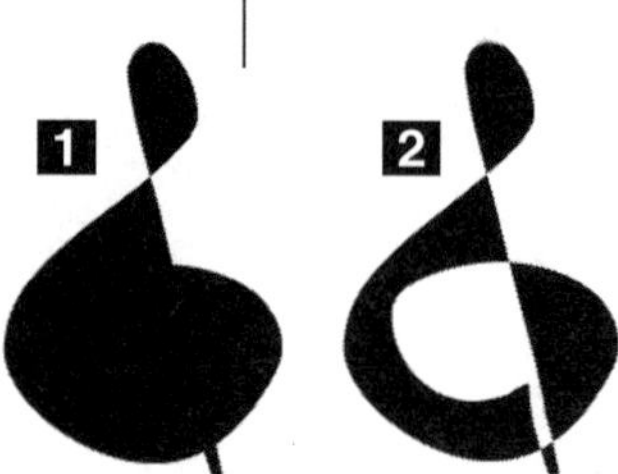

You can also turn a shape's fill on or off or adjust a shape's fill opacity or stroke width using the sliders on the Controls: Shapes palette. Adjustments made on this palette will be reflected in the Set Shape Attributes dialog box the next time it's reopened. Adjustments made in the Set Shape Attributes dialog box are reflected immediately on the Controls: Shapes palette.

Floater Adjuster

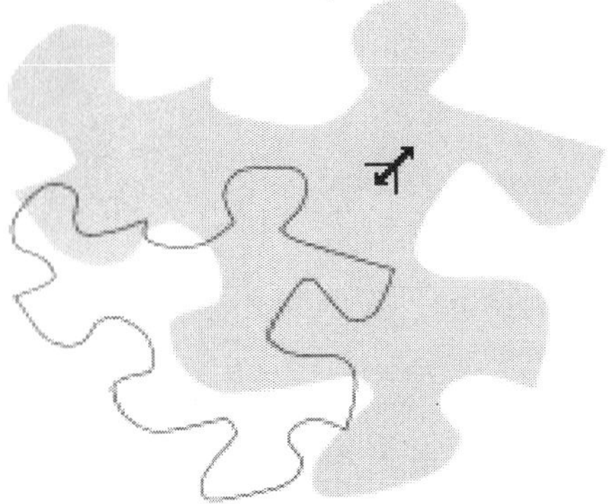

If you turn on the Fill AND Stroke options
You'll probably want to make them different opacities so you can tell them apart. To change the default fill and stroke opacity for shapes, make sure no shape is selected, choose **Shapes menu > Set Default Attributes**, and adjust the **Stroke** and/or **Fill Opacity** slider.

To set shape preferences:

1. To set defaults for all future documents, close all open image windows.
   or
   To set defaults for the current document only, leave it open.

2. Choose Edit menu > Preferences > Shapes.

3. Do any of the following:
   Click **On Draw:** Fill With Current Color or Stroke In Current Color to fill or stroke shapes as they're being created, and if they're left open.
   Click **On Close:** Fill With Current Color or Stroke In Current Color to fill or stroke shapes when they're closed.

   These display options affect both current and subsequently created shapes:
   Click **Big Handles** to display large wings and anchor points for better visibility, or the standard small handles and anchor points.

   To change the default **Wing Color**, **Selected Point Color** or **Outline Color** for selected shapes, click the color icon, then choose a new color from the Art Materials: Color palette.

4. Click OK or press Return.

To resize a shape or shapes:

1. Choose the Floater Adjuster tool (F).

2. On the Objects: F. List palette, click the name of the shape to be modified. Shift-click to select multiple names.

3. Drag a center handle inward or outward to change the shape's height *or* width.
   or
   Drag a corner handle inward or outward to change the shape's height *and* width. Hold down Shift as you start dragging to preserve the shape's original proportions.

   Use the Effects menu > Orientation > Scale command to resize a shape by entering exact percentages.

To rotate a shape or shapes:

1. Choose the Floater Adjuster tool (F).

2. On the Objects: F. List palette, click the name of the shape or shape group to be modified. Shift-click to select multiple names.

3. Hold down Command and drag a corner handle of the selection rectangle in a circular manner.

   Use the Effects menu > Orientation > Rotate command to rotate a shape by entering an exact angle.

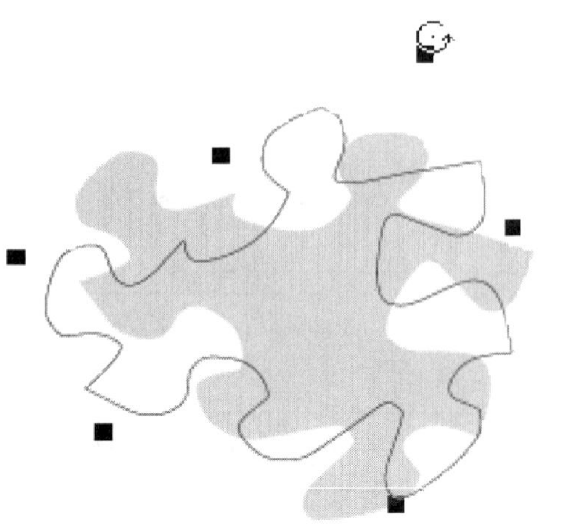

To skew (slant) a shape or shapes:

1. Choose the Floater Adjuster tool (F).

2. On the Objects: F. List palette, click the name of the shape or shape group to be modified. Shift-click to select multiple names.

3. Hold down Command and drag a midpoint handle of the selection rectangle to slant the shape.

   If you want to skew a shape by dragging midpoint *and* corner handles, use the Effects menu > Orientation > Distort command.

   To change a shape's orientation, choose Effects menu > Orientation > Flip Horizontal or Flip Vertical.

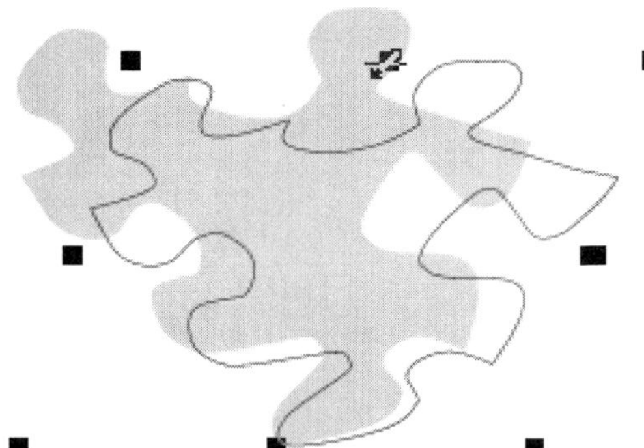

To copy a shape in the same document:

1. On the Objects: F. List palette, click on the name of the shape you want to duplicate.

2. Choose Shapes menu > Duplicate.

   To duplicate a shape and control where the duplicate is placed, choose Shapes menu > Set Duplicate Transform, then enter Translation: H. Offset and/or V. Offset values.

You can also use the Edit menu commands Copy, Cut, and Paste to move shapes to another Painter document or to copy a shape within the same document. See page 96.

Shape Preferences

Drawing Options

On Draw: ☐ Fill With Current Color
☒ Stroke In Current Color

On Close: ☒ Fill With Current Color
☐ Stroke In Current Color

☐ Big Handles

Colors

Wing Color: ▨   Selected Point Color: ■

Outline Color: ▨

[Cancel] [OK]

If you turn on the Fill AND Stroke options

You'll probably want to make them different opacities so you can tell them apart. To change the default fill and stroke opacity for shapes, make sure no shape is selected, choose Shapes menu > Set Default Attributes, and adjust the Stroke and/or Fill Opacity slider.

Floater Adjuster

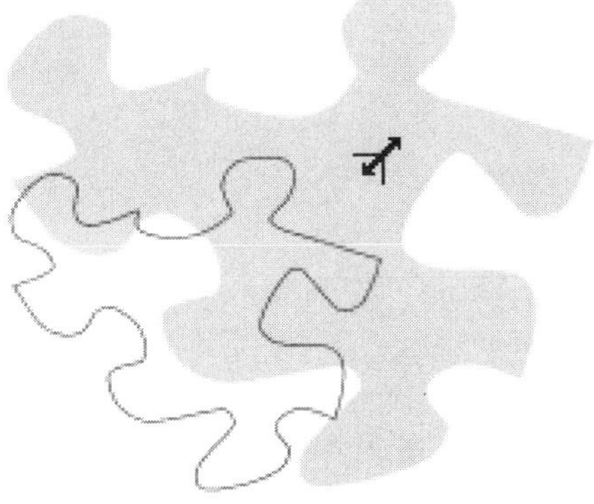

To set shape preferences:

1. To set defaults for all future documents, close all open image windows.
or
To set defaults for the current document only, leave it open.

2. Choose Edit menu > Preferences > Shapes.

3. Do any of the following:
Click **On Draw:** Fill With Current Color or Stroke In Current Color to fill or stroke shapes as they're being created, and if they're left open.
Click **On Close:** Fill With Current Color or Stroke In Current Color to fill or stroke shapes when they're closed.

These display options affect both current and subsequently created shapes:
Click **Big Handles** to display large wings and anchor points for better visibility, or the standard small handles and anchor points.

To change the default **Wing Color, Selected Point Color** or **Outline Color** for selected shapes, click the color icon, then choose a new color from the Art Materials: Color palette.

4. Click OK or press Return.

To resize a shape or shapes:

1. Choose the Floater Adjuster tool (F).

2. On the Objects: F. List palette, click the name of the shape to be modified. Shift-click to select multiple names.

3. Drag a center handle inward or outward to change the shape's height *or* width.
or
Drag a corner handle inward or outward to change the shape's height *and* width. Hold down Shift as you start dragging to preserve the shape's original proportions.

Use the Effects menu > Orientation > Scale command to resize a shape by entering exact percentages.

Set Shape Preferences; Resize a Shape

To rotate a shape or shapes:

1. Choose the Floater Adjuster tool (F).

2. On the Objects: F. List palette, click the name of the shape or shape group to be modified. Shift-click to select multiple names.

3. Hold down Command and drag a corner handle of the selection rectangle in a circular manner.

✎ Use the Effects menu > Orientation > Rotate command to rotate a shape by entering an exact angle.

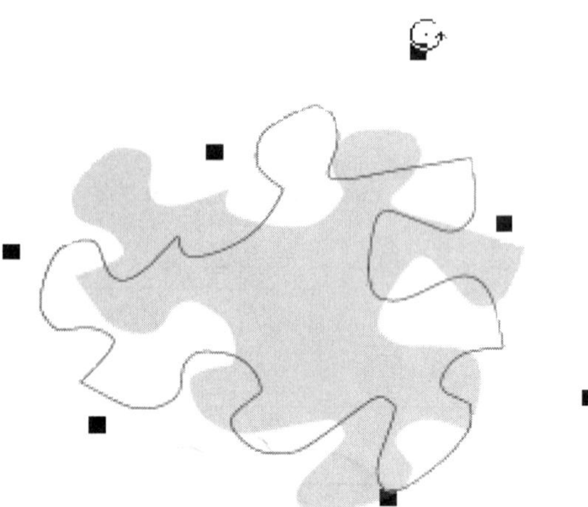

To skew (slant) a shape or shapes:

1. Choose the Floater Adjuster tool (F).

2. On the Objects: F. List palette, click the name of the shape or shape group to be modified. Shift-click to select multiple names.

3. Hold down Command and drag a midpoint handle of the selection rectangle to slant the shape.

✎ If you want to skew a shape by dragging midpoint *and* corner handles, use the Effects menu > Orientation > Distort command.

✎ To change a shape's orientation, choose Effects menu > Orientation > Flip Horizontal or Flip Vertical.

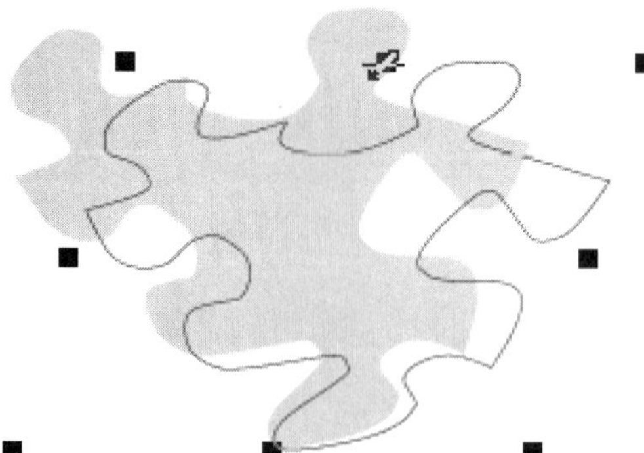

To copy a shape in the same document:

1. On the Objects: F. List palette, click on the name of the shape you want to duplicate.

2. Choose Shapes menu > Duplicate.

✎ To duplicate a shape and control where the duplicate is placed, choose Shapes menu > Set Duplicate Transform, then enter Translation: H. Offset and/or V. Offset values.

You can also use the Edit menu commands Copy, Cut, and Paste to move shapes to another Painter document or to copy a shape within the same document. See page 96.

Rotate, Skew, or Copy a Shape

To align shapes, see page 96.

Shapes are stacked in front-to-back order in the image window (and top-to-bottom order on the Objects: F. List palette) according to the order in which they were created.

To restack shapes:

On the Objects: F. List palette, drag any shape name up or down on the list. You can also restack floaters this way.

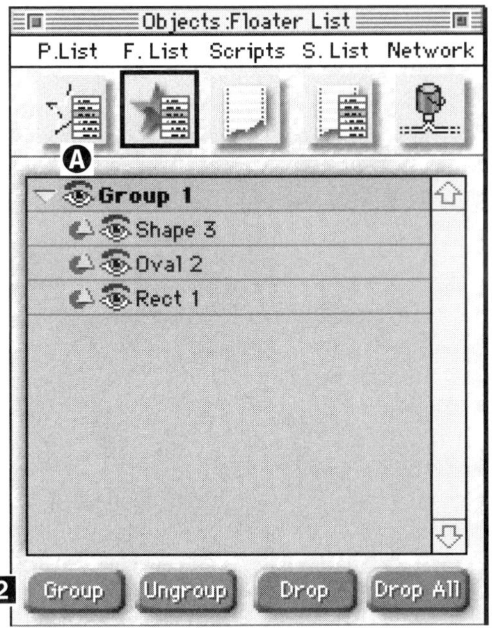

Grouped shapes can be moved or transformed as a unit. You can also blend a whole group with another group (see the next page).

To group shapes into a larger unit:

1. On the Objects: Floater List palette, Shift-click the names of the shapes you want to group.

2. Click Group **2**.

The information on pages 97–98 regarding grouping floaters also applies to shapes.

To hide or show a shape:

On the Objects: Floater List palette, click the eye icon next to the shape name **A**. If the eye is open, the shape is displayed; if the eye is closed, the shape is hidden. Cute.

The Blend command creates a multi-step progression between two shapes or shape groups. The shapes can have different contours and different fills, strokes and opacities. You can blend two open shapes—like lines—or two closed shapes, but you cannot blend an open and a closed shape.

To blend one shape into another:

1. Move two open or two closed shapes apart to allow room for the transition steps that will appear between them.

2. Hold down Shift and click on the two shape or shape group names on the Objects: F. List palette.

3. Choose Shapes menu > Blend.

4. Enter the desired number of steps in the Number of Steps field. The fewer the steps, the less the transition shapes will overlap. Try a low number first.

5. Choose a Ramp type to control the spacing between the transition shapes. In order, the options are:

   ■ Evenly spaced.

   ■ Spacing narrows towards the ending transition shapes.

   ■ Spacing is narrow at the beginning of the blend and increases toward the ending transition shapes.

   ■ Spacing is narrow at the ends and wider in the middle.

6. Choose a Color Space option:

   RGB blends color directly from the starting shape color to the ending shape color.

   Hue CW produces a blend using colors on the color wheel, beginning from the starting shape's color position and moving clockwise around to the ending shape's color position.

   Hue CCW produces a blend using colors on the color wheel, beginning from the starting shape's color

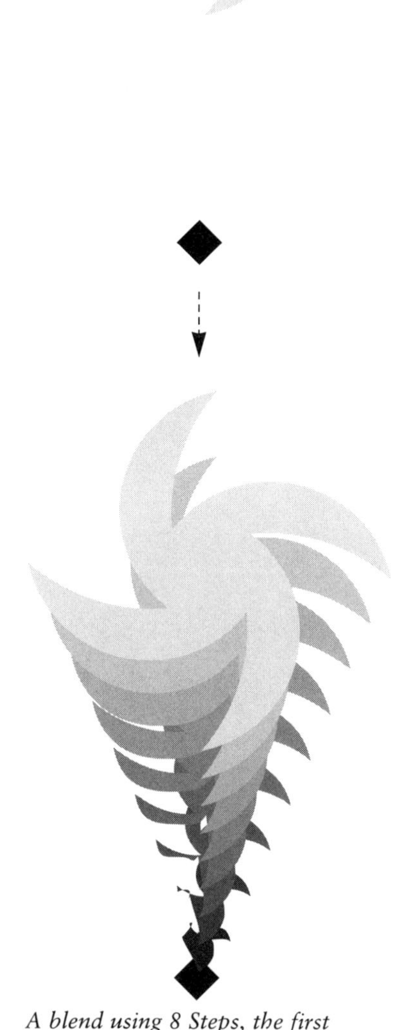

A blend using 8 Steps, the first Ramp Type option (evenly spaced), and a Perspective factor of 1.

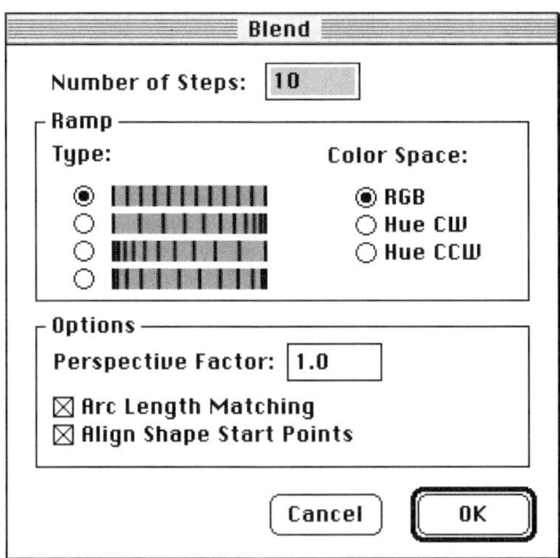

position and moving counterclockwise around the color wheel.

7. *Optional:* Enter a value between .1 and 100 in the Perspective Factor field to control the spacing between the transition shapes. If the ending shape is stacked above the starting shape (in other words, if it's listed above the starting shape on the Objects: F. List palette), enter a Factor above 1.0. If the stacking order is reversed, enter a Factor below 1.0. The Perspective Factor option can be used to tighten the spacing between the ending parts of the blend, as in a natural perspective view.

8. *Optional:* Check the Align Shape Start Points box to prevent the intermediate blend shapes from twisting.

9. Click OK or press Return. A blend group will be created, composed of the intermediate steps, and it will be listed on the Objects: F. List palette.

When the Arc Length Matching box is unchecked, blending shapes must have the same number of anchor points to produce good results. Bug alert: Arc Length Matching, when it's turned on in Painter version 4.0, can cause the application to bomb. We've been told this bug has been fixed in Painter 4.0.3.

You can blend between two shapes to create an illustration of 3D shading from a shadow color shape to a highlight color shape. Place the highlight shape on top of the shadow shape, then select both and apply the Blend command. Use a largish number of steps to produce smooth color transitions.

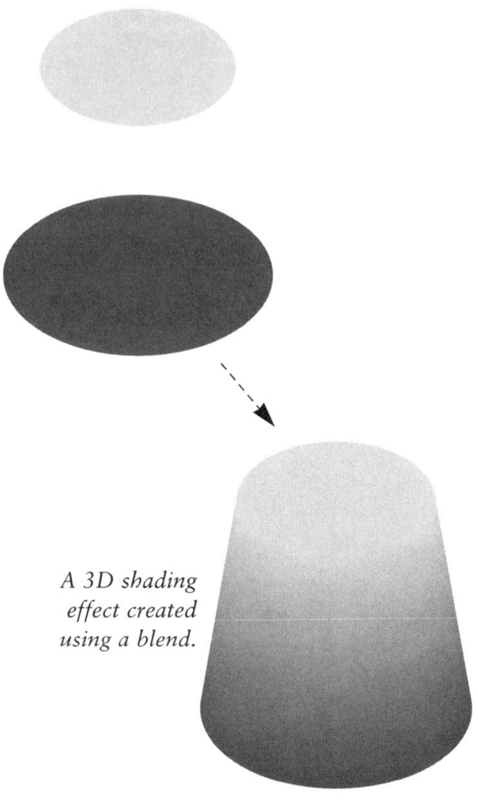

A 3D shading effect created using a blend.

The Make Compound command joins two shapes into one shape. Where the original shapes overlapped, a transparent "hole" is created, through which the underlying imagery is revealed.

To create a compound shape:

1. Choose the Whole Shape Selection tool.

2. Arrange two shapes: place the shape you want to see through in front of a larger shape.

3. Marquee both the shapes.
   or
   Hold down Shift and click on both shapes.

4. Choose Shapes menu > Make Compound. The frontmost shape will "cut" through the backmost shape. The compound shape will have the fill and stroke attributes of the back-most shape.

   The compound name on the Objects: Floater List palette will take the name of the frontmost shape. The other shape used in the compound will no longer be listed.

   Choose Shapes menu > Release Compound to revert a compound back into individual shapes. The names of the original, pre-compound shapes will reappear on the Objects: Floater List palette.

   To add more shapes to a compound, follow the same steps above.

Whole Shape Selection tool

The cutout in the compound is transparent.

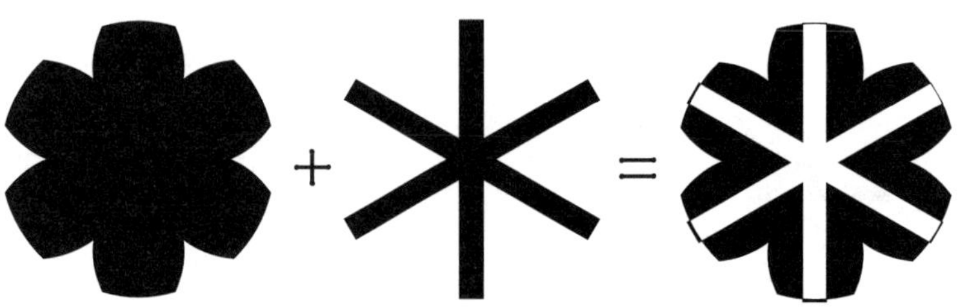

To edit the contour of a selection, convert it into a shape, use the shape editing tools to adjust the contour, and then convert the shape back into a selection.

To convert a selection into a shape:

1. Create a selection. A selection generated from the Magic Wand tool or a Mask command can be used.

2. Choose Objects palette > P. List menu > Convert to Shape. The selection will no longer be listed on the P. List palette; the new shape name will appear on the F. List palette.

To convert a Pen or Quick Curve shape into a selection

With the Pen or Quick Curve tool chosen and the shape name highlighted on the Objects: P. List palette, click Make Selection on the Controls: Shape Design palette.

To convert a shape into a selection:

1. Click the shape name on the Objects: F. List palette.
   or
   Click on a shape in the image window.

2. Choose Shapes menu > Convert To Selection. The shape will no longer be listed on the F. List palette; the new selection name will appear on the P. List palette.

To convert a shape into a floater:

1. Choose the Whole Shape Selection tool.

2. Click a shape name on the Objects: F. List palette.
   or
   Click on a shape in the image window.

3. Choose Shapes menu > Convert To Floater. The circle/triangle icon on the F. List will change to a star icon.
   or
   Apply brushstrokes to the shape or apply any Effects menu > Surface Control command. The shape will automatically become a floater, because these Painter features work with pixel information; a shape cannot contain pixel information, but a floater can. *Note:* If your shape had a stroke and a fill and you apply the Convert To Floater command, two floaters will be created: one for the stroke and one for the fill.

Since there is no such thing as a shapes library, the only way to preserve a shape to use in other documents is to convert it into a selection and save the selection in a paths library.

To save a shape in a paths library:

1. Choose Shapes menu > Convert To Selection to convert the shape into a selection.

2. Choose Objects palette > P. List menu > Paths to open the Paths palette.

3. Choose the Selection Adjuster tool.

4. Drag the selection into the Paths palette drawer front or drawer.

5. Enter a name.

6. Click OK.

Selection Adjuster tool

If you acquire an object from Adobe Illustrator or Macromedia FreeHand, it will appear on Painter's shapes layer.

To acquire shapes from Illustrator or FreeHand:

FreeHand users: Choose File > Save As, and save the file in Illustrator 5 format. Illustrator users: Choose File > Save As, and save the file in Illustrator 5.0/5.5 or 6.0 format. In Painter, choose File menu > Acquire > Adobe Illustrator File, then locate and double-click the file. Objects containing patterns, placed images, or masks cannot be acquired. Gradients will appear as solid colors or in a star configuration, regardless of the original.

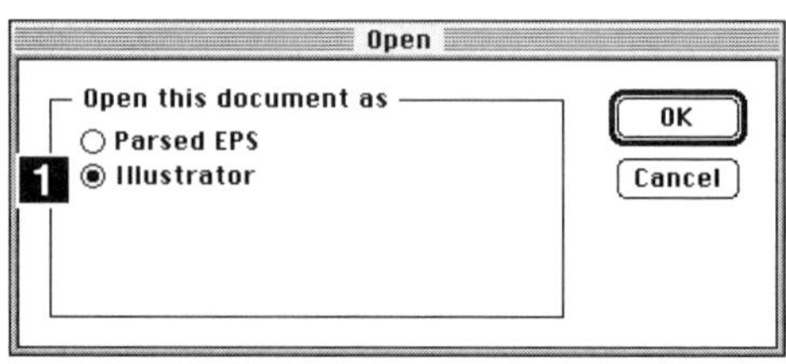

To export shapes to Illustrator or FreeHand:

Choose File menu > Export > Adobe Illustrator File. This command will save shapes (and only shapes) as solid fills and strokes in the Illustrator 6 file format. Opacity levels and composite methods that are applied to shapes via the Controls: Shapes palette will be lost. In Illustrator, choose File > Open, and click the Illustrator option **1**.

For information about outputting shapes, see page 249.

Fills 8

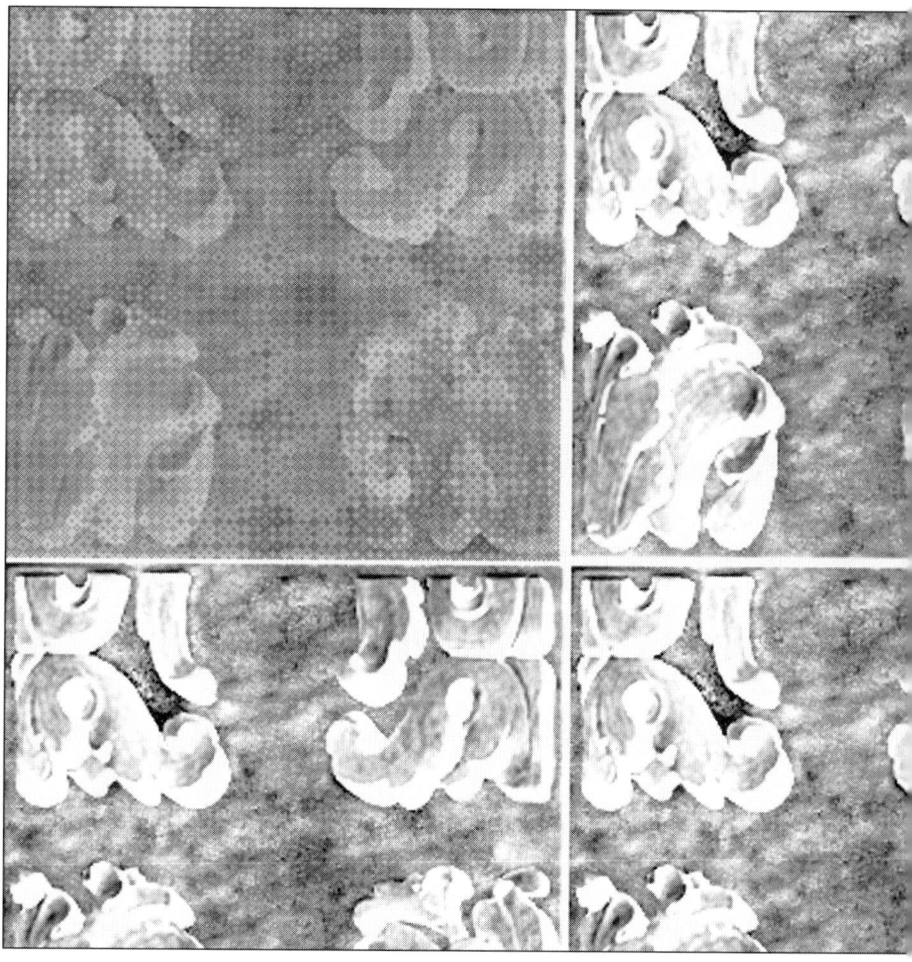

If there is no selection in your picture, the Paint Bucket will fill adjacent pixels whose color is similar to the color you click on. If the picture is blank, the Paint Bucket will fill it entirely with color. If you click inside or outside a selection or click on an active floater with the Paint Bucket tool, color will fill only that area.

To fill with a color, a pattern, a gradation, or a weaving using the Paint Bucket tool:

1. *Optional:* Create a selection or activate a floater to restrict the fill.

2. Choose a Primary color (page 28), a gradation (page 137), a pattern (page 142), or a weave (page 140).

3. Choose the Paint Bucket tool (C).

4. Click What to Fill: Image on the Controls: Paint Bucket palette.

5. Click Fill With: Current Color, Gradation, Clone Source, or Weaving. If you're not working on a clone and you choose Clone Source, the pattern currently selected on the Pattern palette will be used as the fill.

6. Click on or marquee the area of your picture that you want to fill.

To fill with a color, a pattern, a gradation, or a weaving using the Fill command:

1. *Optional:* Create a selection or activate a floater to restrict the fill.

2. Choose a Primary color (page 28), a gradation (page 137), a pattern (page 142), or a weave (page 140).

3. Choose Effects menu > Fill (Command-F).

4. Click Current Color, Pattern, Gradation, or Weaving. You can choose a different color, gradation, pattern, or weave from the Art Materials palette while the dialog box is open.

5. Choose an Opacity.

6. Click OK or press Return.

Ray Rue produced this texture using gradations.

Paint Bucket tool

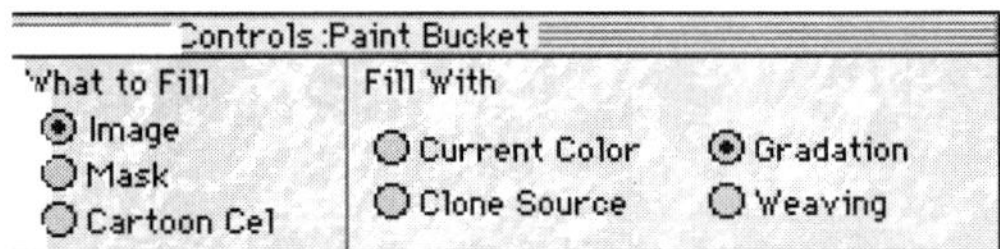

Using the Fill command, you can apply a color, gradation, or weaving at any opacity.

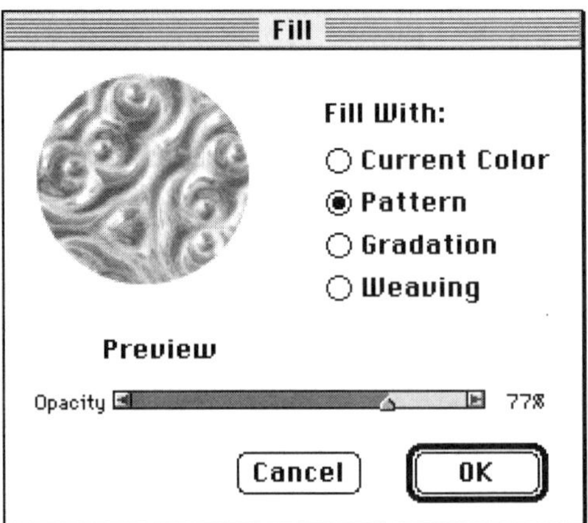

Bernice Mast

Gradations

Use the Art Materials: Grad palette to choose a gradation Type (pattern) and an order for the gradation's colors. Once you choose a gradation, you can use either fill method described on page 136. To capture a gradation from a painting or create a gradation using a dialog box, follow the instructions on the next page.

To choose a gradation:

1. Click the Grad icon on the Art Materials palette **1**.

2. Click a gradation on the drawer front or in the drawer. To create a gradation that uses the current Primary and Secondary colors at the time you use the gradation as a fill, click the Two-Point icon **2**, then choose Primary and Secondary colors (front and back color rectangles on the Color palette). Tear off the Color palette from the main Art Materials palette to preview colors as you choose them.

3. Click a gradation Type (linear, radial, spiral, or circular) **3**.

4. Do any of the following:

   To change the **angle** of the gradation, click on the rotation ring or drag the little red ball **4**a. (To loosen or tighten a spiral gradation, hold down Command while dragging the red ball).

   To change the **order** of the colors, click a different Orders button on the expanded Grad palette **4**b.

   To **save** a modified gradation, click Save on the Grad palette, enter a *new* name, then click OK. **Once a gradation is saved in a Grad palette library, it can't be edited.** If you save a Two-Point gradation, the colors in the palette icon for the gradation won't change, but the gradation will always be applied with the current Primary and Secondary colors.

5. Follow either set of instructions on page 136 to use the gradation as a fill.

Help!

You clicked on the preview square, and now the gradation is rotating aimlessly. Click on the rotation ring to stop it.

To capture a gradation from a painting:

1. Paint a gradation (or open an existing image).

2. Choose the Rectangular Selection tool.

3. Create a skinny horizontal or vertical selection **3**. Only the topmost or leftmost row of pixels will be used.

4. Choose Art Materials palette > Grad menu > Capture Gradation.

5. Enter a name for the gradation.

6. Click OK or press Return. A thumbnail of the gradation will appear on the Grad palette drawer front **6**.

To create a gradation using a dialog box:

1. Tear off the Color palette from the Art Materials palette so you can preview the gradation on the Grad palette and choose colors at the same time.

2. Choose Art Materials palette > Grad menu > Edit Gradation.

3. Do any of the following:

   To **change a color**, click a marker under the color bar, then choose a color from the Color palette.

   To **add a color**, choose a Primary color, then Option-click inside the bar.

   To **remove a color**, click its marker, then press Delete.

   To **change the location of a color**, drag its marker.

   To manually **adjust the amount of a color**, click its marker, uncheck the Linear box, then move the Color Spread slider.

   To **choose a different color space** for a segment, click a square box above it. RGB is the default. Click on a marker to close the pop-up menu.

4. Click OK or press Return.

5. *Optional*: To save the gradation, click Save on the Art Materials: Grad palette, enter a name, then click OK.

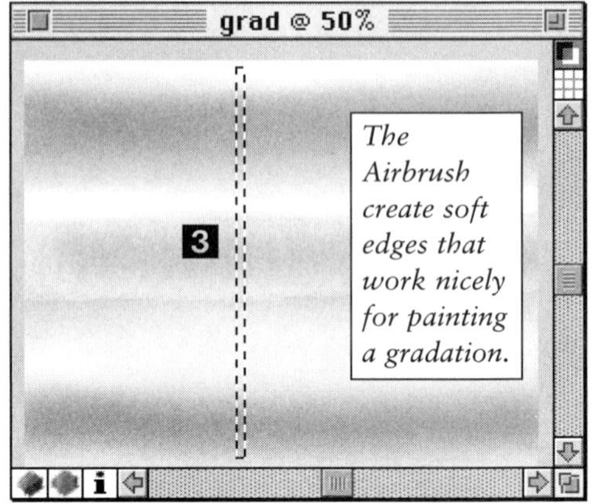

The Airbrush create soft edges that work nicely for painting a gradation.

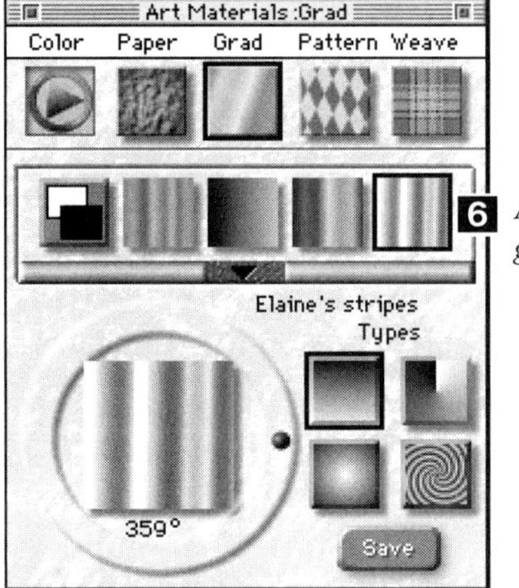

A captured gradation.

You can also edit a Two-Point gradation using the Edit Gradation dialog box. Just click on the Two-Point gradation before you open the dialog box.

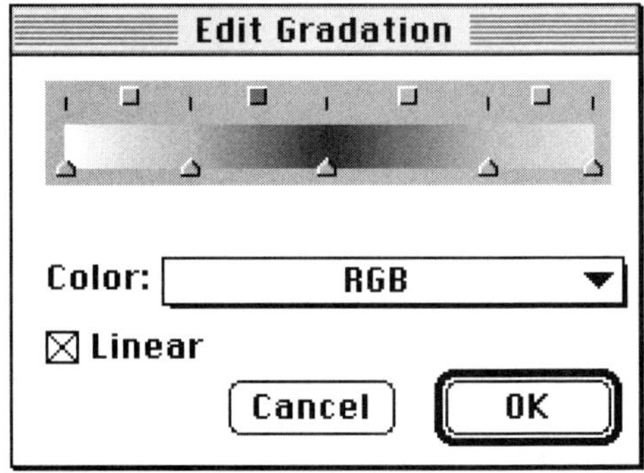

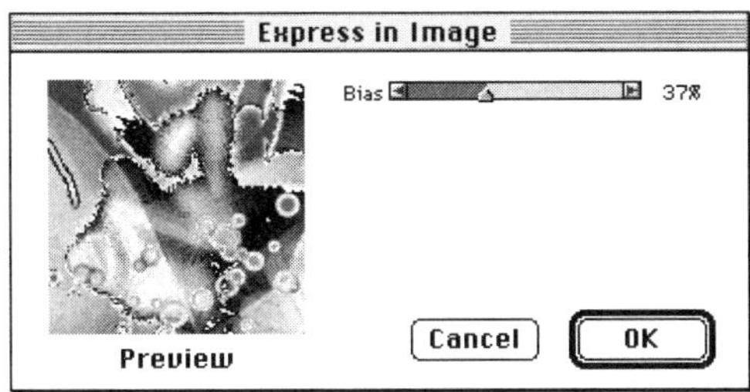

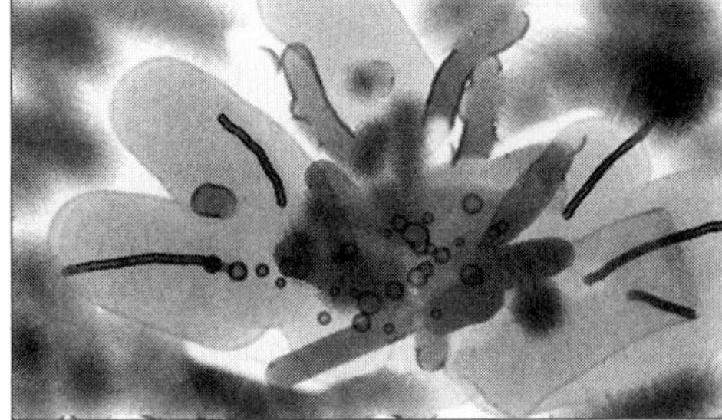

The original image.

After applying the Express in Image command using the captured gradation shown on the previous page and three different Bias percentages:

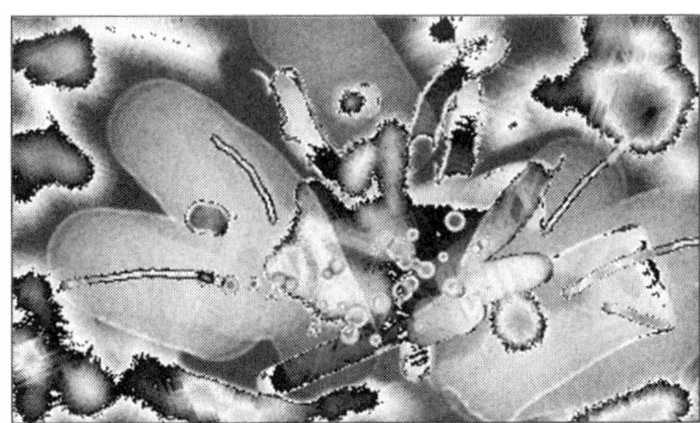

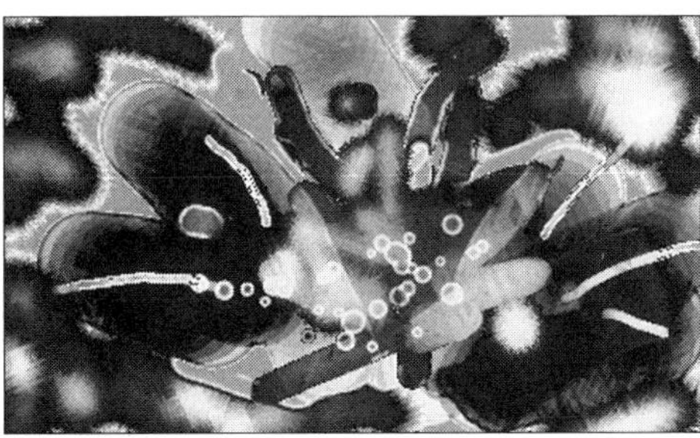

The Express in Image command replaces colors in an image with colors that match them in luminance value in the currently selected gradation.

To recolor an image using a gradation:

1. *Optional:* Select part of a picture to restrict the effect to that area.

2. Click a gradation on the Art Materials: Grad palette.

3. Choose Art Materials palette > Grad menu > Express in Image.

4. Move the Bias slider to cycle gradation colors through the picture's luminance values. (0% and 100% produce the same result.)

5. *Optional:* Choose a different gradation from the Grad palette, or click a different Order button on the expanded Grad palette (the bottommost buttons).

6. Click OK or press Return.

To create or edit a gradation library, see the instructions on pages 21–22.

Weaves

You can choose a preset weave pattern from the Art Materials: Weave palette or you can customize a weave pattern and save it. Once you select a weave, use the Paint Bucket tool or the Fill command to apply it to a selected area.

To choose or modify a weave:

1. Click the Weave icon on the Art Materials palette **1**.

2. Click a weave pattern on the drawer front or in the drawer **2**. To display weaves from a different library, click Library in the Weave palette drawer, locate and highlight the weave library you want to open, then click Open.

3. If you're satisfied with the weave design, follow either set of fill instructions on page 136.

   or

   To modify the weave design before using it as a fill, follow the remaining steps.

4. Close the drawer on the Weave palette and expand the palette.

5. Do any of the following:

   Move the Horizontal and/or Vertical **Scale** sliders **5**a or click the left or right Scale arrow to adjust the width or height, respectively, of the whole pattern. Each increment increases or reduces the scale by 100%.

   To change the thickness of the threads (not the spaces between them) for a three-dimensional pattern, adjust the Scale, then move the Horizontal and/or Vertical **Thickness** sliders or click the left or right arrow.

   Click the **Fiber Type** button **5**b to switch between the two-dimensional and three-dimensional versions of the pattern. (You'll most likely need to make Scale and Thickness adjustments to preview a 3D Fiber Type.)

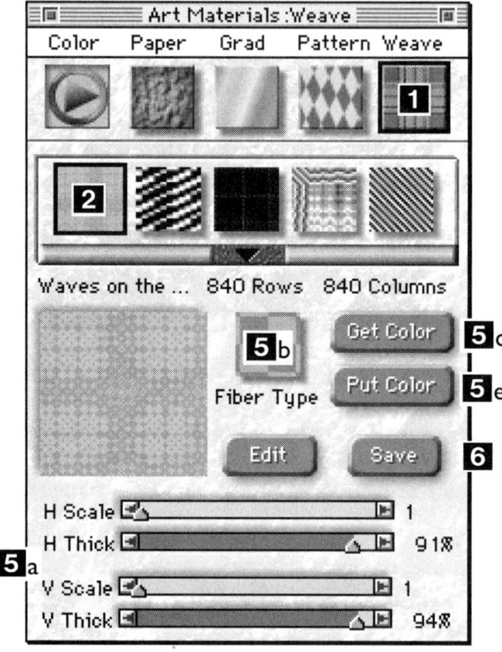

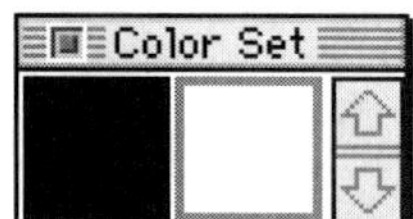

The original color set for Painter's Satin Diamonds weave.

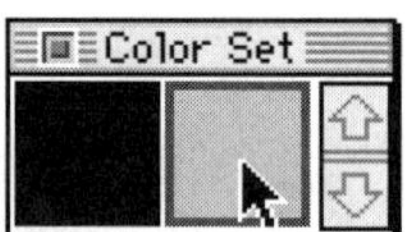

5d *Hold down Option and click a color to replace it with the currently selected Primary color.*

To see the Glass Distortion command applied to a weave, see page 193.

Choose or Modify a Weave

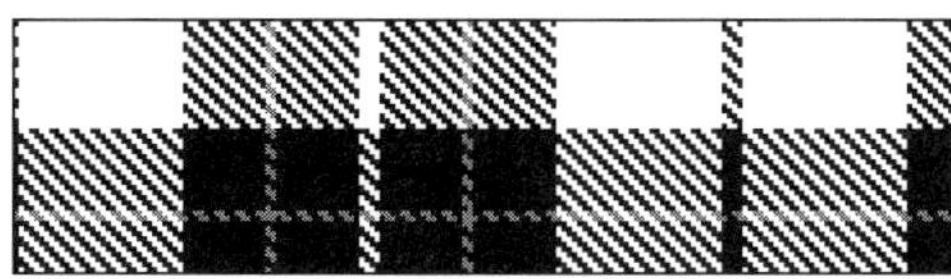

Painter's original Scottish Tartan Brodie B&W.

Same weave, Horizontal and Vertical Scale enlarged to 2 (a 100% increase).

Ray Rue

Ray Rue is a self-taught artist who creates interactive multimedia art using Painter's brushes, Image Hose, lighting effects, and various plug-ins, like Kai's Power Tools and Paint Alchemy. He creates his own trompe-l'oeil wood, metal, and stone textures that he incorporates into his images. Rue is also an illustrator, published poet, non-fiction author, muralist, actor, theater director, stage designer, accordion-player and former Elvis impersonator. We're not kidding.

To **recolor** the weave, click Get Color **5**c. The Color Set palette for the weave will open. Choose a Primary color from the Art Materials: Color palette, then hold down Option and click the swatch on the Color Set palette that you want to replace **5**d. Click Put Color on the Weave palette **5**e. Repeat for any other colors you want to change.

6. *Optional:* To save the weave in the currently open weaves library, click Save **6**, enter a new name for the weave, then click OK. An icon for the modified weave will appear on the Weave palette. (If you don't enter a new name, the modified weave will replace the original.)

7. Follow either set of instructions on page 136 to use the weave as a fill. If you use the Fill command, you can choose an opacity for the weave.

To create or edit a weaves library, see the instructions on pages 21–22.

To design for loom weaving, see pages 142–152 of the Painter 4 User Guide.

Choose or Modify a Weave

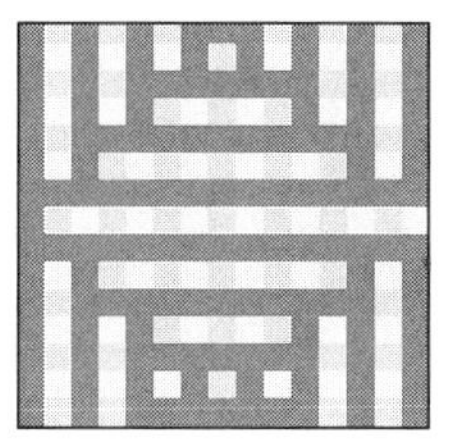

To create an inlaid wood texture (right), Ray Rue filled rectangles in Painter's Shadow Op Art weave (above) with his own light or dark wood texture.

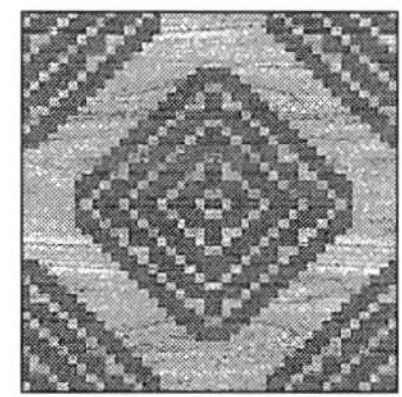

Rue's parquet texture.

Patterns

Are you a textile or wallpaper designer? You'll love the Define Pattern command. As you paint over one edge of your document, the pattern repeats at the opposite edge, creating a perfect wrap-around effect.

Using the Capture Pattern command, you can save a pattern to use as a fill of repetitive tiles in any document. Once a file has been saved as a pattern, it can be opened again and edited.

(The Make Fractal Pattern command is discussed on pages 60–61.)

To choose a pattern:

1. Click the Pattern icon on the Art Materials palette **1**.

2. Click on a pattern icon in the drawer or on the drawer front **2**. To display patterns from a different library, click Library in the Pattern palette drawer, locate and highlight the pattern library you want to open, then click Open.

3. *Optional:* To see a full-window preview of the pattern, choose Art Materials palette > Pattern menu > Check Out Pattern. To edit the pattern, follow the instructions on the next page.

4. Close the palette drawer, and choose a Pattern Type **4**: Rectangular (normal, no Offset); Horizontal (move the Offset slider to stagger tile rows horizontally); or Vertical (move the Offset slider to stagger tile columns vertically). Move the Scale slider to the left to preview the Offset effect on multiple tiles.

5. *Optional:* Move the Scale slider **5** to enlarge or reduce the pattern size.

6. Follow either set of instructions on page 136 to use the pattern as a fill. If you use the Fill command, you can choose an opacity for the pattern.

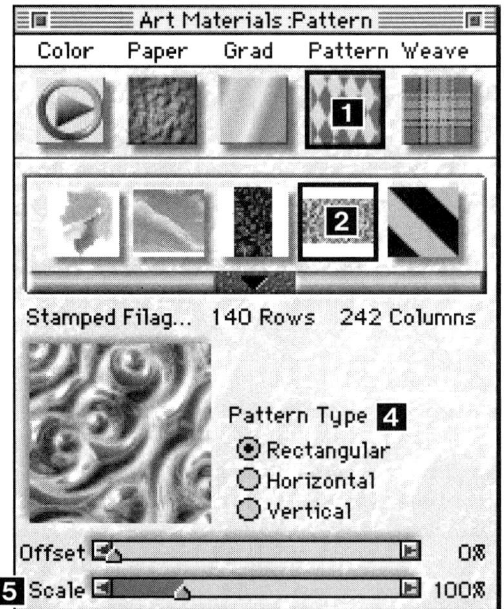

Choose a Pattern

The original pattern.

To edit a pattern:

1. On the Art Materials: Pattern palette, click the icon of the pattern you want to edit.

2. Choose Art Materials palette > Pattern menu > Check Out Pattern.

3. Modify the pattern using any Painter tool or command.

4. Choose Art Materials palette > Pattern menu > Add Image To Library.

5. To save over the existing pattern, don't change the name, click OK, then click Yes.
   or
   To save the pattern as a new pattern, enter a new name for it **5**, then click OK.

After adding a few polka dots.

After the edited pattern is saved, it's used as a fill.

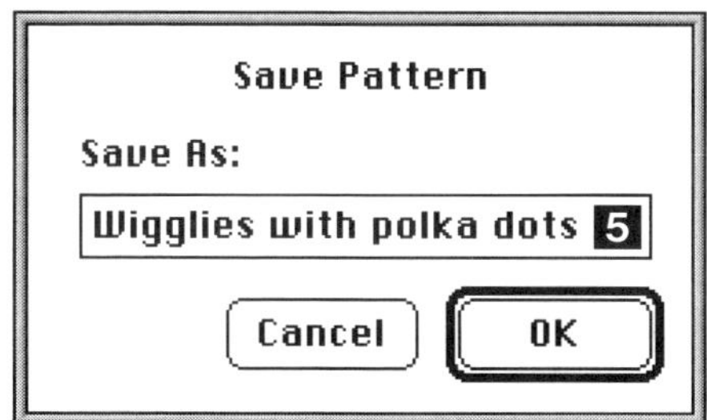

Edit a Pattern

To create a wraparound pattern:

1. Create a new document, and enlarge the image window so you'll be able to draw on and off the edge of the image.

2. Choose Art Materials palette > Pattern menu > Define Pattern.

3. Choose the Brush tool (B).

4. Draw with any brush. The Image Hose works beautifully.

5. To save the pattern in the currently open library, choose Art Materials palette > Palette menu > Add Image To Library, enter a name, then click OK.

6. *Optional:* To use the new pattern as a fill, follow the steps on page 136.

To recolor the pattern, move the Hue slider in the Effects menu > Tonal Control > Adjust Colors dialog box.

To reposition the pattern tiling, hold down Shift and Space bar and drag in the image window. (If the Grabber tool happens to be selected, just hold down Shift.) To blend the seams between tiles, use a Liquid or Water brush variant. Use the Dropper tool (D) to pick up colors from the pattern.

To see how the wraparound effect works, draw from the inside the "live" picture area to far outside it, or vice versa.

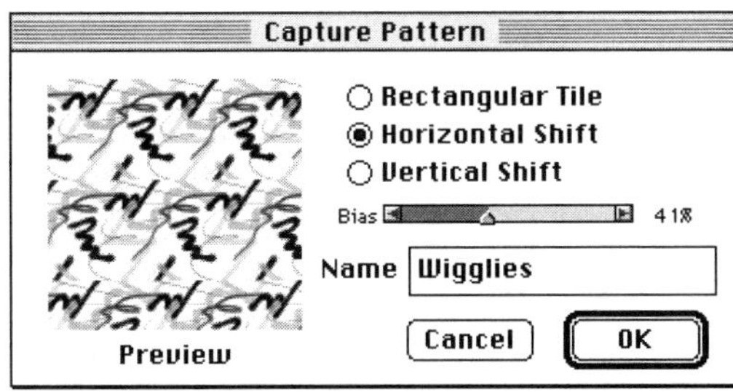

The captured pattern used as a fill.

To capture a pattern from a picture:

1. Open or create a picture to use as a pattern tile. You can use a wrap-around pattern (previous page).

2. To use the whole picture as a pattern tile, choose Edit > Select All (Command-A).
   or
   To use part of a picture as a pattern tile, use the Rectangular Selection tool to create a selection (hold down Shift if you want to create a square selection).

3. Choose Art Materials palette > Pattern menu > Capture Pattern.

4. Choose Rectangular Tile, Horizontal Shift, or Vertical Shift. If you choose either Shift option, you can then move the Bias slider to stagger the tiles.

5. Enter a name for the pattern.

6. Click OK or press Return.

7. Follow either set of instructions on page 136 to use the pattern as a fill. If you use the Fill command, you can choose an opacity for the pattern.

   A captured pattern will automatically become the clone source for painting or for any Effects menu command if you choose Original Luminance from the Using pop-up menu, unless you choose a document as the clone source after you capture the pattern. To paint the pattern in strokes, choose the pattern from the Pattern palette, choose Art Materials palette > Pattern menu > Check Out Pattern, choose the Brush tool, choose any Cloners brush variant or choose a non-cloning brush and the Cloning method category, then paint on another image.

To produce a rubbing from a pattern, see page 161.

Since most Painter strokes are anti-aliased, a normal fill technique might leave small white gaps between the fill and the line work. The cartoon cel fill method prevents this problem. Before you can use the cartoon cel fill method, though, you must create a mask to protect your line work. The Auto Mask command is perfect to use for this step.

To fill using the cartoon cel method:

1. Choose the Brush tool (B).

2. Choose the Scratchboard Tool variant of the Pen brush or any other hard-edged, non-anti-aliased brush.

3. Choose Black as the Primary color.

4. **Draw closed line work shapes. If there is a break in a line work shape, the fill color will leak outside it.**

5. Choose Edit menu > Mask > Auto Mask.

6. Choose Image Luminance from the Using pop-up menu.

7. Click OK or press Return. A mask is now protecting the black line work.

8. Choose the Paint Bucket tool (C).

9. On the Controls: Paint Bucket palette, click What to Fill: Cartoon Cel **9**. *and* Click Fill With: Current Color, Gradation, or Weaving.

10. Choose a Primary color, pattern, gradation, or weave from the Art Materials palette.

11. Click inside any of the line work shapes in the image window.

To display the mask, click the second Visibility (eye) button on the Objects: P. List palette or click the Mask Edit mode icon (image window). Don't click the third Visibility button—you'll lose the mask. If you save the file in the RIFF format, the mask will save with it, even if you remove or erase its matching line work shape. To remove the mask, click Clear on the Objects: P. List palette.

If you use the Lock out color method (next page) without using the cartoon cel fill method, areas may fill incompletely, leaving tiny white dots.

The circles indicate areas to be filled.

Phil Allen

Controls :Paint Bucket

What to Fill	Fill With	
○ Image	⦿ Current Color	○ Gradation
○ Mask	○ Clone Source	○ Weaving
9 ⦿ Cartoon Cel		

The areas are filled.

Dropper *tool*

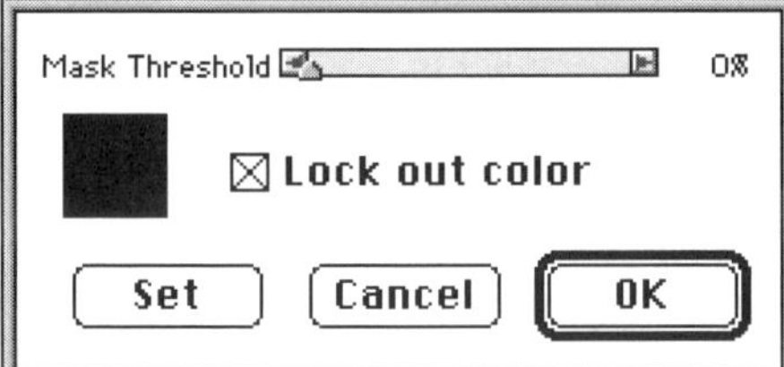

The Lock out color dialog box can be used to protect a solid color area from Paint Bucket fills when What to Fill is set to Image and not Cartoon Cel (on the Controls: Paint Bucket palette).

To lock out a color:

1. Choose the Dropper tool (D), then click on the color in the picture that you want to protect.

2. Double-click the Paint Bucket tool.

3. Click Set to place the current Primary color in the color preview square. The "Lock out color" box will become checked automatically.

4. Click OK or press Return.

To change the Lock out color, choose another Primary color, then click Set.

To turn off the Lock out color feature, double-click the Paint Bucket tool and uncheck the "Lock out color" box.

How to import line art from Illustrator

Save the file in Illustrator 5.0/5.5 or 6 format in Illustrator. In Painter, create or open a file, then choose File menu > Acquire > Adobe Illustrator File. All Illustrator objects will become shapes, and they will be listed on the F. List palette, but only closed shapes can be made into selections. To create masks for the shapes and drop the shapes onto the canvas, check Drop With Mask on the Objects: F. List palette, then click Drop All.

Use the following method in conjunction with the cartoon cel fill method (instructions on the previous page) to protect (lock out) non-black line work.

To lock out non-black lines:

1. Choose the Dropper tool (D).

2. In the image window, click on the lightest shade of line art you want to protect.

3. Note the color's V(alue) setting on the Art Materials: Color palette.

4. Double-click the Paint Bucket tool.

5. Move the Mask Threshold slider slightly above the value (V) percentage that you noted for step 3.

6. Click OK or press Return.

7. Follow the cartoon cel fill instructions on the previous page.

Open line work shapes can be filled using the cartoon cel method if the gaps are first closed using a mask.

To protect open line work for filling:

1. If your image does not contain line work, choose the Brush tool (B), choose the Scratchboard Tool variant of the Pen brush, choose Black as the Primary color, then paint your line work shapes.

2. Choose Edit menu > Mask > Auto Mask.

3. Choose Image Luminance from the Using pop-up menu.

4. Click OK or press Return. A mask is now protecting the black line work.

5. Choose the Mask method category for the current brush.

6. Click the second Visibility button on the extended Objects: P. List palette (bottom row).

7. Use Black as the Primary color and draw on the line work shapes to close the gaps. (Use White if you need to remove the mask.)

8. To hide the mask, click the first Visibility button on the Objects: P. List palette or choose the first icon from the lower left corner of the image window.

9. Follow the instructions on page 146 to fill using the cartoon cel method.

   If you have filled an area with color, don't use the Auto Mask command again—the filled areas will be partially masked. To recreate the mask to protect black line work, choose the Dropper tool, click on a black line, choose Edit menu > Mask > Auto Mask, then choose Current Color from the Using pop-up menu. Click the Mask Edit mode icon in the upper right corner of the image window if you want to view the mask.

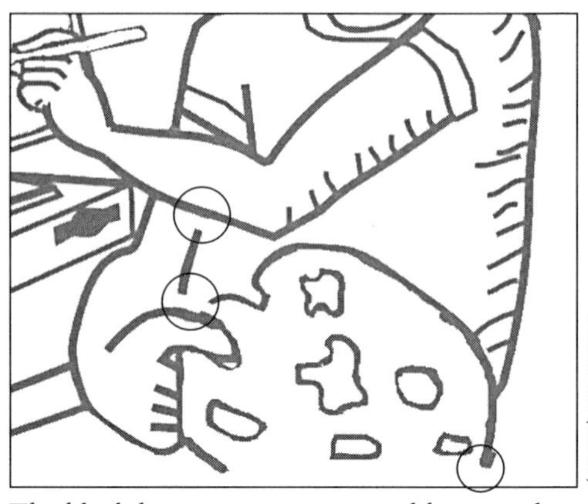

The black lines are now protected by a mask after applying the Auto Mask command using Image Luminance, but the open shapes need to be closed before they can be filled.

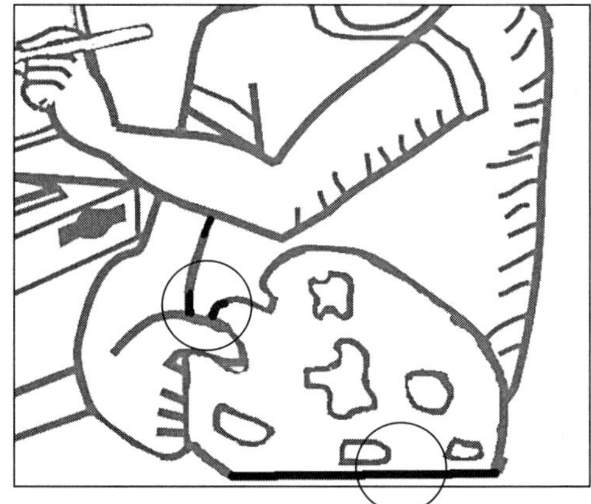

The same image after touching up the mask. Dark gray is used here only to make our point clear—normally you won't be able to differentiate between the Auto Mask and the painted mask.

___

An alternate method

Create the line work as closed shapes first, follow steps 2 through 4 at left, choose the Eraser method category for your brush, then erase where you want the shape to be open—the eraser won't remove your original line work mask.

Masks 9

Fabric Effects, Inc.

Create a Mask from a Selection

Masks

Normally, areas that are covered with a mask are protected from editing. You can create a mask using a Masking brush variant or using any non-Masking brush at 100% opacity with the Mask method category selected. Or, using special Mask commands, you can create a mask based on a color, on a range of colors, on image luminosity values, or on a paper texture. Masks are accessed from the Objects: P. List palette. You can also display a selection path as a mask. In the image window, a mask representation path will have a green dashed marquee to distinguish it from a selection path, which has a black dashed marquee. Floater masks are discussed at the end of this chapter.

To create a mask from a selection:

1. Create a selection. Don't use the Rectangular Selection tool.

2. Click the P. List icon on the Objects palette.

3. Click the second Visibility (eye) button on the extended P. List palette. The selection now displays with color around it.

4. To limit paint strokes to outside the masked area, click the second Drawing button or choose the second Drawing icon from the lower left corner of the image window **4**a.
or
To limit paint strokes to inside the selection, click the third Drawing button or choose the third Drawing icon from the lower left corner of the image window **4**b.

If you open a Photoshop file in Painter 4.0 with a mask in channel #2 (grayscale) or channel #4 (RGB), the mask will become part of the Painter file, but it won't be listed on the Objects: P. List palette right away. Click the third Visibility (eye) button to make the mask name appear on the P. List palette.

If you save a Painter file with a selection path in Photoshop 3.0 format (check the Save Mask Layer box in the Save As dialog box) and then open the file in Photoshop, the mask will appear in channel #4. Any Painter paths will appear on Photoshop's Paths palette. If the Painter document contains more than one selection path, activate the path you're planning to use as a mask in Photoshop before you save the image in Painter.

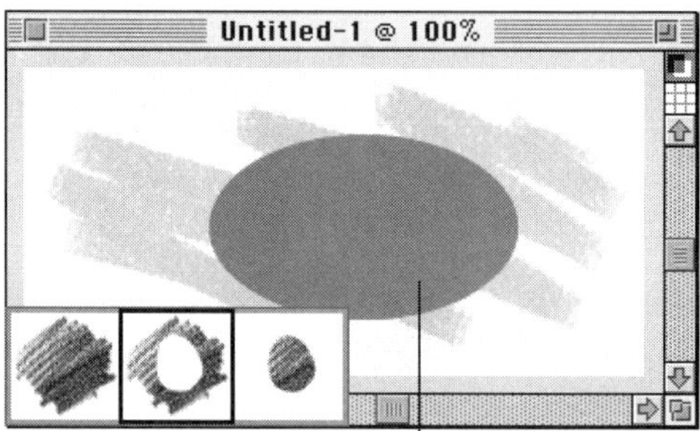

4a *With the second Drawing button selected, the mask protects the selected area.*

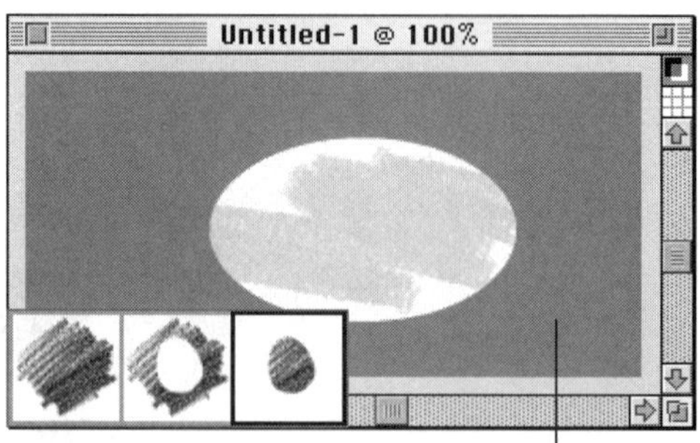

4b *With the third Drawing button selected, the mask protects the unselected area.*

The default Masking brush variants

Grainizer: Large, grainy strokes that reveal paper texture.

Big Masking Pen: Large, anti-aliased, solid circular strokes, clean swipe of mask color. Doesn't reveal paper texture.

Masking Airbrush: Soft spray, default opacity 23%.

Masking Chalk: Smaller version of Grainizer.

Masking Pen: Smaller version of Big Masking Pen.

Single Pixel Masking: Single pixel line. Choose a large display size for your picture when you work with this variant.

A tree trunk is masked to protect it from gestural brush strokes painted outside it.

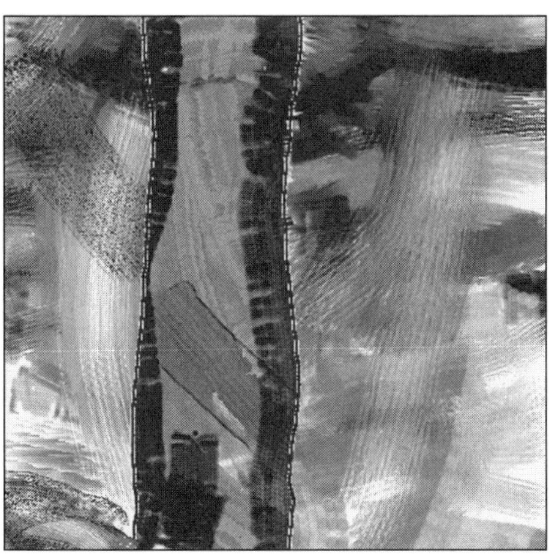

To create a mask using a brush:

1. Click the P. List icon on the Objects palette.
2. Check the Transparent Mask box at the bottom of the extended P. List palette.
3. Choose the Brush tool (B).
4. Choose the Masking brush and one of its variants (see box at left).
   or
   Choose a non-Masking brush, choose the Mask method category, and set the Controls: Brush palette Opacity slider to 100%.
5. Make sure the second Drawing (pencil) button and the second Visibility (eye) button are selected on the extended P. List palette.
6. Paint with Black as the Primary color to create the mask.
   or
   Paint with White as the Primary color to remove the mask.
   or
   Paint with a gray shade between Black and White to create a partial mask. (You may also use the Opacity slider on the Controls: Brush palette to change the mask opacity.)

Reverse these colors if the third Drawing button is selected.

The new mask group name will appear on the P. List palette if you click the third Visibility button on the P. List palette to make the mask into a selection. The mask will have a green dashed marquee when the third Visibility (eye) button is selected. Beware: If you press Return, the mask group will become a selection (black dashed marquee), and if you press Return again, it will become a non-active path. Mask group names appear in green on the P. List.

To reshape a selection using a masking brush:

1. Activate a mask group or a path selection using the Objects: P. List palette.

2. Choose a Masking brush variant or choose the Mask method category for any non-Masking brush.

3. Click the second Drawing button on the Objects: P. List palette.

4. Choose the Brush tool (B).

5. Paint with Black as the Primary color to add to the mask. (Make sure the Opacity slider on the Controls: Brush palette is at 100%.)
or
Paint with White as the Primary color to remove the mask.
or
Paint with a gray shade between Black and White to create a partial mask. (You can also use the Opacity slider on the Controls: Brush palette to change the mask opacity.)

   Reverse these colors if the third Drawing button is selected.

6. Click the third Visibility (eye) button on the Objects: P. List palette to view the mask as a selection. A new mask group will appear on the P. List palette. The original path won't be modified.

7. *Optional:* Press Return to turn the mask representation into a selection. The selection marquee will turn into a black dashed line and the selection name will be listed in blue on the P. List palette.

To modify a mask group

Click the mask group name on the P. List palette, press Return to activate the selection, then follow any of the instructions on page 88.

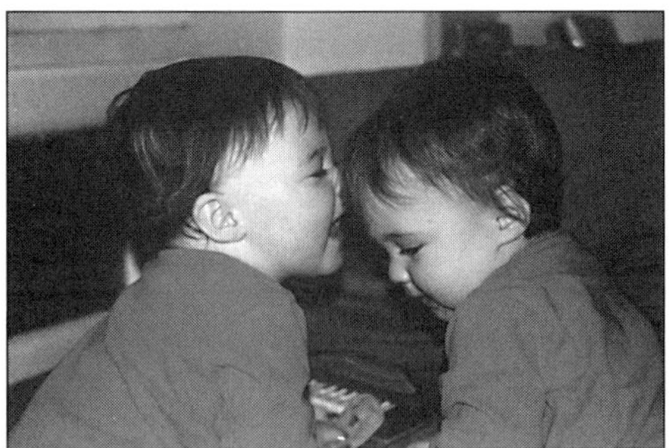

The original image.

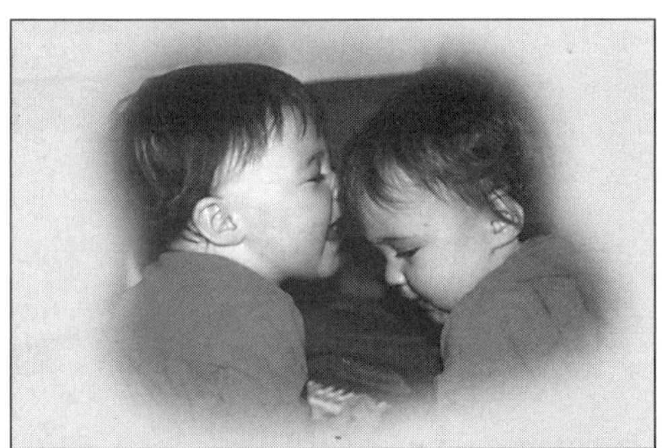

After applying a mask to the area around the figures and then choosing the Feather Mask command.

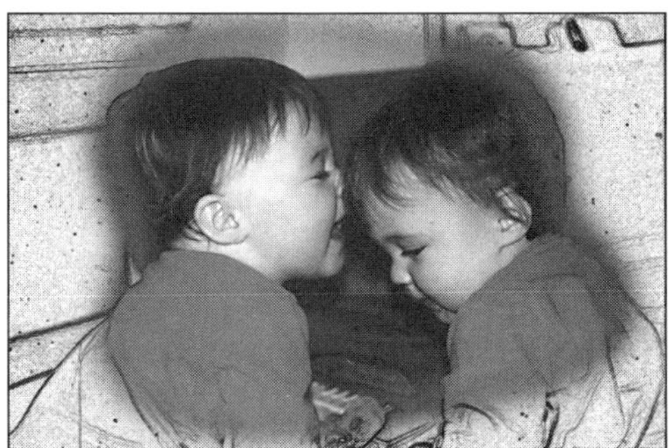

After importing the image and its mask into Photoshop and applying Photoshop's Find Edges filter.

To switch the masked and non-masked areas:

Choose Edit menu > Mask > Invert Mask (Command-Shift-I). This command works on a mask or an active selection.

You can apply the Feather Mask command to a mask group after it is created, whether it is displayed as a selection or as mask color. If you subsequently apply brush strokes or Effects menu commands, you'll reveal the soft transition between the masked and unmasked areas.

Note: If you apply the Feather Mask command to an active selection path, the path will automatically become a mask group, and if you then convert the mask into a selection (by pressing Return), the feather will disappear. To create a feather on a selection path that won't disappear, see page 86.

To feather a mask:

1. Make sure the mask is active.
2. Click the second Visibility (eye) button on the extended Objects: P. List palette to see the feather effect.
3. Choose Edit menu > Mask > Feather Mask.
4. Enter the number of Pixels for the Feather.
5. Click OK or press Return.

To remove a mask:

1. Click the name of the mask group that you want to remove on the Objects: P. List palette.
2. Click Clear on the Objects: P. List palette.

Use the Auto Mask command to create a mask based on a paper texture, luminosity values, or the current Primary color.

To create an Auto Mask:

1. Choose Edit menu > Mask > Auto Mask.

2. Choose a masking method from the **Using** pop-up menu:

   Paper Grain creates a mask based on the raised and lowered parts of a texture. Click Invert to reverse the masked and non-masked areas.

   3D Brush Strokes creates a mask in a clone based on highlights and shadows of 3D modeled strokes in the source picture, *provided* the clone was produced using strokes and the Apply Surface Texture command was applied to it with 3D Brush Strokes chosen from the Using pop-up menu.

   Original Mask creates a mask in a clone based on the mask in the source picture. Use to copy the source image mask into the clone image's mask layer.

   Image Luminance creates a mask based on the the picture's light and dark values. Shadow areas will receive a 100% mask; highlight areas won't be masked. High contrast pictures create well defined mask areas.

   Original Luminance uses the lights and darks in the source picture to create a mask in a clone.

   Current Color masks color areas in the picture that match the current Primary color. Use the Dropper tool to grab a color from the picture first.

3. Click OK or press Return.

4. Click the second Visibility (eye) button on the extended P. List palette to display the mask color.

5. Click the second Drawing (pencil) button to paint around the mask or click the third Drawing button to paint inside the mask.

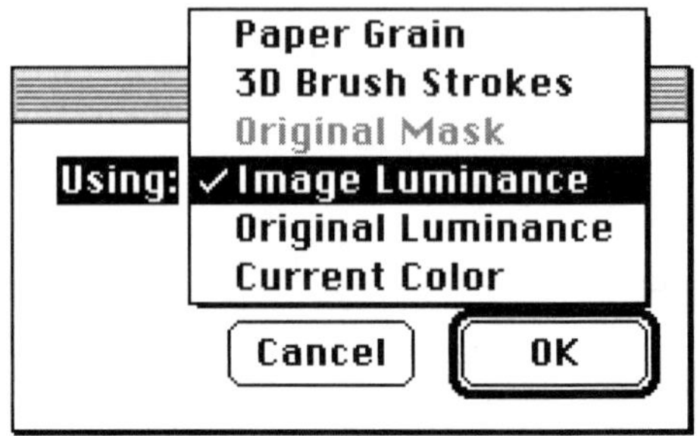

If there is no clone source document and you choose Using: 3D Brush Strokes or Original Luminance, the pattern currently selected on the Art Materials: Pattern palette will be used as the source.

The barn is masked (the white area).

Color Mask

H Extents   20%
H Feather   100%
S Extents   100%
S Feather   100%
V Extents   24%
V Feather   100%
Click in image to set center color.
Preview
Inverted   Cancel   OK

To create a mask based on a color in the picture:

1. Choose Edit menu > Mask > Color Mask.

2. Click on a color in the image window. The H(ue), S(aturation) and V(alue) extent sliders will calibrate automatically based on that color's HSV values.

3. Do any of the following:

   Press and drag in the preview window to preview other areas of the picture.

   Move the H Extent slider to the right to add colors close in **hue** to the chosen color or to the left to narrow the hue range.

   Move the S Extent slider to the right to add colors close in **saturation** to the chosen color or to the left to narrow the saturation range.

   Move the V Extent slider to the right to add colors close in **value** to the chosen color or to the left to create more abrupt transitions.

   Move the H, S, or V **Feather** slider to the right to soften the transition between the masked and unmasked areas.

4. Click OK or press Return.

5. To display the mask in the image window, click the second Visibility button on the Objects: P. List palette or click the Mask Edit mode icon on the image window.

6. Click the second Drawing button to make the unmasked areas editable.
   or
   Click the third Drawing button to make the masked areas editable.

Floaters and their masks

Every floater automatically has a mask that matches its shape. You can mask part of a floater itself or disable the mask altogether. To display and edit a floater's mask, use the Floater Mask Visibility buttons (top row of buttons on the extended Objects: F. List palette). To control how a floater interacts with a mask or an active selection, use the Image Mask Visibility buttons (bottom row of buttons).

The Floater Mask Visibility buttons

With the floater active, click the **Masking Disabled** (first button) to disable the floater mask. The floater's original background displays within the masked area.

Click the **Masked Inside** (second button) to mask the floater itself. Use a Masking brush variant or use any non-Masking brush at 100% opacity with the Mask method category selected to modify the floater's mask. Paint with White as the Primary color to add to the mask and hide more of the floater. Paint with Black as the Primary color to remove parts of the mask (and reveal areas of the floater's original background or restore areas that you may have inadvertently painted out using White). If parts of the floater become exposed as you apply masking brush strokes, beware—you're actually masking parts of the floater.

Click the **Masked Outside** (third button) to mask the floater's background, but not the floater shape itself. This is the default setting when a floater is active. With this button selected, painting with a masking brush with White will remove parts of the floater and painting with a masking brush with Black will expose the floater's original background.

Whatever is visible, including the mask or original background of the floater, will drop into the background if you click the Drop button.

Icon for the row of Floater Mask Visibility buttons.

Masking Disabled button.

Masked Inside button. The floater itself is masked. The background picture will show through the current masked area.

Masked Outside button, the default visibility mode. The floater is visible, but its background is not.

Modify a floater mask using Mask Edit
With the floater active, click the Mask Edit mode icon in the upper right corner of the image window. Paint with black to add to the mask; paint with white to remove the mask.

Floater Masks

THE FLOATER MASK VISIBILITY OPTIONS

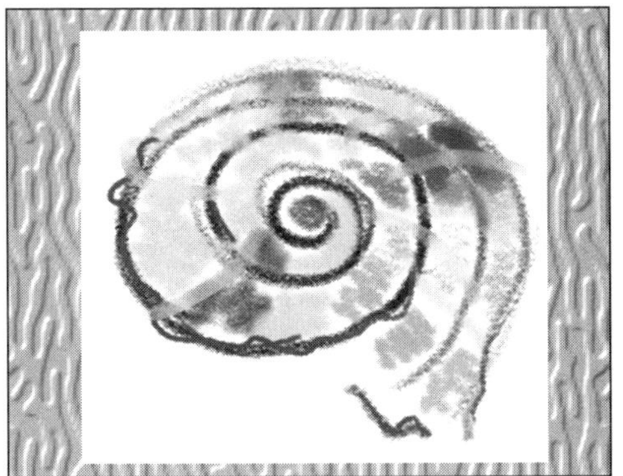

Masking Disabled button. The floater and its original background are visible.

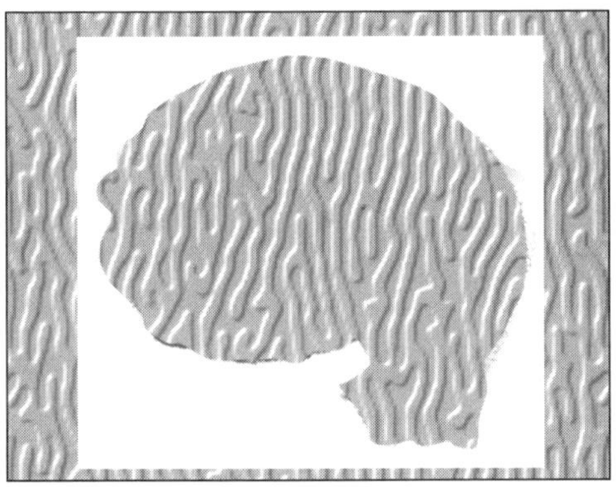

Masked Inside button. The floater is masked.

Masked Outside button. The floater's background is masked.

To unmask parts of a floater that you may have inadvertently covered:

1. Click the third Floater Mask Visibility button so you'll be able to see the floater as you draw with a masking brush.

2. Choose the Brush tool (B).

3. Choose a Masking brush variant.
   or
   Choose the Mask method category for any non-Masking brush.

4. Choose Black as the Primary color to remove parts of the mask and reveal parts of the floater that may have been inadvertently covered. Be careful not to paint outside the floater shape.
   or
   Choose White as the Primary color to hide parts of the floater's original background.

If the original floater was created from the canvas (it didn't originate from the Floaters palette), you can remove masking brush strokes and restore the original floater mask by clicking Restore on the Objects: F. List palette. A bug in Painter 4.0 makes the Restore button unavailable for non-canvas floaters.

Mask part of a floater with a background selection:

1. Create or activate a selection path. Don't use the Rectangular Selection tool.

2. Position a floater so it partially overlaps the selection.

3. Click the **Masked Inside** Visibility button (second button on the bottom row) of the extended Objects: F. List palette to display only parts of the floater that don't overlap the selection.

   or

   Click the **Masked Outside** Visibility button (third button on the bottom row) to display only parts of the floater that overlap the selection.

   Click the Masking Disabled (first) button to have the floater be unaffected by any active background selection.

THE IMAGE MASK VISIBILITY BUTTONS

 *Icon for the row of Image Mask Visibility buttons.*

 *Masking Disabled button. This is the default image mask visibility mode. The whole floater is visible.*

 *Masked Inside button. Only parts of the floater that don't overlap the selection are visible.*

 *Masked Outside button. Only parts of the floater that overlap the selection are visible.*

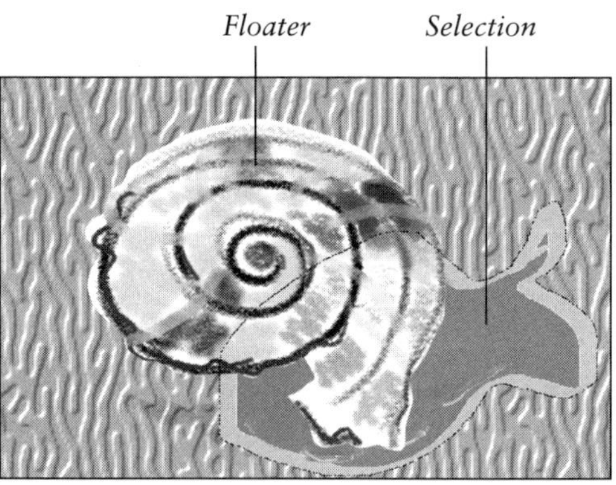

Masking Disabled.

Masked Inside. Only parts of the floater that don't overlap the selection are visible.

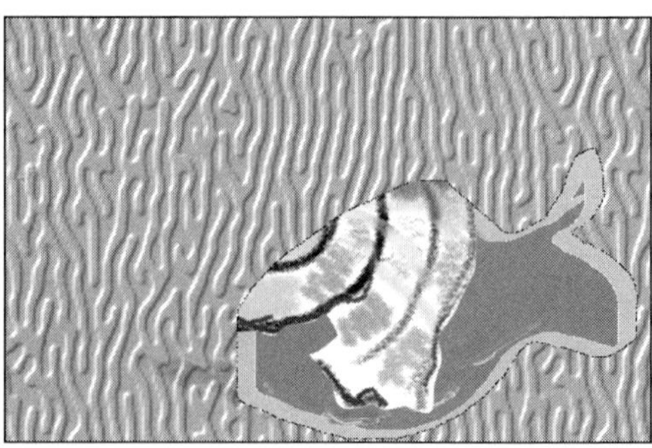

Masked Outside. Only parts of the floater that overlap the selection are visible.

Mask Edit off.   *Mask Edit* on.

The original image.

A pattern pasted into the mask layer.

Diane Margolin

*The final image, after
drawing brush strokes
on the mask in Mask
Edit mode using Masking
Chalk and applying the
Apply Surface Texture
command.*

Mask Edit mode

In Mask Edit mode, the image mask displays in grayscale and the color image is hidden. You can use any brush or any Effects menu command to modify the mask.

To edit a mask in Mask Edit mode:

1. Open a document that contains a mask or use a masking brush to create a mask on the current document.

2. Click the Mask Edit mode icon on the vertical scroll bar of the image window **2**.

3. Choose the Brush tool, and paint on the mask to make it look textured or brushy. Use black to add to the mask; use white to remove masked areas; or use gray to create a partial mask.
   or
   Apply any Effects menu command.

4. Click the Mask Edit mode icon to redisplay the color image.

   If a floater is selected and displayed, only the floater's mask will display while Mask Edit mode is turned on. Deselect and hide the floater if you want to work on the image mask.

   If a mask is converted into a selection (by clicking on the third Visibility button on the Objects: P. List palette and then pressing Return) and the selection is active, the mask will be visible only when Mask Edit mode is on.

Mask Edit Mode

Mask Edit mode and Effects menu commands

On this page and the next two pages are suggestions for ways to use Effects menu commands while your picture is displayed in Mask Edit mode. Feel free to concoct your own formulas.

To remove gray areas of a mask and preserve the black areas:

1. Click the Mask Edit mode icon.
2. Choose Effects menu > Tonal Control > Equalize (Command-E).
3. Move the Black slider to the right to make gray areas black.
4. Move the White slider to the left to remove gray areas.
5. Click OK or press Return.

To soften a mask:

1. Click the Mask Edit mode icon.
2. Choose Edit > Mask > Feather Mask.
3. Enter a value in the Feather field.
4. Click OK or press Return. The edge of the mask will be feathered.

1. The original image.

2. The image pasted into the mask layer, and the Equalize command applied.

3. The Feather Mask command applied.

4. The final image, after applying the Glass Distortion command.

Diane Margolin

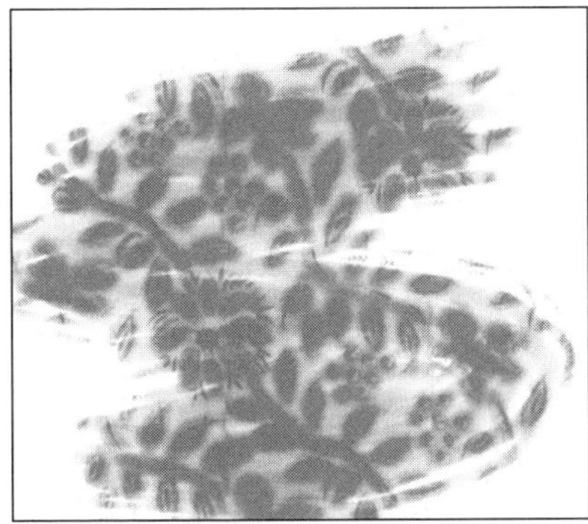

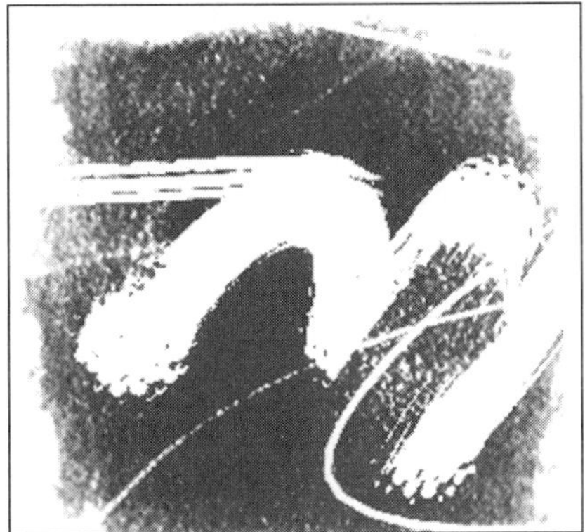

Rubbings.

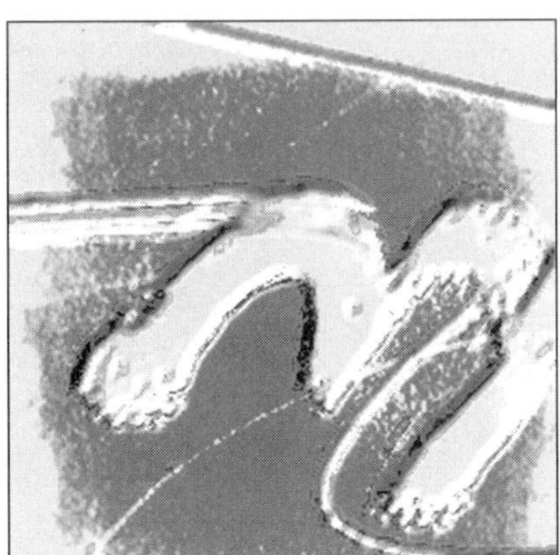

An embossed rubbing.

To create a rubbing of a pattern using a mask:

1. Create a new, blank document.
2. Click the Mask Edit mode icon.
3. Choose a pattern from the Art Materials: Pattern palette.
4. Choose Effects menu > Fill (Command-F).
5. Click Fill With: Pattern.
6. Click OK or press Return.
7. Click the Mask Edit mode icon to redisplay the color image.
8. To create the rubbing, choose a brush, then paint inside the mask (second Drawing button on the Objects: P. List palette), or around the mask (third Drawing button). The Chalk variants work well.

To emboss the pattern using the mask:

1. Follow the previous set of instructions.
2. Click the Mask Edit mode icon.
3. Choose Effects menu > Surface Control > Express Texture, choose Using: Original Luminance, adjust the Gray Threshold, Grain, and Contrast sliders, if necessary, then click OK. The current pattern is now inside the mask area.
4. Click the Mask Edit mode icon to redisplay the color image.
5. Choose Effects > Surface Control > Apply Surface Texture, choose Using: Mask, adjust the sliders for color and lighting effects, then click OK.

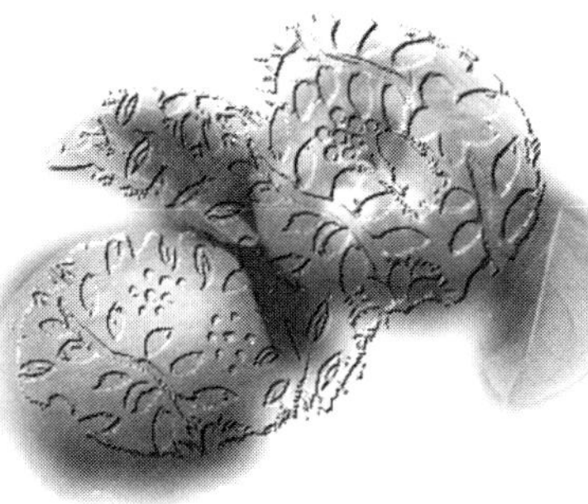

To emboss a pattern on the apples, we drew a mask for the apples, and then followed steps 2–5 above.

To gradually fade a color image to gray:

1. Open an image.

2. Click the Mask Edit mode icon.

3. Choose black as the Primary color and white as the Secondary color.

4. On the Art Materials: Grad palette, choose the Two-Point gradient.

5. Choose Edit menu > Fill (Command-F).

6. Click Fill With: Gradation, move the Opacity slider to about 15%, then click OK.

7. Click the Mask Edit mode icon to redisplay to the color image.

8. On the Objects: P. List palette, click the third Visibility button to convert the mask into a selection. Click the second or third Drawing button to mask one side of the image or the other.

9. Choose Effects menu > Tonal Control > Adjust Colors.

10. Choose Using: Mask.

11. Move the Saturation slider all the way to the left.

12. Click OK or press Return.

To create a 3D effect using a mask:

1. Create an image.

2. To copy the whole image to the mask, choose Edit menu > Mask > Auto Mask, choose Using: Image Luminance, then click OK.

3. Click the Mask Edit mode icon to view the mask, then click the Mask Edit mode icon again to redisplay the color image.

4. Choose Effects menu > Surface Control > Apply Surface Texture.

5. Choose Using: Mask. Move the Softness slider to adjust the 3D effect.

6. Click OK or press Return.

🖌 Tint a 3D image using Effects menu > Surface Control > Color Overlay.

The mask.

Lourekas

The final 3D image.

The canvas image was selected and deleted (after step 3 in the instructions below, left) to produce a shallow, embossed look (below).

The mask. 

The final 3D image.

Diane Margolin

Cloning 10

Peter Lourekas, **Figure & Shroud** *(detail).*

Cloning

Use the Clone command to recreate an entire document exactly as the original. Or use a Cloners brush variant to clone all or part of the source image in its original colors, stroke by stroke, in different media—as a pencil sketch, for example, or an oil painting or a watercolor. When you use a Cloners brush variant, you control stroke direction, number of strokes, opacity, and graininess. Another reason to clone a document is so that if you modify the clone, you'll have the option to use the Straight Cloners variant like an eraser to restore areas from the source image.

Other cloning features include the Tracing command, which you can turn on to trace over a ghosted version of the clone, the Auto Clone command, which does the brush stroking for you, and the Auto Van Gogh command, which automatically recreates an image in quasi-Van Gogh style.

To clone a whole image exactly:

1. Open the picture you want to clone (the source document).

2. Choose File menu > Clone. The clone image will appear in a new image window.

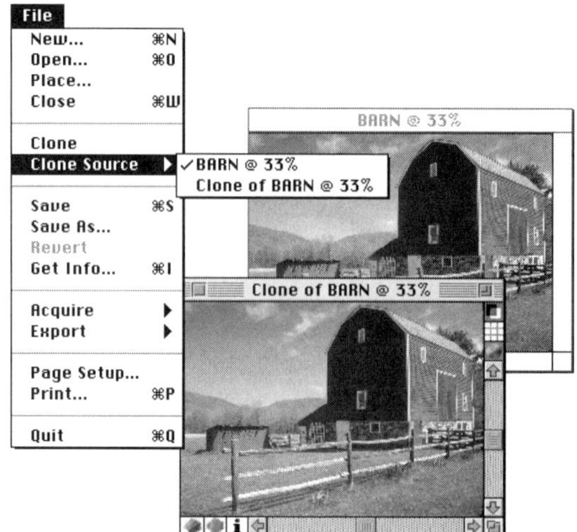

To trace a picture

Clone the image (File menu > Clone). With the clone image active, choose Edit menu > Select All (Command-A) and press Delete. Turn on Tracing Paper (Canvas menu), then draw using a fine point brush, like the Sharp Pencil variant of the Pencils brush or the Fine Point variant of the Pens brush (Cover or Buildup method category).

Tracing contours, Tracing Paper turned on.

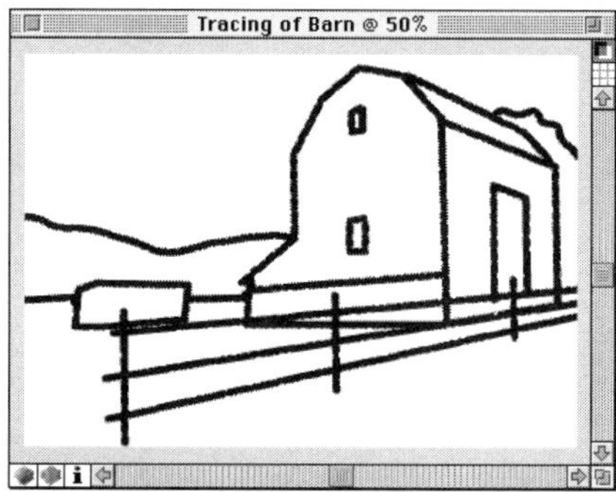

Tracing Paper turned off.

Cloning tips

- If you close the source or the clone document, the source/clone link will be broken. To reestablish the source/clone link, open both documents, click in the clone image window, then choose the source document name from the Clone Source submenu under the File menu.

- To clone from a second source document, open it and choose its name from the Clone Source submenu under the File menu.

- To clone more randomly, experiment with the Clone Location sliders and check the Random Clone Source box on the Advanced Controls: Random palette (see page 72). To add random color, raise the Color Variability setting (Color palette).

- To restore part of the source document in the clone, use the Straight Cloner variant. To restore the entire source image, choose Edit menu > Select All, press Delete, choose the Paint Bucket tool, click What to Fill: Image and Fill With: Clone Source on the Controls: Paint Bucket palette, then click on the image.

To clone manually using brush strokes:

1. Open the document you want to clone (the source document).

2. Choose File menu > Clone.

3. *Optional:* With the clone image active, choose Edit menu > Select All, then press Delete if you don't want to paint on the existing image, or lighten the image using Dye Concentration.

4. Choose the Brush tool (B).

5. Choose a Cloners brush variant.
   or
   Choose a non-Cloners brush and check the Use Clone Color box on the expanded Art Materials: Color palette. Don't choose the Cloning method category.

6. *Optional:* Turn on Tracing Paper to display a light, non-editable version of the image behind your paint strokes. Click the Tracing Paper icon in the upper right corner of the clone image window or choose Canvas menu > Tracing Paper (Command-T).

   Note: For Tracing Paper to work, the source and clone documents must have the same dimensions and resolution, as in these instructions.

7. *Optional:* To establish a custom source point for cloning, activate the source image window, then hold down Control and click on the area of the source image that you want to clone.

8. Draw in the clone image window. Try drawing short brush strokes at first. If you turned on Tracing Paper, turn it off occasionally to monitor your progress. (Just choose the command again or click the icon.)

   Choose a different method category or subcategory for the Cloners brush. If you find the Buildup method category causes strokes to darken too quickly, choose the Cover method category instead. Choose a Grainy method subcategory to reveal the current paper texture under your strokes.

Clone from a Specific Source Point; Cloners Variants

To clone from a specific source point in the same or another image:

1. Choose a Cloners variant or choose the Cloning method category for a non-Cloners brush.

2. Hold down Control and click on the area you want to clone.

3. Draw brush strokes in the same or another image window where you want the cloned imagery to appear.

To see exactly which part of the source document you're cloning from, choose Edit menu > Preferences > General, and check the "Indicate clone source with cross hairs while cloning" box.

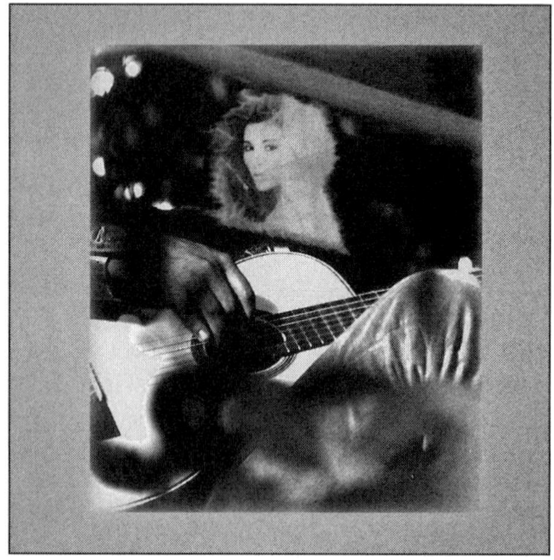

To produce this illustration for a CD cover, Johanna Gillman cloned a photograph of a woman behind a guitar figure.

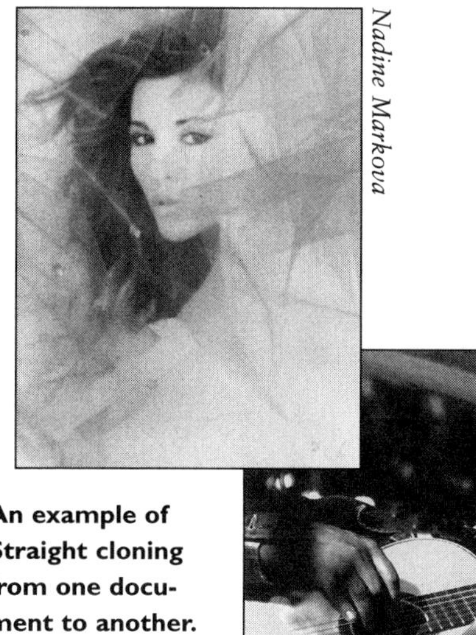

Nadine Markova

An example of Straight cloning from one document to another.

The Cloners brush variants

There are two main Cloners brush variant types—Single Cloners and Multi or Rake Cloners—and of course they produce different kinds of strokes. (The Single, Multi, and Rake Stroke Types are chosen from the Brush Controls: Spacing palette.) Except for the Straight Cloner and Soft Cloner variants, the Cloners brush variants clone in different media than the source picture.

The Single Stroke Type Cloners brush variants (Chalk, Pencil Sketch, Felt Pen, Melt, Driving Rain, and Impressionist)

Chalk. (The original image is on page 168.)

Melt

Pencil Sketch

Oil Brush

match colors from corresponding areas in the source document. A continuous stroke with any of these variants will duplicate the source picture's color and detail, though in different media.

When you use a Multi or Rake Stroke Type Cloners brush variant (Hairy, Hard Oil, Oil Brush, or Van Gogh), the first sampled color is maintained for the full length of the stroke, so it's best to draw short brush strokes with these variants. Non-Cloners brushes also follow this rule of Single versus Multi or Rake Stroke Type when the Use Clone Color box is checked and brush strokes are applied to a clone image.

To clone in the same media as the source picture, use the Straight Cloner variant or use the Cloning method category for any non-Cloners brush. Only the brush shape will vary. (Choose a Grainy sub-method category to reveal texture as you clone.) Choose the Soft Cloner variant to create a soft, airbrushed clone.

Some Cloners method subcategories

Hard Cover. Semi-anti-aliased strokes that cover existing color. The source document is reproduced clearly.

Soft Cover. Soft, anti-aliased strokes that cover existing color. The source document is reproduced clearly.

Grainy Hard Cover, Grainy Soft Cover. Semi-anti-aliased and anti-aliased, respectively. Strokes reveal the current paper texture. **Grainy Flat** also reveals paper texture.

Drip. Distorts the image by pushing color around and produces a wet, crumbly surface texture.

To compare Cloners brush variants
Choose Brushes palette > Brushes menu > Brush Look Designer, draw a brush stroke in the preview window, then note the preview as you choose other Cloners variants from the Brushes palette.

Auto Clone

The Auto Clone command clones automatically, dab by dab, in the Cloners brush variant of your choice. Painter does the brush stroking—you just sit and watch! You can clone right over an existing photograph to make it look more painterly or you can clone onto a blank canvas.

To clone automatically:

1. Open the image you want to clone.

2. *Optional:* To clone onto a blank canvas, choose File menu > Clone, choose Edit menu > Select All, then press Delete.

3. Choose the Brush tool (B).

4. Choose a Cloners brush variant, method category and method subcategory. If you choose a Grainy method subcategory, choose a paper texture from the Art Materials: Paper palette.
   or
   Choose any non-Cloners brush (don't choose the Cloning method category) and check the Use Clone Color box on the Art Materials: Color palette.

5. Choose Effects menu > Esoterica > Auto Clone.

6. To stop the auto cloning, click in the clone image window.

> To clone different areas of your picture using different brush sizes or variants, create a selection before you choose the Auto Clone command. Try using a smaller brush for details, like facial features.

> To add variety and create a less "machine made" look, interrupt the auto cloning, choose a different brush variant or paper texture, or change your brush size, or adjust the Color Variability sliders on the expanded Color palette, and then resume auto cloning.

> Use the Straight Cloner or Soft Cloner variant at a very low opacity to restore details from the original image.

To clone using a recorded brush stroke

Choose the Brush tool (B), choose a non-Cloners brush, choose Brushes palette > Stroke menu > Record Stroke, draw a stroke, then choose Edit menu > Undo Brush Stroke. Activate the clone image window, choose a Cloners brush variant (or choose a non-Cloners brush and check the Use Clone Color box on the Art Materials: Color palette), then choose Brushes palette > Stroke menu > Auto Playback. Click in the image window to stop the Auto Playback.

The original image.

(close-up)

Auto Clone with Hard Oil Cloner variant

Artists brush, Auto Van Gogh variant, Record Stroke, Auto Playback.

Artists brush, Auto Van Gogh variant, Effects menu > Esoterica > Auto Van Gogh.

Let's be honest—Van Gogh Cloning techniques will produce a clone in Impressionistic-like dabs or strokes, but it won't be a Van Gogh.

To produce a "Van Gogh" clone:

1. Open the document you want to clone (the source document).

2. Choose File menu > Clone.

3. With the clone image window active, choose Edit menu > Select All (Command-A).

4. Press Delete.

5. Use any one of the following three methods:

   To draw the brush strokes yourself, choose the Artists brush and the Van Gogh variant, check the Use Clone Color box on the expanded Art Materials: Color palette, then draw short, "Impressionistic" strokes.
   or
   To clone automatically in little orzo-shaped strokes, choose the Artists brush and the Auto Van Gogh variant, choose Brushes palette > Stroke menu > Record Stroke, draw one stroke, then choose Brushes palette > Stroke menu > Auto Playback. Click in the image window to stop the playback.
   or
   To render the clone automatically, but in strokes that follow the forms and lights-and-darks of the source image more closely, choose the Artists brush and the Auto Van Gogh brush variant, then choose Effects menu > Esoterica > Auto Van Gogh.

Embossed or Line Art Clone

To produce an embossed or line art clone:

1. Open the document you want to clone (the source document).

2. Choose File menu > Clone.

3. With the clone image window active, choose Edit menu > Select All.

4. Press Delete.

5. If you want to emboss the clone, choose a Primary color from the Art Materials: Color palette or the Color Set palette, choose Effects menu > Fill, click Current Color, then click OK.

   To produce a line art rendering, leave the clone blank.

6. Choose Effects menu > Surface Control > Apply Surface Texture.

7. Choose Using: 3D Brush Strokes or Original Luminance.

8. Do any of the following:

   Move the Softness slider to the right to blur edges.

   Move the Amount slider to add depth.

   Move the Picture slider to lighten or darken.

   Move the Shine slider to the right to emphasize the highlights.

   Move the Reflection slider to the right to add more color or to the left for a line art effect.

   Move any of the Light Controls sliders, click a different Light Direction button to change the angle of the cast light, or move the light source dot.

   Move the picture in the preview window.

9. Click OK.

   For a beautiful effect, choose a non-Cloners brush and the Cloning method category (or the Soft Cloner variant of the Cloners brush), lower the Opacity to 2 or 3 percent (Controls: Brush palette), then stroke lightly over the clone to restore some of the source image color.

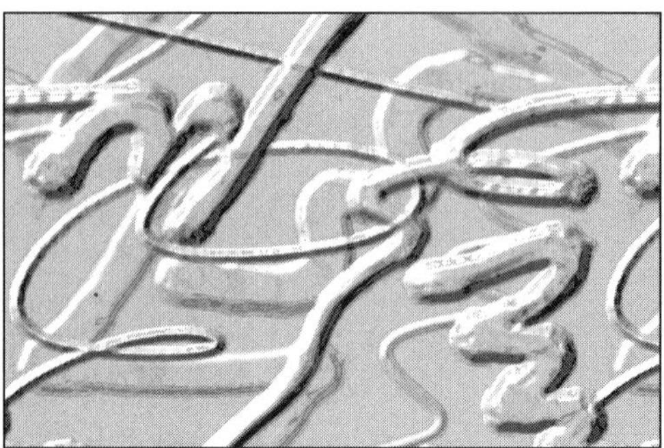

Embossed clone

To remove gray shades in a line art clone, move the Picture slider and the Brightness or Exposure slider to the right. A line art clone works very well as a starting sketch, over which you can apply colored brush strokes. The Straight Cloners variant was applied to this picture in broad brush strokes to restore a few details from the source image.

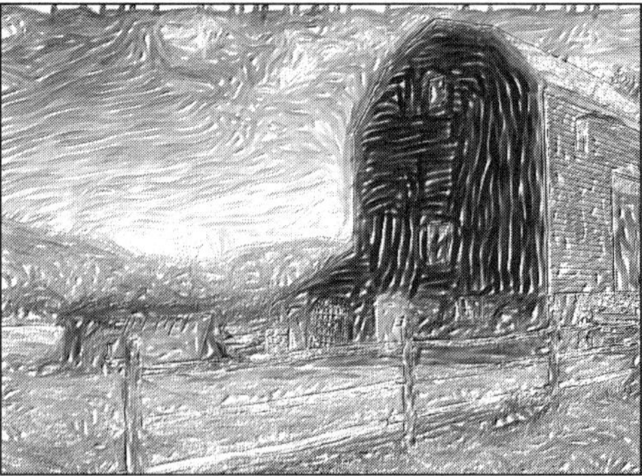

And a third variation: A picture cloned using the Auto Van Gogh variant of the Artists brush and the Auto Van Gogh command, then an impasto texture created via Apply Surface Texture (3D Brush Strokes).

Effects Menu   11

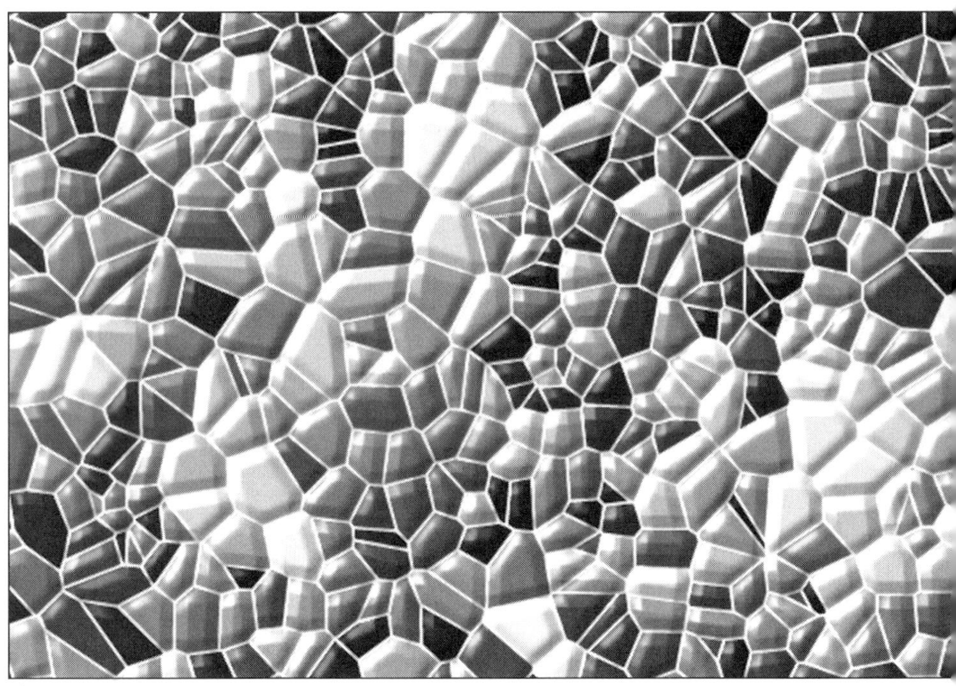

Elaine Weinmann.

Important things to know about the Effects menu commands

- Effects menu (image editing) commands don't work on the Wet Paint layer. To dry brush strokes on the Wet Paint layer, choose Canvas menu > Dry.

- If the dialog box has a preview window, you can press and drag inside it to display a different part of the picture. Most commands preview in the dialog box, but not in the picture, unfortunately.

- You can restrict any Effects menu command to an active selection, a shape, or a floater. To image edit the whole picture, make sure no selection, shape, or floater is active before you choose the command.

- To adjust a clone, make sure the clone window is active and the clone source document name is selected from the File menu > Clone Source submenu before choosing the Effects menu command.

- Shortcuts:

  Command-/ to reopen the last opened Effects menu dialog box.

  Command-; to reopen the second-to-last opened Effects menu dialog box.

  Command-. to cancel a command while it's processing.

- You can choose from the Art Materials palettes—like the Color palette or Paper palette—while the Effects menu dialog box is open.

- Plug-in filters are accessed from the Effects menu (see page 237).

- When adjusting with the Using: Mask option, not all sliders work predictably.

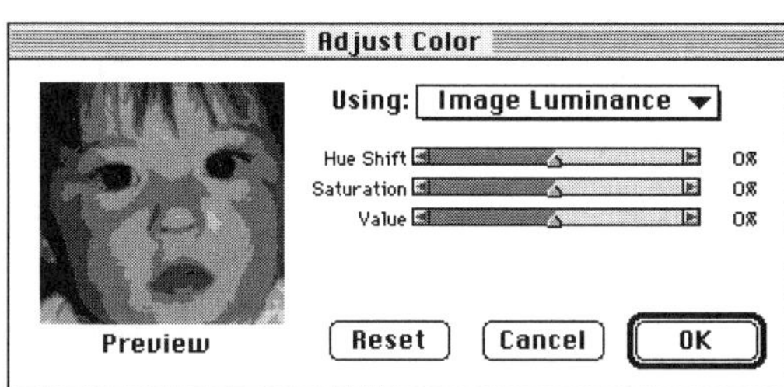

The Tonal Control commands

Use the **Adjust Colors** dialog box to change the dominant color cast, saturation, or value (brightness) of an entire image or of a selection.

To change a picture's hue, saturation, or value:

1. Choose Effects menu > Tonal Control > Adjust Colors (Command-Shift-A).

2. Choose from the **Using** pop-up menu:

   Uniform Color: Adjusts colors without applying a paper texture.

   Paper Grain: Adjusts colors and applies the current paper texture.

   Mask: White areas in the mask are affected, black areas in the mask are not affected, gray areas are partially affected.

   Image Luminance: Adjusts color based on light and dark values in the image.

   Original Luminance: Adjusts color in a clone based on light and dark values in the source image.

3. Move the **Hue Shift** slider to shift the picture's colors along the color wheel.

   Move the **Saturation** slider to adjust color intensity.

   Move the **Value** slider to lighten or darken the picture.

4. *Optional:* Click Reset at any time to restore the original settings.

5. Click OK or press Return.

   Beware of oversaturating a picture if it's going to be printed. Choose Effects menu > Tonal Control > Printable Colors to force the picture's colors into the printable range.

   Move the Saturation slider to the left to make a photograph look hand tinted. Move the Saturation slider all the way to the left to turn a color picture into a grayscale picture.

Use the Correct Colors command to correct a color cast by adjusting the R,G, or B components of an image individually, or to adjust brightness and contrast.

To correct colors:

1. *Optional:* If you want to use the Correct Colors command to reset the White point (lightest part of the image) or the Black point (darkest part of the image), choose the Dropper tool, then click on the color you want to become the darkest or lightest in the image.

2. Choose Effects menu > Tonal Control > Correct Colors.

3. Click the red, green, or blue swatch to adjust that color individually, or click the master (gray) icon to adjust R,G, and B simultaneously.

4. Choose an adjustment method from the pop-up menu, and move the corresponding sliders:

   Contrast and Brightness—Increase Contrast to reduce the midtone values and push luminosity values to the extreme ends of the spectrum. Increase Brightness to lighten the image.

   Curve—Drag from the diagonal line upward to lighten that value range— highlights, midtones, or shadows— or drag downward to darken. The higher the Effect slider setting, the more gentle the curve. Lower the Effect setting to target a specific luminosity range. If you chose a color with the Dropper for step 1, above, click Black Point or White Point.

   Freehand—Draw the curve yourself.

   Advanced—Set the red, green, and blue curves by specifying numbers for five luminosity values.

5. *Optional:* Click Reset if you need to restore the default Color Correction dialog box settings.

6. Click OK or press Return.

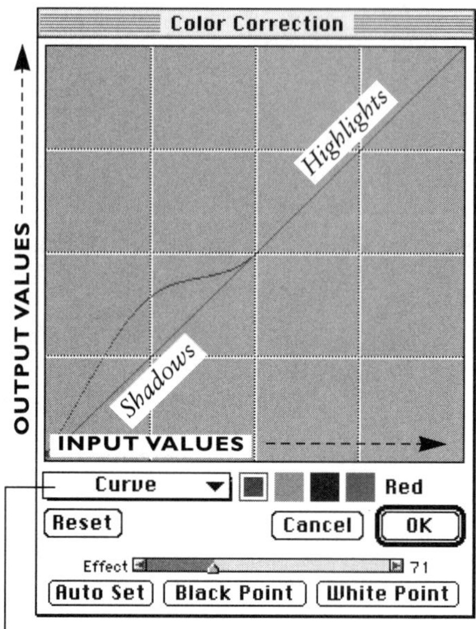

Choose an adjustment method from this pop-up menu.

Correct Colors

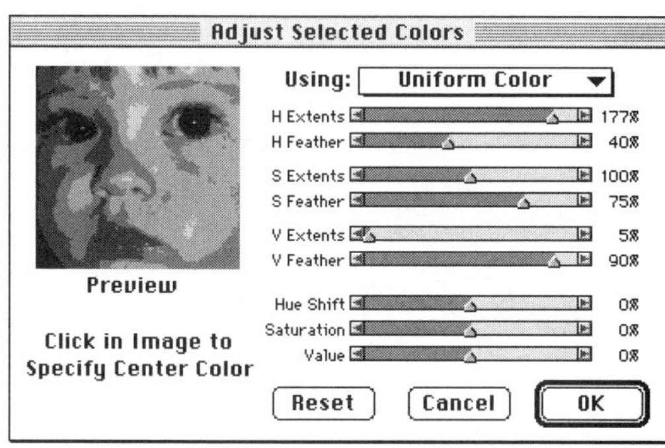

Use the Adjust Selected Colors command to adjust one color or a range of similar colors.

To adjust selected colors:

1. Choose Effects menu > Tonal Control > Adjust Selected Colors.

2. Click on the color in the image window that you want to adjust.

3. Choose from the **Using** pop-up menu:

   Uniform Color shifts colors with the base color being at the center of the slider. No paper texture is added.

   Paper Grain adjusts color *and* adds a paper texture. You can choose a different paper texture from the Art Materials: Paper palette while the Adjust Selected Colors dialog box is open.

   Mask adjusts white areas of the mask; black areas of the mask are unaffected.

   Image Luminance adjusts color based on the picture's light and dark values.

   Original Luminance adjusts color in a clone based on the source document's light and dark values.

4. Move the H (hue), S (saturation) or V (value) **Extents** sliders to widen or narrow the range of colors that are adjusted.

   Move the H (hue), S (saturation) or V (value) **Feather** sliders to adjust how much color adjustment is softened on the edges of color areas.

5. Move the **Hue Shift** slider to recolor the picture with different colors.

   Move the **Saturation** slider to increase or decrease color intensity.

   Move the **Value** slider to lighten or darken the picture.

6. *Optional*: Click Reset at any time to restore only the default Hue Shift, Saturation, and Value sliders settings.

7. Click OK or press Return.

To adjust brightness and contrast:

1. Choose Effects menu > Tonal Control > Brightness/Contrast.

2. Move the top slider (moon icon) to the right to increase contrast or to the left to decrease contrast.
and/or
Move the bottom slider (sun icon) to the right to increase brightness (lightness) or to the left to decrease brightness.

   Changes will preview in the image window immediately.

3. Click Apply.

✒ Click Reset to restore the original Brightness/Contrast settings.

✒ To lighten small areas manually, use the Dodge brush. To darken small areas manually, use the Burn brush. Use with a low opacity at first.

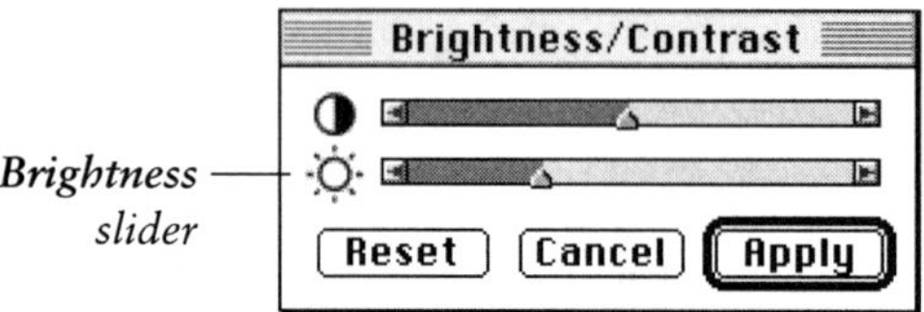

Brightness slider

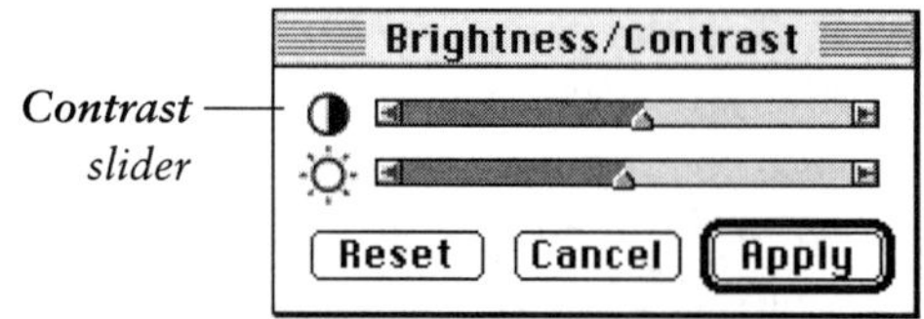

Contrast slider

*The original image: **18th Century Interior** by Ray Rue.*

*The **Brightness** lowered...*

*...and the **Contrast** increased slightly.*

The original image is at left, on the opposite page. The above image is after Equalize adjustments.

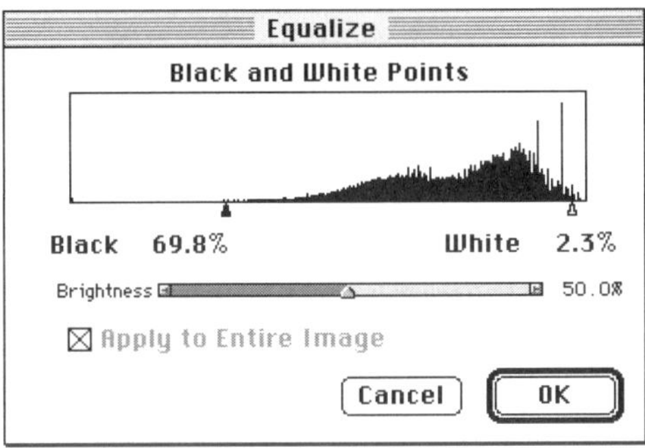

You can use the Equalize command to adjust the brightness and contrast of a picture's highlights, midtones, or shadows individually.

To equalize a picture:

1. Choose Effects menu > Tonal Control > Equalize (Command-E). Automatic adjustments will be made, and will preview in the image window.

2. Do any of the following optional steps:

   Move the **White point** slider to the left to brighten the picture's highlights.

   Move the **Black point** slider to the right to darken the picture's shadows. The white and black points are the picture's darkest and lightest values.

   Move the **Brightness** slider to lighten or darken the picture's midtones (gamma).

3. Click OK or press Return.

   To reduce previewing time, shrink the preview area by selecting a representative area on your picture. Then choose Effects menu > Tonal Control > Equalize and click the Apply to Entire Image box.

To create a negative of a picture:

Choose Effects menu > Tonal Control > Negative.

The original image.

After applying the Negative command.

Posterization reduces the number of color or shade levels in a picture. The fewer the Levels, the more dramatic the effect. Posterization can make a picture more adaptable to screen printing.

To posterize a picture:

1. Choose Effects menu > Tonal Control > Posterize.

2. Enter a number (2–128) in the Levels field. Try a number below 10 first.

3. Click OK or press Return.

4. *Optional:* Choose Effects menu > Tonal Control > Printable Colors to ensure the picture's colors are in the printable range.

Like the Posterize command, the Posterize Using Color Set command reduces the number of color or shade levels in a picture, but in this case, colors from a color set of your choice are substituted based on their closest brightness match to the picture's original brightness values. Apply this command to make a picture look more hand painted, to prepare a file for screen printing or a press that uses a limited number of inks, or to colorize a grayscale image. (Remember, though, spot color separations can't be produced from Painter.)

Color sets are discussed on page 29 and on pages 56–58. Use one of Painter's color sets, like Pastels, or use your own color set.

To posterize a picture using a color set:

1. Open or create the color set you want to become the picture's colors. You can pluck colors from any open picture using the Dropper tool (D) and add them to a color set. Try using a small set first (up to ten colors).

2. Choose Effects menu > Tonal Control > Posterize Using Color Set.

   If the colors in the set have assigned names, you can use the Annotate feature to mark colors on the picture.

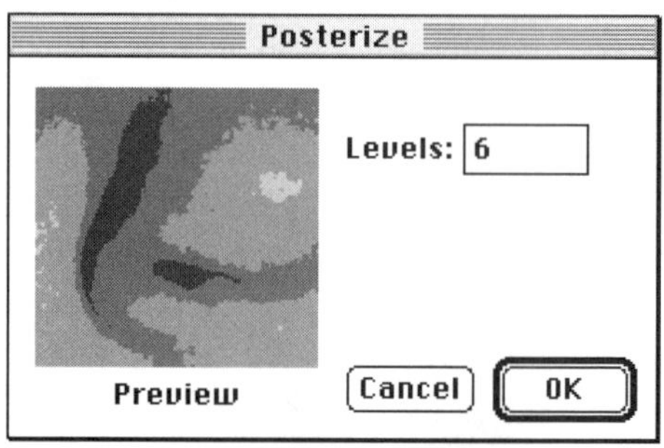

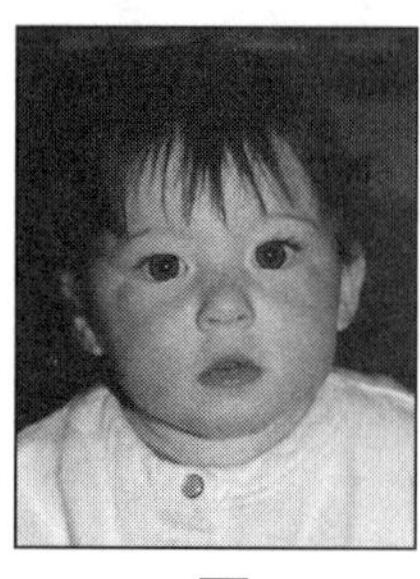

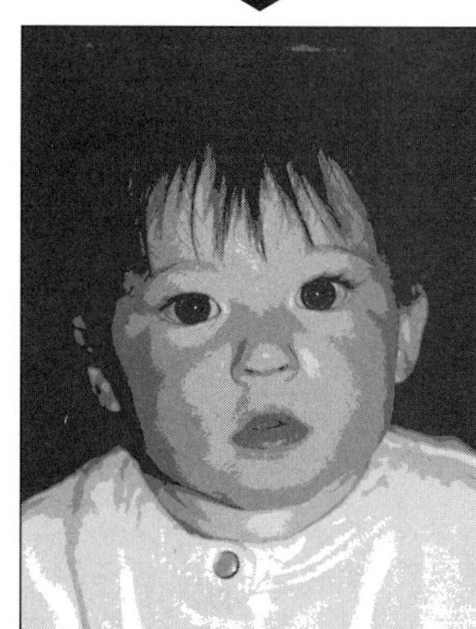

Six-level posterization.

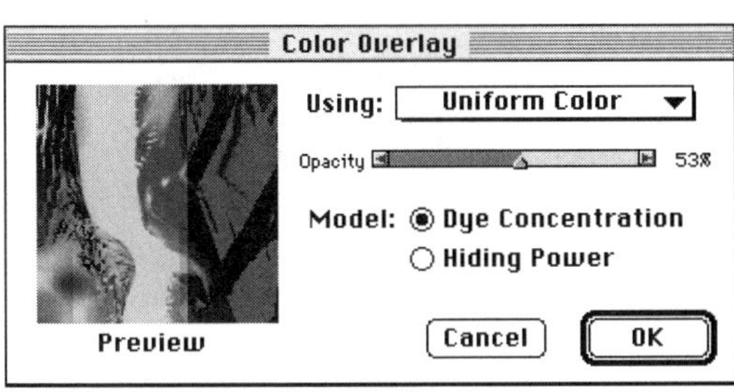

To apply a paper texture to your image

Choose **Paper Grain** from the **Using** pop-up menu when you apply any of these Effects menu commands: **Adjust Colors, Adjust Selected Colors, Apply Screen, Apply Surface Texture, Color Overlay, Dye Concentration, Express Texture, or Glass Distortion.**

To apply a pattern to your image

If you choose the **Using: Original Luminance** option for any **Surface Control** command when no clone source is currently chosen, luminosity values in the pattern currently selected on the **Art Materials: Pattern** palette will be used instead.

The Surface Control commands

Use the Color Overlay command to apply one overall color tint to a picture. You can also apply a paper texture at the same time.

To apply a tint:

1. Choose Effects menu > Surface Control > Color Overlay.

2. Choose a color from the Art Materials: Color palette or from the Color Set swatch palette.

3. Choose from the Using pop-up menu:

   Uniform Color applies a flat tint of the current Primary color. You can choose a different Primary color while the Color Overlay dialog box is open.

   Paper Grain applies the paper texture currently selected on the Art Materials: Paper palette. You can preview different textures while the Color Overlay dialog box is open.

   Mask—white areas in the mask are tinted, black areas in the mask receive no color, and gray areas are partially tinted.

   Image Luminance colorizes the image based on the picture's light and dark values, which are preserved.

   Original Luminance colorizes a clone based on the source picture's light and dark values.

4. Click **Dye Concentration** to make the canvas or paper look as if it's absorbing the tint.
   or
   Click **Hiding Power** to have the tint cover underlying pixels more.

5. Move the Opacity slider to adjust the amount of color that is overlayed.

6. Click OK or press Return.

Easel painters through the ages have used highlights and shadows to create realism. Painter's Apply Lighting command produces believable highlights and shadows by casting one or more light beams on a picture. You can choose a preset lighting effect or you can create your own lighting effect by adjusting any number of variables, such as the light's color, shape, direction, or brightness. If you want the option to reuse a lighting effect that you've created, save it in the currently open Lighting library. To access Apply Lighting, use a Mac that has a Floating Point Unit (FPU), or use a Power Mac.

To apply lighting:

1. Choose Effects menu > Surface Control > Apply Lighting.

2. Click a preset lighting effect **2**. Click the scroll arrows to display other choices.

   Click OK if you're happy with the preset lighting effect. If you want to customize the lighting effect, follow the remaining steps.

3. Do any of the following to customize the lighting effect:

   Move the **Brightness** slider to the right to make the light beam brighter or to the left to make it dimmer.

   Move the **Distance** slider to the right to increase the distance between the light source and where the light beam falls on the picture.

   Move the **Elevation** slider to the right to adjust the angle of the cast light. 90° shines directly down on the image, 10° shines at an acute angle.

   Move the **Spread** slider to the right to widen the light beam or to the left to make it narrower.

   Move the **Exposure** slider to the right to increase the exposure (brightness) of the whole image or to the left to lower the exposure.

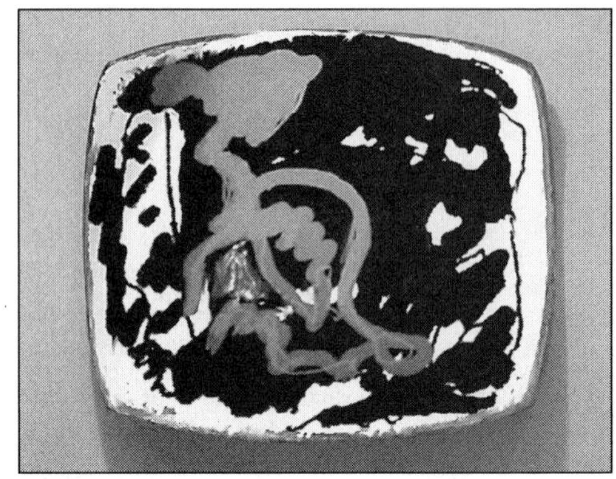

Ron Gorchov, **Delihla.**

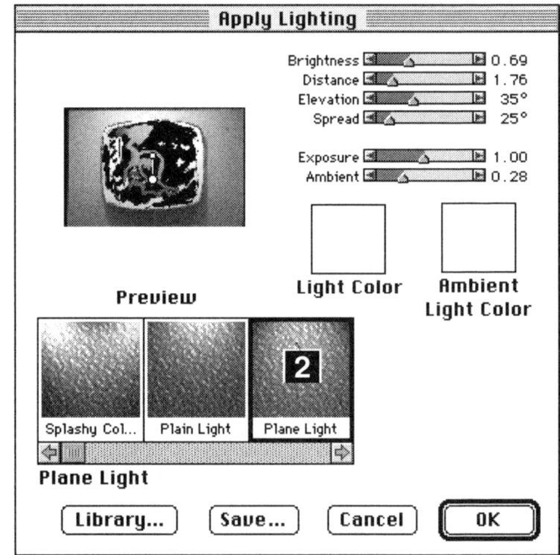

We applied the Readable lighting effect to Gorchov's painting. His version is better, of course.

Ron Gorchov

To produce his traditional media artworks, Ron Gorchov, a 1994 recipient of the Guggenheim Award, usually begins with an actual, stretched, specially curved, and glue-sized linen canvas—convexly curved along the horizontal axis and concave on the vertical axis.

Gorchov uses the computer to develop a visual theme for his work on canvas. In Painter, he opens a CD-ROM photograph of a completed oil on canvas, and then "primes" his electronic canvas at 60% opacity over the existing image using a paint color that simulates traditional white lead. Over a faint ghost of the original image that remains, he paints directly, pastes and rearranges imagery from other electronic images, overpaints, and finally smudges the edges of any visible white lead ground. In addition to oil and chalk brushes, Gorchov also uses a variety of other Painter features: the Apply Lighting and Fade commands, the Lasso tool to cut out shapes, the Distort command to stretch them, and the Water brushes to create smudges and drips. In addition to Painter, he also uses NIH Image, a public domain program designed by Wayne Rasband of the National Institute of Health, which is normally used for medical imaging. It produces surprising color transformations that Gorchov likes.

Once he arrives at a promising theme on the computer, Gorchov turns his back to the computer and recreates the image on real-life canvas. Like a dancer or musician who rehearses a composition, the computer prepares him for his canvas "performance."

Ron Gorchov

Move the **Ambient** slider to the right to raise the light level in the overall image (except the light beam).

To change the light source **direction**, rotate the square end of the light icon in the preview window. Click right on the icon, or else you will create another light source icon.

To **move** the whole light source, drag the round end of the light icon in the preview window.

To **add** another light source, click in the preview window. The new light will have the same color as the current light source.

To **remove** a light source, click on the light icon, then press Delete.

To change the color of a light, click on its icon in the preview window, click the **Light Color** square, choose a color from the Color Picker, then click OK.

To change the color of the area around the light beam, click the **Ambient Light Color** square, choose a color, then click OK.

4. *Optional:* To save the edited lighting effect in the currently open lighting library so you can choose it again from the Apply Lighting dialog box, click Save, enter a name, then click OK.

5. Click OK or press Return.

> You can restore a lighting effect's default settings if you haven't saved it. Just click on a different effect.

> To create or edit a lighting library, follow the instructions on pages 21–22.

The Dye Concentration command is one of our favorites. It darkens (or lightens) colors without making them dull and makes them richer without noticeably changing their hue or making them gaudy. You can apply a paper texture as you adjust dye concentration.

To adjust color intensity:

1. Choose Effects menu > Surface Control > Dye Concentration.

2. Choose from the **Using** pop-up menu:

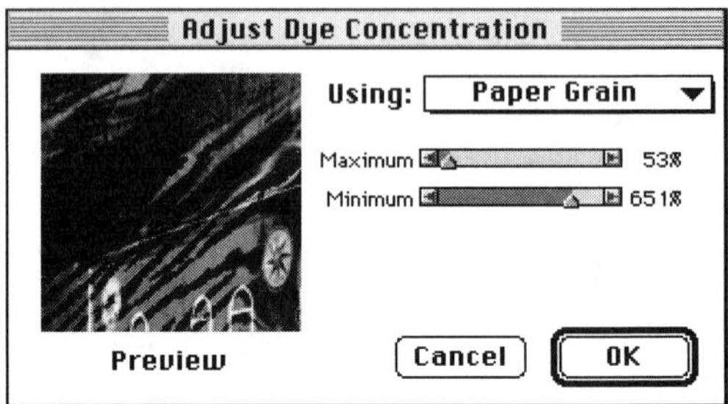

   Uniform Adjustment adjusts color without adding texture. Move the Maximum slider to adjust the intensity of the Dye Concentration effect.

   Paper Grain adjusts color and applies the paper texture currently selected on the Art Materials: Paper palette. You can choose a different paper texture while the Adjust Dye Concentration dialog box is open.

   To emphasize the paper texture more, move the Maximum or the Minimum slider to the right. The farther apart the sliders are, the more pronounced the paper texture.

   Mask adjusts outside mask using the Maximum slider or within the mask using the Minimum slider. Colors are adjusted based on luminosity values in the mask.

   Image Luminance adjusts color based on the picture's light and dark values.

   Original Luminance adjusts a clone based on the source picture's light and dark values.

3. Click OK or press Return.

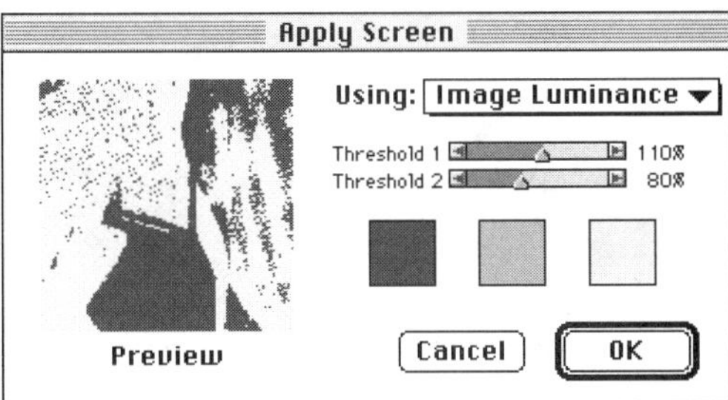

Lourekas

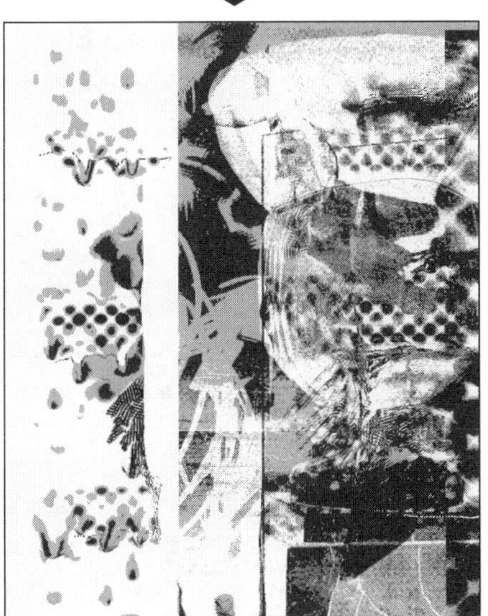

The Apply Screen command reduces a picture's colors to three colors that you specify. You can apply a paper texture at the same time. You can use Apply Screen to colorize a grayscale picture.

To apply a color screen:

1. Choose Effects menu > Surface Control > Apply Screen.

2. Click the first color square, choose a color (drag the horizontal bar to change the brightness of the color wheel), then click OK. Repeat for the second and third color squares.

3. Choose from the **Using** pop-up menu:

   Paper Grain applies the paper texture currently selected on the Art Materials: Paper palette. You can preview different textures with the Apply Screen dialog box open.

   Mask applies the color screen to the black mask areas when the Threshold sliders are to the left of center or to the whole image when the Threshold sliders are moved to the right.

   Image Luminance applies color to the image based on the picture's light and dark value distribution.

   Original Luminance applies color to a clone based on the source picture's light and dark values.

4. Move the Threshold 1 slider to the right to add more of the second color, or to the left to add more of the third color.
   and/or
   Move the Threshold 2 slider to the right to add more of the first color and reduce the second color, or to the left to reduce the first color and add more of the second color.

5. Click OK or press Return.

Apply Surface Texture

Use the Apply Surface Texture command to apply a surface texture to a completed painting or to a selection. Where you draw subsequent brush strokes or use an Eraser brush, however, you'll **remove** the texture. To access the Apply Surface Texture command, use a Mac that has a Floating Point Unit (FPU), or use a Power Mac.

To apply a texture to a whole painting:

1. Choose Effects menu > Surface Control > Apply Surface Texture.

2. Choose **Paper Grain** from the Using pop-up menu to apply the paper texture currently selected on the Art Materials: Paper palette. You can choose a different paper texture with the dialog box open.

   Choose **3D Brush Strokes** to make strokes applied to a clone look more three-dimensional.

   Choose **Mask** to limit the effect to masked areas.

   Choose **Image Luminance** to create a raised surface effect.

   Choose **Original Luminance** to create a raised surface in a clone based on luminosity values in the source image.

3. Move the **Softness** slider to smooth transitions in the texture.

4. *Optional:* Check the Inverted box to invert the Using info.

5. Adjust any of the following Material controls:

   Move the **Amount** slider to the right to intensify the effect.

   Move the **Picture** slider to the right to reveal more of the original picture's color.

   Move the **Shine** slider to the right to create a more reflective surface texture with stronger highlights.

   Move the **Reflection** slider to the right to adjust how the clone source maps onto the clone (see page 186).

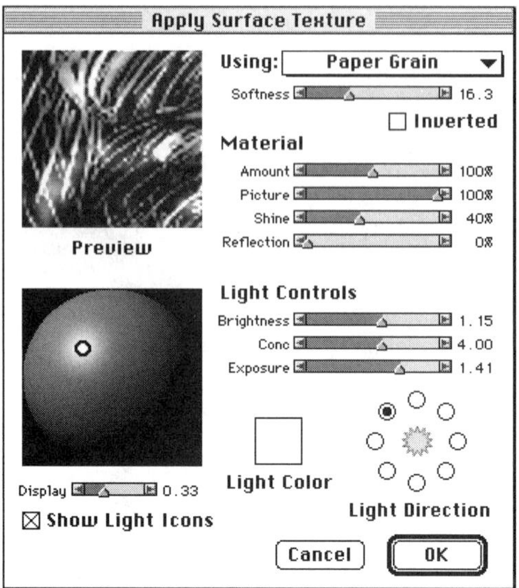

Jacquelyn Martino

Jacquelyn Martino

Two images from Martino's "Blue" series.

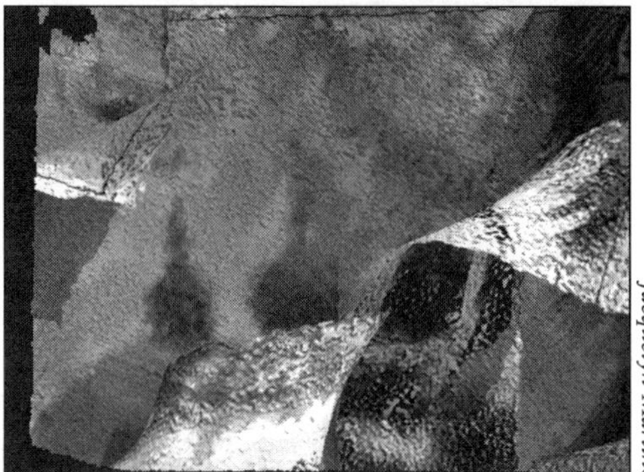

Images from the "Tear" series

Jacquelyn Martino

To produce the pieces on these pages, which are part of an interactive multimedia piece exploring the city of Venice, Italy and issues of time, rejuvenation, and decay, Jacquelyn Martino started with her own Polaroid transfer prints of scenes in Venice. She developed the images further using various techniques, then photographed and scanned them. In Painter, Martino cloned the images using Water Color, Chalk, and Charcoal brush variants (the Use Clone Color box checked on the Color palette) and using the Apply Surface Texture command (Original Luminance). She also used Bleach variants of the Eraser brush to lighten selective areas. The Tear Series images were used as color maps for 3D animations using SoftImage and then imported into Macromedia Director. The Blue Series still images were imported from Painter into Macromedia Director. To activate the multimedia piece, which includes a soundtrack, viewers turn pages of a real-life, handmade book in a candlelit room, which in turn "turn pages" on the computer.

6. Before you adjust any of the following Light Controls, check the **Show Light Icons** box, then **click on a light on the preview sphere to select it.**

Drag the light icon to **move** the light.

Click a different **Direction** button to change the highlight-to-shadow direction.

Don't click a different Light Direction after adjusting other Light Controls—the single default light will be restored and all other lights will be deleted.

Move the **Brightness** slider to adjust the intensity of the light.

Move the **Conc** slider to adjust the width (spread) of the light.

Move the **Exposure** slider to adjust the overall brightness of the image.

Click the **Light Color** square, and choose a different color for the light.

Move the **Display** slider to lighten or darken the preview.

To **add** a light source, click on the sphere. Each light source can have its own Light Controls settings, except for the Exposure setting.

To **delete** a light source, click on it, then press Delete.

7. Click OK or press Return.

To apply a tinted texture, choose Effects menu > Surface Control > Color Overlay, choose Using: Paper Grain, and click Hiding Power.

Using the Reflection slider in the Apply Surface Texture dialog box, parts of a clone source image can be mapped as a surface reflection onto a floater in another image, like a reflection on metal or glass.

To map a reflection onto a floater:

1. Create or open an image to use as the reflection. To make a recognizable reflection, try using a centralized image.

2. Activate the image window that you want to map the reflection onto.

3. From File menu > Clone Source submenu, choose the name of the reflection image you chose for step 1.

4. Choose the Floater Adjuster tool.

5. Select or create a floater onto which you want to map the reflection. The floater's mask will be used in the reflection mapping process.

6. Choose Effects menu > Surface Control > Apply Surface Texture.

7. Choose Using: Mask.

8. Move the Reflection slider to the right to make the clone source image appear on the floater.

9. Move the Softness slider to the right to make reflection spread over more of the floater surface.

10. Adjust any of the other sliders, if desired. For example, you might want to adjust the Amount, Shine, or overall Brightness. These options are discussed on the previous two pages.

11. Click OK or press Return.

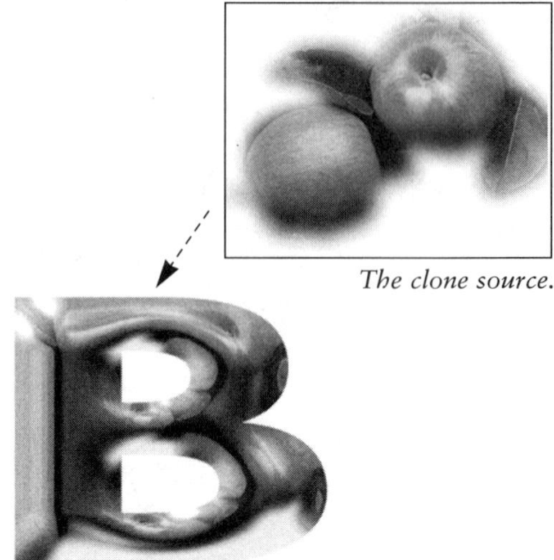

The clone source.

The clone source as a reflection on a floater.

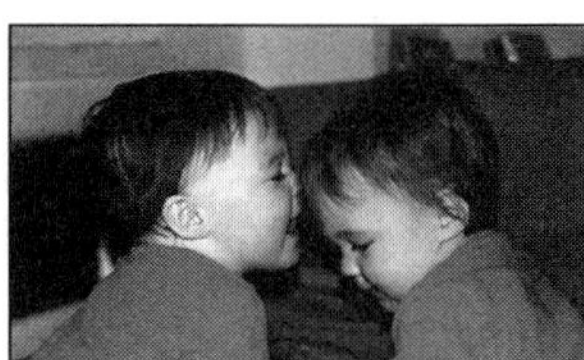

The clone source.

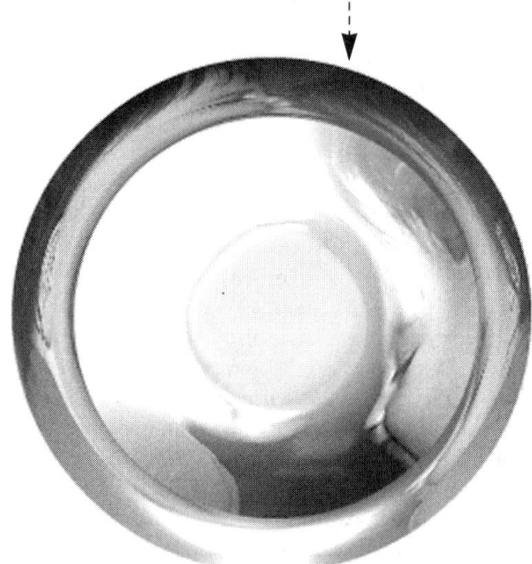

The clone source as a reflection on a floater.

Map a Reflection onto a Floater

Texture combos produced using various methods

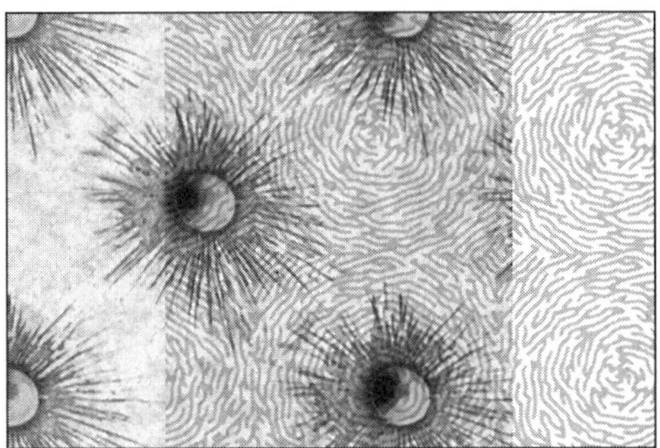

Circles (More Wild Textures file) Color Overlayed at 30% Opacity over Bolt Burst (Walls Library).

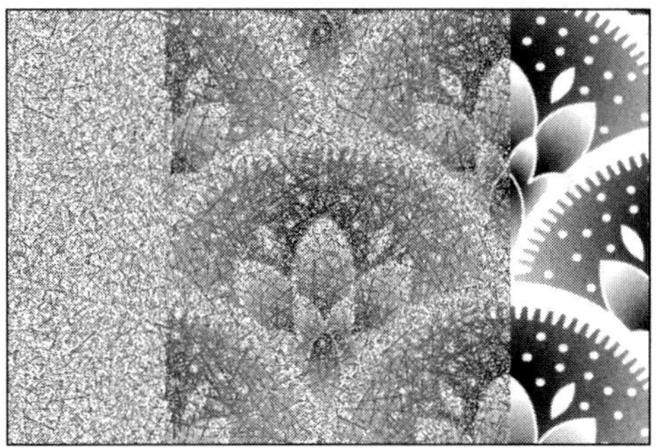

Fiber Fill (Weaves Library) floater (Dissolve Composite Method, 63% Opacity) over Deco Scallops (Walls Library) applied via the Color Overlay command.

Watercolor 2 (More Paper Textures file) at 43% opacity over Wood Squares (Walls Library) at 50% opacity, both floaters.

Texture on the left produced using Fractal Pattern, saved via Capture Texture, and applied to the picture via Apply Surface Texture (Paper Grain; Light Controls used to heighten contrast). Texture on the right produced via Make Paper Texture (Square pattern, Spacing 45), saved to the Paper palette, applied over first texture via Apply Surface Texture (Light Control options).

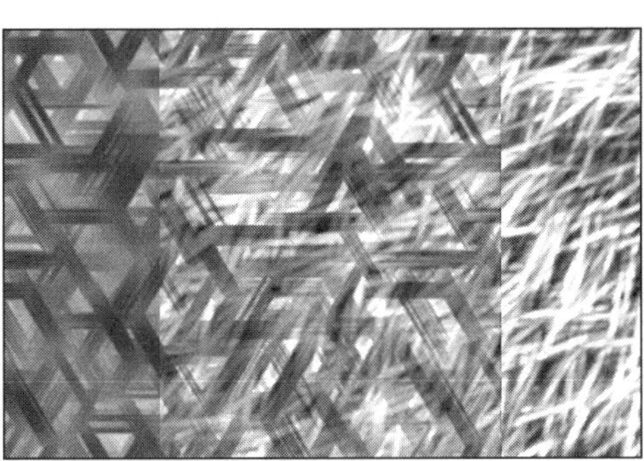

Basket 2 (Weaves Library) floater (Difference Composite Method, 100% Opacity) over Long Grain (Wild Textures) floater (Normal Composite Method, 87% Opacity).

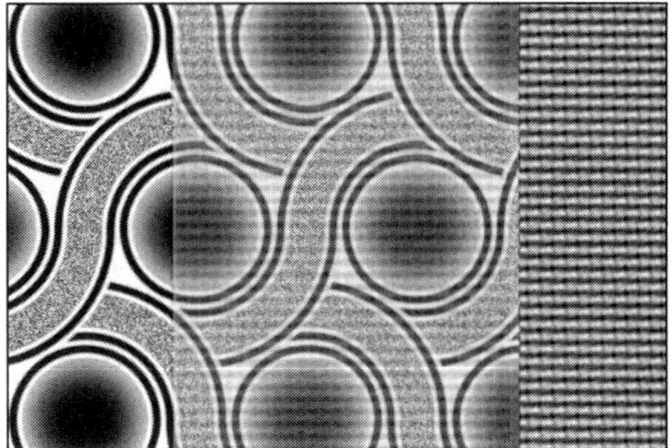

Raw Canvas (Grains) floater (Difference Composite Method, 27% Opacity) over Celtic Circles (Walls Library) floater (Normal Composite Method, 64% Opacity).

To translate a picture into grayscale values (Express Texture):

1. Choose Effects menu > Surface Control > Express Texture.

2. Choose from the Using pop-up menu:

   Choose **Paper Grain** to apply the current paper texture. You can choose from the Art Materials: Paper palette while the dialog box is open. Painter's Dottie and Circles textures are fun to experiment with. Or use a texture that you've created.

   Choose **Mask** to restrict grayscale and contrast effects to inside the mask when the sliders are at their low settings. The paper texture isn't applied.

   Choose **Image Luminance** to apply grayscale values based on the picture's light and dark values.

   Choose **Original Luminance** to apply grayscale values to a clone based on the source picture's luminosity values.

3. Do any of the following:

   Move the **Gray Threshold** slider to control the balance between gray, black, and white. Move the slider to the right to add Black.

   If you chose Paper Grain from the Using pop-up menu, you can move the **Grain** slider to adjust the prominence of the paper texture. The higher the Grain setting, the more White in the picture.

   Move the **Contrast** slider to adjust the number of gray levels in the picture. Move to the right to heighten contrast or to the left to increase midtone gray levels.

4. Click OK or press Return.

   If the original picture was in color, you can restore some color using the Edit menu > Fade command. Or apply the current Primary color to non-Black areas using the Effects menu > Surface Control > Color Overlay command.

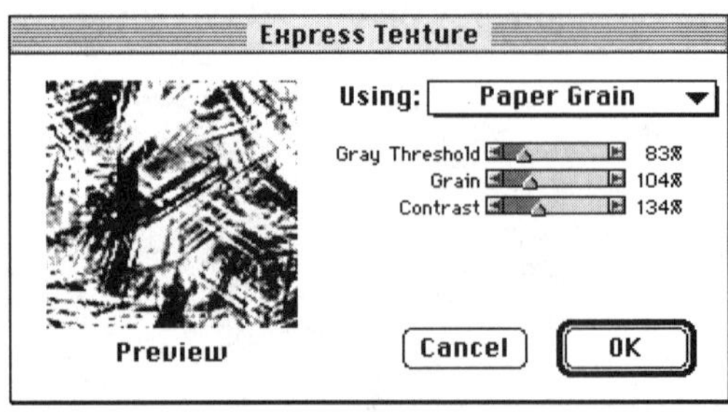

The original picture.

Express Texture (Using: Paper Grain) with Painter's Omniwicker texture (Invert box checked, Scale 133%), Gray Threshold 84%, Grain 72%, and Contrast 88%.

Painter's Omniwicker texture (Invert box checked, Scale 133%), Gray Threshold 83%, Grain 104%, and Contrast 134%.

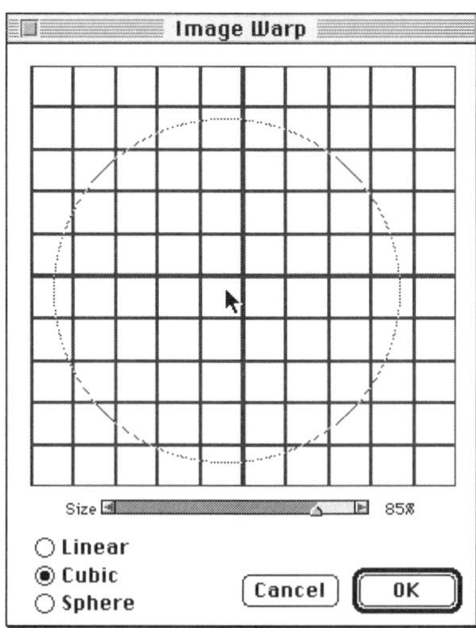

Use the Image Warp command to distort all or part of an image around curvey, 3D shapes. Unfortunately, once you drag in the preview window, you can't undo that image warp except by cancelling out of the dialog box. Hopefully, this limitation will be corrected in a future version of Painter. You can, however, apply multiple image warps at one time.

To warp an image:

1. Choose Effects menu > Surface Control > Image Warp.

2. Click **Linear** to warp as if you were pulling straight up from the top of a cone, like a 3D pyramid.
   or
   Click **Cubic** to pull straight up from a flat surface.
   or
   Click **Sphere** to warp pixels into a three-dimensional sphere.

3. Drag the Size slider to adjust the amount of the warp. Try a fairly high setting first (50% or higher).

4. Drag in the preview window to define the area to be warped. You can add more warps at this point, if you like.

5. Click OK or press Return.

(All 85% Size setting.)

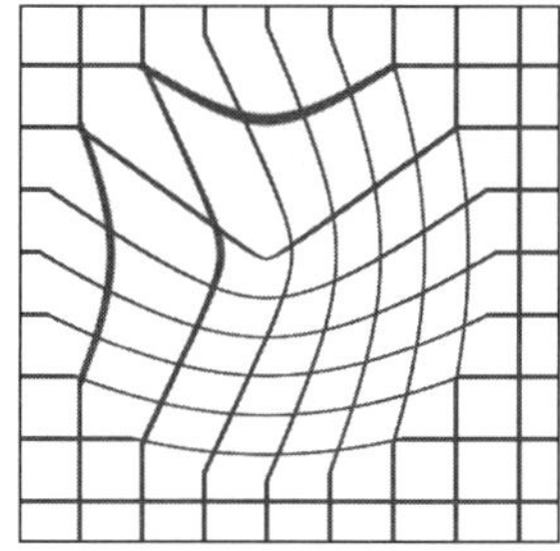

Linear Image Warp

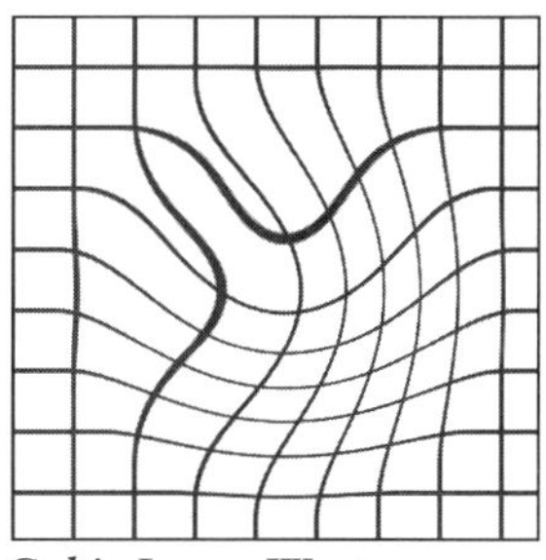

Cubic Image Warp

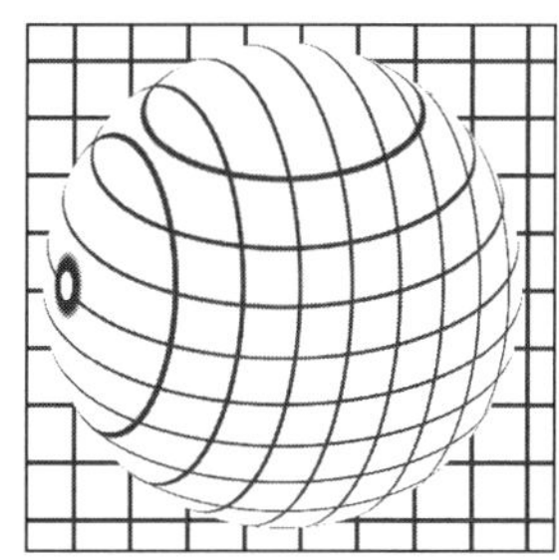

Spheric Image Warp

The Quick Warp command distorts an image based on preset options.

To Quick Warp an image:

1. Choose Effects menu > Surface Control > Quick Warp. *Note:* The Quick Warp command affects the whole image, even if a selection is active. It *will* be limited to a selected floater, though.

2. Click a preset option:

   Sphere makes the image appear to be wrapped around a sphere.

   Bump makes the center of the image appear to bulge towards you.

   Valley makes the center of the image appear to push away from you.

   Swirl spirals the whole image around its center.

   Ripple makes the image look like a reflection on water, with reflection rings radiating from the center.

3. The **Power** slider affects the distortion along the edge of the image with the Sphere option, and it affects the number of rings that are produced with the Ripple option. With other options, this slider's effect is minimal.

   The **Angle Factor** slider controls the amount of overall distortion.

4. Click OK or press Return.

The Distort command isn't on the Esoterica submenu, but we're covering it in this section because it is interesting to compare its effects to the warp commands.

To distort an image:

1. Choose Effects menu > Orientation > Distort.

2. Drag any corner handle.

3. *Optional:* Check the Better (Slower) box for cleaner rendering. Processing takes longer with this option checked.

4. Click OK or press Return. The image will automatically become a floater.

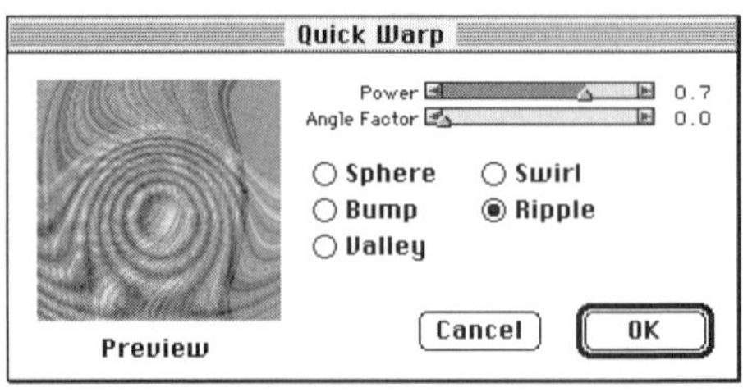

The original image.

Barbara S. Pollak

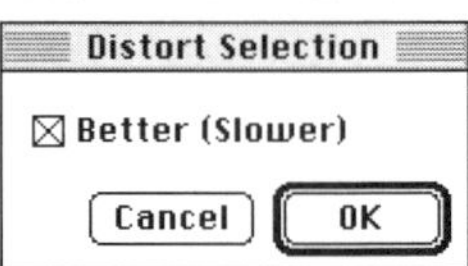

After distorting the teacup.

The Focus commands

The Sharpen command works by increasing the contrast between pixels.

To sharpen an image:

1. Choose Effects menu > Focus > Sharpen.

2. Do any of the following:

   Move the **Radius** slider to the right to sharpen a wider area of each edge. Try a low Radius first to avoid over-sharpening.

   Move the **Highlight** slider to the right to brighten the picture's highlights.

   Move the **Shadow** slider to the right to darken the shadows.

   Move the image in the preview window.

3. Click OK or press Return.

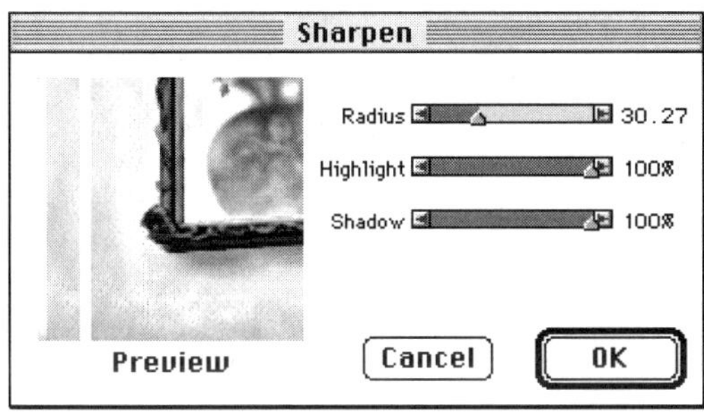

The original image.

After sharpening (30).

Ray Rue, 18th Century Interior

Sharpen

To soften an image:

1. Choose Effects menu > Focus > Soften.

2. Move the Radius slider to the right to increase blurring or to the left to decrease blurring. Try a low setting first.

3. Click OK or press Return.

Barbara S. Pollak

The Soften command applied to the background.

To apply the Glass Distortion command:

1. Choose Effects menu > Focus > Glass Distortion.

2. Choose from the **Using** pop-up menu:

   Paper Grain to apply the paper texture currently selected on the Art Materials: Paper palette. You can choose a different texture while the Glass Distortion dialog box is open. Painter's Rougher, Basic Paper, Medium Fine, and Regular Fine textures produce believable glass effects.

   3D Brush Strokes distorts only areas in a clone to which brush strokes have been applied.

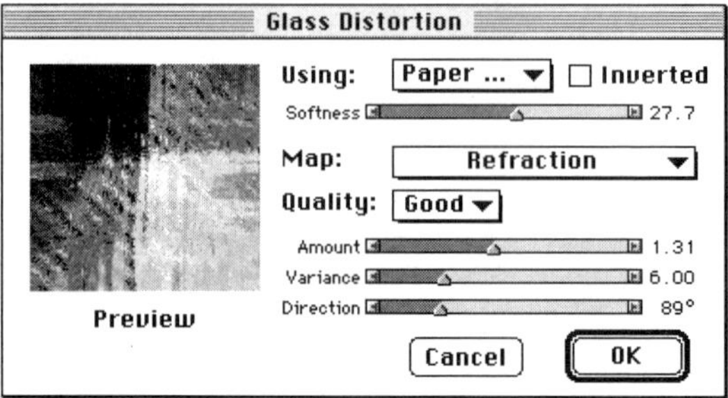

The original weave fill.

After applying the Glass Distortion command, Amount .44, Variance 6: a wool texture!

Another variation.

Mask distorts the image based on mask information.

Image Luminance displaces picture elements based on the picture's light and dark values.

Original Luminance distorts a clone based on the source picture's light and dark values.

Optional: Check the Inverted box to invert the Using info.

3. Choose a type of distortion from the Map pop-up menu. Refraction produces a believable bumby glass effect. Vector Displacement pushes pixels in the Direction chosen using the Direction slider (with Using: Paper Grain, this also produces a bumpy glass effect). Angle Displacement pushes pixels more randomly.

4. Choose Fast from the Quality pop-up menu for faster, but less accurate rendering, or Good for more precise rendering.

5. Do any of the following:

   Move the **Softness** slider to the right to produce smoother color transitions.

   Move the **Amount** slider to the right to intensify the effect.

   Move the **Variance** slider to the right to fracture shape edges more. Try using a low Amount setting and a high Variance setting. Or, to create very abstract shapes, move both sliders to the far right.

   Move the **Direction** slider to control the angle on which pixels are pushed using the Map: Vector Displacement or Angle Displacement option.

6. Click OK or press Return.

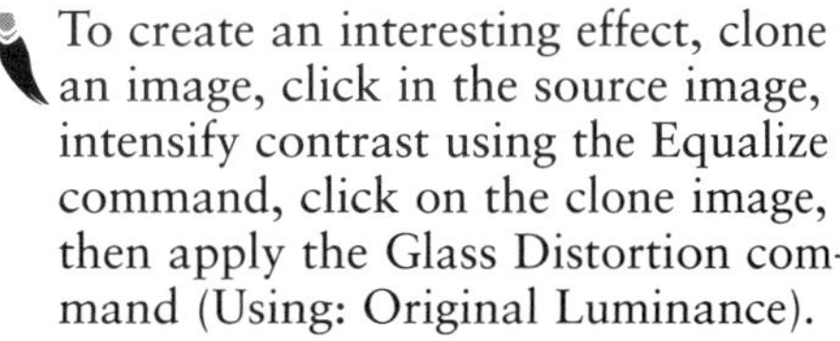 To create an interesting effect, clone an image, click in the source image, intensify contrast using the Equalize command, click on the clone image, then apply the Glass Distortion command (Using: Original Luminance).

To motion blur an object or an image:

1. Choose Effects menu > Focus > Motion Blur.

2. Do any of the following (try Radius and Thinness settings below 20 first):

   Move the **Radius** slider to the right to increase the motion effect (the distance pixels are moved).

   Move the **Angle** slider to change the direction of motion. 0° is horizontal, 90° is vertical.

   Move the **Thinness** slider to the right to blend and smooth edges at right angles to the Angle value and make the Angle less obvious. Too high a Thinness percentage will completely blur the image.

3. Click OK or press Return.

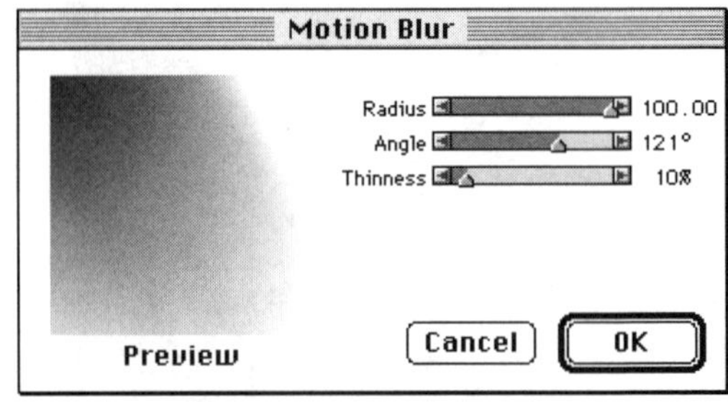

The Esoterica commands

The commands grouped under the Esoterica submenu perform miscellaneous oddball distortions.

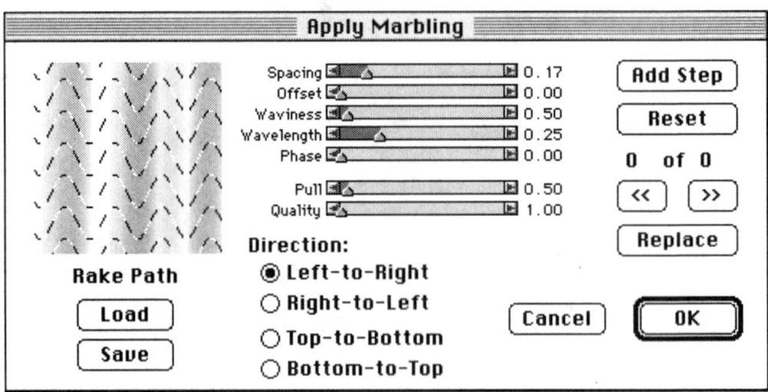

The Apply Marbling command mimics traditional marbling, a process by which a comb or rake is pulled through wet pigments to produce wave patterns.

To apply marbling:

1. Open an image. Apply Marbling works well on an image filled with a gradation or a pattern, or on an image created using the Blobs command.

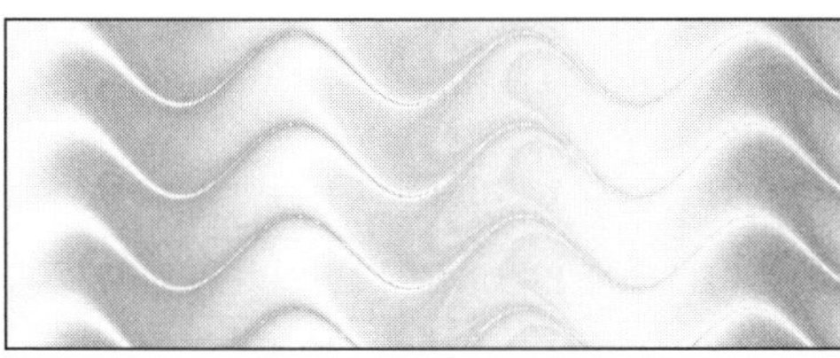

We used a gradient as a starting point for this image and for the images below.

Default Marbling

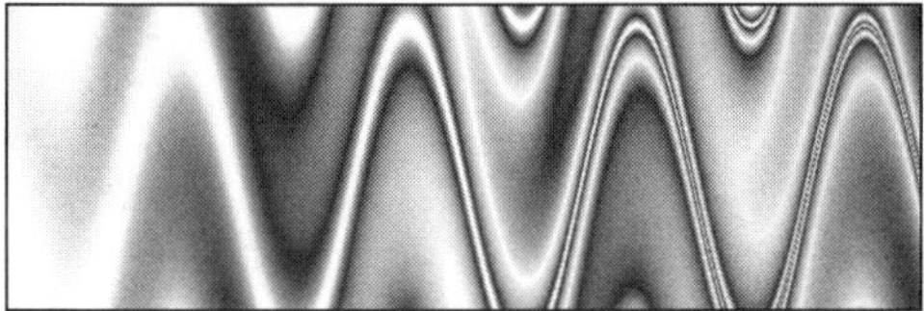

Spacing .51

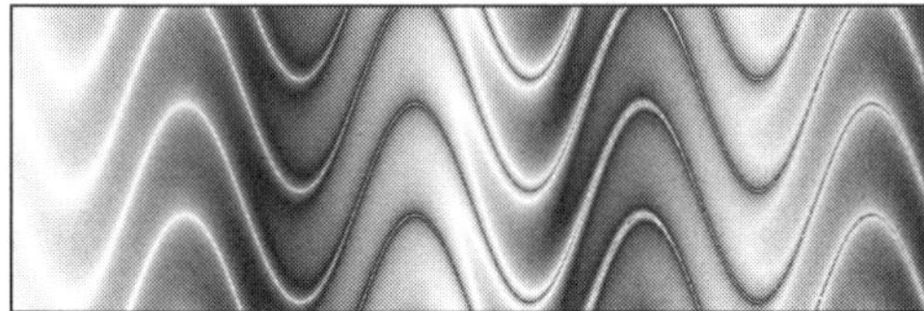

Waviness .89

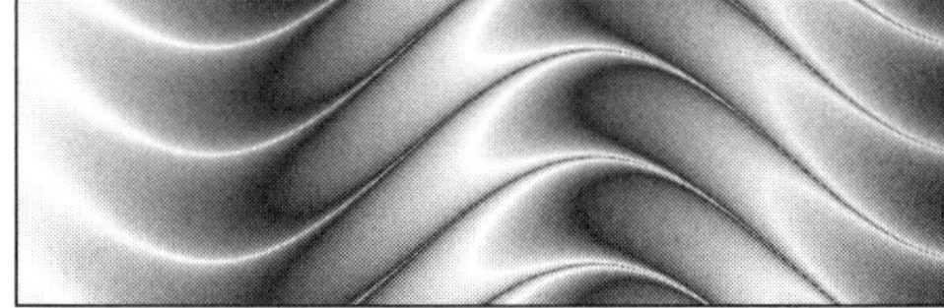

Wavelength .79

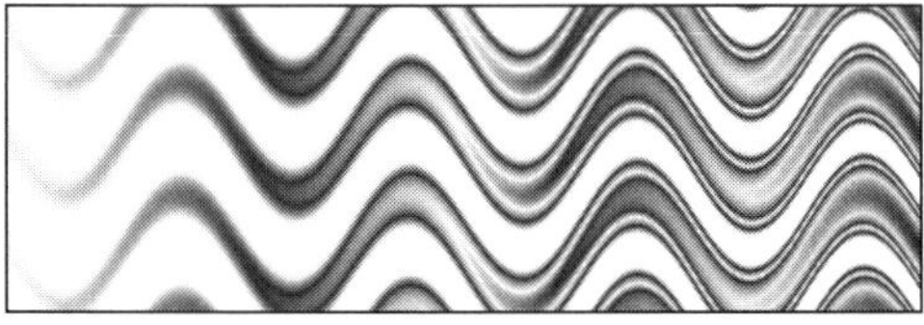

Pull 9

2. Choose Effects menu > Esoterica > Apply Marbling.

3. Adjust any of the following settings:

Spacing: the distance between the rake teeth.

Offset: the amount the rake shifts for each step you add. The rake will shift vertically if you choose the Left-to-Right Direction option, horizontally for the Top-to-Bottom Direction, etc.

Waviness: curve depth. Try a low Waviness setting first.

Wavelength: the length (flatness) of the curves. A high Wavelength will produce gentle curves.

Phase: the position in the curve where the waves start.

Pull: the amount of ink that is pulled. This option doesn't preview.

Quality: anti-aliasing (smoothing). The higher the Quality, the longer Marbling takes to process.

Direction: the direction the wave moves through the picture.

4. Click Add Step.

5. *Optional:* To add more passes of the rake, repeat steps 2 and 3. Try clicking a different Direction button for each pass.

6. *Optional:* To edit any of the steps, click the forward or backward arrowhead to display the step you want to edit, change the settings, then click Replace.

7. *Optional:* To save the marbling recipe, click Save, enter a name, then click OK. (Later, if you want to apply the recipe, just click Load to load it into the Apply Marbling dialog box.)

8. Click OK or press Return. The greater the number of steps, the longer the marbling will take to process.

The blobs command dispenses shapes in liquid, like oil droplets in water. To access this command, use a computer that has an FPU (floating point unit), or use a Power Mac.

To create blobs:

1. To blob a picture element, select an area of an image or activate a floater, then choose Edit menu > Copy.
   or
   To fill the blobs with a flat color, choose a Primary color.
   or
   To fill the blobs with a pattern, choose a pattern.

2. Open the picture you want to blob.
   or
   To disperse the blobs on a blank background, create a new, blank file.

3. Choose Effects menu > Esoterica > Blobs.

4. Choose Fill Blobs With: Paste Buffer to fill the blobs with the current Clipboard contents, or choose Current Color or Pattern. You can choose a different color or pattern while the dialog box is open.

5. Enter the desired Number of blobs, Minimum size, Maxmum size, and Subsample amount. Subsampling is anti-aliasing (smoothing).

6. Click OK or press Return.

The Growth command produces organic forms—tree branches, flowers, parsley, Venetian glass, snowflakes—curved or axial shaped. Experiment with subtle slider adjustments to produce different kinds of shapes.

To use the Growth command:

1. Choose Effects menu > Esoterica > Growth.

2. Adjust any of the following settings.

   Flatness controls how far in toward the center of the shape the smaller branches meet the main trunks.

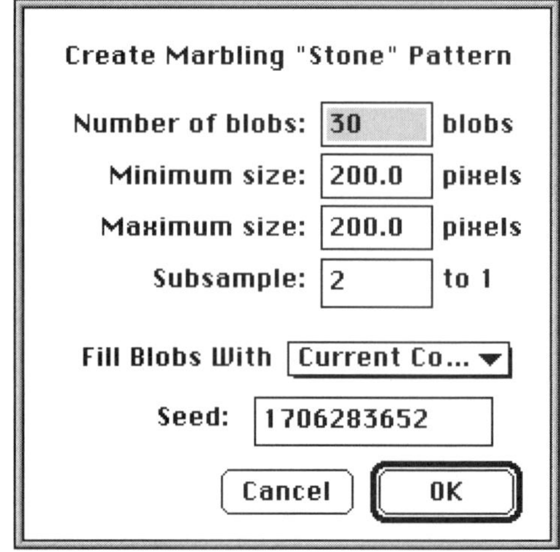

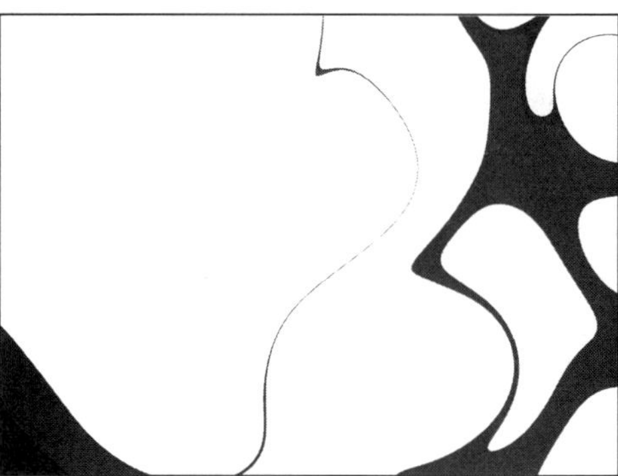

Blobs (Current Color).

The default Growth shape.

Blobs; Growth

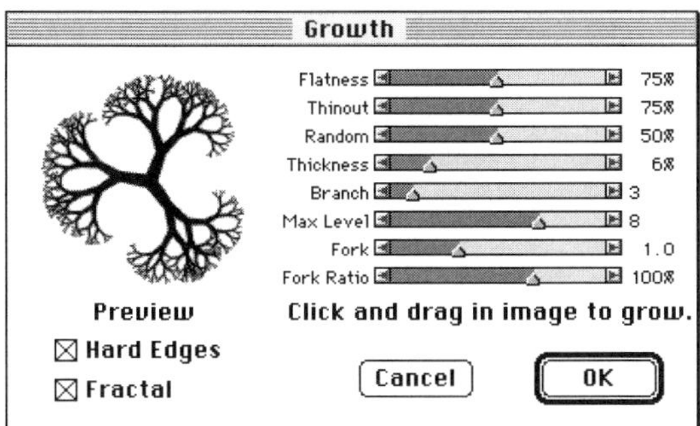

*The default Growth command settings. **To restore the default settings, you must relaunch Painter.***

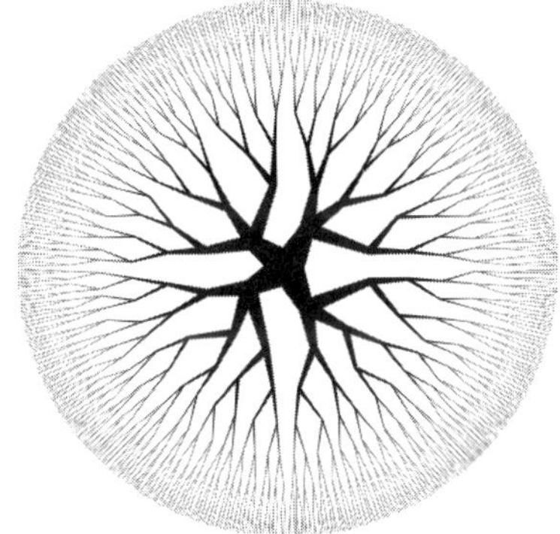

Flatness 92%, Thinout 48%, Random 50%, Thickness 6%, Branch 4, Max Level 8, Fork 1.0, Fork Ratio 100%, Hard Edges checked, Fractal unchecked.

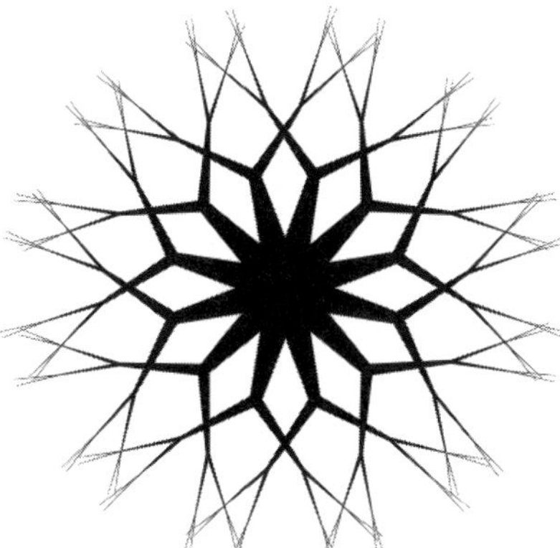

Flatness 72%, Thinout 33%, Random 4%, Thickness 6%, Branch 12, Max Level 4, Fork 1.7, Fork Ratio 29%, Hard Edges and Fractal checked.

Thinout controls whether branches are thickest at the center of the overall shape or at the outer edges.

Random controls whether the branch pattern is symmetrical or asymmetrical.

Thickness controls the overall width of the branches.

Branch controls the number of main branches (1–20) from the center. The more Branches, the more circular the shape.

Max Level controls the number of secondary forks off the main center branches. A high Max Level setting will produce a very complex shape which will preview slowly.

Fork controls how widely the forks spread. The Fractal box must be checked to use this option.

Fork Ratio controls the spread of the outer tips. The Fractal box must be checked to use this option.

Hard Edges: Uncheck to produce softer-edged lines.

Fractal: With the Fractal box checked, branches form cellular, honeycomb-like shapes, especially with a high Fork setting. Uncheck the Fractal box to make forks more symmetrical and the overall shape more circular.

3. Choose a Primary color.

4. Drag in the image window to preview the current shape on your picture. The further you drag, the larger the shape. Repeat steps 2–4 to add more shapes. Or, since Growth shapes can't be removed individually (except with an Eraser brush variant), you may want to click OK after creating each shape to apply them to your image one-by-one. (Click Cancel to remove *all* the shapes that you previewed on the picture and exit the dialog box.)

5. Click OK or press Return to apply all the shapes that you previewed.

Flatness 31%, Thinout 12%, Random 5%, Thickness 9%, Branch 5, Max Level 4, Fork 0.6, Fork Ratio 29%, Hard Edges and Fractal checked.

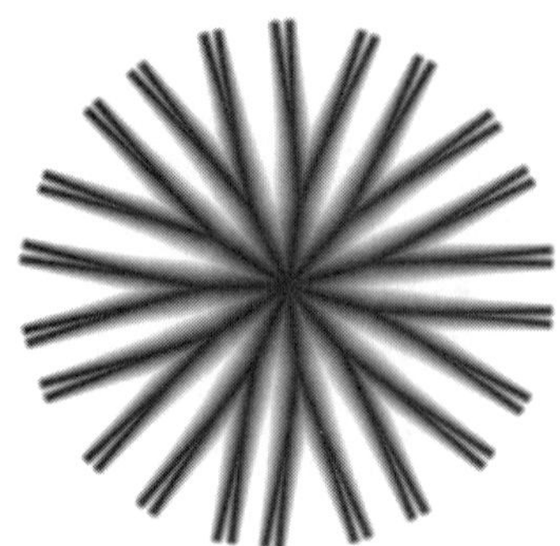

Flatness 76%, Thinout 71%, Random 12%, Thickness 15%, Branch 11, Max Level 5, Fork 0.5, Fork Ratio 25%, Hard Edge unchecked, Fractal checked.

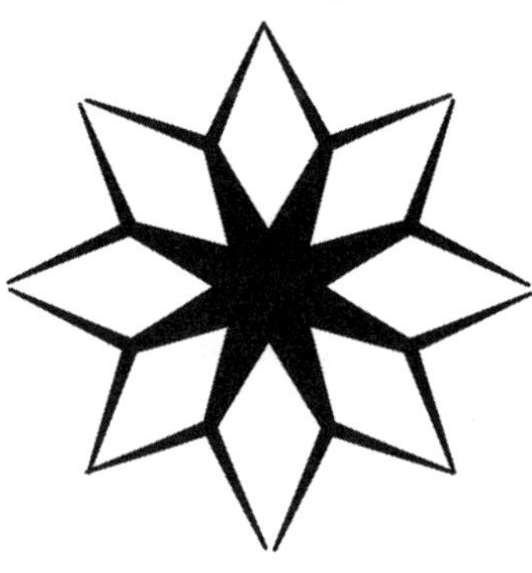

Flatness 87%, Thinout 27%, Random 4%, Thickness 10%, Branch 8, Max Level 2, Fork 1.7, Fork Ratio 25%, Hard Edges and Fractal checked.

Flatness 39%, Thinout 71%, Random 12%, Thickness 15%, Branch 6, Max Level 2, Fork 1.0, Fork Ratio 100%, Hard Edge and Fractal unchecked.

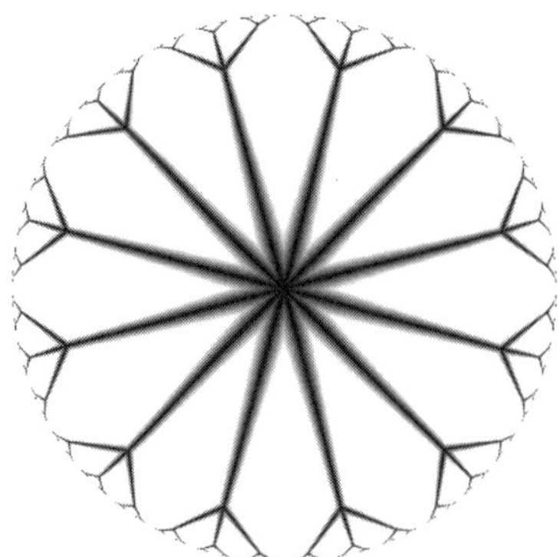

Flatness 17%, Thinout 33%, Random 4%, Thickness 6%, Branch 12, Max Level 4, Fork 1.0, Fork Ratio 100%, Hard Edge and Fractal unchecked.

Flatness 94%, Thinout 86, Random 50%, Thickness 6%, Branch 4, Max Level 8, Fork 1.0, Fork Ratio 100%, Hard Edges checked, Fractal unchecked. Lower the Random percentage to straighten the branches.

Mosaics 12

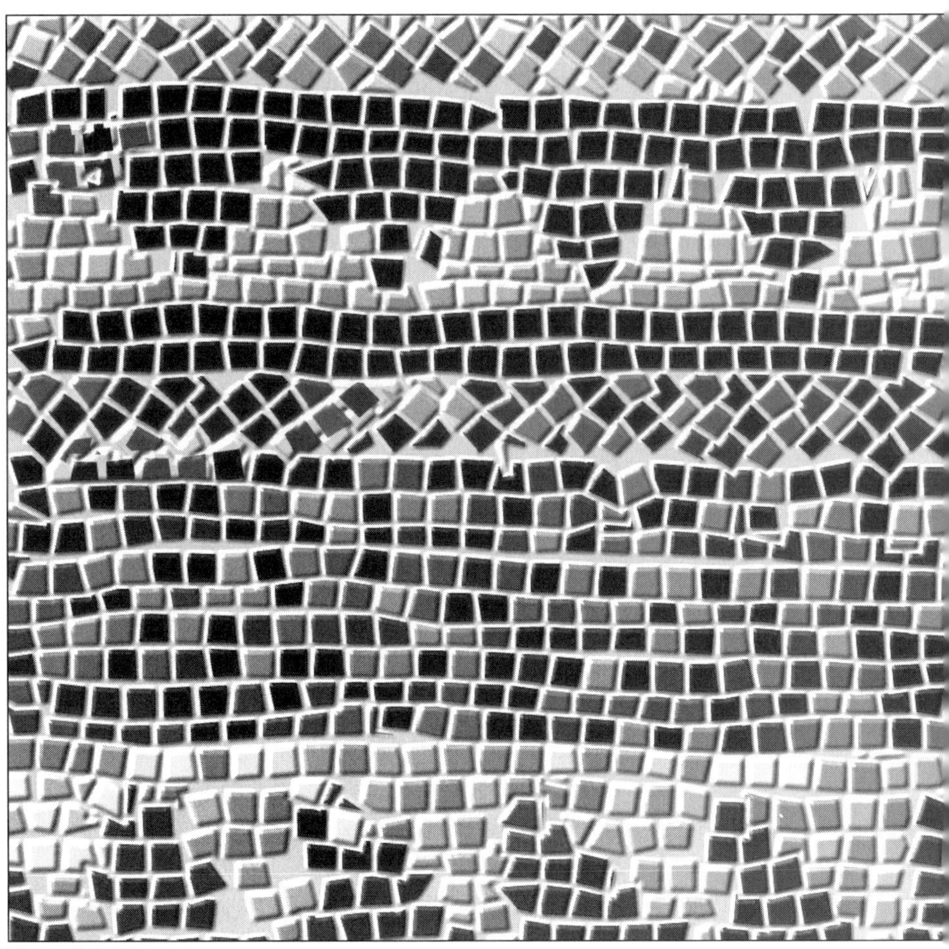

Elaine Weinmann

Mosaics

Painter's Mosaic command produces imagery that mimics traditional mosaic tiling. It doesn't render an image as a mosaic automatically—you actually paint the tiles on using brush strokes.

Mosaics can be applied to a blank canvas or to a clone using colors from the source document, and you can choose a custom grout color for the area behind the tiles. To achieve a high degree of realism, make your mosaic tiles look three dimensional (see page 204). Once they're applied, tiles can be recolored or removed.

You can apply Effects menu commands to, paint on, or create floaters from mosaic tiles. If you re-render the mosaics, though, only the tiles and the grout color will be preserved—not your painted effects.

Since mosaic tiling covers over the entire canvas, you should consider creating the mosaics in a separate document if you want to incorporate mosaics with existing imagery. Copy the mosaic image, and then paste it into an existing Painter document. Or you could create separate floaters from an image, create mosaics on the canvas, and then drop or composite the floaters with the mosaic.

Save your mosaics as RIFFs

A mosaic saved in the RIFF format can be re-rendered or recolored at any time, because tiles are saved as independent objects in this format. Mosaics saved in any other file format become pixel areas on the canvas and can't be revised as mosaic tiles. Additionally, tiles won't be limited to the current file's resolution if they're saved as RIFF; resizing the file and then re-rendering the mosaic won't affect its original quality.

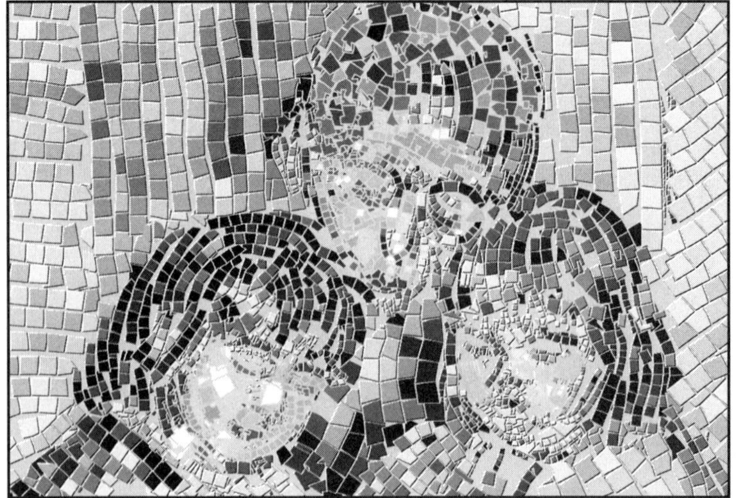

Elaine Weinmann, Bert

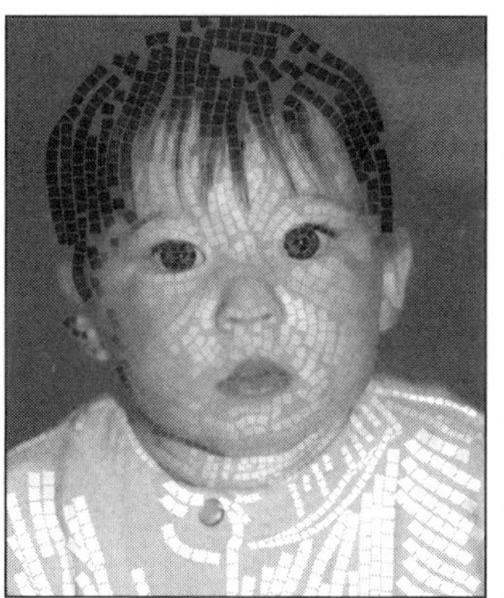

Filling in tiles on a clone of a photograph, with Use Tracing Paper turned on. We used larger tiles to draw the baby's jacket and smaller tiles to bring out details in her face.

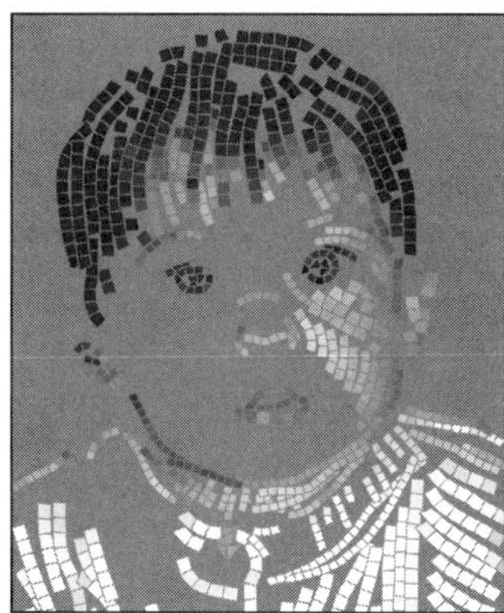

To check our progress, we unchecked the Use Tracing Paper box.

You can create mosaics in a new image or in a clone image.

To create a mosaic:

1. Open the Art Materials: Color palette and/or the Color Set swatch palette so you can choose colors for the mosaic tiles later (step 5).

2. If you want to create a clone for the mosaic so you can trace it, open the document to be cloned, then choose File menu > Clone, and make sure the clone document window is active.
   or
   Create a new document.

3. Choose Canvas menu > Make Mosaic (Command-Option-M).

4. If you're working on a clone image, check the Use Tracing Paper box.

5. Choose a Primary color for the tiles from the Color palette or the Color Set swatch palette. You can choose a different color at any time while the Make Mosaic dialog box is open. Increase the Hue or Value range using the Color Variability sliders on the expanded Art Materials: Color palette to create color shifts from tile to tile.

6. *Optional:* If you're working on a clone, check Use Clone Color box on the expanded Art Materials: Color palette to use colors from the original image.

7. *Optional:* To choose a grout color other than black, click the Grout square **7**, move the slider to the right to reveal colors on the wheel, pick a new color, then click OK. You can change the grout color later on if you want, though doing so will cause the tiles to re-render.

8. Click the Apply Tiles icon **8**.

9. Choose Settings: Dimensions to have exact control over tile and spacing

(Continued on the following page.)

sizes or Randomness for random tile and spacing sizes.

10. If you chose the **Dimensions** setting, adjust any of these sliders:

The Width and Length sliders control the tile width and length, respectively.

The Pressure slider controls to what degree tile width depends on stylus pressure. At a low setting, a light pressure will produce narrow tiles. 100% Pressure will produce tiles of a uniform width, regardless of stylus pressure.

The Grout slider controls the spacing between the tiles. Drag to the right to increase spacing.

11. If you chose the **Randomness** setting, adjust any these sliders:

The Width and Length sliders control how much the tile width and length will randomly vary. Drag to the right to increase randomness.

The Cut slider controls how square the side edge of the tiles are.

The Grout slider controls how much tile spacing will randomly vary.

12. Draw strokes on the image to apply tiles. To create an illusion of volume, try to draw curvy strokes that follow the forms in the original image you're working from. You can use the Undo shortcut (Command-Z) as you're working.

If you're working on a clone, periodically check your progress by unchecking the Use Tracing Paper box.

13. *Optional:* Hold down Control and drag over any tiles you want to delete.

14. Click Done to close the dialog box.
or
Modify the tiling (instructions on the next page).

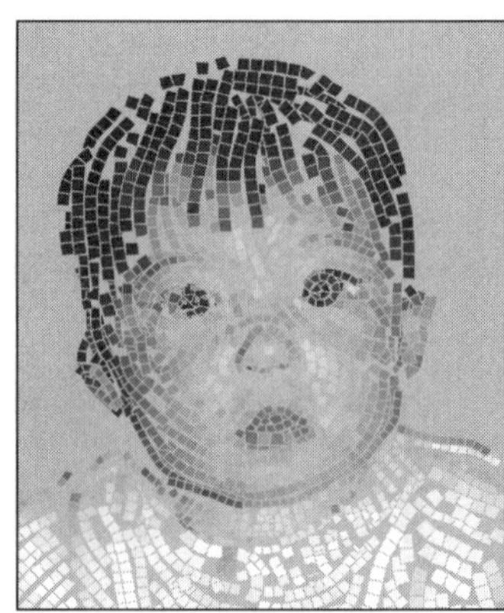

We lightened the grout color to emphasize the skin tones.

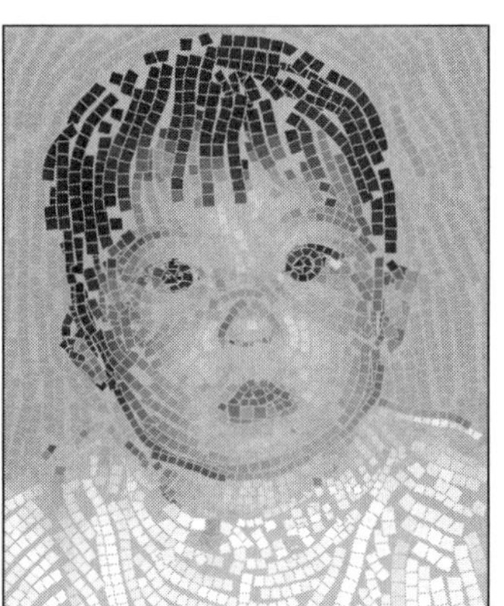

We wanted a simple background for this image instead of the dark background in the original photo, so we unchecked Use Clone Color on the Colors palette and then applied neutral gray tiles.

Weinmann

Tips

■ **To lighten areas of the mosaic, drag over tiles with the Change Tile Color icon and the Lighten option chosen in the Make Mosaic dialog box. To darken areas of the mosaic, drag over them with the Change Tile Color icon and the Darken option chosen. You could also use Painter's Dodge brush or the Apply Lighting command to lighten or the Burn brush to darken.**

■ **Start a mosaic, click Done, then use a Pencil or Brush variant to draw over the mosaic. Then open the Make Mosaic dialog box again, and continue to add tiles, using the sketch as a guide. Finally, choose Re-Render Mosaic to remove the sketch.**

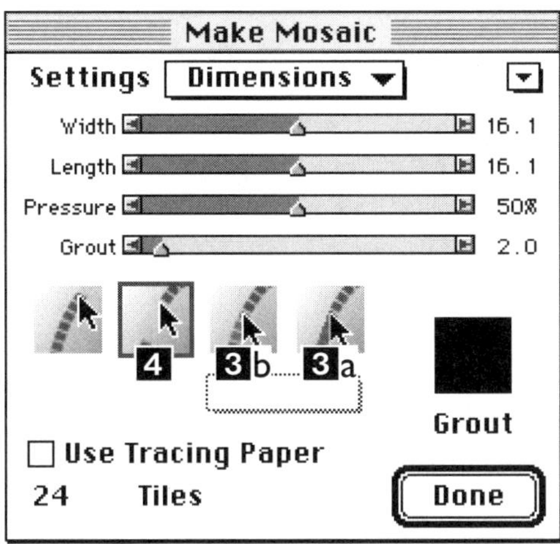

Keyboard shortcuts for recoloring tiles

C Color selected tiles with the current Primary color.

T Tint selected tiles with 10% of the current Primary color.

V Vary selected tile's color based on the Color palette's current Color Variability settings.

Keyboard shortcuts for selecting tiles

A Select every tile in the image.

D Deselect every tile in the image.

With the Select Tiles icon highlighted, **Command-click** on a tile containing a flat color to select any contiguous tiles that contain the same flat color.

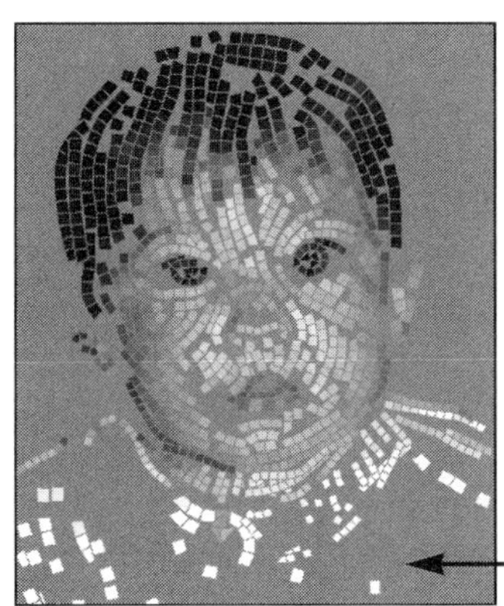

Removing tiles in the baby's sweater.

To recolor mosaic tiles:

1. Open the mosaic image you want to modify. *Note:* The image must have been saved in the RIFF format for the mosaic to be editable.

2. Choose Canvas menu > Make Mosaic.

3. *To recolor tiles using shortcuts:*
   Click the Select Tiles icon **3**a.
   and
   Click on or drag over the tiles in the image that you want to recolor. Selected tiles have a red outline. (To select every tile in the image, press A.)
   and
   Choose a Primary color from the Art Materials: Color palette.
   and
   Use any of the keyboard shortcuts for recoloring tiles listed at left (C, T, or V).

   To recolor tiles by dragging:
   Click the Change Tile Color icon **3**b.
   and
   From the pop-up menu below the Change Tile Color icon, choose:

   Color to recolor tiles you drag over with the current Primary color. Choose a Primary color now.

   Darken to mix black into the tiles you drag over.

   Lighten to mix white into the tiles you drag over.

   Tint to mix 10% of the current Primary color into the tiles you drag over. Choose a Primary color now.

   Vary to apply the Color palette Color Variability settings to the tiles you drag over. Choose those settings now.
   and
   Drag over the tiles you want to recolor.

4. *Optional:* To remove tiles, click the Remove Tiles icon **4**, then click on or drag over any tiles you want to remove.

5. Click Done to close the dialog box.

To create a 3D mosaic:

1. Create a mosaic.
2. Choose Canvas menu > Make Mosaic.
3. Choose Render Tiles into Mask from the pop-up menu in the Make Mosaic dialog box. A mask of the tile shapes will be created.
4. Click Done.
5. Choose Effects menu > Surface Control > Apply Surface Texture.
6. Choose Using: Mask.
7. Adjust any of the sliders. Start with low Softness and Reflection settings.
8. Click OK. Looks like Chicklets!

✎ To turn the mask of the tiles into a selection of the tiles, click the third Visibility button on the Objects: P. List palette. Choose Edit menu > Mask > Invert Mask if you want to select the grout areas.

To stroke or fill a selection with tiles:

1. Create a selection.
2. Choose Canvas menu > Make Mosaic.
3. Adjust the Dimensions or Randomness sliders for tile sizing.
4. Choose Stroke Selections or Fill Selection from the pop-up menu. The selection will be stroked and/or filled with tiles.
5. Click Done to close the dialog box.

✎ To remove the stroke or fill tiling effect, choose Edit menu > Undo while the dialog box is open.

✎ Try applying the Stroke Selections command first, choose a smaller tile size (Width and Length sliders), then apply the Fill Selection command.

✎ If your selection is positioned on top of existing mosaics and the file was saved in the RIFF format, the Stroke Selections or Fill Selection command will insert tiles only into grout areas—not over existing tiles.

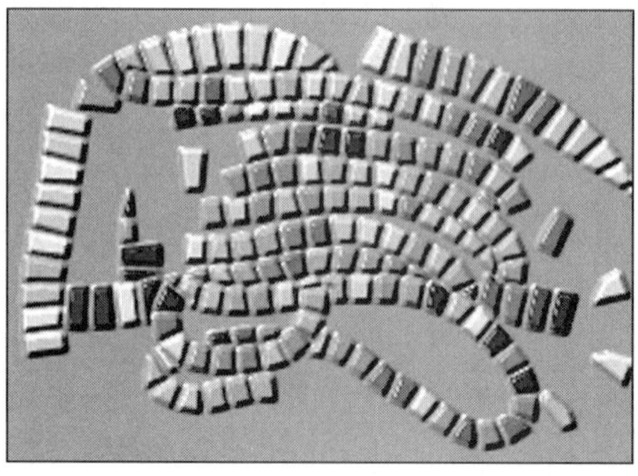

Ray Rue

The Fill Selection command was used to create this image, and then a three dimensional effect was created (instructions on this page).

To cut tiles at the edge of the image
Choose Respect Edge of Image from the pop-up menu in the Make Mosaic dialog box BEFORE you apply tiles to the image. A line the width of the current Grout setting will be created at the edge of the image and tiles will fit within the image boundary. Once Respect Edge of Image is turned off, it cannot be turned on again for the current mosaic. You can turn it on for a new mosaic or after choosing Reset Mosaic from the pop-up menu in the Make Mosaic dialog box, which erases the current mosaic.

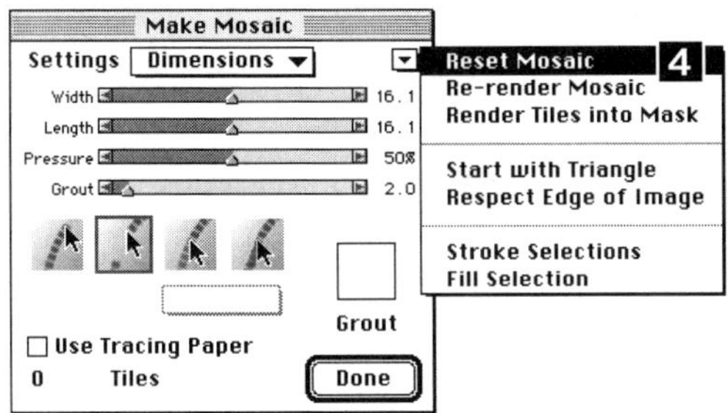

To clear all mosaics and any other pixel imagery from an image:

1. Open the image from which you want to remove the mosaics.

2. Choose Canvas menu > Make Mosaic.

3. The entire canvas is going to be filled with the current grout color, so if you want to change the grout color, click the Grout color square, choose a new color, then click OK.

4. Choose Reset Mosaic from the pop-up menu **4**.

5. Click Yes. Any existing paint strokes will be covered with the grout color. Only floaters and shapes will be preserved.

To restore the image to its state prior to your choosing Reset Mosaic, choose Edit menu > Undo (Command-Z).

To re-create a mosaic at a higher resolution:

1. Create a mosaic at a low ppi resolution, like 72 ppi.

2. Choose Canvas menu > Resize.

3. Uncheck the Constrain File Size box, enter a higher resolution value in the Resolution field, then click OK. The image will be resized and the tiles will look less sharp.

4. Choose Canvas menu > Make Mosaic.

5. Choose Re-render Mosaic from the pop-up menu **5**.

6. Click Done. The tiles will be redrawn at the higher resolution.

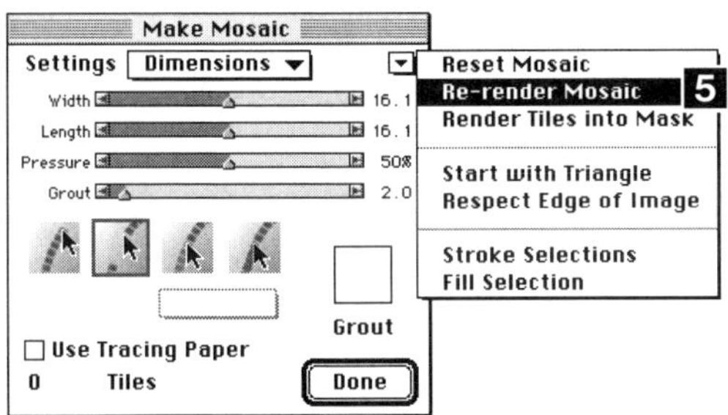

Tessellation mosaics

Using the Make Tessellation command, you can produce non-rectangular mosaic tiles. The tiles can be triangular (Triangles), they can look like cracked glass or pottery (Cracks), or they can be pebble-shaped (Pieces). You can marquee an area on an image and fill it with tessellation tiles or apply tessellation mosaics to a clone using colors from the source image. The Make Tessellation command affects the entire canvas—only floaters are preserved.

To create a tessellation mosaic:

1. Choose a Primary color for the tiles from the Art Materials: Color palette or the Color Set swatch palette. To achieve a variegated effect, adjust the Color Variability sliders on the extended Color palette. You can recolor the tessellation tiles later.

2. Create a new document. (The Make Tesselation command will erase everything in an existing document.)
   or
   To create a tessellation mosaic from a clone, open an image, drop all floaters in the image, choose File menu > Clone, choose Edit menu > Select All, press Delete, and check the Use Clone Color box on the expanded Art Materials: Color palette.

3. Choose Canvas menu > Make Mosaic, move the Grout slider to a low setting, then click Done.

4. Choose Canvas menu > Make Tessellation (Command-Option-V).

5. Choose a tile shape from the Display pop-up menu: Triangles, Cracks, or Pieces.

6. Choose any Add [...] Points option from the pop-up menu on the right side of the dialog box to fill the image window with polygon pieces. **The tiles will be colored when you close the dialog box.** If you're working on

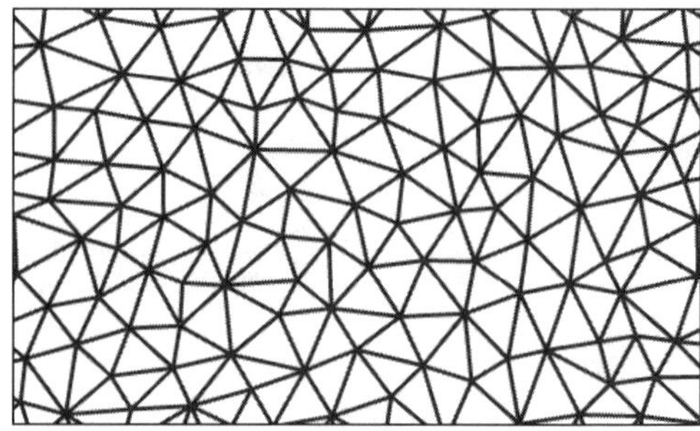

Triangles.

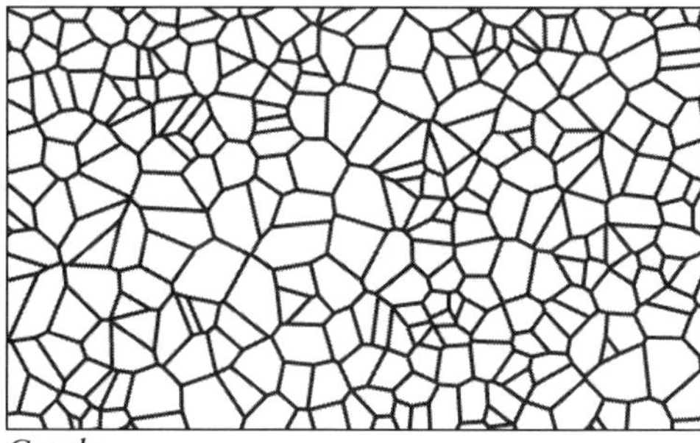

Cracks.

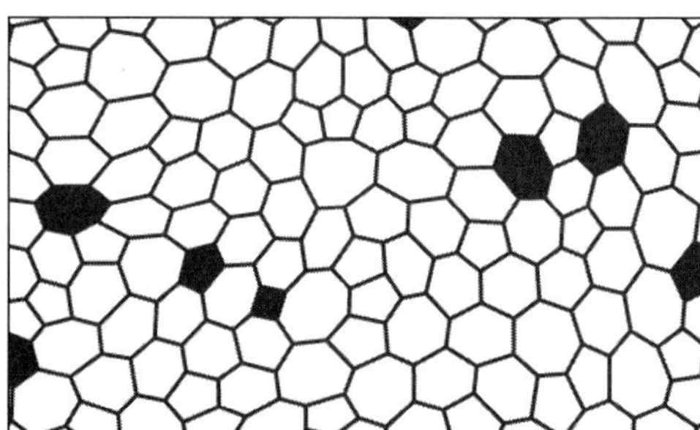

Pieces (Add 500 Evenly-Spaced Points).

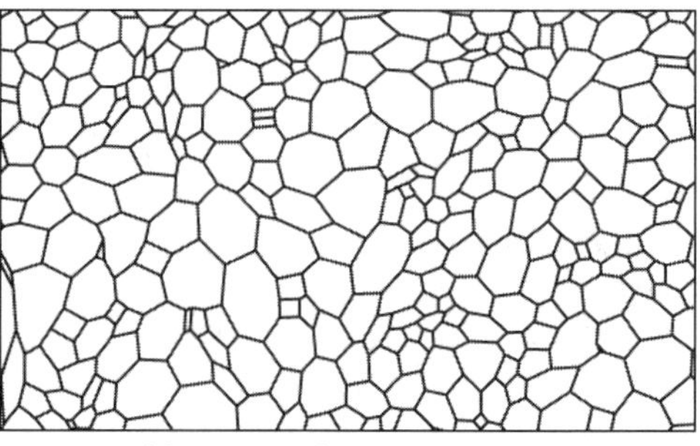

Pieces (Add 500 Random Points).

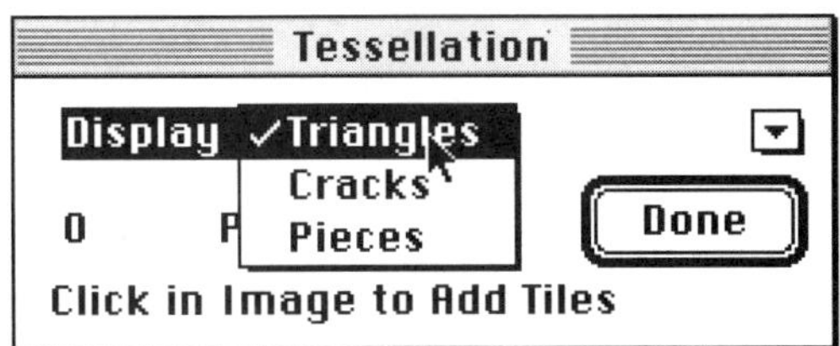

a clone, choose Add 500 Clone Spaced Points or Add 500 Inverse-Clone Spaced Points. Pause while the tessellation lines render in the image window. You can choose the same command again to produce even smaller pieces. Choose Reset to start over with a new, blank canvas.

7. *Optional:* Drag in the image window to subdivide existing tessellation pieces in a linear pattern. This step is useful for defining volume and accentuating details. You can't undo these steps, unfortunately.

8. Click Done to close the dialog box. Painter will render the tessellation into mosaic tiles.

9. *Optional steps:*

   Choose Canvas menu > Make Mosaic, choose a new Grout color for the spaces between the tessellation tiles, or adjust the Grout thickness slider.

   To recolor the mosaic tiles, follow the instructions on page 203. The other instructions in this chapter also apply to tessellation mosaics.

   To make the tesselation look three-dimensional, follow the instructions on page 204. Use low Softness and Reflection settings in the Apply Surface Texture dialog box.

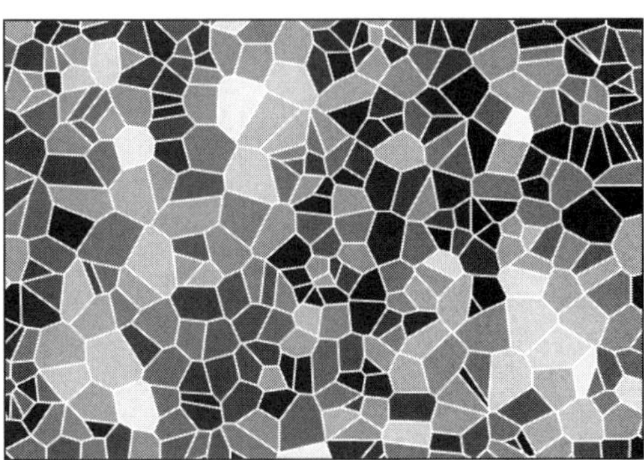

To create this variegated effect, the Color Variability: Value slider (extended Art Materials: Color palette) was moved to the right before choosing the Make Tessellation command. Tiles were further darkened and lightened by dragging across them with the Change Tile Color icon and the Darken or Lighten option chosen in the Make Mosaic dialog box.

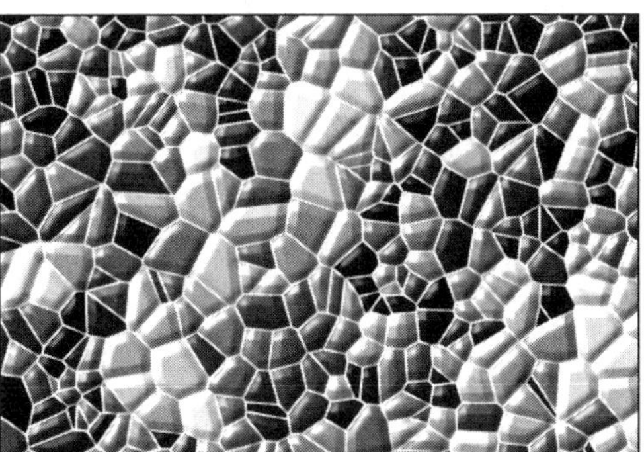

Finally, the Apply Surface Texture command was used (Softness slider moved to the right) to make the tessellation tiles look three dimensional (follow the first set of instructions on page 204).

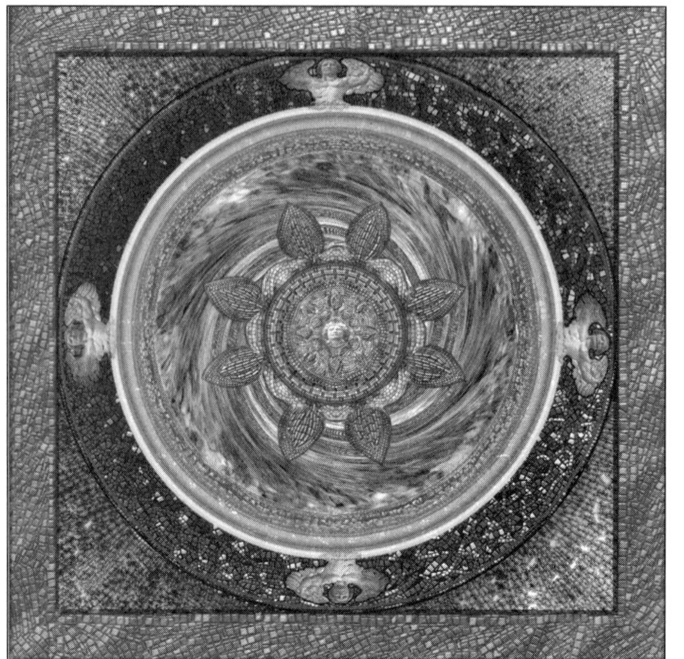

Ray Rue, **Angel.**

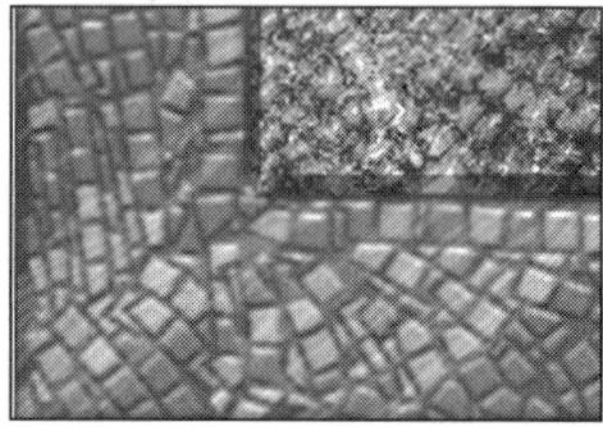

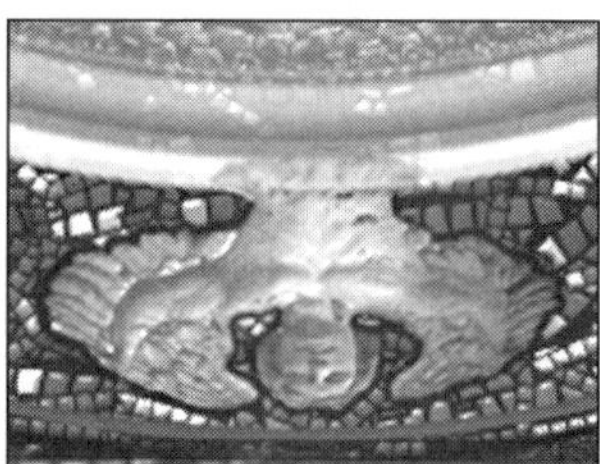

Close-ups.

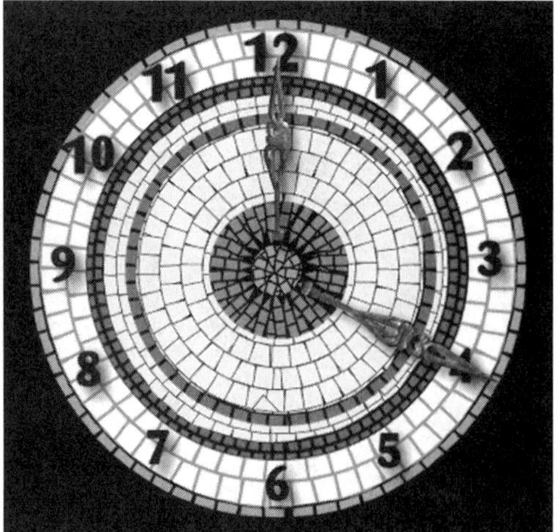

Ray Rue

To start with a triangular tile for each spoke that connects at a common center or corner point, choose **Start with Triangle** *from the pop-up menu in the Make Mosaic dialog box.*

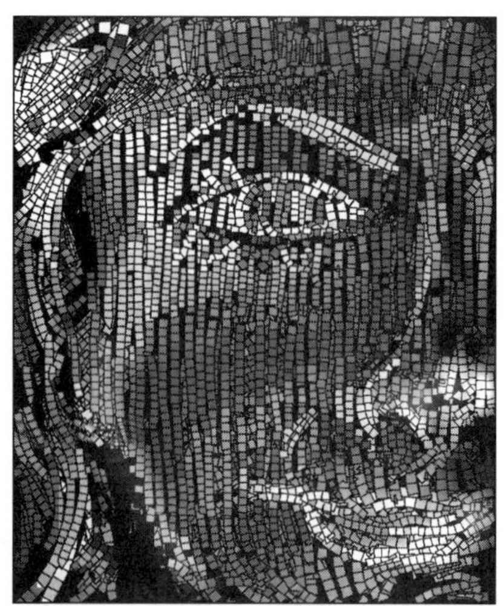

Lourekas

The Dodge and Burn brushes and the Apply Lighting command were used to enhance contrast in this mosaic.

Scripts 13

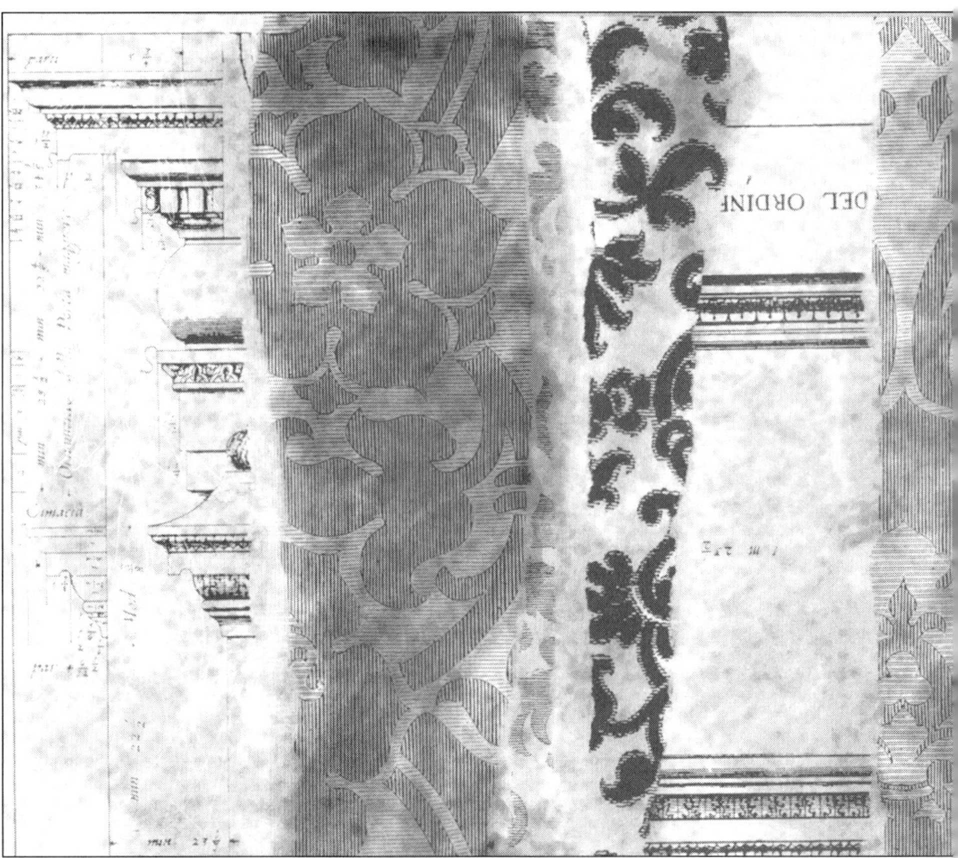

Fabric Effects, Inc.

Scripts

Using scripts—Painter's instant replay feature—you can record and then replay any number of brush strokes or commands. Use scripts to demonstrate how you create your artwork, to replay one image on top of another, to perform repetitive tasks, to create a movie or apply commands to a series of movie frames, to re-create an image at a different resolution, or just to make a record for yourself of how you produce your artwork. And best of all, you can add, delete, or reorder steps in a completed script.

To record a script:

1. Choose Objects palette > Scripts menu > Script Options.

2. Check the **Record Initial State** box if you plan to replay your script using the same brushes and paper textures **2**.

   Uncheck **Record Initial State** if you want to replay your script using one brush and one paper texture that you will select at the time of replay. These Script Options will remain in effect until you change them or quit Painter.

3. Click OK or press Return.

4. Create or open an image window.

5. Click the Scripts icon on the Objects palette, and close the palette drawer.

6. Click the red Record button on the Scripts palette **6** or choose Objects palette > Scripts menu > Record Script.

7. Create your art work.

8. To stop recording, click the square Stop record button on the Scripts palette **8**.

9. Type a name for the script. To assign a keyboard shorcut to the script, enter "\" then a letter of your choice after the script name **9**.

10. Click OK or press Return. The script will be saved in the currently open script library and an icon for it will appear on the Objects: Scripts palette.

To insert pauses in a script as you record it

Use the Shift - (hyphen) shortcut.

Jam Sessions

This is what a script file icon looks like.

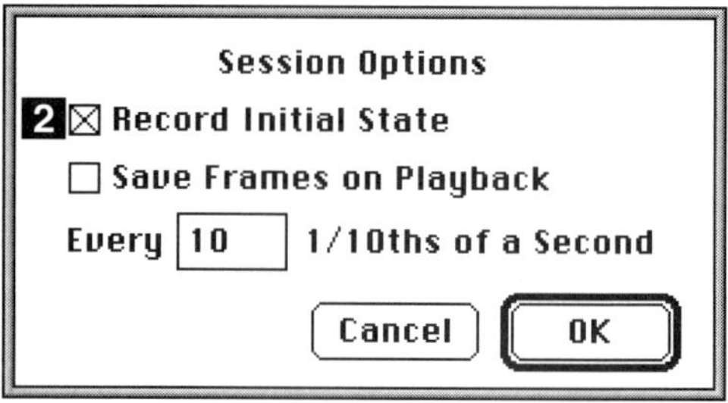

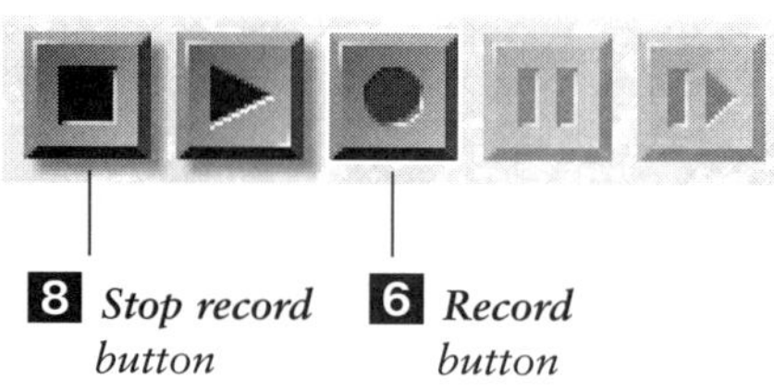

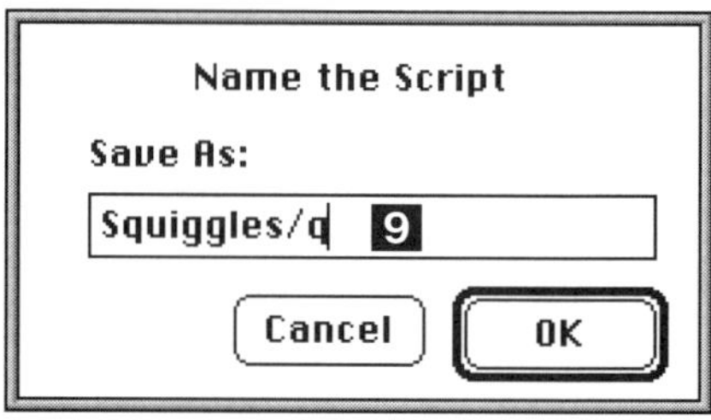

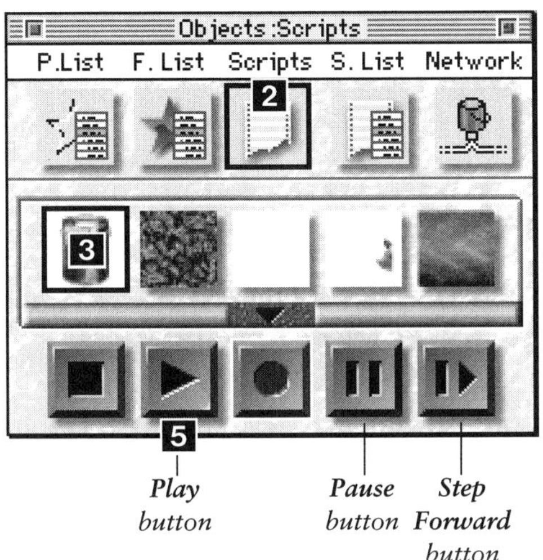

A script can be replayed by itself or right on top of another picture.

To replay a script:

1. Create a new document or open an existing document.

2. Click the Scripts icon on the Objects palette **2**.

3. Click the icon on the Objects: Scripts palette of the script you want to replay **3**. To access a script in a different library, click Library in the Scripts palette drawer, locate and highlight the library you want to open, then click Open.

4. Close the Scripts palette drawer.

5. *Optional:* If you unchecked the Record Initial State box before you recorded the script, you can choose one brush and one paper texture for the replay.

6. Click the Play button **5**. To pause the replay, click the Pause button, then click the Play button or the Pause button again to resume the replay. Click the Step Forward button to fast-forward.

To end the replay before it's finished, hold down Command and press ".".

To replay a script using a shortcut, hold down Command and press "K", then press the letter you assigned to the script. You don't need to highlight the icon on the Scripts palette. *(See step 9 on the previous page.)*

To create or edit a Scripts library, see the instructions on pages 21–22.

To record and replay one brush stroke instead of a whole work session, follow the instructions on page 64. To record a script as a movie, see page 213. To replay a script on a movie, see page 228.

Replay a Script

High resolution files are slow to process and bulky to store. Though it's best to create a picture at its final output resolution, if you need to save storage space and speed up processing, you can record a script at a low resolution and then replay and save the picture later at a higher resolution. Replaying a script at a higher resolution is preferable to increasing a file's resolution via the Canvas menu > Resize command.

To record a script so it can be replayed at a different resolution:

1. Create a new document. Enter the appropriate starting Resolution.

2. Choose Edit menu > Select All (Command-A).

3. Choose Objects palette > Scripts menu > Script Options.

4. Check the **Record Initial State** box if you're planning to replay your script using the same brushes and paper textures.

   Uncheck **Record Initial State** if you want to replay your script using one brush and one paper texture that you will select at the time of replay. These Script options will remain in effect until you change them or quit Painter.

5. Click OK or press Return.

6. Click the Scripts icon on the Objects palette, and close the palette drawer.

7. Check the red Record button on the Scripts palette.

8. Choose Edit menu > Deselect (Command-D).

9. Paint your picture. *Note:* If you find that a very long or complex script causes playback problems, record your picture-making in more than one script.

10. Check the square Stop button on the Scripts palette to stop recording.

11. Enter a name for the Script.

12. Click OK or press Return.

To replay a script at a different resolution:

1. Record your script following the steps at left.

2. Choose File menu > New.

3. Enter the desired Resolution. Don't choose a resolution that is higher than approximately three times the resolution of the original file, or you may end up with color gaps. Also, Painter's brushes have a maximum size, so large brush strokes may not increase proportionally.

4. If you want this document to have a higher resolution but the same width-to-height ratio as the original document, increase the Width and Height by the same amount that you increased the resolution. If you change the width-to-height ratio, the image will become distorted.

5. Click OK or press Return.

6. *Optional:* If you unchecked the Record Initial State box before you recorded the script, you can choose one brush and one paper texture for the replay.

7. Choose Edit menu > Select All (Command-A).

8. Follow steps 3–6 on the previous page to replay the script.

Tips

■ **To save the movie in a different format, choose File menu > Save As, then click "Save current frame as image" or "Save movie as QuickTime" or "Save movie as numbered files."**

■ **If you replay a script recorded as a movie on another open picture, the movie will record over the picture, but it will be saved as a new movie file. Make sure no other movies are open when you replay the script and be sure to check the Save Frames on Playback box in the Script Options dialog box, otherwise the script will simply play back over the picture and will not become a frame stack movie.**

■ **If you replay a script on a new document, the first few frames may be blank, but you can delete them later.**

■ **After recording a script as a movie, choose Objects palette > Scripts menu > Script Options and uncheck the Save Frames on Playback box so future scripts aren't recorded and replayed as movies.**

If you save an existing script as a frame stack movie, you'll be able to edit the frames later in Painter. You can save the frame stack as a QuickTime movie later on.

To record an existing script as a frame stack movie:

1. Create a new document. When you choose dimensions, consider how the script will be played back (whether it will be applied to a movie or played over a picture).

2. Choose Objects palette > Scripts menu > Script Options.

3. Check the Save Frames on Playback box.
   and
   Enter a number in the Every 1/10ths of a Second field. The more frames (the lower the number entered), the smoother the movie playback, but the larger the file size. 10 is the default.
   and
   Click OK or press Return.

4. On the Objects: Scripts palette, click a script icon, then click the Play button (right pointing arrowhead).

5. Enter a name for the new movie.
   and
   Choose a location in which to save it.
   and
   Click Save or press Return.

6. Enter the number of Onion Skin layers you'll want to use.
   and
   Click a Storage Type for the movie: 8-bit gray (256 levels of gray), 8-bit color (256 levels of color with a Macintosh system palette), 15-bit color (32,768 colors) with an 1-bit mask (black and white mask only), or 24-bit color (16.7 million colors) with an 8-bit mask (grayscale).

7. Click OK or press Return. The script will be recorded over several frames of the movie, depending on the length of the script.

To edit a script:

1. If the script you want to edit is not on the Objects: S. List palette, click Open Script on the palette **1**, highlight the script you want to edit (Click Open Library to open a different scripts library), then click Open. (If there's a script open on the S. List, but it's not the one you want to edit, click Close, then click Open Script.)
or
To add instructions to a brand new script, choose Objects palette > S. List menu > New Script, enter a name, then click OK.

2. Click on the instruction you want to edit. Hold down Shift to select multiple instructions. To select all the instructions in the script, choose Objects palette > S. List menu > Select All. (To deselect all the instructions, choose Objects palette > S. List menu > Deselect.)

3. Do any of the following:

   To **remove** the instruction without placing it on the Clipboard, click Clear **3**a. You can't undo this.

   To **move** the instruction to a different spot in the script, click Cut **3**b, select the instruction you want to follow the pasted instruction, then click Paste. (Click Copy instead of Cut if you want to duplicate the instruction.)

   To **display the contents** of an instruction, click the triangle next to it **3**c. Click the triangle again to close it. To **change an element** in an instruction, like a color, tool, variant, or texture, double-click the indented entry and enter the number code that Painter has assigned to the desired command. To choose a new method subcategory, for example, you'll enter "1" for Flat Cover, "2" for Soft Cover, etc. To learn more about script coding, see the second tech note in the Painter Tech Notes.pdf file in the REFERENZ folder on the Painter 4 CD-ROM.

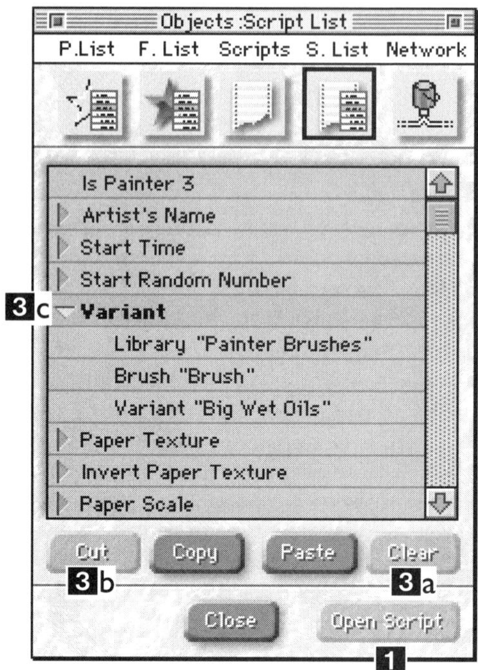

To copy instructions from one script to another

Click Open Script on the Objects: S. List palette, highlight the script you want to copy from, then click Open. (If a script is already open, click Close, then click Open Script on the palette.) Highlight the instructions you want to move, click Copy, then click Close. Click Open Script again, open the script you want to add the instructions to, highlight the instruction you want to follow the pasted instructions, then click Paste.

If you like, you can create a new script to copy instructions to. In fact, a script is automatically created each time you launch Painter and work in the program (it's called "Current Script"), and it's saved for the number of days entered in the "Auto Save scripts for [   ] days" field in the General Preferences dialog box.

Net Painter 14

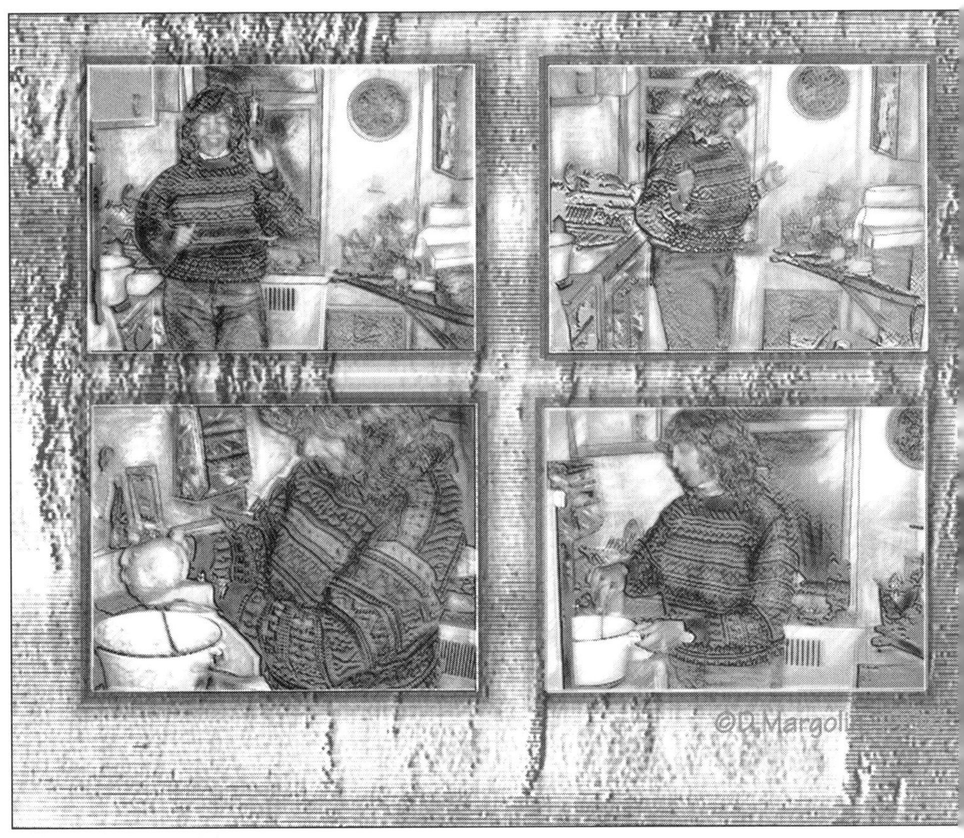

Diane Margolin, **Untitled.**

Net Painter

Net Painter

A Painter image can be shared and edited by several people on a network. One participant can paint while others view the changes, then another participant can paint while the others watch. During a painting session, anyone on the network can type comments in the chat window for other participants to read.

To paint on a network, all the computers involved in the session must be connected via a TCP/IP network. Ask your network administrator if your network is a TCP/IP setup.

If you log on to the network through a modem, you'll achieve faster file and library resource transfers and screen update on a 28.8k bps modem (V.34) than on a lower speed modem.

To set up Net Painter:

1. Log onto the network, then choose Objects palette > Network menu > Setup **1**.

2. In the Network Setup dialog box, enter a name in the User Name field **2**. This name will appear near the top of the Network window. The Host IP address field and the Host Name field will fill automatically with information from the computer's own network setup.

3. Enter up to four characters in the Chat ID field **3**. This ID identifies your comments and will appear in the chat window area of the Network window.

4. Enter a port number in the Port for Painter field **4**. You must agree among the session participants on a number between 1024 and 65535.

5. Uncheck Disable Network Painter **5**.

6. Click OK.

7. Choose Objects palette > Network menu > Setup again to see the IP address.

8. Click OK or press Return.

A few Net Painter tips from Fractal Design

■ To preserve the original file you will share, copy it. You can, if you want, place the copy in the Network Folder. When you have the green light, send the copy to the other participants.

■ You won't see a status bar while a file is being sent on the network, so you should send a chat message before you send the file to notify the other participants that it's on its way.

■ For best results on a PCI-Power Mac, install Open Transport 1.0.7. or later.

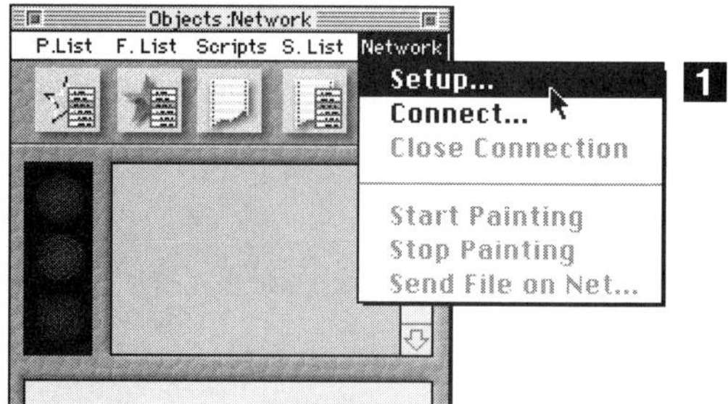

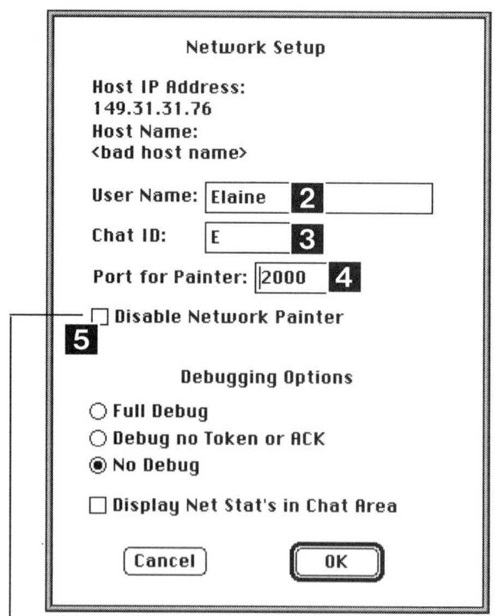

*Uncheck **Disable Network Painter** to use Net Painter. Check Disable Network Painter when you do not want the auto log-in to slow down your private, non-Net Painter sessions.*

Before starting a Net Painter session, make sure that:

1. All the participants are using Painter 4, with the same Undo Level setting (Undo Preferences).
2. All the participants are using the same port number.
3. No participants have any Painter files open.

To connect for a Net Painter session:

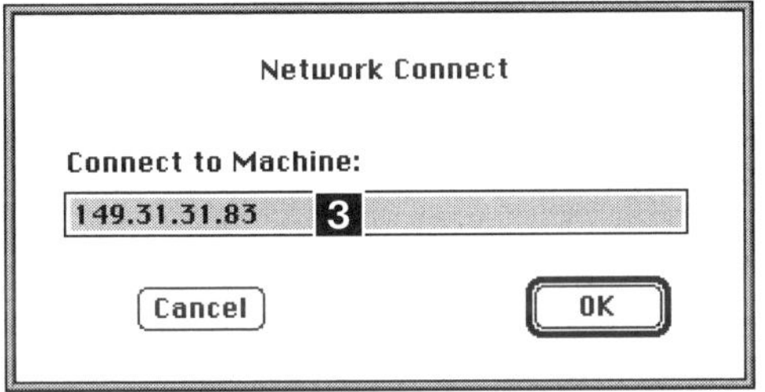

1. Connect to the Network.
2. Choose Objects palette > Network menu > Connect **2**.
3. Enter or accept the IP address of the computer you want to connect to—either the IP address name or the Domain name **3**. Several participants can connect to one computer IP address name or one participant can connect to an already connected computer IP address.
4. Click OK. The names of the participants connected for this session will appear in the Network window. Once one person begins painting or sending a file, the session becomes locked, and no one else can join.

To send a file to other participants in the session:

1. Make sure everyone has connected to Net Painter.
2. Click the green light in the Network window **2**.
3. Choose Objects palette > Network menu > Send File on Net **3**.
4. Locate and highlight the file.
5. Click Open. The file will be sent to the Network Folder (located in the Painter 4 folder) on the connected computers.
6. The person with the green light should now choose File menu > Open, and open the file that was just sent. It will open on all the connected computers.

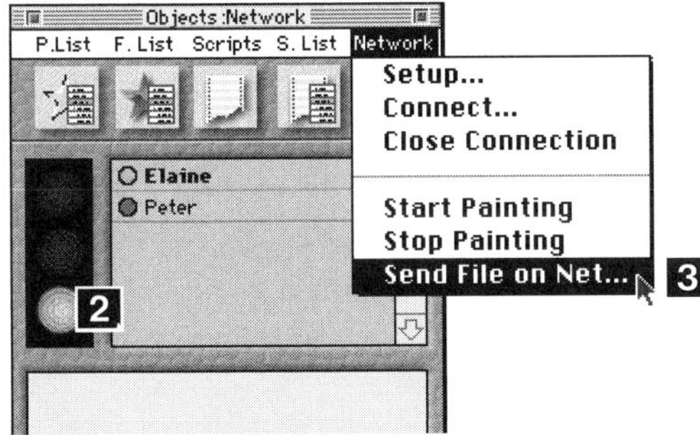

Net Painter

To begin Net painting:

1. On the Objects: Network palette:
    Click the green light on the left side of the Network window **1**.
    or
    Choose Network menu > Start Painting.

    If no one else is painting, you will see a green light by your name.

    If someone else is painting, you will see a yellow light by your name, signifying that you are waiting to paint.

2. If you have the green light, begin painting.

To stop Net painting:

On the Objects: Network palette:
Click the red light on the left side of the Network window.
or
Choose Network menu > Stop Painting.

While you are watching someone else paint, you can send comments to the other participants via the chat window.

To use the chat window:

1. Click on the chat line at the bottom of the Network window **1**. An insertion pointer will appear.

2. Type your message.

3. Press Return to send the message. To send another message, type, then press Return again.

4. Press Return on a blank line to close the text entry. Click the chat line again if you want to type and send a new message.

To disconnect from a Net Painter session:

Choose Objects palette > Network menu > Close Connection **A**. Your name will be removed from the list in the Network window.

Share your resources

If you want other participants to use custom resources that are on your system—like nozzles, brush variants, patterns, paper textures, plug-in filters, floaters, or paths—you must supply them. You can create custom libraries containing the resources you want to share and then send the library files to session participants at the start of the session.

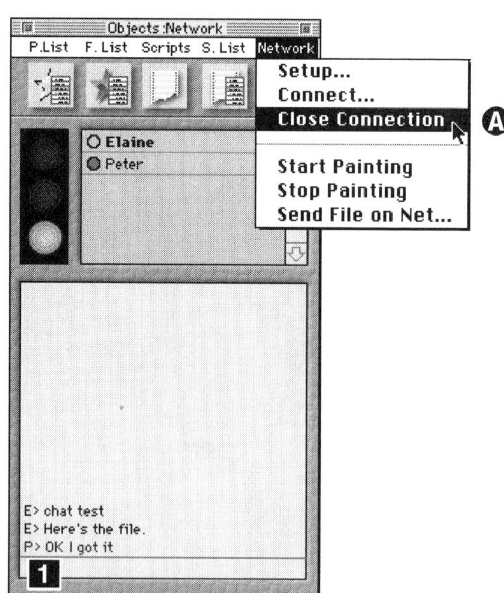

Movies 15

Animation by Philip Sanders (Penny Ward, videographer. Margarita Guergue, dancer).

Movies

Using Painter you can create a movie from scratch or you can edit individual frames of an existing movie using any Painter feature. Even if you've never made a movie before and you don't know anything about animation, try making a movie in Painter. You'll probably find making a simple movie to be relatively easy and fun. You can edit and save your movie in the QuickTime format or in Painter's own frame stack format.

QuickTime movies

QuickTime is a Macintosh system extension that enables applications to use data and resources needed for video. QuickTime runs on both the Macintosh and Windows operating systems, and you can use Painter to import from or export to either platform. A Painter movie saved in QuickTime format can be used in or further edited in a video editing application like Adobe Premiere, Adobe After Effects, or used in a multimedia application like Macromedia Director. (You can also import a series of numbered files from Painter into Director, where each file will become a separate cast member.)

Frame stack movies

A frame stack is a sequence of movie frames that can only be edited in Painter. In the frame stacks format, you can use "digital onion skin paper," which, like traditional onion skin paper that animators use, will enable you to view previous or subsequent frames behind the frame you're currently editing. Frame stack files are larger in file storage size than QuickTime files. When you open and save a QuickTime movie in Painter, it is automatically saved as a frame stack.

Digitizing video using hardware compression

You may encounter problems between hardware and software compressions if you digitize a video on one system and then move the digitized movie to another system. A digitized movie that uses custom hardware compression—like a video add-in board—won't play in software if the hardware isn't present in your system.

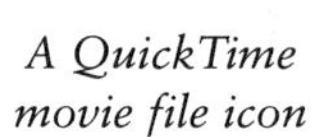

Surfer.QT2

A QuickTime movie file icon

On the Beach

A frame stack movie file icon

Frame editing hints

- **You can use any Painter tool to modify an existing movie. You can even play back a recorded brush stroke or a script on a movie or apply a texture to a movie.**

- **When you move forward or backward to a different frame, Painter saves your changes, and you can't undo a change after you move to a previous or subsequent frame. You can choose File menu > Revert to undo multiple changes to a frame only before you move to another frame. To play it safe, work on a copy of a movie rather than the original (highlight the file name icon in the Finder, then choose File menu > Duplicate).**

- **To learn how to navigate through the frames of a movie, see the next page.**

Movie frame previews. The red arrowhead points to the frame that is currently displayed in the image window. Click a frame thumbnail to make that frame active in the image window, or control frame display using the buttons at the bottom of the palette. The number of frames that preview on the palette and in the image window behind the current frame depends on the number of onion skin layers you chose to use. Click the Tracing Paper icon in the upper right corner of the image window to display/hide onion skin layers.

The Frame Stacks palette

Frame Stacks palette buttons control the playback of movie frames. Up to five sequential movie frame thumbnails can be displayed at a time, though you can only paint on one frame at a time. The Frame Stacks palette opens automatically when you open a movie.

It's a flip book! →

Frame Stacks Palette

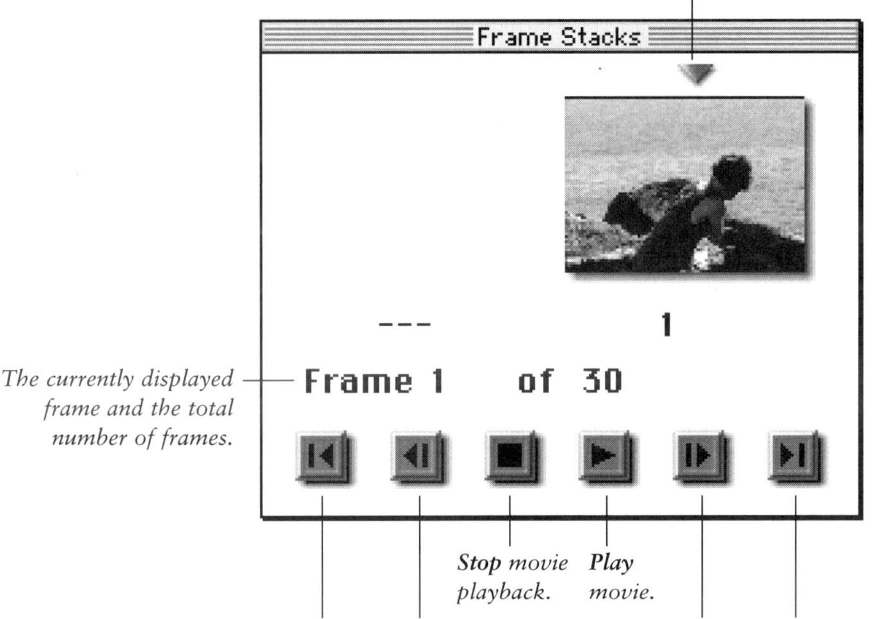

The currently displayed frame and the total number of frames.

Stop movie playback.

Play movie.

Rewind movie to first frame.

Step Reverse to previous frame.

Step Forward to next frame.

Fast Forward to last frame.

MOVIE SHORTCUTS

First frame of stack	Home
Last frame of stack	End
Next frame	Page Up
Previous frame	Page Down
Stop at current frame	Option-Stop button
Stop and return to start	Command-.
Play	Command-Shift-P

Follow these steps to create a new, blank movie (stack of frames), then follow the instructions on page 224, 227, or 232 to fill the frames with imagery.

To create a new, blank movie:

1. Choose File menu > New.

2. Enter Width and Height values and a Resolution of 72 dpi for the new movie. A full-screen movie—which is 640 x 480 pixels—will be large in file size. If this is your first movie, try a frame size of about 320 x 240 pixels.

3. Click Picture type: Movie with [ ] frames, then enter the number of frames that you want the new movie to contain. You can add or delete frames later.

4. Click OK or press Return.

5. Enter a name for the new movie.

6. Choose a location in which to save the movie, then click Save.

7. Enter the number of Layers of Onion Skin you want to use **7**.

8. Choose the Storage Type for the new movie **8**: 8-bit gray (256 levels of gray), 8-bit color (256 levels of color with a Macintosh system palette), 15-bit color (32,768 colors) with an 1-bit mask (black and white mask only), or 24-bit color (16.7 million colors) with an 8-bit mask (grayscale). A 1-bit mask uses only black and white pixels, so shapes will have hard, aliased edges. An 8-bit mask uses many levels of gray, so mask shapes can have soft, gray edges.

9. Click OK or press Return. The first frame of the movie will appear in an image window and on the Frame Stacks palette. The movie will be saved as a frame stack when you close it (choose File menu > Close or click the movie window close box).

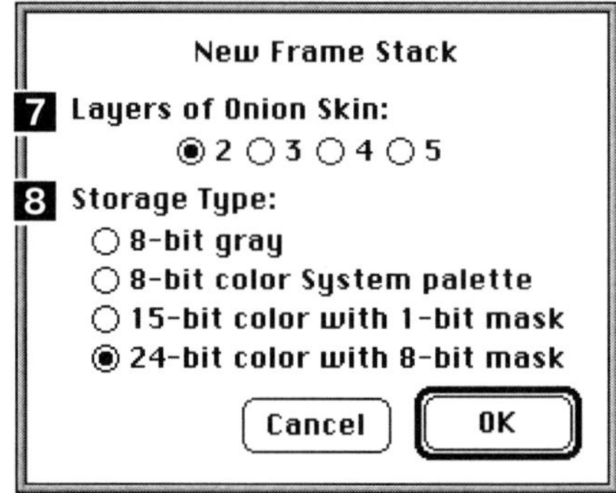

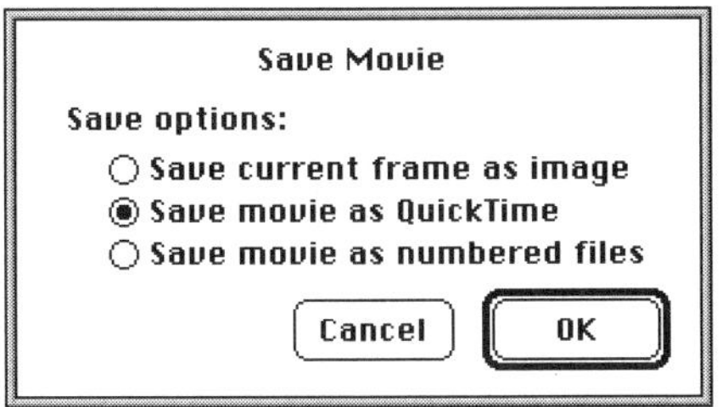

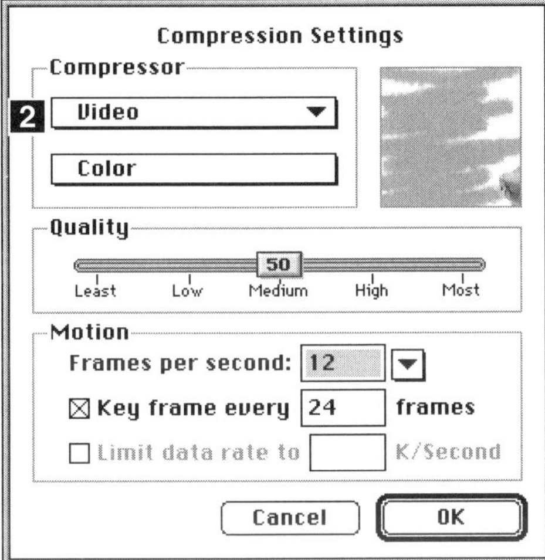

To save a frame stack movie in a different format:

1. With a frame stack movie open, choose File menu > Save As.

2. Click "Save current frame as image" to open the Save dialog box, where you can choose any of Painter's file export formats. Choose the PICT format to export to a multimedia program, like Macromedia Director.
   or
   Click "Save movie as QuickTime," enter a name, choose a location for the QuickTime file, then click Save. In the Compression Settings dialog box, choose a Compressor option **2**, choose a Color depth (if applicable), choose a Quality setting, enter a Frames per second rate, enter a frame interval when Key frames will be saved as complete images (and not just when changes occur in the digital info), then click OK.
   or
   Click "Save movie as numbered files" if you want to save the frame stack as a sequence of named frames starting or ending with a number, and in a different file format. This is the best method for exporting a series of Painter images as PICTs to Director to be used as separate cast members.

   Use Painter to convert a QuickTime movie into a frame stack and then save the frame stack as a series of sequentially numbered frames in the PICT format. The PICT files can be imported all at once into Director as separate cast members.

   If you have trouble importing a movie saved in Painter's QuickTime file format into a QuickTime compatible application, try importing the Painter movie into Adobe Premiere, resave the movie in Premiere's QuickTime format, and then reimport it into the QuickTime-compatible application.

Use the following technique to add hand-drawn elements to a movie in increments. Each new frame will automatically fill with the contents of the previous frame, so you can build on previous frames without having to redraw them.

To use a floater to create repetitive frames:

1. Create a new one-frame movie (instructions on page 222) that contains the desired background imagery.

2. Choose the Brush tool (B), a brush, and a variant, and paint on that frame.

3. Choose Edit menu > Select All (Command-A).

4. Choose the Floater Adjuster tool.

5. Click on the frame to turn the whole frame into a floater.

6. Click the Step Forward (fifth) button on the Frame Stacks palette. A new frame will be created and the floater will be copied onto it.

7. *Optional:* Press any of the arrow keys to move the floater within the frame.

8. Repeat steps 2–6 to create more frames.

9. Paint on the last frame, then click Drop on the Objects: F. List palette. You can now play or rewind the movie.

To move a floater across a movie frame, place a floater on a frame, step forward to the next frame, reposition the floater, step forward again, reposition the floater, etc. Drop the floater on the last frame. Using this method, you can copy the floater only from frame to frame, not the imagery on the background canvas.

To open a frame stack or QuickTime movie:

1. Choose File menu > Open (Command-O).

2. Highlight the name of the movie you want to open.

3. Leave the Open Numbered Files box unchecked, and click Open.

4. If it's a QuickTime movie, you'll need to save it as a frame stack movie. Enter a name, choose a location in which to save it, then click Save.

   For a frame stack movie, click the number of Layers of Onion Skin you want to use .

5. Click OK. The first frame of the movie will be displayed in the image window and on the Frame Stacks palette.

Numbered files are a sequence of related files—one per movie frame—that is saved in a format that can be opened in Painter. For numbered files to be opened as a movie, all the names in the sequence must contain the same number of characters, and they must have the same size and resolution. For example, you could use the names "Movie.01," "Movie.02," etc. for a movie that contains 99 or fewer frames. Change the number of zeros for a movie that contains more than 99 frames.

To open a numbered files movie:

1. Choose File menu > Open.

2. Check the Open Numbered Files box **2**.

3. Highlight the name of the first numbered file you want to open **3**, then click Open.

4. Highlight the name of the last numbered file you want to open, then click Open.

5. Enter a name for the frame stack movie.

6. Choose a location in which to save the movie, then click Save.

7. Enter the number of Layers of Onion Skin you want to use.
   and
   Choose a Storage Type (see page 222).

8. Click OK or press Return. The first frame of the movie will appear in the image window and on the Frame Stacks palette.

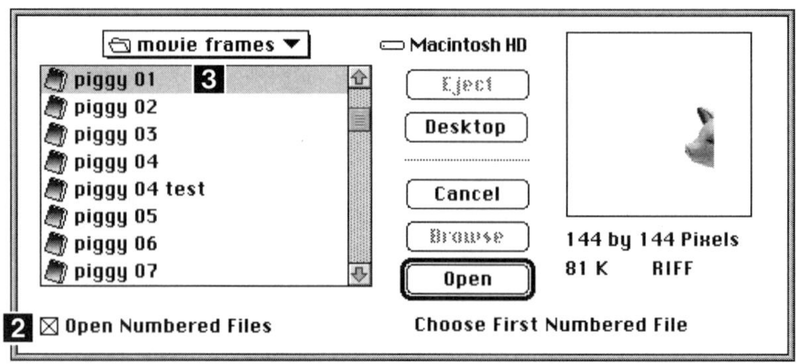

Artist Anna Kogan repainted the mouth on the clock face on this animation.

To paint on movie frames:

1. Follow the steps on page 222 to create a new movie, or open an existing movie (see page 225).

2. Make sure the Frame Stacks palette is open and the first frame of the movie is displayed in the image window (click the leftmost button on the Frame Stacks palette, if necessary).

3. Choose the Brush tool and a Primary color, then paint on the first frame using any brush.

4. Click the Step Forward (fifth) button on the Frame Stacks palette, and draw on the next frame. Repeat to edit other frames.

5. *Optional:* Click the Tracing Paper icon on the vertical scroll bar of the image window to view previous or subsquent frames (onion skin layers) under your current frame as you draw. Click the icon again to turn Tracing Paper off.

   Your file will be saved automatically when you close it. See the "Frame editing hints" on page 220.

To edit a frame stack:

Choose any of the following from the Movie menu:

Add Frames. Enter the number of blank frames you want to add **1**, then click the desired insertion point **2**: before or after a specified frame or at the start or end of the movie.

Delete Frames. Enter the range of consecutive frames to be deleted **3**.

Erase Frames. Enter the range of consecutive frames to be erased **4** (the frame itself will become blank, but it won't be deleted).

Go To Frame: Enter the number of the frame you want to move to.

Clear New Frames: If you click the Step Forward (fifth) button on the Frame Stacks palette when the Clear New Frames option is checked and the last frame of the movie is currently displayed, a new, blank frame will be added to your movie. If Clear New Frames is unchecked and you click the Step Forward button, a duplicate will be made of the last frame of the movie.

Insert (a separate) **Movie:** Choose an insertion point **5** (before or after a certain frame or at the start or end of the movie). In the Open dialog box, highlight the movie you want to insert, then click Open. *Note:* The movie you insert must be saved in Painter's frame stack format and must have the same width, height, and resolution as the movie into which it is inserted.

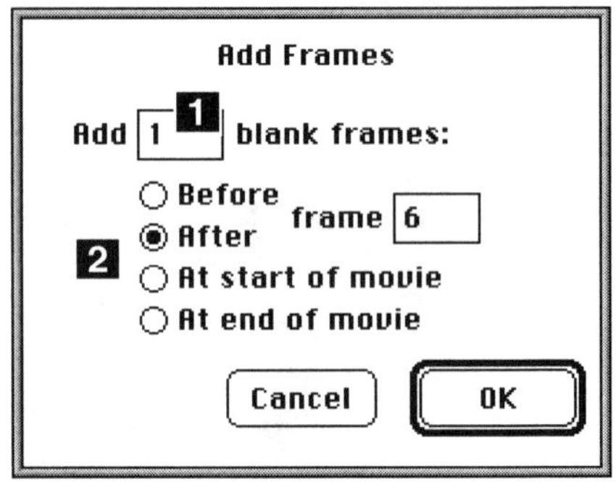

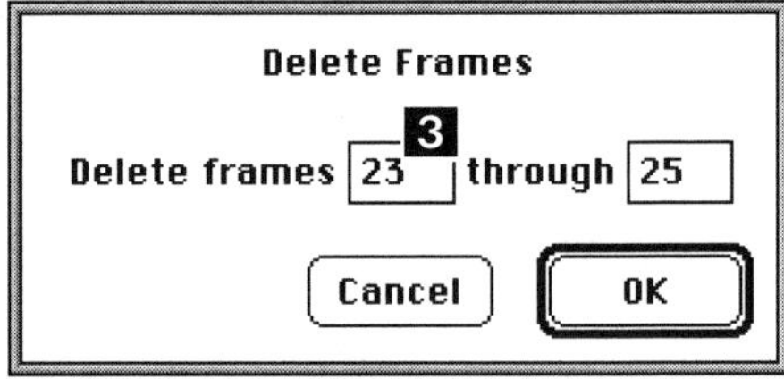

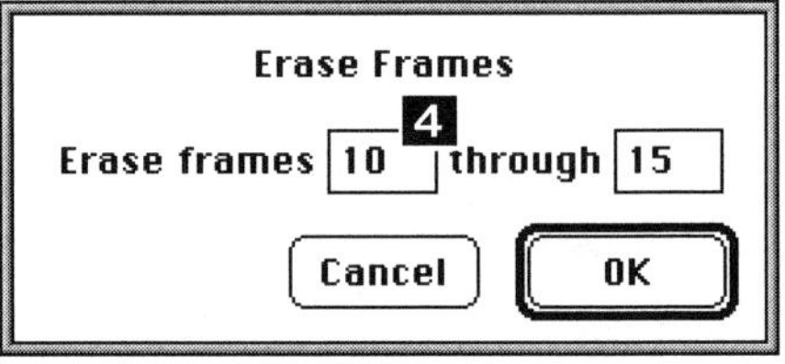

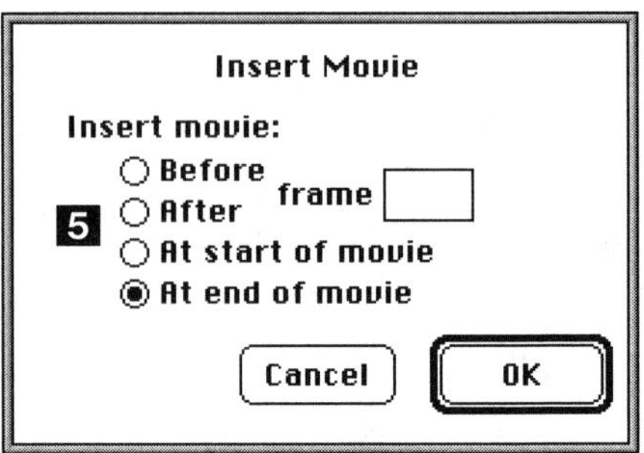

Penny Ward

Philip Sanders

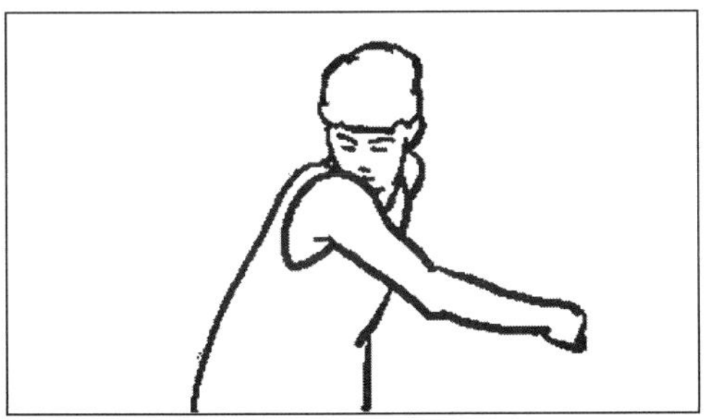

To trace a movie:

1. Open the movie to be the tracing source.

2. Create a new movie with the same dimensions and resolution and number of frames as the open movie. (Press the "i" icon in the lower left corner of the source movie window to display Height, Width, and Resolution info.)

3. Click in the source movie image window.

4. Choose Movie menu > Set Movie Clone Source.

5. Click in the new movie image window.

6. Click the Tracing Paper icon on the vertical scroll bar to make the first frame of the source movie appear faintly behind the new movie frame.

7. Choose the Brush tool and a brush variant to trace with. Choose a hard-edged brush to draw solid line work.

8. Trace over the image in frame 1.

9. Click the Step Forward (fifth) button on the Frame Stacks palette—the source movie will also advance—then trace over the next frame. Repeat on other frames.

 To darken the line work in the tracing to make filling with the Paint Bucket tool easier, choose Effects menu > Tonal Control > Equalize, then move the black point slider to the right.
To apply a command to all the frames in a stack using a script, follow the instructions on page 232. Also be sure to close all line shapes if you plan to use the Paint Bucket tool. See pages 146–148.

(Illustrations continue on the next page)

Trace a Movie

Penny Ward

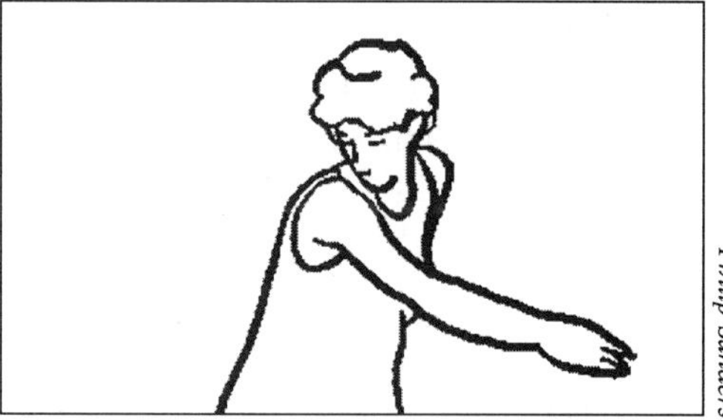
Philip Sanders

Apply a Recorded Brush Stroke to a Movie

A drawback with the Apply Brush Stroke To Movie command is that it applies only part of the stroke to each frame. If you use the **Image Hose** to produce the stroke, though, a complete nozzle file element will appear in each frame.

To apply a recorded brush stroke to a movie:

1. Record a brush stroke using the Brushes palette > Strokes menu > Record Stroke command. If you record the stroke on the movie, choose Edit menu > Undo when you're finished.

2. With the movie image window active, choose Movie menu > Apply Brush Stroke To Movie. Pause while the brush stroke is applied to the movie.

If you use a mask when you apply a brush stroke, you'll have more control over the placement of the stroke.

To apply a continuous brush stroke to a movie using a mask:

1. Open the movie, and make sure Tracing Paper is off.

2. Choose a Masking brush variant.

3. Make sure the second Visibility (eye) button and the second Drawing button on the extended Objects: P. List palette are selected, and check the Transparent Mask box.

4. Choose Black as the Primary color.

5. Draw an entire, continuous masking stroke on any frame of the movie.

6. Click the third Visibility (eye) button on the Objects: P. List palette to turn the mask into a selection.

7. Choose a paintbrush and a Primary color. Make your brush tip size wider than the mask selection so you can easily cover the selection area.

8. Click the third Drawing button to paint inside the mask.

9. Draw a short stroke at the start of the active mask selection.

10. Click the Step Forward button on the Frame Stacks palette.

11. Press Return to activate the mask selection.

12. Draw a slightly longer stroke beginning again at the start of the active mask selection.

13. Repeat steps 10–12 until the entire mask selection is filled in.

14. Press Return when you're finished to deactivate the selection.

15. Click the first Visibility and Drawing buttons on the Objects: P. List palette so future edits won't be restricted to the mask selection.

To apply a continuous brush stroke to a movie using tracing paper:

1. Turn on Tracing Paper: Click the Tracing Paper button at the top right corner of the image window (Command-T).

2. Paint the stroke on the first frame of the series that you want to edit.

3. Click the Step Forward (fifth) button to advance one frame.

4. When you start painting the next frame, paint over and then continue beyond the previous stroke. Repeat on consecutive frames.

You can record a script in which you apply Effects menu commands like Video Legal Colors or a series of brush strokes and then apply the whole script to every movie frame.

To apply a script to a movie:

1. Record a script (see page 210).

2. Open a copy of the movie to which you want to apply the script. (You can't undo applying a script to a movie.)

3. Choose Movie menu > Apply Script To Movie.

4. Locate and highlight the script name.

5. Click Playback. The whole script will be applied to every frame. A long script may take a while to process.

✎ Use the Command-. shortcut at any time to stop the application of the script to the movie.

✎ Record a separate script for individual commands—like Auto Mask, Brightness/Contrast or Posterize—on the first movie frame, choose Edit > Undo, then follow steps 3–5 above to apply each script. Store the scripts in one folder so you can locate them easily and apply them as needed. Some commands may not work reliably if they're recorded in the same script with other commands.

To mask part of a frame

■ Use any Masking brush variant to mask areas on a frame. If you do this on each frame of a movie, you can then clone imagery frame-by-frame from another source within or around the masked area, depending which mask Drawing button you select on the Objects: P. List palette. Or, for a high contrast image, choose Edit menu > Mask > Auto Mask with its Using: Image Luminance option to mask dark shadow areas with a more opaque mask. Repeat this auto masking step on each frame of a movie to create masks for the whole movie.

■ You can also record a script using Auto Mask (Using: Image Luminance) and apply the script to the movie.

■ If all the frames in the movie contain an area of the same flat color, you can use the Dropper tool to pick up that flat color (it will now be the new Primary color) and use Auto Mask with the Current Color option. Record these steps in a script.

To record a script as a movie, see page 213.

Movie 1, a soft landscape background, to be cloned onto movie 2.

Movie 2, the dancer. The Magic Wand tool is dragged around the figure to create a mask so cloning can be limited, via the third Drawing button, to the mask (around the figure).

To clone between two movies:

1. Open two movies. Enter names for the new frame stack documents, if prompted to do so.

2. Click in the movie you will clone from, then choose Movie menu > Set Movie Clone Source.

3. *Optional:* Use the Magic Wand tool on each target movie frame to select a particular area of the frame to limit cloning to only that area.
   or
   To composite one movie onto another using a mask, use the Dropper tool to pick up a flat background color from a frame in the movie into which you want to clone, and then use the Edit menu > Mask > Auto Mask command (Current Color) to create a mask. Click the third Drawing button on the P. List palette. If you want to view the mask, also click the second Visibility button.

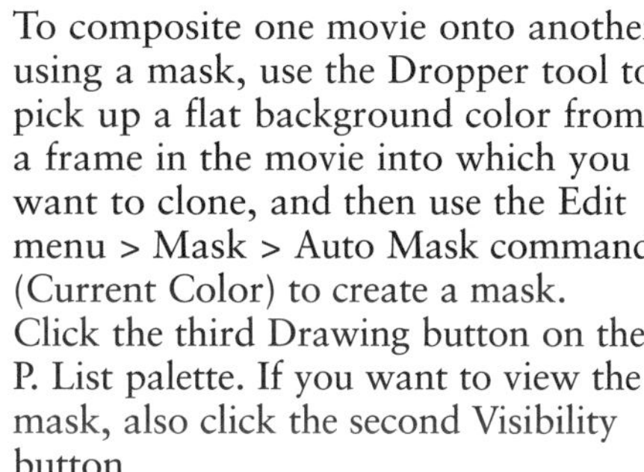

4. Choose a Cloners brush variant. Use the Straight Cloner variant to clone exactly.

5. Click, then press and drag on the clone (target) movie. Areas of the source movie frame will appear in the clone movie frame.

6. Click the Step Forward (fifth) button on the Frame Stacks palette for the clone (target) movie. The source movie will also advance.

7. Repeat steps 3–6 for each frame you want to clone into.

 Record a stroke with a Cloners brush variant, then play it back on consecutive frames. Contents of the cloned areas will vary within the stroke.

Control-click in the source movie to establish a new clone reference point.

To apply a texture to a movie:

1. Record a script in which you use the Effects menu > Surface Control > Apply Surface Texture, Color Overlay, or Dye Concentration command to apply a texture (choose Using: Paper Grain) (see page 210). If you want the grain to move randomly (see step 4), uncheck the Record Initital State box in the Script Options dialog box before you record the script.

2. Open the movie you want to apply the texture to.

3. Choose Movie menu > Set Grain Position.

4. Pick a Grain movement option: Grain Stays Still, Grain Moves Randomly, or Grain Moves Linearly.

   If you choose the Grain Moves Linearly option, enter pixel amounts in one or both Move fields. Enter numbers in both Move fields to make the grain move diagonally. This will work well if the texture has a distinct pattern.

5. Click OK or press Return.

6. Choose Movie menu > Apply Script to Movie.

7. Highlight the script you want to apply to the movie.

8. Click Playback. Pause while the script is applied to the movie. Use the Command-. shortcut at any time to stop it.

To produce this frame sequence, we chose the Grain movement moves Linearly option and entered values in both Move fields in the Frame-to-Frame Grain Position dialog box to move the grain diagonally downward and to the right.

Animation by Philip Sanders (we added the texture).

Apply a Texture to a Movie

Preferences 16

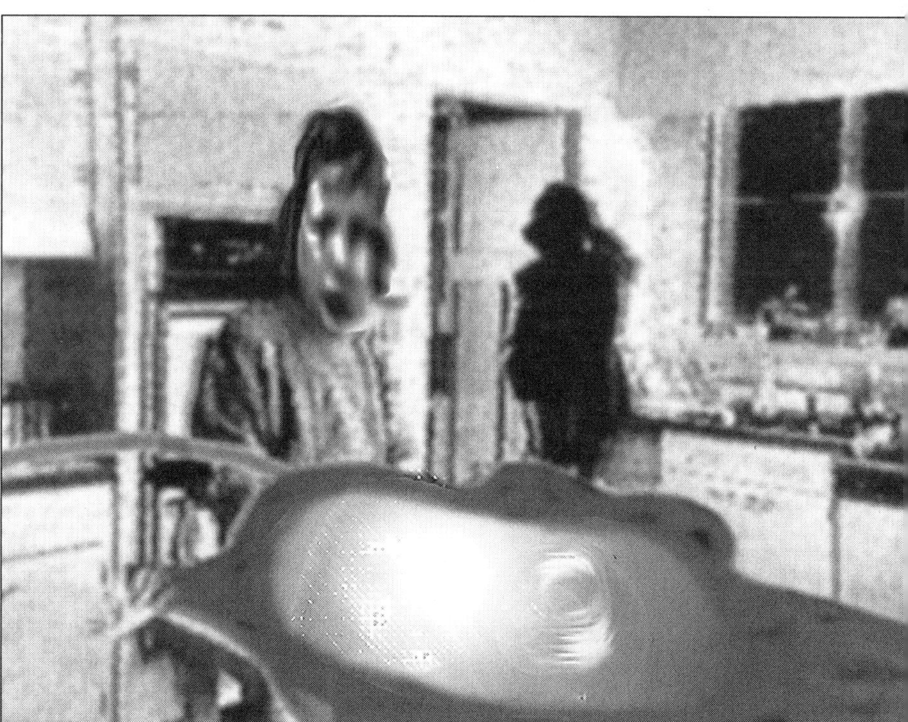

David Humphrey, **Solarized Kitchen** *(detail).*

General Preferences

General Preferences: (Choose Edit menu > Preferences > General)

(Preferences changes take effect when you click OK, except where otherwise noted.)

1 Click **Triangle Drawing Cursor type** to see the cursor more easily on screen. Click **Single pixel** for more precise cursor placement.

Click a cursor **Orientation** button to tilt the triangle to suit your drawing style and left- or right-handedness.

Click a cursor **Color**.

2 A script is automatically created each time you paint a picture, and is saved for the number of days entered in the **Auto-Save scripts for [ ] days** field.

3 Enter the maximum number of pixels in the **Floater pre-feather** field that a floating selection can be feathered using the Feather slider on the Objects: F. List palette. The maximum is 50; the default is 16. The larger the pre-feather amount, the larger the bounding box around the floater. Re-launch Painter to activate this default.

4 Check **Indicate clone source with cross hairs while cloning** if you want to know which area of the source document is being cloned.

5 When **Draw zoomed-out views using area-averaging** is checked, screen rendering when the view size is less than 100% is faster, but less accurate. Uncheck for slower, more accurate rendering.

6 When **Display warning when drawing outside selection** is checked, a warning prompt will appear if you try to paint outside the boundary of a selection.

7 Enter the name of the **Brushes, Papers, Paths, Floaters,** and **Color Set Libraries** that you want to appear in their respective palette drawers each time you launch Painter.

8 Choose a **Temp File Volume** that Painter will use as a scratch disk for virtual memory when available RAM is insufficient for processing.

9 Choose the measurement unit for the Resize dialog box for the current and future documents. (Ruler units are set in the Ruler Options dialog box.)

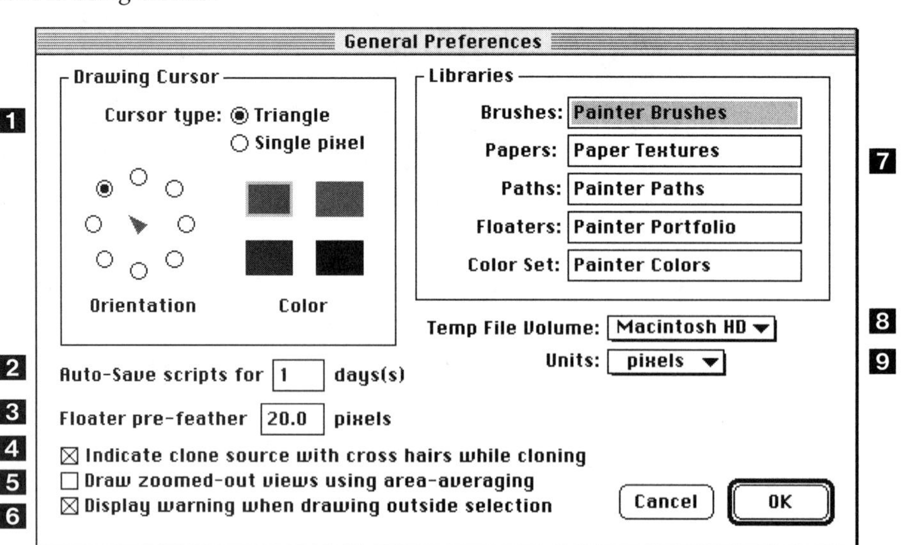

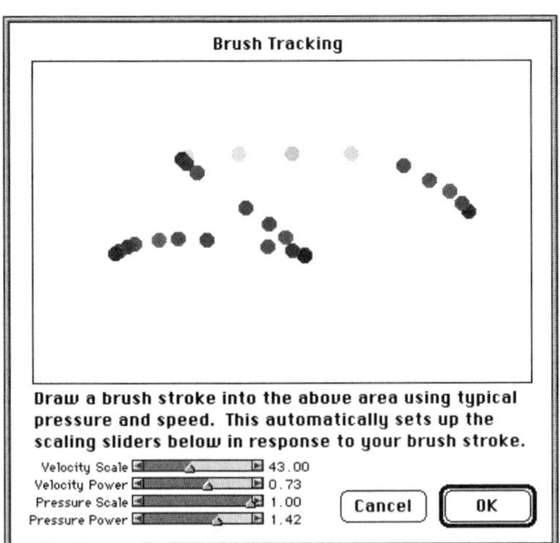

Note: Painter's Brush Tracking dialog box defaults are restored *each time* the application is launched.

To customize stylus pressure and speed:

1. Choose Edit menu > Preferences > Brush Tracking.

2. Draw a stroke in the dialog box using your usual pressure and speed. If you're using a mouse, draw with your usual speed.

3. Click OK or press Return.

🖌 If you're in the mood to draw with an especially heavy or light touch, draw your Brush Tracking stroke that way.

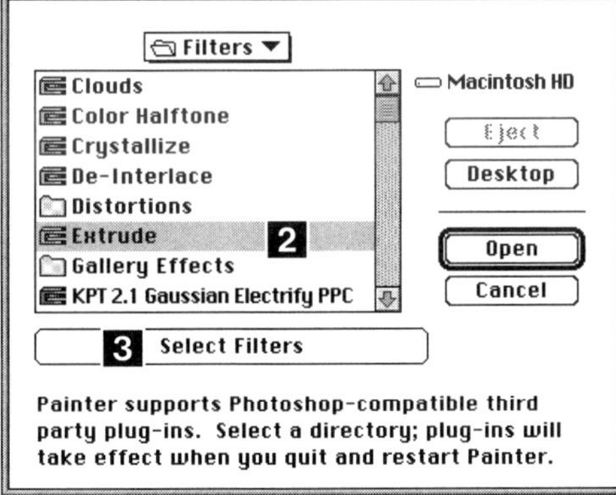

Follow these instructions to make Photoshop or other third-party filter plug-ins accessible from the Plugin Filter submenu under Painter's Effects menu. Painter can access plug-ins from only **one** folder at a time, so place a copy of the plug-ins you want to use in a designated folder of your choice.

To load third-party plug-ins:

1. Choose Edit menu > Preferences > Other Raster Plug-ins.

2. Locate and highlight a plug-in you want to use **2**. To load Photoshop plug-ins, open the Plug-ins folder inside the Photoshop application folder, and then open the Filters folder.

3. Click Select Filters **3**.

4. Choose File menu > Quit (Command-Q).

5. Relaunch Painter.

Undo Preferences are covered on page 14, and Shape Preferences are covered on page 127.

Brush Tracking and Third-Party Plug-Ins Preferences

To change the Painter interface:

1. Open the Art Materials palette (you may be choosing from the Color, Paper, or Pattern palette).

2. Choose Edit menu > Preferences > Interface.

3. Options you can't preview:

   Enter **Rectangular Shadows** X-Offset and Y-Offset values for the shadows under palette icons. Enter a Softness amount for shadow feathering (1-10).

   Enter **Rectangular Pillowing** X-Offset and Y-Offset values for the shadows on palettes sliders and the Primary and Secondary color rectangles. Enter a Softness amount for shadow feathering.

4. Watch any open Painter palettes as you do any of the following:

   Choose a new **Icon Selection Color** (the frame color for highlighted icons) from the Art Materials: Color palette, then click Use Current Color.

   Choose a new **Window Background Color** (the area around the image in the image window) from the Color palette, then click Use Current Color. A neutral color like gray or black is a good choice.

   Choose a new **Palette Background** or **Drawer Bottom** texture from the Art Materials: Paper palette. To display the texture in grayscale, click "in grayscale," then click Use Current Texture. To display the texture in color, choose a Primary and a Secondary color, click "in current colors," then click Use Current Texture. To use a pattern as a palette background, choose a pattern from the Art Materials: Pattern palette, then click Use Current Pattern. (You can select an area of an image and choose Pattern palette > Palette menu > Capture Pattern to create a pattern before you open Interface Preferences.)

5. To save your custom interface preferences, click Save, enter a name, choose a location, then click Save.

6. Click Done.

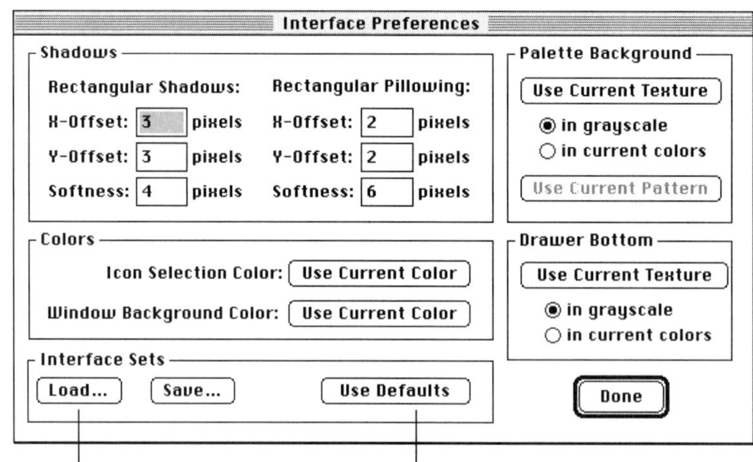

*To load a saved interface, click **Load**, then locate and double-click an interface. Additional Painter interfaces are located in the INTRFACE folder inside the Goodies folder on the Painter 4 CD-ROM.*

*Click **Use Defaults** to restore Painter's default Interface Preferences.*

Output/Export 

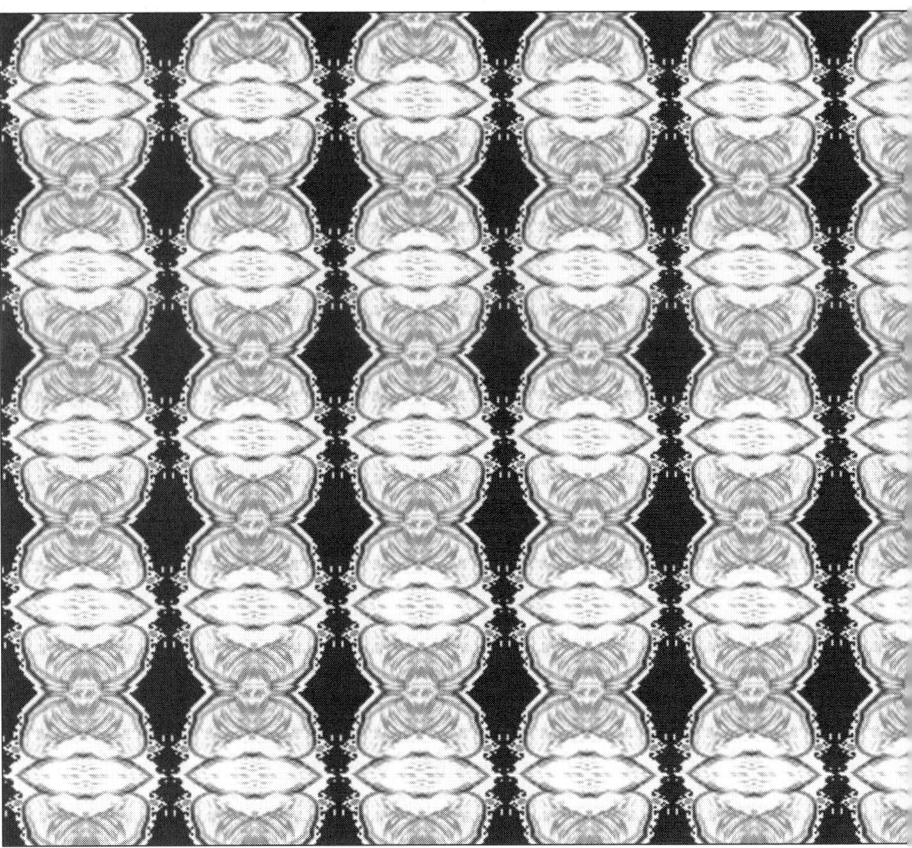

Diane Margolin.

Composite Color Printers

Output devices

Standard size composite color printers

Composite color printers—like thermal wax, color laser copier, and dye sublimation—print the whole image on one sheet of paper. Composite color prints can be used as intermediary "comps," as final output, or even as proofs for press output if the printer is carefully calibrated to the film output device.

Thermal wax printers produce colors by printing Cyan, Magenta, Yellow and Black dots, usually at a resolution of around 300 dpi. Unfortunately, mixed color areas on thermal wax prints usually look very dithered, color accuracy is poor, and you must choose from a preset selection of paper stocks. To prepare your document for a thermal wax printer, save it at a maximum resolution of 150 ppi.

Fiery color laser copiers—like the Canon CLC—output computer files using a RIP (raster image processor). They produce continuous-tone color prints with no discernible dots. Colors are usually fairly accurate, though sometimes a little on the dark side, and you must choose from a preset selection of paper stocks. To prepare a file for a laser copier, save your file at a maximum resolution of 150 ppi in the Photoshop 3.0 format in Painter, and then save it again in the EPS format in Photoshop. (Double-check this with your service bureau.)

Scitex IRIS ink-jet printers produce very smooth continuous-tone color prints, and, if the IRIS is calibrated properly, fairly accurate color. Unlike many other printers, some IRIS models print on a variety of paper types—like cotton rag, glossy, and watercolor—and even onto fabric. The water soluble inks used to produce IRIS prints are environmentally sound, but, unfortunately, they also smear very easily with water. Your service bureau can laminate your IRIS print with a special coating that will provide some protection. Most IRIS inks are also fugitive, which means they will fade if they're exposed to light.

<hr>

Output tips

- If you're planning to color separate or color composite print your picture, you should choose paint colors with the Printable Colors Only box checked on the Art Materials: Color palette. To make doubly sure your picture is printable, choose Effects menu > Tonal Control > Printable Colors to convert all colors to printable (CMYK) colors, or convert your file to CMYK Color mode in Photoshop.

- Ask your service bureau or print shop which file format to use for your target printer, and ask if they have any special instructions. If your service bureau doesn't output from Painter, save your file in the Photoshop 3.0 format.

- If your picture is in color and it contains photographic imagery, save your document at a resolution that is twice the printing press screen resolution using the Canvas menu > Resize command. If you created the image from scratch in Painter and it doesn't contain precise line work, one-and-a-half times the screen resolution will probably suffice.

- For slide output, no CMYK conversion is necessary, because a film recorder is an RGB device. Film recorders can output 2,000 or 4,000 pixels per line, depending on the desired quality and enlargement. Some service bureaus recommend using a Gamma of 2.2 when creating an image for slide output. Ask your service bureau what pixel dimensions and resolution to choose in Painter.

The maximum IRIS printout size is approximately 36 by 50 inches. Save your document in Photoshop 3.0 format in Painter, and then save the file again in the EPS format in Photoshop at a resolution of 150 to 300 ppi, depending on how sharp you want the printout to be. But don't just take our word for it— verify this procedure with your service bureau.

Large format composite color printers

The Vutek printer generates large-sized output (four feet wide by any length) on gessoed canvas. Vutek acrylic-based inks are permanent, and you can paint right on the canvas printout if you like. Save your file at a resolution of 18 ppi (yes, 18 ppi) in Painter in any file format that Photoshop reads, like Photoshop 3.0.

The Versatec printer outputs onto poster-size rolls of paper. The paper stocks that you can choose from may be limited (check with your service bureau). Save your file in Photoshop 2.5 or 3.0 format in Painter, and then save it in TIFF or EPS format in Photoshop.

Some output services, like Supersample Corporation, print water-based fabric dyes onto fabric using an ink-jet device. These dyes are more permanent, brighter, and produce a wider range of colors than standard printing inks. The printer resolution is 300 dpi and the maximum printout size is 36 inches wide by two to three yards long. To prepare a file for fabric output, save your file in the TIFF format at a resolution between 100 and 150 ppi. A low resolution is appropriate for printing on fabric, which doesn't have a crisp surface like paper. Supersample Corporation recommends saving your file in Photoshop in Indexed Color mode. You can use the Posterize Using Custom Color Set command in Painter to reduce the number of colors in the image. Your output service may even recommend specific colors for you to use.

Color separations

For printed color work, you'll need to get high resolution film output (color separations), from which your print shop will produce plates for the final press. When a picture is color separated, one sheet of film is produced for each of the four process color inks—Cyan, Magenta, Yellow and Black—that are used for printing. For imagesetter output (1270–4000 dpi), save your file at twice the screen resolution of the final press, and save your file in the EPS format from Painter or from Photoshop.

Painter doesn't produce the best color separations because you can only work and save in RGB color mode—not CMYK color mode—and you can't tweak Painter's monitor, printing ink, or separation parameters. You can specify dot gain, monitor gamma, and halftone screen frequency and angle settings in Painter's Page Setup dialog box, but programs like ColorStudio and Photoshop offer greater control over these separation parameters and so are a better choice for producing separations.

If you decide to color separate from Painter, save your file in the EPS-DCS format, which produces a file for each color component (C, M, Y, and K) and a low resolution preview file. **You can't reopen an EPS-DCS file in Painter**, though, so be sure to save a copy of the file in a format that Painter opens.

Painter doesn't produce spot color separations. To reduce the number of colors in a document for screen printing, see the "To posterize a picture using a color set" instructions on page 178 and "To annotate colors on a picture" on page 245.

Color proofing devices

There are several reasons to proof your computer artwork before it's printed. Firstly, the RGB colors that you see on your computer screen won't match the printed CMYK colors unless your monitor

---

If you decide to color separate your Painter file from Adobe Photoshop...

Ask your print shop the following questions so you'll be able to choose the correct scan resolution (if you're using a photograph in your Painter picture) and the appropriate File menu > Preferences > Printer Inks Setup and File File > Preferences > Separation Setup settings.

What lines per inch setting is going to be used on the press for my job? This will help you choose the appropriate scanning resolution if you use scanned imagery or choose the appropriate file resolution for a hand-painted image.

What is the dot gain for my paper stock choice on that press? Allowances for dot gain can be made using the Printer Inks Setup dialog box. Dot gain adjustments can be made in Painter, but it may be simpler to do all your adjustments in Adobe Photoshop.

Which printing method will be used on press—UCR or GCR? GCR produces better color printing and is the default choice in the Separations Setup box. (GCR stands for Gray Component Replacement, UCR stands for Undercolor Removal.)

What is the total ink limit and the black ink limit for the press? These values can also be adjusted in the Separations Setup box.

Note: Change the dot gain, GCR or UCR method, and ink limits **before** you convert your picture from RGB Color mode to CMYK Color mode. If you modify any of these values after conversion, you'll have to convert the picture back to RGB Color mode, adjust the values, and then reconvert to CMYK Color mode.

Calibration tip

Order a laminated color proof (Chromalin or Matchprint) from color separations of a picture and then calibrate your monitor using Photoshop so it matches the proof as closely as possible. Better still, create a color set in Painter and a sheet of sample swatches, and then order a Matchprint for the swatches. Calibrate the monitor to the printout, and you'll have a reliable color set. For the color to be consistent, though, be sure to use the same prepress shop for your final output!

is professionally calibrated. Secondly, obtaining a proof will give you an opportunity to correct the color balance or brightness of a picture, or catch output problems like banding in gradations. And finally, most print shops need a proof to refer to so they know what the printed piece should look like. Digital (direct-from-disk) color proofs—like IRIS or 3M prints—are the least expensive color proofs, though they're not perfectly reliable. An advantage of using an IRIS print, though, is that you can color correct your original electronic file and run another IRIS print before you order film. A more accurate but more expensive proof is a Chromalin or Matchprint, which is produced from film (color separations). Matchprint colors may be slightly more saturated than final print colors, though. The most reliable color proof, and by far the most expensive, is a press proof, which is produced in the print shop from your film negatives on the final paper stock.

Video and Multimedia

RGB is the native computer color model that is used to display images on screen. Choose Effects menu > Tonal Control > Video Legal Colors to convert your image into NTSC colors, which will reproduce reliably in video. For video, save your file in the PICT file format (the Macintosh native, on-screen image format), or the BMP file format (the Windows native, on-screen image format), depending on your target video platform, and save your file at 72 ppi—the monitor's resolution. You can save a Painter movie in QuickTime format or as numbered files (see Chapter 15, Movies). To output from a Macintosh to videotape, you will need a video board to convert the digital information to analog information (the 8500 Power Mac excepted). Images intended for video output should have a Monitor Gamma of 2.2 (Page Setup).

To print a Painter file:

1. Choose File menu > Page Setup. (You can proceed directly to step 3 next time you print from Painter if the current Page Setup settings are correct.)

   If your picture is larger than the Paper size you have selected and you want Painter to shrink the image to fit on the paper, check the Size to Fit Page box.

   For PostScript color printing, let your print shop enter Printer/Press Dot Gain and Halftone Screens values.

   Change the Monitor Gamma only if you've calibrated your monitor with a calibration device that uses a different number. (Photoshop's Gamma control panel has a setting of 1.8.)

2. Click OK.

3. Choose File menu > Print (Command-P).

4. Click Color Quickdraw only if your printer uses Quickdraw, and not PostScript.

   Click Color PostScript to output to a PostScript composite color or grayscale printer.

   Your service bureau or print shop will click Separations if you request color separations.

   Click Black and White to output to a black-and-white or grayscale PostScript laser printer.

5. Click Print or press Return.

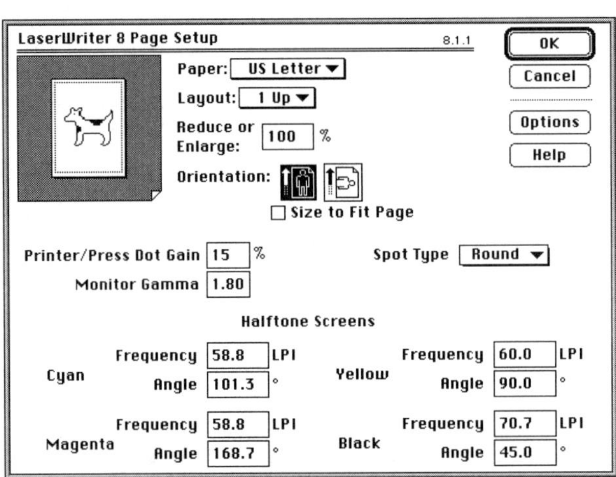

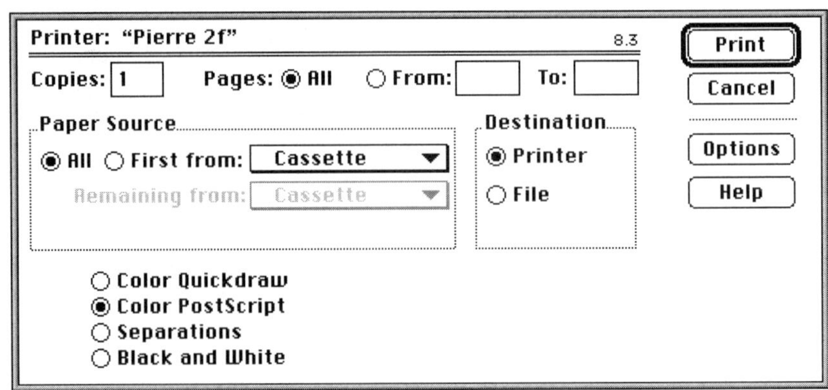

Color Set		
Yellow Proc	108 Yellow Lt.	109 Sunshine
110 Mustard	114 Butter	116 Chop's Hair
104 Green Gold	388 GreenYello Lt	377 Green Yello Drk
375 Speck's Shirt	368 Green Leaf	376 Green Yel. Med
353 Green Lt	354 Green Med	346 Mint
348 Green Drk	322 Turq Drk	320 Turq Med
319 Turq Lt	3272 Aqua	312 Cyan Warm
311 Chop's Shirt	2975 Sky Bright	2985 Sky Deep
300 Sky Dark	286 Blue Royal	534 Chop's Pants
Chop's Pants Brite	264 Violet Lt	265 Violet
2597 Purple	Purple Medium	530 Pink Violet
2583 Speck's Pants	513 Berry Drk	514 Berry Lt
211 Bubble gum	213 Artms'Dress/...	215 Rose Drk
1925 Cool Red	485 Warm Red	701 Blush
1565 Skin 1/Peach	180 Skin 2	1807 Skin Outline
1385 Artemis' Hair	157 Orange Lt	1585 Orange Deep

Rodney Alan Greenblat's custom process color set. To standardize his color output, Greenblat created and output a sample color chart using his custom colors, made sure they printed correctly, and now chooses from this color set when he paints.

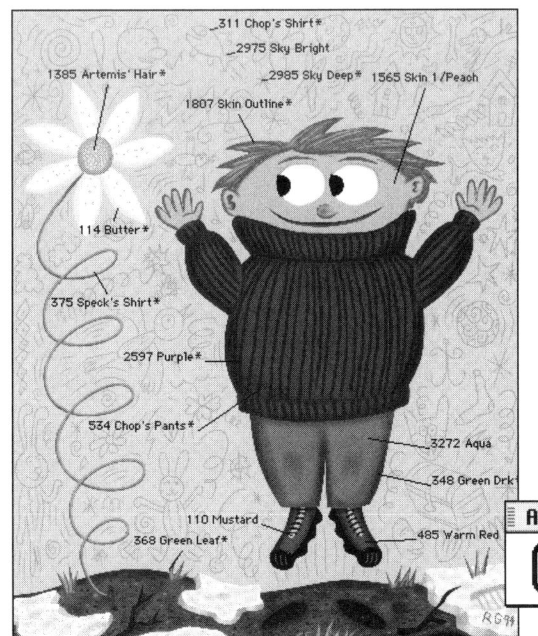

*Rodney Alan Greenblat's **Springing**, with color annotations.*

To use the Annotate command, you must paint using colors from a **color set**, the colors must have **assigned names**, and you musn't change their names after you've annotated them. Also, you must save your picture in the **RIFF** file format to preserve the annotations.

To annotate colors on a picture:

1. Make sure the color set you used to create the painting is the Current Color Set. If it's not, choose Art Materials palette > Color menu > Adjust Color Set, click Library, then locate and open the picture's color set. The Color Set swatch palette doesn't have to be open.

2. *Optional:* Use the Canvas menu > Canvas Size command to add more pixels around the picture to make more room for the color tags.

3. Choose Canvas menu > Annotations > Annotate.

4. Press and drag a short distance over a color area you want to annotate. Repeat for other colors.

5. Click Done or press Return.

▗ Choose Canvas menu > Annotations > Hide Annotations to hide annotations.

▗ To delete a color tag after you've clicked Done, make sure annotation display is on (Hide Annotations will be listed on the Canvas menu > Annotations submenu) choose Canvas menu > Annotations > Annotate, click on the tag, then press Delete.

▗ An asterisk next to an annotation indicates the color is a close—but not an exact—match.

To prepare a Painter file for QuarkXPress:

Choose File menu > Save As, choose EPS from the Type pop-up menu, check the "Save PostScript data into preview file" box **1**, and leave the Data options box unchecked to save it as a Binary file.

An EPS-DCS file consists of five files, one each for C, M, Y, and K, and a low resolution preview file. **You can't reopen an EPS file in Painter**, though, so be sure to save a version of it in another file format using the File menu > Save As command if you think you might want to work on it again in Painter.

If you don't want to create an EPS file and you have Photoshop 3.0, you can save your file in Photoshop 3.0 format in Painter (uncheck the Save Mask Layer box to save without masks), open it in Photoshop, and then save it as a TIFF. This method was used for the images in this book. Remove the file's paths and extra channels in Photoshop. (If you have trouble reopening a TIFF in Painter, save it in Photoshop 3.0 format first.)

To prepare a Painter file for PageMaker:

Choose File menu > Save As, choose EPS from the Type pop-up menu, check the "Save PostScript data into preview file" box, and check the "Data Options: Hex (ASCII) picture data" box. Remember, you can't reopen an EPS file in Painter.

To prepare a Painter file for Photoshop:

Choose File menu > Save As, then choose Photoshop 3.0 from the Type pop-up menu. An active mask group or path on the Objects: P. List palette will become a mask in Channel #4 in Photoshop if you also check the Save Mask Layer box, and any feathering on the mask will also be saved in the same Photoshop channel. Painter selection paths will appear on the Paths palette. If the Painter file contains floaters, each floater or floater group will be assigned its own layer in Photoshop.

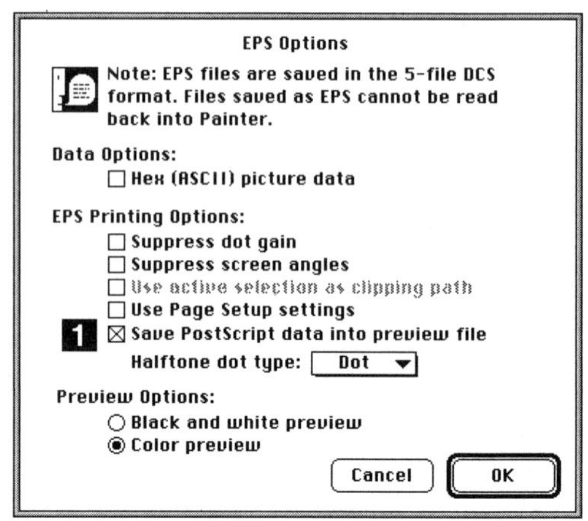

To export shapes to Illustrator or FreeHand, follow the instructions on page 134.

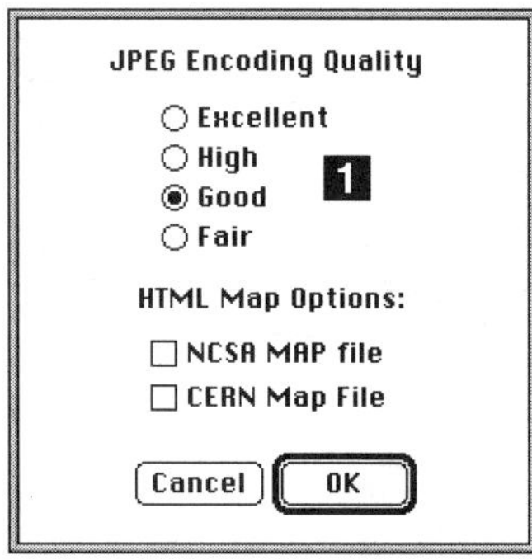

World Wide Web

To send a file via modem or to display it on the Internet's World Wide Web using more than 256 colors, choose File menu > Save As, and choose JPEG from the Type pop-up menu. Since some image detail is lost with this format, it works best on photographic-type images that contain gradual shade variations. Images containing flat areas of color or type will be more compromised. (GIF is a better format choice for these types of images.) If you save a file in the JPEG format, you'll need to choose a compression option (Encoding Quality) **1**. The higher the quality, the lower the degree of distortion, but the less the file will be compressed and the longer it will take to transmit. Save your picture in the JPEG format after it's finished—not while you're working on it—so it won't be recompressed over and over. Leave the HTML Map Options unchecked.

Another format you can choose to display your picture on the Internet's World Wide Web is GIF, which uses a maximum of 256 colors with a transparency option. (GIF is also the better format for displaying a 24-bit color image on an 8-bit monitor.) For GIF, you'll need to choose color options for the file, such as the Number of Colors **2** and an Imaging Method. To reduce the file size and speed up downloading, choose fewer than 256 colors (click Preview Data to preview). Choose Imaging Method: Quantize to Nearest Color to have Painter choose nearest colors, or choose Dither Colors for smoother color transitions when the number of colors is fewer than 64. Check the Interlace GIF File box to make your picture render in successive low resolution passes until the higher resolution rendering is completed. If you're creating an image map, ask your Internet service provider which Map Options to check. NCSA is the usual choice for Macintosh-based image maps.

To make parts of an image transparent

Create a mask for the image area that you want to display, but don't want to be transparent. In the Save As GIF Options dialog box, check the Output Transparency box, and click Background is WWW Gray to make transparent areas gray or choose Background is BG Color to use Painter's current Secondary Color for transparent areas. Use the Threshold slider to control the minimum shade at which transparency will start. With the Threshold at zero, only areas of 100% black in the mask won't be transparent. At 50%, areas of the mask between 50% gray and 100% black won't be transparent. Click Preview Data to preview the GIF. Transparent areas will preview as a lattice pattern.

Image Map for WWW

An image map is a graphic file on the Internet's World Wide Web that contains areas that act as buttons (hot spots). By clicking on a button, Web users are automatically linked to another Web page.

To create an image map:

1. If you don't have an existing floater that you want to use, create a graphic to use as the image map, choose the Rectangular Selection tool, select the area in the image that will become the button, choose the Floater Adjuster tool, then click on the rectangle to turn it into a floater.

2. Activate the floater on the Objects: F. List palette, then click Trim.

3. Double-click the floater name on the F. List palette.

4. Check the WWW Clickable Region box.
   and
   Enter a URL address for the floater.
   and
   Choose a Region type. Choose Rectangle Bounding Box for fastest server response to a click.

5. Choose File menu > Save As.

6. Choose GIF or JPEG from the Type pop-up menu.

7. Choose an HTML Map Option. Ask your Internet service provider which option to use.

8. Click OK or press Return. Painter will create a data file that describes the location and links of the buttons in the graphic that will be used by Web software to display and interpret the graphic. For the map to be fully interactive, you'll have to go outside Painter. The image map must be placed in an HTML page and a CGI program will be needed to interpret mouse clicks for the Web server.

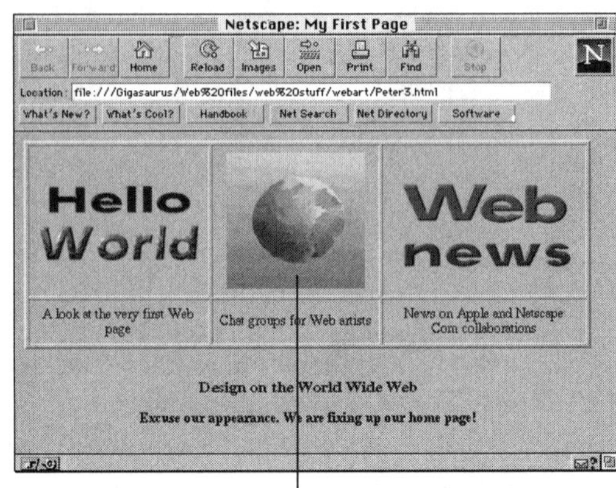

An image map viewed in Netscape's browser. The globe and the words "Hello World" and "Web news" are image map buttons.

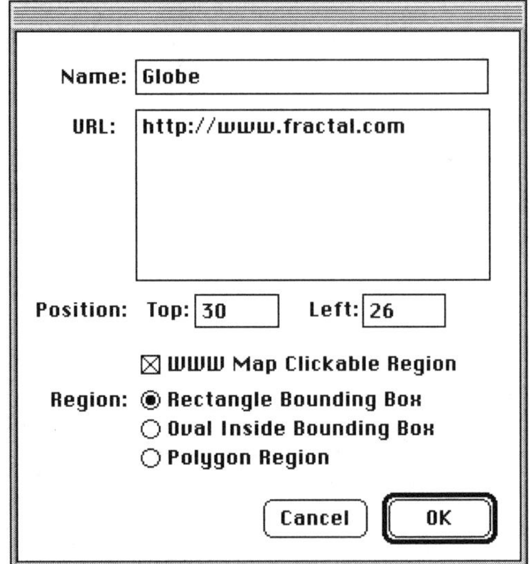

Read more about it!

See the Painter 4 tutorial for a more detailed discussion of image maps and for instructions on using the template HTML file GRTEST.HTM—located in the Tutorial folder—to preview Web graphic images in a browser.

Outputting shapes

Shapes are PostScript descriptions of objects, whereas other elements in Painter are pixel-based. When a shape has 100% opacity and the Normal Composite Method, it doesn't intermix with any pixel-based areas and will print as a PostScript shape.

A shape that is transparent or composited with pixel areas must be rasterized (converted into pixels) in order to be output. If the file is output on a sufficiently high-resolution printer, the rasterizing process won't be noticeable, and the shapes will look okay.

If you get a limitcheck error when you try to print a complex shape on a high-resolution printer, try adjusting the Flatness setting in the Set Shape Attributes dialog box (double-click each shape name on the Objects: F. List palette). Ask your service bureau for an appropriate flatness setting for the shape.

Specialty output services

Cone Editions Press
Powder Spring Road
East Topsham, VT 05076
802-439-5751
Archival IRIS prints

Image Transform
106 Southwest 2nd Avenue
Des Moines, IA 50309
515-288-0000
Fax 515-288-6403
(See info at right)
Archival IRIS prints, canvas prints, billboard size output

Nash Editions
nashed@aol.com
310-545-4352
Fax 310-796-1418
Archival IRIS prints

Supersample Corporation
350 Great Neck Road,
Great Neck, NY 11021
516-482-4386
(See info on page 241)
Fabric prints

Vutek Company
Richard Noble, ordering agent
Noble & Company
899 Forest Lane
Alamo, CA 94507
510-838-5524
Canvas prints

(X+C) The Color Space
200 Varick Street
New York, NY 10014
212-366-6600
(See info at right)
Archival IRIS prints, canvas prints, billboard size output

Image Transform

Image Transform produces output for fine artists using archival inks and papers at a variety of output sizes. For small- to medium-size outout, they can output on their customized IRIS printer using archival inks on 100% neutral ph rag paper. Save your Painter file in the EPS or TIFF format, 100–150 ppi resolution, and at the final printing dimensions. Before you output the file, Image Transform recommends that you do the following in Photoshop: Choose File menu > Preferences > Printer Inks Setup, and choose SWOP uncoated. Then choose File menu > Preferences > Separation Setup and set the Black Generation to Light. These Preferences settings will make your screen image closer to the IRIS printout. Finally, "proof" your image in Photoshop (choose Mode > CMYK Preview), and adjust the color, if necessary.

Image Transform uses the Translock print system for large output (up to 100 by 400 feet) on vinyl, canvas, or special adhesive-backed wallpaper. The file resolution should be 300 ppi, but the file does not have to be saved at the final output size. The printer uses ACO dyes that are guaranteed to be permanent.

For very large output—flags, banners or theater backdrops—Image Transform can print directly onto sailcloth (300 thread count). Save your file at 75–150 ppi.

(X+C) The Color Space

(X+C) The Color Space also does large format (35 by 50 inches) fine arts prints using their IRIS inkjet printer and special archival inks. They also use a patented coating on rag paper or fabric to control ink absorption. Save your file in the EPS or TIFF file format at 150 ppi for a very painterly image, or at 150–300 ppi for imagery that contains file lines or text.

(X+C) The Color Space also outputs on vinyl, canvas, theater scrims, mylar, or sail cloth using an inkjet Scitex Outboard billboard printer and MEK inks. They claim this method produces more accurate color ink delivery than other billboard type printers. Print sizes are 63 inches wide by any length. Save your file in the EPS or TIFF format at 22 ppi.

Crackerjack Speed Tips

These suggestions won't make an artistic genie pop out of a bottle, but they may help to liberate you from technical constraints and from the frustration of waiting for effects to process, which in turn will clear the way for image-making to flow more freely. The less you get bogged down in technical snags, the more you can concentrate on painting.

- Use floaters so you can paint on image elements and move them around easily without affecting the background and conversely, so you can paint on the background without affecting the floaters.

- Use keyboard shortcuts. Start by memorizing just a few, and gradually add more to your repertoire. Some of the most useful shortcuts you can learn are the shortcuts for choosing individual tools.

- Work at the lowest resolution possible, bearing in mind the resolution required for your final output device. Unless you have a screamer of a Power Mac, high resolution files will test your patience.

- Create color sets for the colors you use most frequently so you can grab them quickly and so you don't have to re-mix them at each work session.

- Save your custom brushes in a brush looks library, or save them as new variants.

- If you copy or cut a large or high res image to the Clipboard, copy or cut a smaller-size image to the Clipboard when you're finished pasting the high res.

- Limit the number of elements in each library. And store all your libraries, movies, and color sets in the same location so you don't have to hunt for them when you need to open or edit them.

- Allocate as much RAM as possible to Painter. If total available RAM is limited, consider allocating more RAM to Painter and working with fewer applications open at a time.

- Set your Undo levels (Edit > Preferences > Undo) to a maximum of seven or eight. Undo levels tie up memory.

- Make your image window larger than your image so you don't accidentally click or drag in the Finder.

- Restore a brush's default settings quickly by Option-clicking its icon.

- Discover the power of cloning. Clone your document if for no other reason than so you'll have the option to restore areas from the source document.

- Screen your calls...order takeout.

- Save path shapes in a paths library and floaters in a floaters library so you can reuse them at any time and on any image.

- Choose Drawing and Visibility options from the lower left corner of the image window so you don't have to hunt for the Objects: P. List palette or the Objects: F. List palette. (Doesn't the palette you're looking for always seems to be buried behind a zillion other palettes?)

- If you need to erase strokes, choose the Eraser variant for your current brush instead of switching to the Eraser brush. Ditto for masking. For erasing or masking, always remember to check the Controls: Brush palette Opacity slider setting.

- If you use a Water Color variant or any other brush with the Wet variant chosen, you'll be able to erase brush strokes on the Wet Paint layer without affecting linework or other kinds of brush strokes in the background, and you'll also be able to erase background strokes before you dry the wet strokes.

- To mix a color that is similar to an existing color in an image, click on the existing color with the Dropper tool and then adjust its saturation or value using the Art Materials: Color palette.

- Record and replay brush strokes or scripts to accomplish repetitive tasks. Or use scripts so you can remake a picture using different commands or art materials.

- Use the Image Hose to quickly fill areas with repetitive shapes.

- Use the Fade command to partially undo a modification instead of using the Undo and Redo commands.

- Nag nag nag Fractal Design Corporation to create a brush variants palette for assembling and choosing frequently used or customized variants, like the way the Color Set palette is used to organize color swatches.

Speed Tips

Keyboard Shortcuts

Palettes (display/hide)

Tools — Command 1
Brushes — Command 2
Art Materials — Command 3
Objects — Command 4
Controls — Command 5
Color Set — Command 6
Display/hide all previously open palettes — Command H

File menu

New Picture — Command N
Open — Command O
Close — Command W
Save — Command S
File Information — Command I
Print — Command P
Quit — Command Q

Undo/Redo

Undo — Command Z
Redo — Command Y

Tools

Magnifier — M
Floater Adjuster/Selection Adjuster — F
Pen/Quick Curve — P
Oval Shape/Rectangular Shape — O
Brush – Freehand — B
Brush – Straight Lines — V
Paint Bucket — C
Dropper — D
Rectangular Selection/Oval Selection — R
Text — T
Direct Selection/Whole Shape Selection — A

Image window

Zoom in — Command + or Command Space bar-click
Zoom out — Command – or Command Option Space bar-click
Screen Mode toggle — Command M

Use Grabber when another tool is selected — Space bar
Center image — Space bar-click
Rotate image — Option Space bar-press and drag
Un-rotate image — Option Space bar-click
Constrain rotate image to 90° — Option Shift Space bar-press and drag

Clipboard

Undo — Command Z
Cut — Command X
Copy — Command C
Paste (Normal) — Command V

Paint

Load Image Hose nozzle — Command L

Brush Controls
Resize Brush — Command Option-press and drag
Build Brush — Command B
Reset brush defaults — Option-click brush icon
Constrain Straight Lines Draw Style to 45° — Shift
Choose Opacity 1-0 keys (1 = 10%, 2 = 20%, etc.)

Wet Paint
Post-diffuse strokes — Shift D

Cloning
Establish clone source location — Control-click
Tracing Paper toggle — Command T

Color sets

Add current color to Set — Unlock color set, then Command Shift K
Replace color in set — Option-click swatch

Dropper

Use Dropper with Oval Selection, Rectangular Selection, Brush, Floater Adjuster, or Paint Bucket tool selected — Command

Gradations

Tighten/loosen spiral — Command press-and-drag angle adjuster (red ball)
Edit Gradation — Command Shift B

Keyboard Shortcuts

Canvas

Resize Image — Command Shift R

Selections

Select All — Command A *or* double-click Rectangular Selection tool

Deselect — Command D
Reselect — Command R

Rectangular Selection tool

Constrain to square — Shift
Adjust current selection rectangle — Control
Edit Rectangular Selection — Command Shift E

Oval Selection tool

Constrain to circle — Shift

Magic Wand

Add color to selection — Shift-click

Lasso

Close path — Enter

Selection Adjuster tool

Duplicate — Option-click *or* Option-press and drag
Move path one pixel at a time — Arrow keys
Delete selected path(s) — Delete
Render/un-render selected path — Return or Enter
Resize/preserve aspect ratio — Shift-press and drag corner handle
Skew — Command-press and drag side handle
Rotate — Command-press and drag corner handle

Path List palette

Select/deselect multiple — Shift-click path names
Path attributes — Double-click path name
Drawing button 1 (unconstrained draw) — Shift 1
Drawing button 2 (draw outside) — Shift 2
Drawing button 3 (draw inside) — Shift 3
Visibility button 1 (view canvas) — Shift 4
Visibility button 2 (view mask) — Shift 5
Visibility button 3 (view selection) — Shift 6

Floaters

Drop currently selected floater — Command Shift D
Change opacity — 1-0 keys (1 = 10%, 2 = 20%, etc.)
Duplicate floater — Option-click *or* Option press and drag
Move floater one pixel at a time — Arrow keys
Hide/display marquee — Command Shift H

Group — Command G
Ungroup — Command Shift G
Floater attributes — Double-click floater name
Select/deselect multiple floaters — Shift-click floater names

Shapes

Open Set Shape Attributes dialog box — Highlight shape name, then press Return
Group — Command G
Ungroup — Command Shift G

Pen tool

Make curve point into corner — Click on last point
Make corner point into curve — Drag last point
Delete last created point — Delete

Rectangular Shape tool

Constrain to square — Shift

Oval Shape tool

Constrain to circle — Shift

Direct Selection tool

Select starting point of shape — Home
Select endpoint of shape — End
Select previous point in shape — Page Up
Select next point in shape — Page Down
Equal length handles — Shift-press and drag handle

Masks

Invert Mask — Command Shift I
Clear Mask — Command U
Measure mask density — Shift-click with Dropper tool
Auto Mask — Command Shift M

Effects

Last Effect — Command /
Second-to-last effect — Command ;
Fill — Command F
Equalize — Command E
Adjust Colors — Command Shift A
Color Talk dialog box — k
QuickWarp — Command Shift F
Lighting Mover — Command Shift L

Mosaics

Make mosaic	Command Option M
Select any contiguous tiles containing the same flat color	Command-click tile containing flat color
Delete tile with Apply Tiles icon selected	Control-click tile

Select Tiles icon

Select all tiles	A
Deselect all tiles	D
Change selected tiles to current color	C
Tint selected tiles with curent color	T
Apply Color Variability settings to selected tiles	V

Tesselations

Make tesselation	Command Option V

Scripts

Replay script	Command K, then user-assigned letter
Record a five-second delay in script	Shift -

Movies

Play movie	Command Shift P
First frame of stack	Home
Last frame of stack	End
Next frame	Page Up
Previous frame	Page Down
Stop at current frame	Option Stop button
Stop and return to start	Command .

QuickTime

Small frame grab with QuickTime	q
Large frame grab with QuickTime	Q

This book weighs over 500MB, and it
contains over 800 pictures!
(And we didn't use the word "cool" once!)

We designed, wrote, tested, rewrote, partially illustrated, and, yes, argued passionately about this book, but it would be empty and spiritless without the contributions of artwork from the artists listed below. It was a pleasure and a privilege for us to meet with them, and we're enormously grateful for their generosity in sharing their work.

Phil Allen
424 East 83rd St., 5W
New York, NY 10028
212-873-3553
Omuck@aol.com
Painter
18, 146, 148, color plate

Caty Bartholomew
198 Seventh Avenue, Apt. 4R
Brooklyn, NY 11215
718-965-0790
catyb@aol.com
Artist, educator
41

Jaime Davidovich
152 Wooster Street
New York, NY 10012
212-254-4978
jaimetango@aol.com
Mixed media artist
color plate

Fabric Effects, Inc.
RSL Digital Consultants
Richard Lerner, President
20 West 20th Street
New York, NY 10011
212-627-2070
rslerner@eworld.com
*System design and hardware/
software integration; fabric
design, hand painting, dyeing,
and silkscreening; computer
assisted design and manufacture. Fabric Effects images in
this book are by Mandy
Leonard. (212-229-1401)*
30, 48, 149, 209, color plates

Johanna Gillman
GG Designs
65 West 90th Street
New York, NY 10024
212-580-1046
ggdesigns@aol.com
Painter, graphic designer
166

Ron Gorchov
Starin Place
RD1 Bx7C
Fultonville, NY 12072
212-334-0419
Painter
25, 51, 180, 181, color plates

Steven Gorney
280 Riverside Drive, Apt. 2E
New York, NY 10025
212-866-2373
Illustrator, designer, educator
41

Rodney Alan Greenblat
Center for Advanced Whimsy
61 Crosby Street
New York, NY 10012
Fax 212-219-1758
rodney@voyagerco.com
*Author, designer, and illustra-
tor of children's books and
interactive multimedia*
**1, 80, 81, 83, 90, 245, color
plates**

(Continued on the next page)

Would you like to submit artwork for future editions of this book, or our Photoshop or Illustrator QuickStart Guides? Please mail your paper output to Peter Lourekas, c/o Communication Design Dept., Parsons School of Design, 66 Fifth Avenue, New York, NY 10011. We will review every submission very carefully and thoughtfully. **Paper output only, please!**

Directory of Artists

Directory of Artists

David Humphrey
439 Lafayette Street
New York, NY 10003
212-780-0512
Painter
7, 43, 53, 91, 235, color plates

Anna Kogan
KUB Inc.
30 West 21st Street
New York, NY 10010
W: 212-924-7700
H: 212-633-9240
Multimedia, 2D/3D animation, illustration
227

Diane Margolin
41 Perry Street
New York, NY 10014
212-691-9537
DiMargolin@aol.com
Illustrator, graphic designer, painter, educator, developer of a collection of over 1,000 original patterns and textures for computer artists.
36, 39, 49, 115, 159, 160, 162, 215, 239, color plates

Jacquelyn Martino
jam67@columbia.edu
Interactive multimedia artist
184, 185

Bernice Mast
mastmedia
201 East 30th Street
New York, NY 10016
212-683-1879
Home furnishings textile designer and digital video producer
46, 72, 137

Barbara S. Pollak
1370 5th Avenue
San Francisco, CA 94122
415-731-0722
pyro406@aol.com
Painter, illustrator
190, 192

Ray Rue
343 East 66th Street, Suite 22
New York, NY 10021
212-794-1210
Illustrator, painter, stage set designer
55, 62, 63, 101, 114, 136, 141, 176, 191, 204, 208, color plates

Philip Sanders
563 Van Duzer Street
Staten Island, NY 10304
718-720-0388
sanders@cgart.trenton.edu
or ps@acfcluster.nyu.edu
Artist, educator
219, 221, 229, 230, 233, 234

Nancy Stahl
470 West End Avenue, 8G
New York, NY 10024
Voice 212-362-8779
Fax 212-362-7511
NStahl@aol.com
Illustrator
37, color plates

Extra special thanks to the following individuals:

The entire Peachpit Press staff, and in particular, Roslyn Bullas, Kate Reber, and Nolan Hester for their various contributions toward getting this book off the ground.

Mark Zimmer, John Derry, and Laurie Hemnes of Fractal Design Corporation, for patiently answering our technical questions, and to Daryl Wise for providing us with resources.

Philip Sanders, for his very substantial artistic and technical contributions to the Movies chapter.

Ray Rue and Diane Margolin for their commissioned illustrations.

Hilary Dyson for copyediting.

If you'd like to share any Painter, QuarkXPress, Photoshop, or Illustrator tips or tricks with us, or pat us on the back, or recommend future titles for us to write, or make suggestions or corrections for future editions of any of our books, E-Mail us at: Pixbill@aol.com.

A

Acquire,
    Adobe Illustrator File, 134
    for video, 24
Add Image to Library (pattern), 143, 144
Add Nozzle to Library, 111
Adobe Illustrator File (Export), 90, 134
Adjust Colors, 173
Adjust Color Set, 29, 57–58
Adjust Selected Colors, 175
Advanced Controls palettes,
    Rake, 70
    Random, 72
    Sliders, 73
    Water, 74
    Well, 71
Airbrush, default variants, 43
Align floaters or shapes, 96
Annotate colors, 245
Apply Brush Stroke To Movie, 230
Apply Lighting, 180–181
Apply Marbling, 194–195
Apply Screen, 183
Apply Script To Movie, 232, 234
Apply Surface Texture, 45, 170, 184–186
Artists brush, default variants, 46
Auto Clone, 168
Auto Mask, 146, 148, 154, 232
Auto Playback, 64
Auto Van Gogh, 46, 169
Average Points, 125

B

Bézier curve shape, 118
Bleach, 50
Blend (shapes), 130
Blobs, 196
Blur, Motion, 194
Brightness/Contrast, 176
Bristle palette, 69
Browse, 7
Brush Controls,
    Bristle palette, 69
    Looks, 35
    Nozzle, 110–111
    Size palette, 66
    Spacing palette, 68
Brush, default variants, 32, 44–45
Brushes,
    3D, 45
    Airbrush, 43
    Artists, 46
    brush-and-paper combinations
      (Brush Look Designer), 35
    Build, 34, 66
    Burn, 54
    capture, 63
    Chalk, 39
    change icon, 62
    change name, 62
    Charcoal, 40
    choose, 26
    Cloners, 165–169
    Crayons, 42
    create new category, 62
    dab spacing (Spacing palette), 68
    Dodge, 54
    Eraser, 49–50
    Felt Pens, 42
    Liquid, 52
    look, 35
    Masking, 151
    method categories and subcategories,
      32–34
    multicolored, 58
    oil, 44–45
    opacity, 27
    paint flow (Well palette), 71
    palette, 26
    Pencils, 38
    Pens, 40–41
    rake (Rake palette), 70
    reshape (Size palette), 66
    save variant, 63
    size, 34, 66
    Sliders palette, 73
    stroke character (Bristle palette), 69
    tip profiles, 67
    variant, new, 63
    Water, 51
    Water Color, 47–48
    Water palette, 74

Tint, apply overall, 179
Tools palette, 12–13
Tracing Paper, 164, 165, 227, 229, 232
Trim floater, 100, 110

U

Undo options, 14
Undo Preferences, 14
Ungroup,
   floaters, 98
   shapes, 129
Use Clone Color, 165

V

"Van Gogh" cloning, 169
Variability, color, 58
Video, 24, 220, 243
Video Legal Colors, 28, 243
View Grid, 19, 41
View/Hide Annotations, 245
View Mask, 82, 151, 159
Visibility buttons (image mask), 5, 82, 151

W

Water brush, default variants, 51
Water Color brush, default variants, 47–48
Water palette, 74
Weaves, 140–141
Well palette, 71
Wet Fringe, 74
Wet Paint, 47, 74
WindowShade option, 11
World Wide Web, 247
Wraparound pattern, 144

Z

Zoom to Fit Screen, 15